Praise for
In Search of the Perfect Job, Second Edition

"This update of Lowstuter's very impressive first book cleverly and straightforwardly leads the reader down the path to a satisfying and lucrative executive position. The book is practical, straightforward, and focused. It reads sensitively, and at times even humorously, yet always gives the reader the confidence that this is one serious book."

—Andrew B. Panega
EVP, Chief Human Resources Officer,
R.R. Donnelley & Sons Company, Inc.

"Having screened 6,500 executives and studied their 65,000 job changes, I'm sure that almost all could have benefited from reading this book. I applaud Lowstuter for creating the finest book available on career management."

—Dr. Brad Smart
Author of *Topgrading: How Leading Companies Win by Hiring, Coaching, and Keeping the Best People*

"This is a great read and really fine advice. Lowstuter lays out a framework on transition issues with great clarity. Too many people have no clue about what is involved in a career transition . . . this book provides both strategy and practical advice."

—Peter D. Crist
Chairman, Crist Associates

"This is a powerful, must-read guide for executives. *In Search of the Perfect Job* is a great resource for every executive who is in the market or those who want to be prepared when they get that unexpected call from a recruiter."

—Jeffrey J. Childs
Senior Vice President – Human Resources,
U.S. Cellular Corporation

"Clyde Lowstuter has effectively captured the essence of finding the perfect job. This book 'tells it like it is' in an open, direct, and down-to-earth style. Lowstuter's book flows well and is hard to put down. With his sense of humor, it is a fast and absorbing read."

—Jack Clarey
Partner, Clarey, Andrews, and Klein

"Lowstuter's book brings contemporary thinking to the vastly changed world of landing big jobs. He hits the mark by providing easy-to-understand insights and proven tactics that work both on and off the job."

—Matthew P. Gonring
VP Global Marketing and Communications
Rockwell Automation

"This is a terrific read and will be a tremendous help to those serious about moving their respective pegs up in the executive suite! Clyde's book is by far the best 'all in one reference guide' for how to plan and execute a search strategy which will lead to superb results. Readers have the confidence that when they follow these approaches, they are employing proven tactics to land that perfect job."

—Dan O'Hara
President, O'Hara Associates

"Lowstuter speaks the language of senior executives and provides practical advice on how to market their most important product: themselves. His writing style is poignant yet sensitive. His examples are real and entertaining. This is a book that every executive should have handy...before they have to make a change *and* after."

—James A. Crawford
Global President – Medical Products Practice,
Ken Clark International Search

"*In Search of the Perfect Job* is a career management tool of the highest order and needs to be on every executive's bookshelf! It is insightful, thought-provoking, and possesses the power to transform your career and your life! Lowstuter has done an amazing job of distilling and harnessing the golden nuggets we all need to produce uncommon results."

—Kevin A. Price
Senior Service Industry Executive

"Lowstuter provides a comprehensive strategy and practical tools to land that meaningful and richly rewarding position. *In Search of the Perfect Job* transcends job hunting and equips readers to lead inspiring and authentic lives. Throughout, I felt like he was speaking directly to me."

—Mark W. Naidoff
President & CEO, consumer products company

"There is no need to take the job search journey alone. As your personal career coach, Clyde Lowstuter, provides you with thought-provoking guidance that will solidify your skills and accelerate your career search success."

—Susan Snowden
President, Snowden Marketing and Strategy Consulting

IN SEARCH OF THE PERFECT JOB

Second Edition

8 STEPS TO THE **$250,000⁺**
EXECUTIVE JOB THAT'S RIGHT FOR YOU

CLYDE C. LOWSTUTER
PRESIDENT AND CEO ROBERTSON LOWSTUTER, INC.

WITH **CAMMEN B. LOWSTUTER**

McGraw-Hill

New York / Chicago / San Francisco / Lisbon / London / Madrid / Mexico City / Milan / New Delhi / San Juan / Seoul / Singapore / Sydney / Toronto

The McGraw·Hill Companies

This book is dedicated in loving memory to my late partner and co-founder of RL, David P. Robertson. He was a brilliant, compassionate, creative, and powerful man with an absolutely wicked sense of humor. He inspired everyone he met and transformed hundreds of lives. I miss him still.

Here's to you, Dave.

1 2 3 4 5 6 7 8 9 10 FGR/FGR 0 9 8 7 6

ISBN-13: 978-0-07-148588-3
ISBN-10:   0-07-148588-0

Product or brand names used in this book may be trade names or trademarks. Where we believe that there may be proprietary claims to such trade names or trademarks, the name has been used with an initial capital or it has been capitalized in the style used by the name claimant. Regardless of the capitalization used, all such names have been used in an editorial manner without any intent to convey endorsement of or other affiliation with the name claimant. Neither the author nor the publisher intends to express any judgment as to the validity or legal status of any such proprietary claims.

McGraw-Hill books are available at special quantity discounts to use as premiums and sales promotions, or for use in corporate training programs. For more information, please write to the Director of Special Sales, Professional Publishing, McGraw-Hill, Two Penn Plaza, New York, NY 10121-2298. Or contact your local bookstore.

Library of Congress Cataloging-in-Publication Data

Lowstuter, Clyde C.
   In search of the perfect job: 8 steps to the $250,000+ executive job that's right for you/Clyde C. Lowstuter; with Cammen B. Lowstuter. — 2nd ed.

      p. cm.
Includes bibliographical references and index.
ISBN 0-07-148588-0 (alk.paper)
1.   Job hunting. 2.   Executives–Recruiting. I. Lowstuter, Cammen B. II. Title.
HF5382.7.L69 2007
650.14–dc22
                            2006033896

CONTENTS

FOREWORD

Are you serious about relaunching your career? If so, you've just found a remarkably comprehensive and easy-to-use tool for optimizing the process. *In Search of the Perfect Job* is a personal owner's manual that will lead you through the maze of choices and decisions that culminate in a successful job search. I'm living proof that the author's compass works, having personally benefited from his direction during my own career transition 10 years ago.

Clyde Lowstuter is one of the most prominent authorities—if not *the* authority—in the outplacement industry. For over 25 years, he has helped thousands of executives get reconnected. *In Search of the Perfect Job* consolidates his vast experience, creative ideas, practical tools, and important perspectives into a comprehensive guide. Simply put, it is an *open me first!* tool for any job search.

Irrespective of the circumstances, losing your job is unsettling, and it stimulates the full range of fears and emotions. It can be downright debilitating. The trick is to make it exhilarating. Even if your departure is on positive terms, landing the right new career opportunity requires a complete change in mind-set, a well-defined plan, and a new daily routine.

Getting started is the key. Recovering from the devastating devastating news and "getting your head on straight" is when executives need all the help they can find. While out-placed executives invariably want to jump right into interview mode, *In Search of the Perfect Job* provides a much broader foundation and a work plan for orchestrating a successful career transition. Having watched a close friend mistakenly take the first opportunity presented, I'm convinced a type A focus on getting a new job must be preceded by introspection, a thoughtful plan, and proper perspective.

A candid, in-depth discussion with yourself is a difficult and unfamiliar task for most people. To make it easier, Clyde shares his own personal story of being fired from his job. His honest account of his anger, humiliation, and family situation is both revealing and thought-provoking. He shares the feelings many people experience but are hesitant to admit. Exercises in the first few chapters encourage readers to face the unvarnished truth about their own situations and personalities. This approach inspires an authentic, results-oriented perspective which enables readers to more successfully navigate the real world of job search.

Beyond these first critical steps, *In Search of the Perfect Job* is packed with valuable exercises, tools, positive self-talk, and vivid examples. For instance, following Clyde's format helps reshape a factual, five-page résumé into a hard-hitting, concise, results-oriented resume that will get the phone ringing. Another particularly helpful section relates to tactful negotiation of a job offer. This is a very stressful time point, and job offers can sour with poor strategy and word choice. *In Search of the Perfect Job* offers a range of tactful and persuasively worded responses for elevating a good compensation package into a much better one.

Finally, the chapter on auditioning your job references and preparing for tough interview questions is simply outstanding. These are not trivial steps in a job search. *In Search of the Perfect Job* painstakingly explores both of these challenges and offers thoughtful approaches.

So, go for it! Take control of relaunching your career. *In Search of the Perfect Job* is as important an investment as you will ever make in both yourself and your future career.

Joe Herring
Chairman and CEO
Covance, Inc.

PREFACE: EMPLOYMENT REALITY

Denial Is More Than a River in Egypt

It's common for people who have involuntarily exited their companies to grudgingly admit that they had been in denial of their employment reality. Invariably, they had employed an amazing array of coping mechanisms to survive or convince themselves that the increasing emotional outbursts toward/from the boss was no big deal. In fact, that is exactly what happened to me.

It's not the lack of technical competency that gets people terminated. Rather, it is the lack of commitment, fit, personal chemistry, and organizational endorsement. Like water seeking its own level, people have the ability to contribute to their organization's success if given a chance at their competency level. Staying in an organization is largely a function of getting egos out of the way and setting aside past upsets and recriminations. Correspondingly, if competencies are reasonably equal, it is the job seekers' commitment, fit, personal chemistry, and organizational endorsement that results in them being hired and staying in their organizations.

My company, Robertson Lowstuter, is an executive development consulting and coaching firm specializing in equipping talented executives to achieve what they want (and need) in their careers. Since 1981 we have coached thousands of executives who were suboptimized in their roles. They often felt frustrated, unhappy, undervalued, and underutilized. One COO client* of ours indicated that for the last three years in his company he felt like he was driving slowly through a dense fog. He was familiar with the road but couldn't see the terrain clearly enough to drive as well as he knew he ultimately could. That's how it feels when you are not aligned with your boss or the organization's culture.

Many clients admitted staying with their companies long after they knew they should have left. Some were actively looking, and they just hadn't found the right opportunity. Others felt the board would terminate their boss before they would be fired, so they would be spared. Many did not see clearly the extent to which their relationships had deteriorated. Still others felt that they could turn the situation around if given enough time, successes, and the right boss.

When I Zigged ... and My Boss Zagged

When I was first terminated, I was in denial—big-time. I was unconscious as to the reality of my situation. I ignored how distant my boss and I were toward each other. I knew we had differences of

---

*Point of clarification: When I use the term "client" I am referencing an executive who is in outplacement with my firm. While the fee is paid by an organization ("sponsor"), we consider the displaced executives our "clients," as we are 100 percent focused on their well-being. While other firms might call people in career transition "candidates for reemployment," we do not.

opinions, but I was clueless as to how, not so subtly, combative my boss and I had become. I zigged and he zagged.

I believe that you get what you create. I created getting zapped a number of years ago from a job and company I loved, not because of the lack of commitment or competency, but because of the lack of chemistry with my boss. I likened being zapped to wetting two of my fingers and sticking them into an electrical outlet. I was shocked at being terminated with no performance discussion or attempt at raising my awareness and turning me around. I had no notice, just BAM! The shock ran through my body like an electrical current. It was, to say the least, jolting (no pun intended).

As Charles Dickens said, "It was the best of times; it was the worst of times." I thought I was living an idyllic life. We were in northern Wisconsin on the border of the upper peninsula of Michigan with a beautiful setting: a heavily wooded seven acres lot on a river. It was a wonderful refuge from the intense 100 percent travel I had experienced for a few years as an organization consultant for Ernst & Ernst (now Cap Gemini Ernst & Young), a global public accounting and consulting firm.

Unfortunately, there came a time when my company needed to streamline and, ultimately, downsize. Like every traumatic situation, I can still remember every minute detail with crystal clear clarity.

One morning after I had heatedly hammered out some additional severance concessions from my boss to better support some senior executives who were about to be terminated, he turned to me and said, "By the way, Clyde, you're fired, too." I laughed, thinking it was merely gallows humor, given the conversation we were having. But only after seeing his pale, waxy complexion did I realize that he was serious. I remember sitting back down in a lump, feeling a rush of emotions: shocked, dazed, hurt, angry, sad, fearful, shamed, vengeful, bitter, and most of all violated and used.

"Excuse me, but you must be thinking of another Clyde Lowstuter. I'll go get him because you can't be referring to me!" My emotional roller coaster was predictable and classic: a prolonged disorientation alternating between red-hot anger and profound sadness. I blamed my boss; I thought he was a jerk and I was a victim. I was so ticked I couldn't see straight.

Ironically, there was no chance for appeal to those senior executives with whom I worked closely. *I'm sure everyone is scrambling to survive at a time like this*, I thought. What was really upsetting was that my last year's performance review was deemed excellent. And now! Nothing except sudden and perfunctory dismissal with zero opportunity for appeal. Intellectually, I understood that this was a business decision, but it felt deeply personal. At some intuitive level I knew that I was more than merely my job. However, my identity was so closely aligned to my work that I was not able to see the firing objectively. Plus, I worked long and hard hours, sacrificing my family time in favor of the company. I felt crushed, angry, embarrassed, used, and discarded. I was also really, really scared. I had never lost a job before. I was devastated.

I'm not telling you this as a way of reliving painful memories. Rather, I am sharing my experience with you as I have heard stories similar to my own repeated countless times from the lips of others. I learned that the best way to deal with a trauma of this magnitude is to give it a voice and not to suppress it. It is helpful to acknowledge the trauma's existence, accept complete responsibility for it, learn from it, and move on with your life. One step at a time. Breathing in. Breathing out.

Traumatic situations will always be with you. Tough, unsettling times represent opportunities for profound learning and personal growth. The hard stuff of life strengthens us. Steel is tempered only after repeatedly being immersed in the blast furnace. Such tempering in our lives and careers enables us to move on to bigger and better things, more confidently and boldly.

It is true that I probably was difficult to manage. I spoke up rather straightforwardly when asked my opinion. While younger than my boss, I felt I had a much broader range of practical experiences given the years of consulting throughout North America. He would suggest something, and I often countered with an alternative strategy based on my experience. He wanted to move forward on a specific project right away, and I remember saying there was more groundwork that needed to be done. I zigged and my boss zagged. I moved forward and he stood still. When he moved one direction, I told him what I thought of his idea by moving down another path. So, in reality, I got exactly what I had created in the relationship; I wrote the script, and my boss played out his role. I'm convinced that he did not see me endorsing him, so why should he endorse me by confronting me on my interpersonal ineptness or by giving me a more generous severance package or a longer notice? Before my termination, my boss was probably as frustrated with me as I was with him. It's a shame neither one of us had the foresight to stop the destructive cycle once we were in it.

In my termination meeting, I was dimly aware that my boss was trying to minimize my feelings, as he mouthed platitudes about this being the best thing for me and acknowledged that this was a tough decision for him. I thought, *Big deal. I don't give a rip about how you feel or how much sleep you lost last night; you still have your job. I'm out in the street, battered and bruised! How tacky. You want me to feel sorry for you? What a jerk.*

I remember thinking at the time that everything seemed to be moving alternately in slow motion and at 250 miles an hour. My head throbbed with a scratchy, tingly sensation that quickly developed into a thunderous roar, drowning out my former boss's explanation of the severance benefits and what the company wanted me to do with regard to my current programs and projects. I felt the rush of tears come to my eyes, and the need to remain strong overshadowed the emotion. As I lowered my head to conceal the humiliation and rage, I noticed with mounting alarm that I could not feel my fingers nor move my arm.

I felt nauseous and could taste the bile rising in my throat. I knew I had to regain control of my mind and body to fully understand the details of my severance package. But it was no good; I couldn't hear, and I could barely see my boss, as the room was spinning out of control. I rose to my feet and lurched for the door. Only later did I realize that I was in the beginning of a major migraine and stress attack.

I stumbled out of my boss's office clutching the carefully worded severance letter full of legalese, facts and figures about months of pay and benefit conversion. There was nothing about my contributions and sacrifices. I found myself floating in slow motion in a sea of flashing and blinding lights filled with alien shapes and sounds. The pain in my head overshadowed my termination as the will to survive took over.

Wow, I sighed. *From hotshot to nothing in a couple of minutes. Guess I'm not that great, after all. Maybe I have been living a lie. Maybe my confidence is all an illusion. No! That's not true. I've got a beautiful wife and an adorable infant son who think the world of me. For sure, though, my world has shifted, and much of what I knew to be reality feels unreal now.*

Not surprising, within a matter of days, the projects I was working on were absorbed by others or dropped. It was as if the projects that were deemed to have a high priority several weeks ago now seemed to be contaminated, as if to imply that anyone assuming responsibility for this work would suffer the same fate. Consequently, there was little passion or commitment to see these programs through to completion.

Within a week of my departure, I also found something else about organizations that I had not experienced before. No matter the extent of the support and endorsement I had inside the company, once I got zapped, the organization closed ranks around itself and isolated me, the tainted one. Granted, there was a fair amount of sympathy for my plight, but there was not sufficient hue and cry to overturn the decision. I discovered that it's not personal; rather, it's a form of survival instinct. As hard as it was for me to realize it, the company needed to operate like this to keep on moving so it did not grind itself to a halt agonizing over these kinds of decisions once they were made.

Being zapped was very rough on me. I thought of myself as confident, assertive, and competent, yet all that was shaken to the core. I got migraines, gained weight, lost weight, and fiddled away the modest six weeks of severance, with no outplacement. Quite frankly, Carolyn, my wife, silently wondered if I could ever fully recover to work again. Apparently, I was a lot further gone than I was aware. I vaguely remember spending a full day in my canoe on the river on our property. I was pretending to fish, when in fact I was merely trying to heal my fractured soul. Carolyn refers, to this time of me being "flatlined" with no discernible brain waves. Years later she remarked that I was way beyond just being spaced out—I was deep into the ozone. While that was apparently true (though it wasn't so obvious to me), it wasn't for the lack of trying to get back on track. I was just badly beaten up in the process, not unlike being run over by a truck and living to tell the tale. Sure, my boss could have told me months before that fatal day that we were on a collision course. He could have had the courage to confront me honestly and indicate that my behavior was unacceptable. Of course, he could have terminated me more effectively (and compassionately), but he didn't. I'm convinced he didn't because he was no longer in support of me and he was worried of how I might react. The possibility also existed that he *did* tell me to modify my behavior and I was too stubborn or blind to see what needed to be done. While I acknowledge the possibility this might have happened, I know that my boss did not confront me on our rapidly deteriorating relationship in a manner that I could really hear and act upon.

While I knew my company was experiencing financial difficulties, I never thought that my job was in jeopardy; others' jobs perhaps, certainly not *mine*. Granted, budgets had been steadily cut in the last 18 months, and all nonessential programs or projects were either eliminated or severely scaled back. Even so! Not Clyde's job! He was the guy you turn to when you wanted something done. How arrogant of me.

Unfortunately, the termination of our relationship was unnecessarily messy, on both of our parts. The more adverse reaction my boss received internally from his peers, the more he tried to justify his actions. When I heard about some of his explanations, that made me even more angry, and I got hooked emotionally all over again. I only wish I had been able to create the much-needed emotional distance to put my upset into perspective.

Clearly, I was stuck. It was only through the tireless loving support from my family and friends that I was able to survive and get back on track.

The ownership of my dismissal went through some distinct cycles, not unlike my emotional roller coaster. My boss fired me. I thought he was wrong, myopic, inflexible, and had difficulty sharing authority. Clearly, he did not know how to handle bright, high-energy, creative professionals. I blamed him.

Once I pushed through all the blame and the emotion, I realized that there was much more personal power in my accepting complete responsibility for how my career and life looked, rather than rationalizing my termination by blaming. The "context" of fault requires that someone be wrong and that roles of victim and persecutor be assigned. I didn't want to blame anyone anymore.

When I finally worked this out for myself, I realized that I had wasted a lot of energy making my old boss wrong and me right. In the final analysis, I was disruptive to what he wanted and needed for his department, regardless of how talented I felt I was. While he had made a business decision, it felt deeply personal. He wasn't wrong; he was absolutely right to terminate me if there wasn't a fit. I'm only sorry neither one of us had the courage, insight, or interpersonal skills to candidly discuss the status of the relationship. Had we been able to do so, a tremendous amount of trauma and angst (on my part) would have been avoided.

So, this is my story. While it is years in the past, it is with me always, as I have integrated this painful experience into my life's guiding principles of taking accountability for my actions and living authentically. The most powerful discovery for me was that I created my life and career the way I desired, albeit at the unconscious level. I did not get zapped for the lack of competence. I got zapped for the lack of personal chemistry, fit, and endorsement from my boss. I got what I deserved. Nothing less; nothing more. My upset was around reality crashing headlong into my sense of entitlement. It was painful having to grow up and take responsibility for how my life looked. I *chose* to take the job; no one forced me to do so. In hindsight, it was obvious that I *chose* to not support my boss more and, in doing so, lost the endorsement I once had. I *chose* to join an organization that was, metaphorically, loping along at 35 mph when my hard wiring had me racing along at 85 mph. Culturally and operationally, we were not an ideal fit. A famous line from the musical *Man of La Mancha* comes to mind: "Whether the rock hits the pitcher or the pitcher hits the rock, it's bound to be bad for the pitcher."

I was living the metaphor; I was the pitcher, and my boss was the rock.

It still amazes me how blind I was and how caught up in my own "stuff" I was that I did not see the unintended impact of my behavioral choices. Even after so many years, it embarrasses me to realize how entitled to an easy career I apparently felt. As I write these words, I shake my head at how clueless to my own disempowering beliefs and behaviors I was. To all those people back in those days, especially my old boss, please forgive my naïveté and inflated sense of self-worth.

This book reflects the lessons I learned from personally being zapped many years ago, as well as lessons learned from the executive coaching, team building, and career transition my colleagues and I, at Robertson Lowstuter, have been engaged in with thousands of executives since 1981. As you read this material, you may think you are being described in the examples or you may relate personally to some of the clients mentioned. I suspect that the truth of some of the vignettes and some of my experiences might even resonate with you.

I invite you to read this book with positive expectancy, while diligently completing each worksheet. I crafted this book so that every question in every worksheet is a good interview question. If you proceed with an open mind and a keen desire to master your career and your life, I know you will be challenged to shift your perspectives and enlarge your vision of what is possible. I hope that you will push against the edges of your comfort zones. When you are nervous and are inclined to resist modifying your thinking or behavior, you are probably face-to-face with those hard-earned beliefs that define you. There is nothing wrong with having such beliefs, as they bring a measure of certainty, stability, and comfort to you. In fact, as humans, we seek to create harmony and balance in our lives. Without it chaos reigns. However, we know that the outer edge of this comfort zone is where the real learning and personal growth occurs. If you are committed to learning about yourself and others while living on the "edge" and are open to modifying how you think, feel, and act, you will definitely broaden your behavioral response repertoire. In effect, you will have a broader array of behavioral options from which to choose.

Since my life-altering experience those many years ago, I have made it my life's mission to operate more openly, honestly, and authentically. I try to always take what I do seriously, though not myself.

You were right, Jerry. Being terminated was a good thing.

Thank you for allowing me to be your career coach on your personal journey of self-discovery. I hope that you will enjoy the trip and experience greater authenticity, boldness, confidence, creativity, and success.

Best wishes for an exciting trip and for your continued careering success. May you always . . .

***Create Uncommon Results!*®**

Clyde C. Lowstuter

ACKNOWLEDGMENTS

This book is a collaborative effort of many—Robertson Lowstuter staff, clients, and friends—sharing their hard-earned learnings and breakthroughs. I have always thought of RL as an executive learning laboratory where people discover, stretch, risk, and grow.

A huge thank you to Cammen Lowstuter for being such a great collaborator who taught me (sometimes kicking and screaming) how much more powerful it is to look at things differently. Without her, this book would not have the insights and balance it has. I always thought of Cammen as my muse, though with hob-nailed boots.

We are indebted to our client organizations with whom we have been privileged to serve. Thanks to the numerous clients and friends who have taught me the lessons contained herein. It's been an honor to partner with everyone on this journey. A special thanks to those who have educated me and been a valued resource. Thanks to James Terry and Rob Sarkis, both good friends and talented IT professionals who educated me on the Internet and allowed me to utilize some of their writings. All examples, vignettes, résumés, letters, etc. have been inspired by or are modifications from actual clients, though their names and companies have been omitted or changed.

I want to especially thank my colleagues at Robertson Lowstuter from whom I learned many lessons and personally grew. These are the pros that are on the front lines coaching clients in new roles or in transition. They've been great contributors and champions of this second edition: Dan Barber, Sharon Noha, Ken Kempka, Ron Hirasawa, Sandy Mitsch, and Linda Balkin. I owe Paul Duski big thanks for allowing me to blend his insights on networking with my own, as well as Dr. John Moriarty's expertise on competency-based interviewing. I greatly appreciate Jennifer McNiven and Laurie Powles for their able assistance and comments, and Kaye Lyons, all great RL associates who were instrumental in enabling me to pull this work together.

To Carolyn Lowstuter, my love, colleague, partner, and inspiration, and also to Nathan and Katrina Lowstuter, whose input, and unqualified support throughout this journey were a wellspring from whence I drew my courage, ideas, and resolve.

Thanks to the Davenport clan for allowing me such a wonderful refuge in which to work on the last two chapters at their breath-taking and joy-filled Texan ranch. Blessing to ya'll.

Without the encouragement, guidance, and huge patience from my friends at McGraw-Hill, this book would not have come into being. Thank you all: Mary Glenn–Editorial Director, Melissa Bonventre– Associate Editor, Maureen Walker–Senior Editing Supervisor, and Joanne Slike–Copy Editor.

STEP 1
INNER VIEW

CHAPTER 1

TAKE CHARGE OF YOUR CAREER AND YOUR LIFE

Now What?

At this moment, your life has probably taken on several new dimensions. Regardless of your circumstances, if you are committed to a career change, then right now you are working for yourself—to find a new job. **Your job is to get a job**. This means you will have to manage your resources (time, energy, creativity, focus, finances, enthusiasm, and commitment) as if you yourself are a business. The way you handle these limited resources has taken on greater importance than ever before.

The metaphor that comes to mind is rowing a boat. If you are part of an organization, there are lots of people rowing besides yourself. So, if you take a break from rowing, the boat will continue to move forward. Since you are operating solo in your career search campaign, and not with other rowers, you are solely responsible for creating and sustaining your own forward momentum. If you stop rowing (i.e., stop networking or interviewing or lose your drive or confidence), your rowboat will definitely slow down and soon stop. If you are committed to forwarding your search, you have to sustain your focus, energy, and belief in yourself.

What's the Right Opportunity for You?

What kind of opportunity are you looking for? Probably one that can utilize your skills and abilities to their maximum and bring in a competitive wage, and one in which you'll be happy. Finding this special job may be tough, and it may be one of the most challenging goals you've ever set for yourself. Will you work hard for your own success?

Only you can determine if you're worth the effort.

How much *are* you worth?

Career Ownership—It's the Major Leagues Now

Chances are that you do not relish the prospect of looking for a new job. It's usually a hassle, regardless of your age, track record of accomplishments, credentials, how well you fit in your organization's culture, or your need to leave. As you look forward, there are so many career options and paths to explore and choose from. It's not surprising that it might even be a bit overwhelming and unnerving. Do you continue following the career path you have been on? Does it make sense to shift your sights to larger corporations? Many executives report that they have been able to accomplish greater things in small to mid-cap companies. Might that be of interest to you? What about exploring entrepreneurial ventures? Obviously, there are pros and cons to each and every venue. What is important is that you discover what is right for you. The whole concept of assuming complete responsibility for the development and success of your own career path, and not relying on a company to define it, is like moving up from the minor league to the majors. You are stepping into an arena of greater challenges, but also greater rewards. You'll be required to dig deeper into your innate and learned talents, capabilities, drive, and commitments.

After many years of successfully coaching executives, I know, without a shadow of a doubt, that the *process* of career transition is important. The first two chapters of this book are about getting grounded in who you are and managing your emotions. You may be itching to skip ahead to writing a knockout résumé or learning the secrets of power interviewing. While you certainly can do that, your overall search efforts will be most effective if you lay the foundation first, getting prepared, if you will. My goal is to help you get fully grounded in those wonderful capabilities, skills, and personality traits that you hope others clearly see, especially in an interview or networking meeting. Obviously, this will not happen if you are embittered or if your self-confidence is shaken. If your emotions are askew, you will not perform at your best. Knowing yourself and managing your emotions are crucial to a successful career search campaign.

 CEOs want to hire the best . . . the most confident, the most bold, and the most courageous. They want to hire talented people who will significantly contribute to their organization's growth and profitability.

This book will help you unlock more of your potential and discover those areas of your life that roadblock you, as well as those that empower you. Through a series of interactive exercises, you will create a focus for your career and identify those organizational environments and working relationships that are best for you and those in which you will flourish. This book is a roadmap for how to achieve your career dreams, one that you can tailor to meet your own unique needs.

It is time to wake up and take control. I will guide you to a place where you can more effectively manage your life and career, but you have to want it. Sports psychologists say that talent being equal, continuous success is mostly mental. The famous former New York Yankees catcher and "philosopher" Yogi Berra once said, "The head game is 90 percent mental."

The following exercise, Worksheet 1, "You've Created Where You Are," recognizes that you have always been in charge of your career—albeit perhaps at the unconscious level. As you answer the questions, you'll see what I discovered years ago.

The key to personal power is taking ownership of your career and your life.

The sooner you take ownership of your emotions, the sooner you can display to the world your talents with a quiet confidence that radiates throughout your demeanor. After all, a desperate person can be picked out at 100 paces. Panic, fear, and desperation ooze out of every pore. Ultimately, **people take their cues from you**. If you interact with people from a negative emotional state, they will see your every insecurity and flaw. If you consider yourself a victim, you will remain powerless. Accepting ownership and mastering these emotions will access your personal power. Notice how I used the word "master," not "ignore." Submersing your emotions is analogous to holding a fully inflated beach ball under water. It's difficult, and it requires a lot of concentration and energy. The reality of a submerged beach ball—and your submerged emotions—is that eventually they will explosively surface, and probably in the least desirable way.

WORKSHEET 1

You've Created Where You Are

To help you see that you have been in control of your career and your life all along versus someone else managing you, please answer the following questions. If you have been involuntarily separated, please consider these questions in the past tense.

Yes	No		
____	__✓__	1.	Are you as happy as you would like to be in your job?
____	__✓__	2.	Are you as productive as you know you could be?
____	__✓__	3.	Are you as creative as you know you have been previously?
____	__✓__	4.	Is your advice sought after as much as it once was?
__✓__	____	5.	Do you get along with your boss as well as you would like?
__✓__	____	6.	Do you trust and respect your boss?
__✓__	____	7.	Have you updated your résumé or thought that perhaps you should?
__✓__	____	8.	Have you ever thought about what it would be like to be employed somewhere else?
__✓__	____	9.	If you could conduct a very discreet search without anyone finding out, would you do so?
__✓__	____	10.	If you had access to a foolproof game plan for successful job changing, would you be interested in it?

Scoring the Worksheet

If you answered no to two or more of questions (1 through 6) or yes to two or more of questions (7 through 10), chances are very good that you have already left your organization—psychologically and emotionally, that is.

While you may physically still be at your company, your heart and mind may be somewhere else. Your commitment to turn the situation around or reestablish the relationship with your boss may seem less important than it once did.

If the intensity you once felt and the enthusiasm you once exhibited about your organization is consistently less than before, then you have made the decision to withdraw or disengage from being 100 percent committed at your workplace, albeit unconsciously. It may be time to move on.

At some conscious level, you "managed" your job and the people around you the way you wanted—even though it might have felt like career sabotage and resulted in your being criticized or even terminated.

When My Submerged Emotional Beach Ball Surfaced

Remember the story in the preface about my being zapped from my job in northern Wisconsin? I thought that I had successfully dealt with all my emotional demons when I began to actively look for a job. Not so. Once I woke up to the fact that I needed to get my life and career back on track, I just started interviewing. Apparently, I had not fully mastered my emotions; I merely submerged them. I guess that I was still harboring a lot of anger, as it burst forth unexpectedly as I was leaving the parking lot of O'Hare Airport in Chicago. I had just finished a great interview and was exiting the circular parking structure when all of a sudden I was instantly broadsided by red-hot anger. In the blink of an eye, I was beating the steering wheel with all my might and yelling incomprehensively. As quickly as the emotional outburst occurred, it was over. I was astounded and more than a little frightened. I pulled into an empty space as soon as I was able and grabbed a few big gulps of fresh air. In a heartbeat, I surmised that I had been denying the existence of residual anger. After all, I took accountability for blowing up my role. I no longer blamed my boss. Yet I had apparently been denying how frightened and angry I still was that I had to look for work during an economic recession.

Your Emotional Roller Coaster—Hang On!

Whether you have voluntarily or involuntarily left your company, or if you are merely beginning to contemplate a career change, you may have a number of conflicting feelings: fear, anger, shock, disbelief, self-doubt, denial, betrayal, guilt, depression, shame, or even a feeling of freedom or excitement. Relief is often an emotion people experience as well. Many people report to us that they feel as if a "50-pound weight has been lifted off their shoulders."

All of our executive clients have experienced and felt what you are feeling when they found themselves in your situation. What you might be feeling is normal and common to all of us. Most of us living (or hanging on) through periods of uncertainty or trauma (such as job loss) usually go through a series of emotional stages. (See Figure 1-1.)

Do not worry about being discouraged or about feeling emotionally out of control. Most people experience a wide range of emotions. As outlined in the figure, the five main emotions are mad, sad, shame, fear, glad. Denial is part of being mad. These emotional swings are normal, and they do shift. It is very much like being on an emotional roller coaster with many ups and downs.

Beware of letting these emotional moods control you for an extended period. Guard against becoming paralyzed by your fears. The time when you might be most discouraged is when you most need your courage and determination to come out of the situation as a winner. If you find yourself emotionally flatlined, like I was when I was terminated, don't beat yourself up. Give yourself some emotional distance from your

Figure 1-1   Your emotional roller coaster.

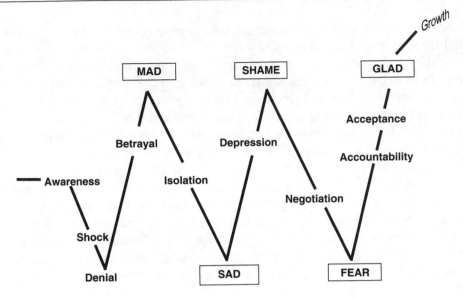

disempowering thoughts. Take a short break to get energized and to shake off negative thinking. I have always found that a good remedy is to engage in some form of physical activity. Doing so will give you some emotional healing as you look forward with positive expectancy. Whenever I am stuck or stalled on an issue, I seek to ask myself empowering questions, such as:

- What two main outcomes do I want to create?
- What are the next three steps I need to take to be successful?
- What is my greatest positive learning?
- What do I need to do to rise up and take charge of my career and my life?
- What will my life be like if I *don't* change?
- What will my life be like if I *do* change?

Since awareness is such a large part of gaining control of your emotions, let's talk about your possible ups and downs. (I should mention that I experienced all, not just some, of the emotional stages during my wild and seemingly never-ending rollercoaster ride.) Lest you think that because you have voluntarily left your company or have decided to initiate a job search you are immune from such emotions, think again. Anytime reality smacks you in the face and your expectations are greater than what you create there is an opportunity for emotional upset. So, lighten up. Relax and work hard at this process.

If you were involuntarily terminated, the moment you were notified of your changed status (*Awareness* in Figure 1-1), you were in *Shock*. Your first and natural reaction may have been *Denial*, "This can't be true. This isn't happening!" When the reality of your job loss began to sink in, you may have felt a sense of *Betrayal* and became *Mad*, experiencing anger, "How dare they do this to me! It's not fair! I'm going to get even!"

Once your anger subsided, you might have experienced *Isolation*, and been *Sad*, and fallen into a *Depression* like I did. Most executives raise questions about their self-worth and technical competence. "What do I do now? Perhaps I did deserve this. Obviously, I'm not as good as I thought I was." Additionally, it's not uncommon for you to feel some *Shame* surrounding your exit, especially if you are concerned about what other people will think. *Shame* is rooted in the feelings of guilt and humiliation. The emotions that tend to immobilize people and sap their energy the most are sadness and shame. These emotions were key contributors to my being "flatlined" for two months. While I felt victimized by my former boss, my powerlessness remained.

Interestingly, people often engage in *Negotiation* with themselves: "If I do 'X' then 'Y' will occur." There is a subtle but profound difference between self-negotiation and action planning. The former is filled with false hope and wishful thinking, whereas the latter is reflective of an executive taking charge of his or her career.

The acute ambiguity of your situation may be generating a fair amount of real *Fear*. There are a thousand questions to answer, many from your own family. Additionally, you have all of your own questions and conflicting emotions.

While these emotional states are normal and can be pretty intense, most individuals can push through their emotional ups and downs and achieve a level of *Accountability* in which they recognize that they created their personal and professional reality, albeit perhaps at the unconscious level. *Acceptance* occurs when you assume complete ownership for the state of your career. While it might be painful for you to stop blaming others, I personally found that I was *Glad* and relieved, because I stopped being a victim and started taking action. In fact, these epiphanies for me (and for thousands of clients before you) were a profound *Growth* experience. Such insights can be incredibly liberating and sobering.

When you are in an "accountability" state, you can face your personal situation squarely as a problem to be solved or a hurdle to be overcome. Healing occurs when you accept that your situation is not unusual and that you are not alone (even though you may feel lost right now). As you acknowledge this, you are beginning to get on top of the situation. It sometimes helps to have the perspective that your termination was a business decision, not a personal one. Granted, it may certainly feel deeply personal, as mine did when I got zapped.

Our personal experience in dealing with many executives over the years is that you can move through all of these emotional states, from awareness to accountability and growth in the blink of an eye—or you may get stuck in being mad, sad, or feeling fear or shame for a long period of time or go back and forth to earlier states. The reality is that your emotional states are fluid. They are ever-changing. You may feel that you have created emotional closure on your last job/company and that you have regained your confidence only to have an incident trigger you riding your emotional roller coaster again. This on-again, off-again emotional ride is common to most executives actively seeking to make a change. It is not surprising that you may even feel more off balance if you have prided yourself on your ability to objectify things within your business realm. My counsel is to lighten up. Don't be so demanding on yourself. It's OK to be human and vulnerable. Acknowledging your emotional vulnerabilities is a powerful method of integrating and embracing your "wholeness."

Seek professional counsel if you find that you are stuck in an unhealthy emotional state for long periods of time and cannot seem to positively move forward. Invariably, executives need to give themselves permission to grieve and emotional space to heal.

Whatever emotional state you happen to find yourself in is OK. I ask that you not focus on or be concerned if you are in an emotional upset, now or even later in your job search. Being upset and having emotions is a natural part of life. To deny that you are upset is to deny a large part of who you are, of your uniqueness. Practice getting in touch with your feelings and with your "inner voices"—the thoughts that rattle around in your head at night or in stressful times.

When I was dealing with my own self-worth issues upon being terminated, I was hearing my negative self say, "Clyde, if you were really successful, you would not have been terminated! If you were as together as you portrayed yourself, you would not have stress attacks and these intense periods of self-doubt. Competent people brush off things like this and move on confidently. Don't be such a wimp!"

What a pack of disempowering beliefs—lies—I told myself!

WORKSHEET 2

Emotional/Career Reality Check

- What were your top five biggest career disappointments in the last 12 months?

- What feelings did you attach to these disappointments?

- How did you think and behave differently toward your boss?

- What was the impact on the relationship with your boss and how did it influence your commitment to your organization?

- What did you do (or didn't do) that created these disappointments?

- What would you do differently if confronted with similar situations in the future?

- What's one thing that you could do differently today?

WORKSHEET 3

Venting—A Safety Release

To gain the most value from this exercise, please be totally frank with yourself. Now is the time to vent a bit. Let some of those bottled up emotions out. Answer the following questions as completely and as thoroughly as you can.

- What happened with your job? What happened at your company?

- What happened to your relationship with your boss?

- What have you learned?

- How do you feel about your boss? Company?

- What are all the positive things you can do right now?

Master Your Emotions and Regain Control

You may observe that you are creating a lot of negative or critical messages for yourself which, ultimately, get in your way and undermine your ability to deal with this significant change in your life. To master your emotions and regain control in your life, we encourage you to follow a three-step process:

1. Do not suppress or deny these unconscious messages; rather, acknowledge their existence. ("Hmm, I am really angry," or "I'm feeling very unloved right now").
2. Physically re-create the body language you have had in times when you were feeling empowered and successful. Move around in your chair or stand, remembering when you were successful, confident, bold, and feeling particularly competent. Get in touch with how your body feels and responds to these emotions as problems to solve and challenges to be met.
3. Acknowledge your emotional state, begin to move into action ("Hmm, I am really angry *and* I am going to work on my résumé!"), and reaffirm your ability to generate success. ("This is tough, but I've overcome greater obstacles before.") You'll find that forward motion, coupled with this kind of openness and positive reaffirmation, will help create a level of quiet confidence.

WORKSHEET 4

Repackaging Your Insights

Review the responses you created in the previous worksheet and rephrase them as if you are responding to a prospective employer. Notice any differences in how you feel as you shift your language to assume complete responsibility for your exit from your company. (Remember, you do not have to be formally out of a job to feel disconnected to your organization.)

Practice reading your responses out loud with conviction—as if you are talking to an employer. Watch for shifts in your emotions and attitude. It's OK to discard "stuff" in your life, if it is not working for you.

- What happened at your company?

- What have you learned?

- How do you feel about your job? Your boss? Your company?

- What are all the positive things you can do right now?

Take Charge of Your Life . . . and Career

Thousands of individuals are caught unaware, just like I was, when their careers end abruptly in termination or face forced early retirement. Even though, in hindsight, I had seen quite a few warning signs that indicated that my job was in jeopardy, I chose to ignore them, as I did not consider them as serious threats.

As I type these words, I think back to a recent conversation I had with an outplacement client of ours. He had been a victim of his company's recent massive downsizing. He commented that many long-service people in his former company were surprised and devastated when their jobs were eliminated. He indicated that many of the people who remained were walking around in a daze, unproductive and frightened to death. Our client couldn't fully understand how people missed the obvious signs that their division or jobs were going away when their budgets disappeared or when their colleagues to the left and right of them were terminated. I gently reminded him of my situation, as I denied and minimized the importance of these obvious signs. Obvious to all but the affected person.

Even in the midst of massive restructuring and downsizing, executives have the ability to build or diminish their endorsement (and stay or leave) based on how they behave and the choices they make. Accordingly, decisions are made to keep some people and let others go. People get terminated, drift aimlessly, or become overwhelmed by some unmet need or by some emotional nuance of mad, sad, fear, or shame. Conversely, many executives are glad and relieved to have exited their organizations.

The questions that you might be posing may very well be the following:

"If people really, truly feel that way, why don't they just change jobs or careers and get their lives back on track?"

"Why would normal people hang around in a job or in company where they no longer feel that they are contributing?"

"Don't they know that when they stop 'playing the political game,' they have already left the organization, though they still remain?"

"Why would individuals remain in toxic working relationships with their bosses or when their self-worth is constantly undermined?"

Good questions. The point is that we are dealing with normal individuals in somewhat abnormal times. If you are feeling out of control in your job while watching other less competent people take charge and gain favor, you may feel you are in a weakened position to do anything about it. Ironically, the time when we *need* to feel most confident is the time when we often *feel* the weakest and the most unsure of ourselves. Besides, we don't always know when we are in trouble. Witness my own situation years ago when I was not aware of the impact of my zigging and my boss's zagging.

To make a commitment to revitalize your career in the face of what you may feel is rejection by your boss or a less-than-stellar career rise requires an exceptional amount of personal courage, power, and strength. I know, firsthand, the struggle, and I honor your dedicated commitment to your success.

Who Are These People Who Exit Their Organizations?

They are you and me.

"These people" are all of us who have ever been anxious about the stability of our careers or have ever lost our jobs, for whatever reason. "These people" represent each one of us who have been committed to our careers. We've been committed to doing the best we can to contribute to our organization's growth and profitability. We are bright, talented, and capable. We've been successful before in our career and we'll be successful again.

Authenticity—The Heart of Personal and Leadership Success

My belief is that personal and leadership success is significantly enhanced when executives operate authentically.

> Authenticity is the single most important determinant for personal and leadership success.

Our operational definition of authenticity is the congruence or alignment of a person's needs, thoughts, feelings, and behavior. Being authentic is operating out of one's genuine or natural self. It's what happens when a person is fully expressed and transparent while taking accountability for his or her impact, intended and unintended.

Being fully expressed is not a license to intimidate or steamroll over a less confident person. The spirit of authenticity is loving and accepting yourself while extending the same graciousness toward others. Now, lest you think I am some kind of pushover regarding performance standards, I'm not. I have just decided, to the best of my ability, to take the emotion out of performance discussions. My intention is to focus on the roadblocks to a person's success. Rather than beat someone up about a performance gap, I recommend that you err on focusing on the ramifications versus the recriminations. In effect, help this person assume accountability for the achievement of results to serve the organizational good, the quality of professional relationships, and the depth of organizational endorsement.

When there is a performance issue, it is helpful to look at three dimensions:

- *Unknowing*. The person is both able and willing but is unaware of the performance shortfall.
- *Unable*. The person does not have the capability to perform the work, regardless of the motivation to do so. This is a training and knowledge gap that needs to be filled if the person is to be successful in this role.
- *Unwilling*. If the person's life depended upon it, could he or she do the work? If the answer is "yes," then we have an attitude, not a competency issue.

Hopefully, once the issue is made clear, the person will take the needed corrective action. Bosses also need to be open to the possibility that they did not fully explain their performance expectations. Many executives are probably more guilty of this than they'd care to admit. As bosses, we naturally assume that people will pick up on our subtle behavioral cues and piece together their marching orders. Ironically, many leaders believe they have already mentioned a course of action but in fact only imagined the conversation. Or if they did have the conversation, they were so obtuse they were unclear or misleading. Setting clear expectations and priorities eliminates a host of potential performance issues.

Achieve Optimal Performance and Personal Satisfaction

Who wouldn't want to perform flawlessly and enjoy solid professional relationships? Through our executive coaching and in team building retreats, I have been privileged to witness transformational gains in relationships, confidence, and satisfaction when authenticity is present and when it envelops technical knowledge, task skills, and interpersonal/leadership skills.

I once had a client who was not fully expressed. In fact, the newly appointed CEO of one of our client organizations was teetering on the brink of terminating Fred, his CFO. The CEO didn't completely trust Fred. Why? Fred held back. Fred was not very forth-coming in staff meetings and in one-on-one discussions. His analyzing style personality fit his role of CFO well, as he was an expert at keeping confidences—so much so that his colleagues felt that he was holding back on information from which everyone could have benefited. He seemed intimidated and outgunned by his peers, especially in those times when it was important to show up with a powerful and bold demeanor. Because of his shy and retiring manner, Fred's interpersonal style was one more of reflection and of quiet deliberation. His concept of acting responsibly was voicing an opinion when he felt strongly about something. He acknowledged that he was often uncomfortable, as the CEO surrounded himself with blunt, hard-charging subordinates.

In one of our coaching sessions Fred seemed even more nervous, distracted, and wound up. He didn't seem to be operating very authentically. His work and personal relationships had suffered, and it seemed that he had lost the trust of his peers at the office. Fred didn't have an ulterior motive or hidden agenda; he was just super intro-spective and was completely unaware of his unintended impact. Part of helping Fred access his authentic self was to ask him to give me an example of when he felt most alive, most self-confident and self-assured, and most comfortable on or off the job. Fred replied without hesitation, "the beach." He regaled me with stories of him growing up at his family's long-time summer home on Lake Michigan. With a little encouragement on my part, as Fred continued to open up, he became more animated and passionate. As he relaxed, his gestures became more fluid and his voice even became deeper and richer in its tonality. In turn, Fred learned a valuable lesson. He accessed more of his authentic self when he tapped into those memories of when he felt most genuine, relaxed, supported, and accepted for who he was.

Would you like to tap into more of your powerful, confident, emboldened authen-tic self? If you'd like to, I invite you to complete the following exercises, Worksheet 5: Come Alive and Worksheet 6: Authenticity.

WORKSHEET 5

Come Alive!

Write about a specific time and place in which you felt most alive, most self-confident, self-assured, and most comfortable—on or off the job. What people were with you? What were you doing? Be specific. Elaborate on your feelings and the thoughts you might have had that buoyed you and made you feel complete and whole.

WORKSHEET 6

Authenticity

- In your experience how do authentic people behave?

- Identify a person, living or dead, real or imagined, who would exemplify living an authentic life as we've defined it. Once identified, write down the behavior of this person you deem to be authentic.

- What behavior that you identified above can you adopt to access more of your own authenticity?

Why Don't People Operate Authentically?

If operating authentically is the single most important determinant to personal and leadership success, then why don't people behave that way?

I believe that the three main reasons why people do not operate authentically are as follows:

1. *Lack of role models*. Simply put, you might have grown up in a family that was not authentic. Additionally, you may have had few fully authentic school or business professionals to emulate. By way of example, I'm sure that you have run into inauthentic colleagues who were bullies or engaged in corporate politics. In such circumstances people do not communicate or behave openly or straightforwardly.

2. *Lack of feedback*. Everyone needs honest feedback that is considerately given and provides insight as to effective behavior. The lack of feedback causes people to drift and "perform" with little or no guidance. I liken it to playing football with no score, no touchdown markers, or no yard lines.

3. *Disempowering beliefs and fears*. If you have self-limiting or disempowering beliefs about how your relationships should look, what you are capable of, and what you are entitled to, you will probably live a frustrating life that is not very authentic, affirming, or joy-filled.

Bottom line: You are most powerful, bold, and confident when you are operating fully authentically. Boldness, confidence, and enthusiasm are all contagious. People want to be around people who are emboldened.

You Are Not Alone . . . and Never Have Been

The way you deal with losing a job depends on two factors: Your internal and external support systems. Internal support includes your personal empowering beliefs and feelings of self-worth, self-confidence, and the values you hold. External support relates to your family and friends and the kind of support they provide to you.

Often, people are not aware how much their beliefs and feelings influence how they relate to the world around them. When people feel unappreciated, unaffirmed, or ashamed, many things in their world trigger an emotional response. Everything looks and feels out of synch. Ironically, during the times when we are most emotional and need to be comforted is when we push away from the sources of support, encouragement, inspiration, love, peace, comfort, and harmony.

Have you ever experienced a big upset in your life and you know that if you involve others and acknowledge it to them, you might find the answer or some measure of peace, but you don't feel like doing so?

What Will I Tell My Family and Friends?

You may be thinking . . .

I am seriously contemplating changing careers doing something different from what I am doing now. The opportunities for advancement are limited here, and I do not want to put my career on hold for three to five years. So, I am beginning to look in the marketplace for a challenging role in which I could contribute to a company's growth and profitability.

Or you might be thinking . . .

I have just lost my job, and I am really embarrassed. If I am embarrassed, my family, friends, and relatives will feel ashamed as well. Maybe the best approach is not to tell anybody.

 Ironically, the time when you need to reach out to others the most is often the time when you least feel like doing it.

Tell your family and your close friends the truth. They will want to know how they can help. After all, what are friends and family for if not to assist you when you have a need?

If you are having some difficulty knowing what to say, here are examples of some language you may wish to try:

Things at work aren't exactly the best right now. Given the declining sales and the threat of a takeover, I have decided that I'd better initiate a search for the right job, before I have to do so involuntarily.

Or,

As you may or may not know, my company has recently gone through a reorganization, with a number of positions being consolidated or eliminated. Unfortunately, I was impacted. While I am disappointed that my career at my company is over, I am enthusiastic about new career opportunities that might lie ahead before me.

As for your *other* friends and acquaintances, we recommend that you *delay informing them* of your status or intent until you have a clear career direction in mind. While it is true that vast percentages of positions are found through personal contacts, it is vital that these valuable leads be informed at the appropriate time and in the appropriate manner.

Sure, you may feel down or out of step with those around you, but that is when you need to rely on your family and others for support and to help stimulate you into action. In some cases, you will have to help them adjust; it may be a new experience for them, too. If your approach is rational, confident, and future, results-oriented, they will follow suit.

Relax. Finding the right position for you may be difficult, but it is not the end of the world. Keep in mind: You've been successful before now in numerous ways; you'll be successful again.

CHAPTER 2

CREATE YOUR LIFE THE WAY YOU'VE ALWAYS WANTED

Changing Jobs Is Like Playing Par Golf

It's true. Job changing is like playing par golf. It's simple, though not easy. And therein lies the rub. Because we think something is simple, we assume that it is easy. Actually, the career search process *is* simple. Create a résumé, interview, negotiate the best offer, and accept. What can be simpler than that? Simple, though not easy.

As you already know, changing jobs is itself a full-time job. It is also a process, often described as a process of becoming . . . a journey, rather than a final destination. You will find that your search for the perfect job is one in which you have already been engaged and will continue throughout your career. While the material contained in these chapters are specifically geared to one's career search strategies, they also relate to the ongoing management of your career.

Paddle, Paddle, Paddle! Tapping into Your Personal Power

Carolyn, my wife, loves to canoe on quiet, still lakes. It reminds her of that wonderful movie, *On Golden Pond*. In the movie the lake is often serene, peaceful, and gentle. She especially loves early mornings as the dawn's mist envelops the shoreline and hugs the water's placid surface. I have to admit, it is beautiful. My experience canoeing on Golden Pond is a great time for reflection. Taking stock. Planning the future. Not much fuss. No strain. Just gliding along. I view my precious time on Golden Pond similar to my getting grounded and laying the foundation for some creative endeavor or demanding project. Indeed, that's the goal of the first few chapters of this book: to ready you for your career search launch.

Have you ever been on white water—canoeing, kayaking, or rafting? While chilling out on Golden Pond is serene, I often prefer more excitement. In my view, there's a time to collect your thoughts and prepare, and there's a time to act. The adrenaline rush that comes from tackling a Class 4 or Class 5 rapids definitely falls into the category of taking action and suits my temperament better. As an Explorer Scout, I grew up on the wild rivers traversing the Appalachia Mountains, so I loved the challenge! The first time I took Carolyn white-water rafting was a Class 5. Looking back, what was I thinking? We were about to push the raft off into the Arkansas River southwest of Denver. The sound of the surging water was deafening. The Arkansas was boiling and hurtling by at an unbelievable rate—2,600 cubic feet per second, the guide gleefully told us with a grin. He shouted at us that if the river were any faster, they would not be allowed to run rafts down the river.

As the guides previously told us of the danger and read us their liability waivers, we signed our lives away. After donning wet suits, nylon splash jackets, helmets, neoprene booties, and gloves, we were cinched into heavily padded life vests. We could walk, but we could barely breathe, the vests were so tightly cinched.

The first rule of white-water rafting is that everyone paddles. Regardless of any person's skill level, the guide commands the boat. The commands are yelled with a fury that needs to be heard over the din of the river's roar. For the thin-skinned, the guide's delivery would seem as though he were manic and furious with us all. Not so. Commands are simple. They are shouted, "Paddle, paddle, paddle!" While there are some nuances—"Right paddle!" "Left paddle!" "Back paddle!"—the goal is to attack the river. You never want to be coasting. You cannot be laid-back in white water because you cannot steer unless you are traveling faster than the water. With a Class 5, it is an all-out assault. Everyone must be aligned and paddle in unison. Get out of synch, and the raft flips. People could drown or be swept away down river to suffer serious injuries. If you are not prepared to attack the river and instantly obey commands for the greater good, stay off the river. This is not a time or place for amateurs playing half-heartedly.

Battling the surging Arkansas River was challenging and exhilarating—and terrifying. After one particularly thrilling set of falls and boiling set of rapids, I remember yelling an unintelligible "Yee-Ha!" I turned to Carolyn to affirm how thrilling this heart-pounding run was for her. Her face was drained of color and her eyes wide with terror. Wanting to bring her out of her fear, I yelled over the deafening roar, "Isn't this the best?" Not unexpectedly, through gritted teeth Carolyn mouthed, "You owe me for life." After four hours of running this beast of a river, we were battered, bruised, and bloody. We were glad to come to the journey's end, especially Carolyn, who still talks to me!

What does my white-water rapids story have to do with executive job changing? I liken the executive career search process to hurtling down steep falls on a Class 5. You have to take charge of the process. You must master your deep-seated fears and rise above them, managing yourself. There are no dress rehearsals or do-overs. You have to "own your place in the raft." Let nothing—discomfort, hassle, or rejection—knock you out of your raft. You belong on this fast-paced journey you have created for yourself.

Mastering your career search campaign is like mastering a Class 5. Once you're on the river, there is no turning back. The only option is forward. And it is "paddle, paddle, paddle!" As your guide in the raft, I say to you, "Paddle on!"

Commitment

Mastering a Class 5 rapids and mastering the career search process starts with you being committed to it. This means you remain skeptical, yet open. *Skeptical* in that you should rarely take things at face value; rather, you should assess the applicability for yourself . . . while being open to the possibility of it working for you. My recommendation is that you should experiment and modify things accordingly. Be alert to the common tendency to engage in "Yes, but . . ." "Yes" acknowledges the presence of a particular course of action or opinion, while "but" successfully eliminates all other options. Be open to the possibility of something being valid and be open to experimenting with new beliefs, approaches, or behaviors. Being open may also require you to more deeply assess whether you actually need to exit your organization or whether you need to shift your attitude or enhance your interpersonal skills.

If you are not enthusiastic and optimistic about mastering the search process, how *do* you make this shift? First, raise your awareness of the thoughts and feelings you have when you think about job hunting. If you have negative thoughts and feelings, you will unwittingly sabotage your search efforts. On the other hand, if your thoughts and feelings about job changing are positive and optimistic, there is a greater probability of success, as everything is aligned to achieve the result you want.

You might find that your operating style is one in which you often become defensive to an idea outside of your comfort zone. If you experience yourself resisting or countering with a lot of "Yes, buts . . ." to my recommendations or observations, I invite you to respond with "Yes, and . . .!" Attach some positive action with your "Yes, and . . ." For example, "Yes, I have not been effective at networking to date *and* I am going to learn!" This "and" helps you focus on the possibilities of another point of view. Commit to mastering the approaches recommended in this book. I challenge you to experiment with these suggestions as possibly a more effective method for connecting. Sigmund Freud is credited with saying, "Insanity is doing the same thing repeatedly, expecting a different result." If you find yourself murmuring, "Yes, but . . ." you have not taken ownership for finding a solution that effectively works for you or enhances your boldness, confidence, or enthusiasm. If you're like most people, I suspect that you'll be startled at the number of times you actually say, "Yes, but . . ." I know I was.

If you are seriously considering leaving your employer and conducting a career search, answer the following questions:

- <u>How well are your needs being met in your current role or organization?</u>
  - What are your career needs?
  - If your career needs are being met, how are they being met?
  - If they are not being met, what is getting in the way of them being met? How serious are these issues?
  - What are the top five reasons why you took this job, and what were you most excited about?
  - How are you inadvertently derailing your career and the relationships in your current company?
  - What can you do differently to create meaningful business relationships and significant career experiences?
  - If you thought of those people whom you like least in a positive light, how might your behavior change, and what impact might you have on them?
  - How would this shift influence your decision to stay or leave?

- <u>How committed to achieving mastery of the search process are you?</u>
  - How willing are you to write out responses to each worksheet?
  - To avoid a "stutter-start" search campaign, what is your sense of urgency to diligently apply and learn everything that is relevant to your getting connected in a new job?
  - What are those things that might help or hinder your achieving mastery?

Some People Have All the Luck!

Ever wonder why some people have greater control over their lives and why they appear to be happier than others? If you asked them, you would probably discover that their happiness, personal control, and achievements relate to the:

- Kinds of questions they ask.
- Meaning they attach to things.
- Extent to which they assume responsibility for how their life and career look.
- Commitments they make.
- Willingness to operate flexibly.

Does your ideal life seem out of reach? Achieving the ideal life is not all that unreasonable, given that you always get what you create. And, indeed, haven't you been operating like this all your life?

To some people, having to change jobs (whether it is voluntary or involuntary) is incredibly upsetting. Yet for others it is an exciting time—one of renewal and hope for something better. Granted, every person's situation is unique, but what makes people react so differently to a similar event? Simply put, it is the meaning they attach to it.

How you represent some event to yourself—how you believe something to be—will significantly influence how you feel about it. For instance, if you were not happy in your job and you found another position more suited to your personality and skills, it is a pretty good assumption that you felt pleased with your decision and excited about your move. On the other hand, if you were terminated from your job that you did not like and by a boss you did not respect, you probably experienced both relief and some pain (anger or sadness). If you are mad, your anger may be more about the company terminating you versus your giving notice to leave the company. They beat you to the punch. Granted, some of the pain may be the anxiety of not knowing what the next step is. If you are like most people in an uncomfortable job or boss-subordinate relationship, you probably wanted to be rid of the hassles and the upset and just do the work. As the on-the-job hassles increased, I suspect, so did your frustration and your desire to be rid of the problem. Who knows? You may have created leaving yourself, just as I did when I got zapped; although I was not aware of it at the time.

I profoundly learned, firsthand, that when I experienced my job loss, there was also the opportunity for significant gain. Eventually I asked myself these questions:

- What's the learning here?
- What can I put to use from this shockingly painful experience?

Since I was so late in bouncing back emotionally, many of my insights came more slowly than I'm sure yours are dawning on you. Ultimately, I learned the simple, commonsense fact that . . .

> The greater your self-mastery and your commitment to your outcome, the greater your resolve will be to let nothing stand in your way.

The successful achievement of any goal will depend upon two key factors: (1) the clarity of the desired outcome and (2) the level of personal commitment to the task. Mastery of self-management, authenticity, focus, and commitment are all major success factors.

Determine what you *want* and *need* in your life and your career in specific terms, not generalities. Goals such as wanting a better job, more money, fewer hassles, better relationships, and reduced stress are too general. Besides, you may *want* more money, but what you might really *need* is better control over your finances. Specific goals enable you to focus on the outcome you desire with greater clarity and determination. The metaphor that comes to mind is taking a picture with a high-quality 35-mm camera. In the hands of a bumbling amateur like myself, you might be able to distinguish that the out-of-focus picture is a house, but not much beyond that. Conversely, a professional can create an incredibly crisp and powerful photograph of the same subject by precise focusing. Likewise, once finely focused, your goals have the potential to mobilize you into action and enable you to achieve your desired outcome.

Once you become committed to your success, you *can* achieve your dreams. The extent to which your thoughts and actions are focused—that is the extent to which you will master the needed skills and create action that will lead to your achieving your goals.

It is also important to be aware of when, how, and why you sabotage your commitments so that you can make choices and reaffirm your commitments. Like cheating on a diet, failure to be fully committed to your outcome is not necessarily final, but it does have its costs.

It's time to fine-tune your strategy, remain flexible, and pursue stretch goals. Not only do you need to know where you presently are and where you are headed, but you also need to be able to quickly adapt your behavior when you are off track. Every one of us has a built-in adaptive sense in which we are able to make adjustments to how we are responding to our environment. When you sit up, walk, run, gesture, or read, you are making countless adaptive behavioral changes to achieve a result that you might only be subconsciously aware of. Your challenge (and opportunity!) is to heighten your awareness and adaptive skills to keep yourself on track while maintaining a high sense of urgency.

I recommend that you pursue stretch goals worthy of your efforts which will challenge you to be the best you can be while providing a sense of true accomplishment when you achieve them. You will probably find that as you become more experienced in setting and achieving stretch goals, you will have raised your expectations, performance, and outcome. This is analogous to a mountaineer gazing at a mountain's peak when she is at its base. While she climbs, the mountaineer shifts her route as she encounters obstacles until she is finally at the peak she earlier spied. However, that initially visible mountain peak is but an interim stop en route to the mountain's true peak. So, "the peak" should be with you as you set new outcomes and achieve your goals at an ever-increasing rate. Be like the mountaineer standing at one peak en route to another, committed to realizing your dream, one peak at a time.

Guidelines to Pursue Your Stretch Goals

1. **Identify your unfulfilled dream.** You know what it is; it's what you daydream about. Your dream wakes you up in the middle of the night. It's the sense of self that stays with you for years.
2. **Take baby steps to fulfill it.** Learn what you need to know and the sacrifices you

have to make. Meet the people who know what you need to know and who are willing to share of themselves.

3. Think about what your life will look like if you achieve this—or if you don't. How will you think, feel, and act when you achieve this or if you never pursue your dreams?

4. In your calendar, block out time and *begin* the process.

5. The point being—begin.

CHAPTER 3

RECONTEXTUALIZE: IT'LL ROCK YOUR WORLD!

Nasty Creatures, Those Roadblocks

Your psychological or emotional roadblocks stop you or, at the very best, slow you down from achieving the kinds of gains you are capable of and desire. While these roadblocks are invisible, they are as real as if they were made out of wood and steel.

The meanings that you attach to things will significantly influence how you think and feel about them. If you view something that has happened to you as incredibly unfair, you will feel victimized and indignant about it. Conversely, if you feel that the identical event is appropriate and fair, you will probably view this as a normal part of living and move on. For some people, not receiving a promised promotion is a tremendous loss of face, prompting an immediate job search. For others, the promotion loss is a sign that perhaps they did not build the level of endorsement needed for the promotion. So instead of a failure, it is viewed as a learning experience.

If there is something in your life which is not working well or if you have been involuntarily separated from your company, rather than looking at this event as a major failure, focus your thoughts on what you can gain from this new condition. Certainly there has been a loss, but there is also the opportunity for significant gain if you attach new meaning to your situation.

I want to help you *recontextualize your roadblocks*. By that I mean to redefine or reframe how you think about your disempowering beliefs. A disempowering belief set in a new context becomes empowering; that is, it is recontextualized.

Figure 3-1   Recontextualize your roadblocks.

Roadblock/ Disempowering Belief	Recontextualized	Empowering Belief
I'm too old . . .	becomes . . .	I'm a seasoned executive!
I'm unemployed . . .	becomes . . .	I'm free to search for the perfect job!
I'm a job hopper . . .	becomes . . .	I'm experienced in diverse industries and companies.
I'm too young . . .	becomes . . .	I have plenty of energy and many productive years ahead!
I don't have a master's degree . . .	becomes . . .	I have practical experience.

My Top Three Roadblocks

1. _____	becomes	_____!
2. _____	becomes	_____!
3. _____	becomes	_____!

Push Through Your Self-Limiting Beliefs

Hunting for a job can be very stimulating as well as often lonely and frustrating. You interview for positions that are perfect for you, and yet it seems impossible to convince the interviewers of your capabilities. In addition to these normal challenges that confront every job seeker, you will also discover that you (like all of us) have a number of self-limiting beliefs that are getting in the way of achieving your potential. These roadblocks to your success are of your own making and are rooted in what you believe to be true.

It does not matter whether or not anyone else believes it; rather, it is how you perceive things. If you believe you are too old, then you are. If you believe that no company is hiring now, then they won't.

When the search takes three times as long as you'd like and it seems to require four times the amount of patience you thought you had, it is easy to erect the roadblock or self-limiting attitude that says, "I will never get a job again." Or, you blame the tough economy, so you stop networking and merely hang around waiting for the phone to ring. Based on those two beliefs or roadblocks, it is no wonder why people's searches take so long.

It is not uncommon to feel that you will never make it, that you will be unemployed forever. Having your career search stall out on you is no big deal; everyone experiences it. So, expect it.

If you diligently follow the guidelines in this book, you will eventually pull out of the tailspin. However, you can become deeply stuck when you don't believe in yourself anymore or if you don't have faith in the action plan you have laid out for yourself.

Sometimes when you get rejected, your resolve can crack and you begin to doubt if you will ever land the right job for you. If you are currently employed and are actively looking, it may feel like the right job is eluding you, almost within grasp but not quite. At times, the sensation of life's circumstances being stacked against you can be overwhelming, whether it is on your job, in your career search, or in your personal life.

If you believe in yourself and deem yourself to be worthy, are committed to your personal success, and trust your skills, you will assuredly find the strength and courage to successfully get through this complex process we call a career search campaign.

Out, Out, Damn Spot!

While paying homage to William Shakespeare's *Macbeth*, I say to you, "Out, out, damn self-limiting beliefs!" Like most things, it is easier said than done. That being said, I do have a process that will enable you to identify your self-limiting or disempowering beliefs and their impact on your success.

You Get What You Focus On . . . and Believe

Your brain is a remarkable computer that not only has a tremendous capacity to store and retrieve data but also has the capability to provide solutions to your most puzzling conditions, provided you ask good questions. Unfortunately, many of us start off with ideas which hold us back and keep us from operating as fully as we might otherwise. We call these thoughts disempowering beliefs. The best way to eradicate these beliefs is to call attention to them so that the next time they pop up in your life you can acknowledge them, recognize that they are an illusion, and realize that you are no longer under their spell.

The Big Lie

When you are on your own emotional roller-coaster ride, ask yourself the question, "What is the big lie, or disempowering belief, that I believe right now that is undermining my confidence in myself?" At some point in our life, we were told the big lie as if it were the truth. Our big lie always has an element of truth in it, which is the reason why we so readily believe the veracity of it. At the unconscious level we believe that these disempowering beliefs that get in the way of our achieving our potential are valid. Right or wrong, good or bad, none of us operate at 100 percent, 100 percent of the time.

As we all know, most of our beliefs and behaviors are learned at our parents' knees. Tragically, our parents (and mentors) were often not equipped, themselves, to reject the big lies that *they* were told when they were young. Hence, not all messages that we internalized from our parents are empowering. Indeed, many of the core beliefs and values by which we live our lives are not the messages that they intended—nor are they particularly helpful to us. So we continued to believe lies that we were flawed or that our wonderfully unique traits and characteristics were of little value. These messages of "you're not bright or capable enough, or you'll never be able to" were delivered by well-intentioned but inept role models, and they often deeply undermined our confidence, creativity, authenticity, and joy.

 Your worth is rooted in your own self-esteem, no one else's.

Regardless of the conditions under which you were raised, take accountability for your career and your life. *Kill entitlement in all forms!* If your world is not filled with happiness, personal creativity, and joy, then assess your attitude. My belief is that when you shift your attitude, you rock your world! It was the motivational speaker Zig Ziglar who once said, "Your *altitude* is related to your *attitude*."

If you are not producing the results you want in your career, don't blame others or seek to be rescued. Ask yourself, "What can I do to achieve my goals?" Then go do it!

Peel Back the Layers of Your Understanding

1. Turn to Worksheet 7, "Inventory Your Disempowering Beliefs" and complete it fully.
2. Reread every phrase that you wrote down and underline only those words that are negative or inhibitors to your boldness, confidence, creativity, and enthusiasm. These represent some of your disempowering beliefs. Select the top five and write these in the top left column, "DISEMPOWERING BELIEFS," in Worksheet 8, "Beliefs, Behaviors, and Results." For example, you may have written disempowering beliefs regarding your job search, such as "discouraged," "unfair," "overwhelmed," or "exhausting."

3. Jot down three to four DISEMPOWERING BEHAVIORS you would exhibit if you were completely operating out of your disempowering beliefs. Put these comments in the middle, top column labeled "Disempowering Behaviors." For example, if you acted on the disempowering belief of being "discouraged," your disempowering behavior might be "listless" and "hesitant."

4. Write down three to four UNINTENDED RESULTS you most likely will create if you are fully operating out of your disempowering beliefs and disempowering behaviors. If you are living the big lie, then I suspect that your unintended results could reflect how your life looks. Write these comments in the top right column. Example: Your unintended result from the above example would be a less than powerful first impression. Now that we've examined the big lies, let's examine the *empowered truths*, that which is possible when you tap into your personal power.

5. Write down seven to eight INTENDED RESULTS that you want to see. These are the results that you most likely will create if you are fully operating out of your empowering beliefs and empowering behaviors. Please record your comments in the bottom right column. For example, let's say that instead you wanted to create a truly dynamic and engaged first meeting as your "intended result."

6. Jot down seven to eight EMPOWERING BEHAVIORS you would exhibit if you were completely operating out of your empowering beliefs. This is the behavior you exhibit when you are operating "in the zone," that magical place when you are fully expressed and authentic. When you are operating in the zone, you are relaxed and powerful, playful and wise, vulnerable, and a compelling leader. Put these comments in the bottom middle column labeled "Empowering Behaviors." For example, to realize a dynamic and engaged first meeting, how would you need to act? That's right: emboldened and fully expressed.

7. Capture the seven to eight most prominent EMPOWERING BELIEFS that you would have to hold to be able to achieve your intended results. Ask yourself the question, "What *really* is the *truth* that I am not allowing myself to believe?" Your goal is to let more truths and empowering beliefs emerge. End this exercise with the commitment to live your life in your truth and not mired in the disempowering messages you might have heard. For example, to be fully empowered, what must you believe about yourself? That you are capable, and competent, and more than able to conduct an effective career search campaign.

"Whether you believe you can or you believe you can't . . . you're right!"
Henry Ford

WORKSHEET 7

Inventory Your Disempowering Beliefs

Write down a series of single-word descriptors that honestly captures how you think and feel. Be brutally honest with yourself. Don't pull any punches; this exercise is for your benefit.

- When you think about job hunting in general, what comes to mind?

- When you think about having to extensively network, what comes to mind?

- When you think about being repeatedly rejected for jobs you could perform, how do you feel?

- When you think about the possibility of having to relocate or burn through your savings, what comes to mind?

- When you think about having to negotiate what you feel you are worth, how do you feel?

WORKSHEET 8

Beliefs, Behaviors, Results

Instructions: To complete this worksheet, follow the seven steps outlined in the previous section, Peel Back the Layers of Your Understanding.

DISEMPOWERING ➡ BELIEFS	DISEMPOWERING ➡ BEHAVIORS	UNINTENDED RESULTS
Example:	Example:	Example:
• Discouraged • Belief that it's "unfair" • Overwhelmed • Exhausting • Entitled to easy search	• Listless • Hesitant and tentative in making networking calls • Make up excuses • Blame others; don't take accountability for self	• Isolated from others • Few, in any, calls from contacts or recruiters • Search that is elongated, intermittently successful, or dead

EMPOWERING ⬅ BELIEFS	EMPOWERING ⬅ BEHAVIORS	INTENDED RESULTS
Example:	Example:	Example:
• Am bright, strategically agile, experienced, and more than capable, competent, and able to conduct an effective search. • Will generate 500% ROI on my compensation costs; I'm a valuable commodity	• Relaxed, confident, playful, authentic, and vulnerable • Powerful, wise, thoughtful, and inspiring leader • Insatiably curious, observant, and probing • Fully expressed and challenging	• Dynamic first meetings • Feeling of confidence, boldness, and enthusiasm • Effectively build networking contact list • Masterfully interview and negotiate offers • Secure the perfect job

WORKSHEET 9

Discover What Works and What Doesn't

This exercise will help you break through some of your roadblocks and identify actions which will positively influence your life and help you manage it better.

1. What are the top three things that are *working well* in your life, and how can you strengthen them?

2. What are the top three things that are *not working well* in your life, and what can you do to turn them around *and* enjoy the process?

3. What **THREE ACTIONS** can you take to develop and strengthen a trusting and respectful relationship with the people you work with, especially your boss?

4. What are six ways you can keep your commitment to positive action and reduce self-sabotage?

   A.

B.

C.

D.

E.

F.

Gain Perspective and Move the Action Forward

Truly successful executives have mastered strategies that they consciously and regularly employ. The following are five such strategies:

1.   Develop Superior Credentials

During your job search, create a powerful résumé and attention-getting marketing letters that distinguish you from others. Refer to Chapter 7, "Your Résumé: The Killer App," for tips in creating distinctive, results-oriented credentials. Ask yourself:

- What have I accomplished in the past 12 months?
- How have I differentiated myself from others?

If you are currently employed, seek out ways you can strengthen your credentials by enhancing your knowledge, skills, abilities, and contributions on the job. Ask yourself:

- How have I contributed to the organization, my colleagues, and myself?
- What are those traits and abilities that I'd like to continue, stop, and start?
- What am I committed to achieving during this year and the next year?
- How will I benefit from realizing these goals?

2.   Model Success . . . and Find Your Own Niche

Identify people whom you deem to be successful in that skill or knowledge area you want to master. Learn from them as you develop your own style, unique to you. If at all possible, contact them. Ask what specific behavior they engage in or thoughts they hold to be successful. Write it down, verify with them what they do, and then model their successful behavior. Do what they do, think the affirming thoughts they think, and feel what they feel.

Identify significant professional and personal goals that stretch you beyond your comfort zone. If you are nervous, that's a good sign, as you are probably up against one or more of your self-limiting beliefs. As you strive to achieve your stretch goals, if you are not producing your intended result, examine your beliefs and behavior. You may find that you may not be modeling or replicating "success" behavior/thoughts closely enough. Try again until you produce positive results and can generate powerful affirming feelings anytime you desire. Caution: I am not recommending that you mimic the style of others nor adopt theirs as your own. Rather, use the learning as a springboard for your own individualized approach that is authentically yours.

3.   Visualize and Create Success

Strive to create and manage those emotions that you desire—from being energized to being joyful, resourceful, confident, open, dynamic, bold, creative, innovative, and even wise.

Visualize an event or a time in your life that captures the emotion you want to be able to re-create easily, say, feeling really confident. Concentrate on a specific scene in which you were confident and zoom in on what you were doing, how you were moving and talking, gesturing, laughing, and smiling. Note who else was with you in this scene. Open your mind up and imagine yourself in the scene as an observer. Notice how much more bright and crisp everything looks. While keeping the energy and confidence high, "pop" yourself into the scene and actually experience what you only observed earlier. Feel the excitement and the power of being highly confident. Notice how you were carrying yourself. While remaining at your high-confidence level, make a fist and flex your bicep, hold for a moment, then release. Squeeze your fist again and as you do, raise your confidence level higher each time you squeeze your first. Squeeze your fist again while you allow your confidence to soar. Repeat this process often to recapture these empowered feelings so you can feel confident, really confident, anytime you choose . . . just squeeze your fist. This technique is called "anchoring" and "positive pairing." You are *anchoring* your feelings of confidence with the squeezed fist (or some gesture that works for you) and *pairing* the positive feelings to this physical act.

4.   What's Your W.O.W. Experience?

Before you yank your hair out in frustration during your job search, remind yourself of a time when you had a difficult task and you succeeded beyond your expectations. In other words, when you had a W.O.W. experience, or a "wonderfully outrageous win."

My own personal W.O.W. was writing the first edition of this book. I had written and self-published numerous learning systems and workbooks, yet I never had anything published by a bona-fide publisher. So to me, my W.O.W. was huge!

5.   Learn, Understand, and Apply Behavioral Models

Behavior models help us take a complex topic, such as how humans behave, and simplify it through a representation or model. Models make real the abstract, not unlike how the clay model of a car is the designer's concept put in physical form so that we can see what only he previously saw in his mind's eye.

If you master the behavioral models identified in this book, you will have made significant, positive shifts in the way you think, feel, and act. Obviously, if you make these kinds of changes, you may just significantly alter your life.

WORKSHEET 10

Your W.O.W. Experience

(W.O.W. = Wonderfully Outrageous Win)

- Identify one of your significant W.O.W. experiences.

- What made it a W.O.W. experience?

- What personal attributes did you draw upon to achieve this W.O.W.?

- How did you feel when it was over?

- What W.O.W. experience is still unrealized for you? What will you do?

Back at the Ranch . . . Completing Your Company Projects

This section is relevant for you, if:

- You have been notified that you are exiting your company, yet you are still on assignment.
- You want to pass on projects that you currently have underway.

You're Out—Yet Still In

If you are exiting the organization yet you remain, you may be in a delicate position. Self-management will be essential. You don't want to get emotional and blow things up in the workplace. It is imperative that you manage all your relationships impeccably, as it is no time to burn bridges. You will have to balance doing your job and winding down while beginning to pull together your career search campaign. Clearly, you have one foot in and one foot out of the organization.

You're Out—And You Want to Finish Up

When you are interrupted suddenly during a project or activity, particularly one in which you have dedicated considerable effort, planning, and energy, you are often somewhat unbalanced until you get to close that chapter in your work life. Most people want to complete what they have started.

Your normal desire to complete assignments sometimes creates several weeks of anxiety following a job loss (or the decision to voluntarily leave the company). This may appear as a recurring concern about a responsibility to an important project and what may have happened to it or who took over the task to which you were so dedicated. (Could anyone really care for your project the way you did?) Even more sobering is the thought that your efforts will not be picked up by anyone, that your work will be ignored, or that your work may not have mattered to anyone but yourself. You might also desire to "protect" your staff from the emotional uncertainty or any recriminations that might follow your departure.

You and your work mattered. Your staff mattered. However, the situation obviously changed and priorities shifted. Projects that were previously important to the company in financially stable times often become categorized as "nonessential" to the business survival when profits have slipped. While intellectually you may know all that, emotionally you may still be frustrated because you may want to manage the effective transition of your project rather than just abandon it. Or you just want to move forward and put this behind you. Whatever your perspective, it is essential that these recurring concerns be put to rest so they do not interfere with your forward progress in a well-managed career transition. To that end, I've created Worksheet 11: "Completing My Prior Work Projects."

The following exercise is designed to help you complete any projects, responsibilities, assignments, or worries that you were handling at the time of your voluntary or involuntary departure.

Complete this worksheet for yourself, not for your current or former company.

Instructions:

1. Write down a brief description of each project, assignment, responsibility, problem, or activity that you will leave or have left incomplete upon your departure. Include anything you may be worrying about now or may be concerned about in the future.
2. Describe the item, indicate what you have done so far, list the steps that you had planned to take, and mention the people you would suggest as the most logical to handle things so that the item can be satisfactorily concluded.
3. Picture yourself confidently sharing this worksheet with your current/former boss. Imagine your boss thanking you for your concern and promising to effectively handle your suggestions in light of the organization's changing needs.

A Note of Caution:

If you actually do decide to communicate this information to your former or current boss, do it for your own sense of completion only. You may wish to e-mail it versus communicating face-to-face, as the initial reaction may not be what you expect. In other words, your boss may not have an overwhelming positive response to your suggestions, and it is important for both you and your boss to save face. If you send it expecting gratitude and it does not happen, you may have unwittingly added to your frustration and upset.

If you do complete this worksheet and you still want to send it, do so to finish your responsibility for any loose ends there might be. You do not want to continue to carry any post-job concerns with you, like extra baggage, into your search for that perfect job.

WORKSHEET 11

Completing My Prior Projects

The following is a list of actions, projects, assignments, or responsibilities that I was handling at the time of my departure from the company. Additionally, each item's current status is identified, along with items left unfinished, suggestions about importance level, and individuals who may be prepared to complete the assignment. These items are prepared primarily to complete my thinking about assignments I was handling. If this information is also helpful to the company, then I am pleased.

ITEM: _____

Describe the action, project, assignment, or responsibility.

- This item is important because:

- Current status (what's finished):

- What still must be done:

- Individuals who may help in finishing the item:

CHAPTER 4

CHALLENGES AND OPPORTUNITIES FOR YOUR SPOUSE/PARTNER

Being in the Passenger's Seat

You might feel that the emotional roller coaster you are on is unique to you. While that is true, your partner also experiences similar emotions. One of the spouses we met described this process as similar to sitting in the passenger's seat of a car driving a little too close to the vehicle in front of it and trying to brake with the visor and steer with the rear view mirror. Another partner described his experience as feeling disconnected: "I felt like I was sitting in the back of a long bus driving through a dark tunnel. I was not only in the dark, but I couldn't even see where we were headed. I had no concept of where we were at any point in time. It was a very scary, fearful, and disorienting time for me." Fear is, indeed, very disorienting and severely limits anyone's ability to operate effectively.

In Your World—Two Kinds of People

Mary was devastated. Her husband, Del, was forced out of the company by the president just 12 months after Del was promoted to EVP and just before his tenth anniversary with the company. Mary found this bitterly ironic because the previous year the president had thrown a big celebration dinner recognizing Del's outstanding contributions and achievements that led to his promotion.

And now, look what had happened—Del got terminated. Sure, the company had lost some major accounts, but it had always been able to recover before. What was the big deal? Was Del asked to leave to reduce the overhead expenses, or did this have anything to do with Del and the president not really getting along? She was positive that Del didn't do anything so terribly wrong that he had gotten fired, or perhaps he wasn't telling her everything.

After his promotion last year, Del was under increasing pressure from all sides to deliver more and perform better. Gone were his mentors and peers that he could open up to and ask advice. In his new role, Del was more isolated and not as happy as he had been previously. He certainly didn't feel he was contributing like he had before. He knew it, and the president knew it. His termination was both shocking and a relief. Even though he had terminated many people in his career, Del had never been terminated before.

Immediately following his termination, many people were stunned and embarrassed, which made Del even more self-conscious. While Del quietly struggled through his emotional upset, Mary was emotionally crushed. As a loyal corporate partner, she took Del's termination as a major slap in the face and was not about to look at this situation positively or optimistically. That would appear to be giving in. Mary reasoned that the only way to be vindicated was for Del to be reinstated with a public apology. Short of that, she was going to remain bitterly angry to show others how wronged she and Del were.

In the three weeks following Del's termination, only five people called to offer their condolences and only three couples stopped by to visit. "You really know who your friends are!" seemed to be Mary's most-heard refrain. Once a gracious and open woman, Mary became embittered and sour, complaining to anyone who would listen how unfair the company had been to Del and that all their problems were the direct cause of the president firing her husband.

Deeply hurt, Mary drove away those who sought the most to provide support. This created additional emotional baggage for Del at a time when he was least able to handle it.

What Mary should have realized was that people were taking their cues from her. Since she was continually upset and acting out the victim role, her friends eventually withdrew, as she was, simply, too uncomfortable to be around. On the other hand, if Mary had helped Del take responsibility for the action, had become committed to moving forward, and had initiated some supportive calls herself, then her life would have looked decidedly different.

If you or your partner have recently been let go or fear this might happen, life may seem very complicated to you right now. You will discover that people seem to fall into two categories: people you expect to support you and people you do not expect any support from. Since so much of how we relate to the world around us is done on the unconscious level, it is important to understand how unrealistic expectations inhibit us from being successful. See Table 4-1.

Table 4-1   Your Expectations

The Way It Really Happens	People You DO Expect Support From	People You DO NOT Expect Support From
When You Get Support, You May Feel . . .	Connected Accepted Complete/Whole Supported	Delighted Surprised Affirmed
When You DO NOT Get Support, You May Feel . . .	Ashamed Rejected Beat Up Contaminated	Neutral Ambivalent

Finding Out Who Your Friends Really Are

If you discover that the majority of your friends and business acquaintances fall into the category of supporting you, great! However, if you are upset because some of your former friends are not supporting you the way you'd like on the job or even acknowledging that you or your partner got zapped, it's time for a reality check.

People generally do not know how to handle grief or trauma well. When a significant loss occurs (loss of a marriage, loved one, health, or job), either to us or to someone else, we most often feel awkward or self-conscious. Your friends, neighbors, relatives, and business acquaintances will often seem to ignore your plight because they do not want to make it worse for you. Indeed, to help keep your mind off the subject, some people will pretend you or your spouse's being zapped never happened. If you are still at your company, you may need to reexamine the extent to which your recent behavioral shifts have affected your relationships. If they have, you probably could benefit from apologizing and then proceed enthusiastically from that point forward.

Ironically, while your friends may have a strong desire to avoid talking about your termination (or demotion), you probably have an equally strong need to receive support or, at least, acknowledgment that your friends are standing by in case you need help or company.

The Problem

When this situation of avoidance occurs, be alert to the normal tendency to make others wrong in your relationship ("I guess they aren't my friends after all!") and yourself miserable ("Perhaps, I wasn't as good as I thought.").

The Cure

Go to the people from whom you need support and acknowledge your situation. Even though you know that they know, this face-saving method will help relieve you from the unnecessary burden of guilt or anger you might be feeling toward another. Try something like the following in a phone call or a face-to-face visit:

As you may or may not know, my company has recently reorganized, with a number of positions being consolidated and eliminated. Unfortunately, I was impacted. While I might have been able to remain in the organization in a lesser capacity, I have elected not to put my career on hold for several years. To that end, I am looking for a challenging career opportunity with the company's full knowledge and support. I just wanted you to know that.

While I am disappointed that my career is over at the ABC Company, I am also looking forward to what the future holds. I hope I can count on you for support. Thanks. I would like to get back to you later and share my plans for my next step. Would it be alright to call you sometime in the future and to also send a résumé to you?

Lessening the Fear Your Spouse/Partner Feels

Your spouse or partner occupies a unique place in your career search. While he or she is not going to be developing your credentials or conducting interviews for you, your partner is directly impacted and involved nonetheless. This section has been written for you, as well as for your partner. We encourage you to specifically share this section and to discuss it together.

From a Spouse's View

Involving the spouse or partner in the career transition process looks different for each couple. Some partners have careers that also need to be considered in the mix, especially if relocation is necessary or desired. In those cases, the spouse may also need to develop a résumé and create a strategy to get relocated into a new career as well.

From my own life-altering job loss years ago, my wife and RL (Robertson Lowstuter) partner, Carolyn, helped me understand that most spouses hold stronger emotions than their partners. Accordingly, they may need time, space, and open and supportive communications to work through their hurt and anger toward a company or a boss. It usually feels very brutal and unjust after the dedication and long hours spent on behalf of the company—often at a sacrifice to the family. I know this is how Carolyn felt when I lost my job early in my career. As you may know, job loss is one of the top losses that you will ever experience—right up there with loss of health, loss of a loved one, or loss of a marriage. So, involuntary termination can be devastating and an emotional roller coaster. That is part of the challenge; both partners are experiencing different emotions at different times throughout this process. Partner with your spouse, allow for venting, and equip him or her with positive coping skills that keep the communication less emotional and more supportive. Fears, uncertainty, and ambiguity, along with the sensation of being in the passenger seat with little control, make this process a challenge. A spouse or partner is vital in helping the displaced executive get centered, grounded, and confident to tackle the job campaign.

Damage on the Job and Off

We are sure it is no surprise to you to hear that when one part of your life seems to be in disarray, other parts may seem to be strained as well. This holds true for both your partner and yourself. If the job is working great and you are feeling empowered, your personal life may seem to be richer and more full. Conversely, your personal life has probably taken a beating if for some time you have not had full endorsement from your boss and colleagues, if you have not been contributing to the extent you know you could, or if you have noticed others have been migrating away from you. If you have experienced any of these shifts (or others like them) that have eroded your feelings of self-worth and professional competency, you may have an opportunity to clean up some damage with the people in your life you least want to hurt or alarm.

Although you might not feel that you were (or are) the primary author of any upset with your partner, you must be committed to resolving it. While the uncertainty of your company's downsizing may have triggered fear in your partner and may have created tremendous financial worries, bitterness, or cynicism, you need to "own" the cause of the upset. Why? Because you are the one who was working there and whose job was in jeopardy. So, if you can objectively consider yourself both the source of the problem and the source of the solution, you can effectively take action.

Expressing and Withholding Emotions

Have you ever experienced or witnessed how quickly parents get hooked emotionally when their child is unfairly picked on or taken advantage of at play or at school? If you have, then you can identify with the flood of protective emotions your spouse or partner may be experiencing.

It is not uncommon for our loved ones to experience emotions in a more pronounced way than we do in a career campaign—deeper sadness, greater bitterness, more blame, more intense vindictiveness, or more obvious relief. Remember our passenger's seat analogy? Even though you have been directly impacted, at least you can diffuse your emotions by working diligently on your job search. You are, in effect, in the driver's seat. Your partner, unfortunately, may feel somewhat removed from this process or hampered from working through all of the issues.

You may even find yourself withholding many of your emotions or thoughts because you do not want to disturb the other. Some of the feelings are best left unsaid, but many others need to be shared because if you (or your partner) withhold these things from each other, you run the risk of withdrawing from the very person whose support you need the most. You may find that your partner will not reveal what he or she is feeling so as to remain strong, protect you from being distracted, or refrain from generating further upset. Ironically, withholding generally creates the opposite effect. One spouse we knew indicated that she was so upset with her husband for losing his job she refused to speak to him for two weeks because every time she did, she either yelled at him or cried. In our discussions, she acknowledged that she was tremendously fearful and angry about the family's finances and their children's college fund being in jeopardy. Conversely, our client felt that sharing all of his concerns and deepest fears would set his wife off. However, she already had felt and experienced all the emotions and blackest of thoughts, so his not sharing just reinforced her greatest fears rather than eliminating them. Once they were able to vent, laugh, and cry a bit, much of the fear went away because neither of them had to "hide out" anymore. Ultimately, our client's campaign seemed to powerfully accelerate after fully communicating and involving his spouse more in the process, with the final outcome resulting in a fine opportunity in the person's preferred industry.

Emotional Upsets Your Partner May Be Experiencing

- Your partner may feel that you, as the employee, are genuinely a nice person and you have just been emotionally hurt and deeply wounded, and your partner feels both angry and protective.
- Your partner may feel that your boss who should leave the company gets to remain. It's not fair!
- Part of your partner's identity, status, and business perks was derived from your title or position, and he or she may feel that has been threatened or ripped away.
- Your partner wants to remain strong for you. Your partner may not openly share concerns or fears because he or she does not want to alarm you.
- Your partner may *feel* ostracized or snubbed by the community and may be cut off from meaningful social or business connections because of the embarrassment or discomfort others feel.

- Your partner may be overwhelmed by financial plans that are threatened and in jeopardy.
- Your partner might be concerned that your children may be harassed or shunned in school and perhaps even told that you did something wrong.

14 Tips for Partners and Displaced Executives During Job Loss

1. *Expect the unexpected, and don't read too much into emotions.* They happen for a number of reasons. Recognize your partner's emotional reactions as valid and that they may be quite different or quite similar to your own emotional roller coaster. Don't make him or her "wrong" because the feeling is different, uncomfortable, or inappropriate, given your perspective.

2. *Communicate your own fears or concerns, balancing them out with your knowledge and confidence that things will be okay.* It is easy to hide out from one another and live in that unspoken silence, which includes the fear of exacerbating the upset. It's common to have your fear spill out into your comments and undermine the very thing you want to occur: having your partner be bold, confident, and enthusiastic. Commit to your partner that you'll do the best you can in your career search, and ask for support.

3. *Balance your concerns with a positive expectancy of your partner landing that perfect job.* Acknowledge the unique talents and strengths that your spouse or partner in transition has. It is helpful if you have a good friend that allows you to vent and diffuse residual anger so that your communication can be more positive and supportive with your spouse.

4. *Provide meaningful affirmation.* As there is a lot of natural rejection in the process of looking for employment, seek ways to provide true and meaningful affirmation. Express appreciation for the support your partner has given to you, acknowledging that it may have been rough for both of you.

5. *Be a valuable sounding board.* Executives can greatly benefit from having their spouses or partners act as a sounding board as to the fit of the environment or position. In our firm, we often involve spouses or partners in helping brainstorm the template for the ideal job. Having that focus keeps people from jumping too quickly into a wrong environment because they are lured by job title or salary. Finding the next right job for the client's operating style and capabilities is the goal. Spouses have a network, too, that can be useful to their partners. Spouses often are supportive of doing company research for their partners if they want to play a more direct role in the campaign.

6. *Be interested and involved. Don't interrogate.* It's highly desirous for spouses or partners to be genuinely interested. My only request is to ask questions in a manner that is supportive and does not feel like interrogation. Like so many other things, there's often a subtle balance between encouraging motivation and being overly pushy. The first helps; the second hurts. And, like most things, the reaction is in the eye of the beholder.

7. *Visualize a successful outcome.* If the spouse and client could read the last chapter of the book and know right now how his or her job story will end, he or she would approach the process very differently. We encourage them to act like they do know. The majority of our clients land great jobs with an increase in pay and responsibility, so why should you be any different? *If you knew you could not fail, what would you think and feel and how would you act?*

8. *Manage your expectations of exactly how this process will look and where the jobs may be found.* Attach new meaning to (or recontextualize) the events that are disappointing. As a spouse or partner, you might be able to help by minimizing distractions or undue pressure or by creating more structure for your loved one. There is an old adage that has a ring of truth in it: "*I married you for better or worse, but not for lunch.*" Stay-at-home spouses or partners often have a hard time continuing their same routine with their displaced executive partner at home.

9. *Manage conflicting emotions.* We often do not know how to manage conflicting emotions. It's paradoxical. Your departed executive spouse may feel beat up and relieved at the same time. As the executive's spouse or partner, you might feel afraid and at the same time confident that you'll make it through this.

10. *Reach out to others, continuing to add value.* Many executives acknowledge the blessing their careers have been to them, and they are desirous of giving back to society in some way, of making a difference and finding greater fulfillment. While most do not elect nonprofit or education institutions and return to corporate jobs, some use this time of transition to volunteer or sit on nonprofit boards. One displaced client took a few months off to volunteer in a soup kitchen in New Orleans for Hurricane Katrina victims. We encourage these efforts as a healthy form of self-expression and being less self-focused—provided it's part of a deliberate strategy (running toward) and not a means of escaping (running away from) responsibility.

11. *Encourage exploring career options.* In addition to corporate roles, many executives actively explore the viability of entrepreneuring (buying or building their own business) or joining a private equity firm as a portfolio general manager. Interestingly, more than 75 percent of our clients investigate this entrepreneurial option, as it is so fully accepted these days, though a much smaller percentage of

executives actually become entrepreneurs. Many displaced executives see entrepreneurship as an alternative path to their corporate jobs, which can be another tough place for a spouse. They often do not share the same risk profile and have a harder time wanting to invest their savings at a time when there might still be large expenses looming on the horizon (such as children still in college).

12. *Maintain a strong belief in yourself and be committed to nurture your physical, emotional, mental, and spiritual well-being while you enhance your confidence.* This will minimize your being beat up and damaged in the process. It is part of the revitalizat0ion process.

13. *Assume complete responsibility for the way your career and life look.* Do not blame others, and note when you are unconsciously choosing to be a victim. Then choose to reenter a powerful emotional state in which you feel confident, powerful, and in control.

14. Involve your partner in this process and demonstrate that you are confident in your abilities and in this proven job search process. Plan your work, work your plan, communicate fully and genuinely, and never, never give up.

STEP 2
STRATEGIES AND OPTIONS

CHAPTER 5

CAREER STRATEGIES AND OPTIONS

So, What *Do* You Want to Do with the Rest of Your Life?

To me, answering this wonderful question is a breath of fresh air. So, what *do* you want to do with the rest of your life ... and career? Developing and following a meaningful career strategy is a major step in integrating your dreams with your reality. I liken the undertaking to the assembly of a 1,000-piece jigsaw puzzle. Lots of pieces, many nuances, and more than one false start as you assume one course of action only to realize that it is not the right strategy. For some, the jigsaw-type task is daunting and terrifying. For others, the anticipation is stimulating and affirming. I will walk you through this process and you'll end up having learned more about yourself and your career options. You'll also become personally more grounded, confident, and emboldened. In short, this chapter will help you highlight your experiences, capabilities, interests, passions, and motivations in order to focus on your objectives for your next career move.

Most executives are interested in identifying their career options and in discovering what's possible beyond their current career path. Others know exactly what their next career move is. They are interested in connecting in a similar role, company, or industry. Regardless of your chosen career path, you need to be able to effectively articulate the nuances of your skills and abilities so as to generate an income, whether you work for an employer or for yourself.

Your self-assessment will help identify aspects of life, both on and off the job, which tend to motivate you, as well as employment environments in which you are able to optimally contribute. Through this process of self-discovery, you will have the opportunity to examine, evaluate, and discuss the many parts that compose the total *you*.

Have fun with these exercises. Experiment. Fantasize about a career path. You may find yourself saying, "I could never do that!" or "It's not financially viable" or some derivation of a mental roadblock that keeps you from fully exploring an option. Keep in mind that an option that you envision may not be your true option; rather, it might be a pathway leading to your ultimate career path. Look to learn, not resist. Be insatiably curious. Ask yourself, "What does this reveal? How does this relate to my background, and where else might it lead?" All of these exercises have been developed and field-tested by thousands of executives in career transition before you. We know they will help you identify your highest priorities and most salient skills.

> Most people have definite opinions about what you should do in your career search. This is your search, not anyone else's. Your search strategies and career goals need to resonate with you: your personality, your passions, your capabilities, and your commitment.

Your Core Personal Values

It is worthwhile for you to identify those core personal values that define you, drive you, and support you in your career and your life. It's been my experience that we are not always cognizant of those values that shape who we are and influence how we function. They are often part of our unconscious selves. We take them for granted. They are just part of who we are, in much the same way that we are not really aware of the oxygen content in the air until something radically different occurs to bring our attention to it. By learning to operate at a more conscious level, we are able to make the right career decisions for the right reasons. Additionally, questions about your personal values and leadership tenets will invariably be part of in-depth interviews.

The following exercise is an opportunity for you to identify your core personal values and explore your career options in light of your life's values and objectives. This allows you to raise your awareness of those roles, relationships, and environments that will optimize your talents and where you can be happy and fulfilled.

So What? By completing Worksheet 12 "Core Personal Values," you'll raise your awareness of the source of your satisfaction when you are fully living your values. My rule of thumb for this exercise is that if you have a gap of two or more points between one of your top values and how satisfied you are living that value, then that may be an indicator of some disquiet, anxiety, or frustration. Invariably, if you are not satisfied in some area of your life, I contend that you are experiencing some form of blockage. Correspondingly, as you develop practical strategies that narrow these value gaps, you will find the key to greater personal and professional congruency, confidence, and satisfaction.

WORKSHEET 12

Core Personal Values

Identify: Circle all those values that resonate with you.
Rank: Rank order your 10 top values (1–10).
Living: Identify how satisfied you are living your values (10 = High; 1 = Low).

Rank		Living	Rank		Living	Rank		Living
	accuracy			determination			partnership	
	achievement		9	emotional health	5		passion	
	acknowledgment			environment			perseverance	
	aliveness/vitality		4	family	7		personal growth	
	authenticity			focus			power	
	autonomy			friendship			privacy	
	balance			full expression		2	purpose/meaning	5
	beauty			fun			quality	
	boldness		1	harmony/peace	5	5	resilience	
	certainty			health/well being	5		respect	7
	choice			honesty			risk-taking/	
	clarity			insight			adventure	
	closeness			intelligence	6		romance	
	collaboration			joy		3	security	5
	commitment			leadership			spirituality	
	community		7	love	6	10	success	7
	completion			loyalty	5		tradition	
	connection			mastery of team			trusting	
	contribution			openness			vulnerability	
6	creativity	1	8	organized	7		wisdom	

Package Your Strengths and Developmental Needs

Preparation for a job search requires that you develop a clear understanding of those behavioral traits that influence how you think, feel, and operate, as well as your technical skills and leadership competencies. This will provide insight into you as a person and the kind of job/environment in which you best operate and contribute. Accordingly, you will be able to talk about yourself appropriately, confidently, candidly, and convincingly without embarrassment, awkwardness, or hesitation when you network or in interviews.

Strengths are those behavioral traits that contribute to your success, seem to work for you, and get your needs met. You want to portray your *developmental needs* as those strengths carried to an extreme or used inappropriately, or behavior seen by a person with whom you do not have a trusting relationship. Rather than labeling them "weaknesses," developmental needs is a much less harsh way of describing those areas you might wish to improve.

In the next series of worksheets, you will be asked to identify the following:

- Personal strengths
- Examples of applied strengths
- Developmental needs
- Brand You, Inc.

Are you ready to dive deeper into what you need to know and articulate? Great! Let's go exploring.

WORKSHEET 13

My Personal/Professional Strengths

Review the following list and CIRCLE the all the words that you identify with or that your close business associates might select when describing your strengths. After you have circled all the relevant strengths, please go back through the list and HIGHLIGHT YOUR TOP 10 STRENGTHS.

accomplished	cost-effective	frank	observant	resourceful
adaptable	courageous	friendly	open-minded	respected
alive	courteous	generous	opinionated	respectful
ambitious	creative	genuine	optimistic	results-oriented
analytical	daring	global	orderly	scientific
anticipative	decisive	good natured	organized	self-reliant
approachable	demanding	gregarious	outrageous	shrewd
argumentative	democratic	happy	outspoken	sincere
articulate	dependable	helpful	partner	smart
artistic	detailed	honest	patient	smooth
assertive	determined	human	people-oriented	sociable
astute	diplomatic	humorous	perceptive	sophisticated
authentic	disciplined	imaginative	perfectionist	straight-forward
bright	discerning	independent	persistent	strategic
calm	discreet	individualist	personable	supportive
carefree	distant	initiator	persuasive	sympathetic
caring	driving	innovative	pleasant	systematic
charismatic	easy	inspiring	polished	tactful
coach	effective	intense	positive	talented
compatible	efficient	introverted	pragmatic	thinker
competitive	eloquent	intuitive	precise	thoughtful
conceptual	energetic	kind	probing	tolerant
confident	enthusiastic	liberal	productive	tough-minded
confrontive	exacting	logical	proud	verbally skilled
conscientious	expansive	loyal	provocative	visionary
conservative	extroverted	mentor	purposeful	winner
considerate	fair	methodical	questioning	
consistent	firm	modest	quick	
consultative	flexible	motivator	realistic	
constructive	focused	mover	reflective	
cool	forceful	objective	reliable	

Other Strengths: _____

WORKSHEET 14

Examples of Applied Strengths

Transfer your top 10 strengths from the previous worksheet, and provide an example that would illustrate how you applied your strengths on the job. Ultimately, we will use some of these supporting examples in your résumé development (Chapter 7) and also in preparing for competency-based interviews (Chapter 18).

MY TOP STRENGTHS

1. Bright

2. _____

3. _____

4. _____

5. _____

6. _____

7. _____

8. _____

9. _____

10. _____

A SUPPORTING EXAMPLE

1. Conceived of a new product that will generate $17 million in third year sales.

2. _____

3. _____

4. _____

5. _____

6. _____

7. _____

8. _____

9. _____

10. _____

What's Inside the Boss's Head?

The following are some examples of what a potential boss might be thinking:

- Who are you *really?*
- How well can you do the job?
- How well will you fit into the organization?
- How much can I trust you; will I be able to rely on you?
- How well do you know yourself?
- What is the unvarnished truth as to why you are looking?

Your Strengths Gone Awry

The following formula can be used to describe your weaknesses as overplayed or overextended strengths when you are in an interview or on a networking call.

1. State your strength.
2. State the excess of the strength.
3. Describe how it shows up.
4. Describe how you manage it so it's not a problem.

Example:

Strength: "As mentioned, I set high performance goals for my team."

Excess: "I'm aware that sometimes I can become impatient if things aren't moving as fast as I'd like or if it seems that people aren't pulling their own weight."

How it shows up: "When I feel pressure around deadlines, I become much more focused on results. My team and I look for blockages and move to resolve them. Also, I don't have a problem challenging my people to perform."

How I manage it: "I have learned to communicate my expectations and timetables more fully and have people keep me posted on a project's status on a regular and ongoing basis. When I use this approach, my developmental need is not a problem—it's a safeguard."

Developmental Needs Are Overplayed Strengths

Strengths overplayed become vulnerabilities.
"Sometimes I can be seen as..."

Strength	Vulnerability
Bright	Having all the answers
Ambitious	Results at any costs!
People-oriented	Not moving quickly enough on tough people issues
Task-oriented	Not considerate enough of others' feelings
Detail-minded	A bit of a perfectionist
Decisive	Somewhat impulsive
Hardworking	A workaholic who overcommits
Setting high performance standards	Demanding of myself and others to succeed
Practical	Conservative, using tried-and-true approaches
Innovative	Using nontraditional methods
Sensitive	Emotional . . . I become deeply committed

WORKSHEET 15

My Developmental Needs

Transfer your top 10 strengths from Worksheet 13 onto this worksheet. Review the examples below; then complete the formula for your top overplayed strength.

Personal Strengths	Developmental Need–Overplayed Strength	
Bright	Seen as…	"Having all the answers…"
Ambitious	Seen as…	"Driven to succeed…"
People-oriented	Seen as…	"Not being tough enough…"
Task-oriented	Seen as…	"Not considerate enough of others…"
Detail-minded	Seen as…	"A bit of a perfectionist…"

1. _____
2. _____
3. _____
4. _____
5. _____
6. _____
7. _____
8. _____
9. _____
10. _____

Strength: _____

Excess: _____

Shows up by: _____

Managed by: _____

WORKSHEET 16

My Personal Self-Description

Write a several-paragraph description of yourself in short phrases and sentences. List as many characteristics as you can, including your behavior, core personal values, likes, dislikes, principles, beliefs, attitudes, convictions, points of view, philosophy about life and business, strengths, developmental needs, leadership styles, and so on. Remember to use short words and phrases; this is not intended to be a writing exercise nor your autobiography. Uncomfortable articulating the most powerful way to describe yourself? Here is your chance to become emboldened and confident as you prepare this response, as every interviewer will ask you to describe yourself, one way or another.

Brand You, Inc.—Create Your Competitive Advantage

To find a great job, you have to market yourself. I know, I know. Your parents may have told you it is impolite to brag. However, it's not bragging if you are telling the truth about your skills, capabilities, and accomplishments. It's not bragging if you have added significant value to your organization. So, tell the truth, the whole truth, and nothing but the truth.

The best way to avoid feeling self-conscious about marketing yourself is to consider yourself a highly desirable product. *If you do not believe in yourself, why should anyone else?* To succeed, you have to effectively package yourself. And that starts with getting excited about *you*. Perhaps for the first time in your life, you are going to have to market yourself like a company markets a product—using every appropriate tool and resource to gain attention and respect in the marketplace. You are now Brand You, Inc.

Learning how to sell yourself to your networking contacts or to a company as a potential employee is simply the best investment in yourself you will ever make. But you have to make the choice to put the time and effort into the task. If you are still employed, please be alert to the fact that as you adapt your behavior in preparation to conduct the search for the perfect job, you may find yourself becoming more empowered at work. You may find that as you begin to master your emotions and perspectives, your relationships become more complete and your interpersonal skills more effective. Who knows? Perhaps as you ready yourself to run in the job-hunting race you will discover that you work in a place which is pretty good, though not perfect, and that you are increasingly more in control of your work environment than you previously thought.

The four main components of your relationships and roles within any organization are as follows:

1. *Position and Duties.* The actual duties and responsibilities that you perform.
2. *Direct Managers.* The people you work directly for, as well as your boss's managers.
3. *Peers and Subordinates.* Your coworkers, subordinates, and other individuals evaluated as occupying lower positions in the organization.
4. *Organization and Culture.* The style and personality of the overall organization, as well as the "personality" of the department in which you worked. Organization culture deals with the organization's values, policies, and operating style.

The following exercises are designed to help you:

- Identify those factors you want to have in your next job, as well as those you want to avoid experiencing.
- Establish a values checklist so you can evaluate potential job offers against each other.
- Zero in on specific areas in the interview that are of particular interest. The

WORKSHEET 17

"Liked Best–Liked Least" Career Factors

Brand You, Inc.

- What *brand* are you? (How would your best friend describe you? What image do you project?)

- What do you have to *offer?* (Your skills, passions, capabilities, etc.)

- What specifically are your distinctive *advantages?* (What extra value do you create that differentiates you from others?

- Provide examples and describe when you have been especially authentic, bold, confident, enthusiastic, and credible?

information that you reveal here will objectify those factors that you should gravitate toward and away from.

In each of the following categories, list as many things as you can that you liked best and liked least in your most recent position. After you have completed this, go back through the exercise again, listing the same items for your previous jobs, until you have covered all of the significant jobs you have held for the past 10 or so years. There is no need to go back beyond 15 years, as your most recent jobs are the most relevant.

When it is complete, you will have a comprehensive list of the kinds of actual duties and responsibilities within jobs, relationships, and organizational environments that you enjoy and cause you to grow and be nurtured, and those that you don't like and probably want to avoid in the future. We think of these as opposite ends of a continuum: those environments, roles, relationships you should gravitate toward versus those that you should gravitate away from. The organizations and roles you should gravitate away from are what I consider toxic. Working in a toxic environment is dangerous to your mental, physical, and relational well-being. If the environment is something you can change by being more collaborative, cooperative, and adaptive, then stay and grow. If staying means compromising your core values and becoming diminished and defeated, then flee as quickly as possible! Indeed, you may find that to maintain your sanity, you may need to jump ship at the first opportunity that looks reasonable, though you know this job is merely a convenient stepping stone to a more appropriate fit.

This list of things you liked best and liked least, along with the insights you gleaned from your core values checklist, will be used later in the chapter in Worksheet 22, "Position Selection Criteria," as you create the template for your ideal job.

Position Selection Criteria

As you completed each of the preceding exercises, you no doubt began to decide (or remember) those parts of your job and company that you really want to have in a new job or company. Refer back to those things that you Liked Best.

For those elements that you really want to avoid, refer back to those things you identified as Liked Least and rephrase them in a positive manner. The following is an example of how to turn negatives into positives or how to state what you want to see in the job.

WORKSHEET 18

Position and Duties

What I Liked Best	What I Liked Least

What are the most important attractions and considerations for you now with regard to the kinds of duties and responsibilities you would like in your next position?

_____

_____

_____

_____

_____

WORKSHEET 19

Direct Managers

Qualities I Liked Best	Qualities I Liked Least

What are the most important attractions and considerations for you now with regard to the kind of supervisors or bosses you most want to have in your next position?

_____

_____

_____

_____

_____

_____

WORKSHEET 20

Peers and Subordinates

Characteristics I Liked Best	Characteristics I Liked Least

What are the most important attractions and considerations for you now with regard to the characteristics of peers and subordinates you want to see in your next position?

_____

_____

_____

_____

_____

WORKSHEET 21

Organization and Culture

Characteristics I Liked Best	Characteristics I Liked Least

What are the most important attractions and considerations for you now with regard to the corporate culture, organizational characteristics, and values in your next assignment?

_____

_____

_____

_____

_____

Turning Negatives into Positive Selection Criteria

Liked Least...	Positively Worded Becomes ...	Position Selection Criteria (I want...)
Combative Board of Directors		Active, collaborative board members
Boss always played favorites.		Everyone treated fairly and uniformly.
Stuck in dead-end job.		Promotional opportunities are present.
Workload is a backbreaker.		Workload is balanced and evenly paced.
Under-paid.		Equitable pay with the opportunity to earn significant bonuses for performance.

Hopefully, you will be faced with the difficult task of deciding among several fine job offers. These worksheet 22, "Position Selection Criteria" is an attempt to help you *objectively evaluate job offers and quantify their value*. Additionally, these criteria identify those areas or topics in the interview you want to get detailed information about. This approach will enable you to more effectively distance yourself from the many emotions that influence career decisions. For instance, if you are an enthusiastic person, you run the risk of being unduly influenced by your potential boss's contagious enthusiasm, even though the position may not be your best career move.

If your criteria for the ideal job are present, you will more likely be favorably impressed by this opportunity, not only emotionally but also intellectually.

The "Position Selection Criteria" worksheets are a guide and should not completely displace your gut instincts. While your ratings for a given company may say "Go," your feelings about the job or the relationships in the company may say "Whoa." You may find that some criteria are so important for you that if they are not present, the company (or offer) is considered to be knocked out of consideration. The potential for career growth and advancement is certainly an issue worth considering. As is wealth accumulation, if that is highly important to you.

Through the use of the Worksheet 22 "Position Selection Criteria" you have the opportunity to more objectively evaluate those factors (and opportunities) that are important to you in your career.

Instructions

1. Using the following format, list those things (criteria) you want in a position. This process will help you sort through the many issues that influence making a career decision.
2. Review the following pages of our fictitious job seeker, Michele Cannon, for ideas on a format. Please do not merely copy Michele's list, although some of her criteria may dovetail exactly with your own. Your goal is to develop your own list, personalizing those things that you want in a job.

3. *Absolute scale*. Reread all of your position selection criteria and assign a rank to them according to what you want and need. Do not worry too much about being completely accurate; this is not a test, and these priorities can shift as you gain more experience with this exercise.

4. *Company evaluation*. Since the evaluation of positions in companies only occurs after interviewing, you may put this section aside for now. Please feel free to add to this list throughout the course of your job search. This criteria list will be used later in Chapter 21, "Offer Negotiations, Gain Leverage, and Get the Package You Deserve."

   To objectively evaluate a company before or after receiving an offer, read each of your selection criteria and assess its availability. Decide on a ranking, and write it down for every item on your list.

5. After you have assessed each individual criterion, evaluate any significant gaps in your Absolute Score and your Company Score. For instance, turn to Michele Cannon's list and note that her first criteria, "Active, collaborative board members" was rated a "1." Obviously, Michele considers this dimension pretty important.

6. Accordingly, Michele's interviewing strategy with her first company was to determine the extent to which the Board of Directors were active, collaborative, and supportive versus combative and unreasonably confrontive. Michele scored Company 1 a "3," as she perceived this criteria to be present "only occasionally." Given that Michele deemed this dimension to be "essential" and it only showed up occasionally, this is what we would call a significant difference. Based on this difference, Michele would circle "3," as she needs to seriously evaluate why that is the case and to see if other significant negatives exist. The reason for the lower rating may simply have been that Michele failed to ask penetrating questions that would have revealed this critical data. No matter the reason, to be satisfied that she fully explored this dimension, Michele gets to zero in on this issue and ask more probing questions.

Probing Questions Michele Can Ask:

1. Describe the composition of the board.
2. How would you describe each board member and his or her personality?
3. What formal and informal roles do each board member play?
4. What is the most pressing agenda of the board and of each member?
5. How did the board view the previous incumbent's performance for whose role I'm interviewing?
6. Describe how the planning process works and who is involved in corporate strategies and department plans.

7. Who determines what programs and projects get worked on and receive funding?
8. What latitude will I have with regard to this role, including project leadership and capitalization?

Note that Michele has circled several criteria in which she either didn't get enough data or she noted a significant difference between her absolute scale and what she discovered in the company. Accordingly, Michele ought to speak to the hiring authority to ascertain the presence/absence of her important criteria.

A word of caution: make sure that your probing questions are carefully woven into the broader context of the interview so as not to appear fixated on one criteria or so that the conversation does not take on the tone of an interrogation. Indeed, while you want to uncover these high priority criteria, you want to suspend judgment until after the interview, lest you appear to be negative or inappropriately critical.

We recommend against multiplying or adding your absolute scores with the company scores. While this quantification may make you feel better, it is statistically worthless. Why? For two reasons. First, you probably have not gone through the laborious process of weighting and validating each item. Second, it is virtually impossible for you to be completely objective in the scoring process because you, like others before you, will react more favorably to one company (and criteria) over another.

Evaluation Key

My Absolute Scale

1. Essential for me in the job
2. Important for me in the job
3. It would be nice to have
4. Not of major significance

Company Evaluation

1. Clearly available in this job
2. Probably available in this job
3. May be there occasionally
4. Clearly *not* available in this job

Figure 5-1   Position selection criteria.

Michele Cannon's Criteria	My Absolute Scale	Companies Interviewed			
		Company 1	Company 2	Company 3	Company 4
I. Positions and Duties					
Active involvement with Board of Directors	1	③			
Competitive compensation package	1	2			
Challenging and complex	1	1			
Opportunity to greatly contribute	2	2			
II. Immediate Managers					
Authentic collaborative and cooperative leaders	2	③			
Boss communicates openly and honestly	1	③			
Bold, confident, enthusiastic, sense of humor, and good self-esteem	2	③			
III. Peers/Subordinates					
Authentic, open, honest, transparent, positive	1	2			
Well educated and highly competent.	2	2			
Capable and driven to succeed for the greater organizational good	2	3			
People are collaborative and very cooperative	1	③			
IV. Organization					
Promotions are available	1	③			
Products are competitive	1	2			
Apolitical climate and one that challenges everyone to do their best	1	2			

WORKSHEET 22

Position Selection Criteria

Companies Interviewed

Criteria	My Absolute Scale	Company 1	Company 2	Company 3	Company 4

WORKSHEET 23

My Ideal Job

The goal of this exercise is to give you an opportunity to capture some of the parameters of your ideal job. Presumably, you have identified various "ideal" elements of the position, relationships, organization environments, industries, and geographic locations in which you operate most effectively, distinct from those which do not work for you. As a general rule of thumb, the more restrictive you are, the longer and more difficult your search.

Now describe your next ideal job.

(Job title, duties, location, opportunity to contribute, and kind of company/industry).

WORKSHEET 24

Your Drivers and Goals

- What are the main motivators in your life? What drives you?

- As you look ahead in your career, what things are you especially *looking forward to* and why?

- As you look ahead in your career, what things would you *like to avoid* and why?

- Immediate (one to three years) goals:
Professional-
Personal-

- Long-term (five-plus years) goals:
Professional-
Personal-

- What financial goals do you have? How much on/off target are you? If off target, what do you need to do to get on target?

- What are your geographical preferences for living and working?

- What is your life's purpose or personal mission?

- Describe where, when, and how the passion in your life shows up.

- What is missing in your life, the presence of which would make you more fulfilled?

Mind-Mapping Your Career Options

Congratulations! You have come a long way in identifying those factors that make up the many parts of you. I'd like to introduce you to a form of brainstorming called mind-mapping. We'll be utilizing all the information and musings from all the questions you have answered in this and preceding chapters. In essence, you are going to map out a number of options for your next career move.

First, what is mind-mapping? This brainstorming technique is a nonlinear method of capturing data. Imagine a spiderweb. After anchoring their web, most spiders spin their webs starting in the middle and working outward. In the case of mind-mapping, think of a series of options spinning away from the center. The farther out from the center, the greater the detail you'll identify.

Figure 5-2 is an example of mind-mapping my options if I won a $200 million lottery. You can see where my fantasies take me in this situation. The fact that I identified buying a private island does not mean that I necessarily would. Rather, one of the options available to me is to buy a private island, though I might ultimately give it a "C" priority in light of the other things I want to do with my newfound wealth. A great question to ask me would be, "What does having a private island represent for you?" Perhaps, I want peace, tranquility, and privacy in a warm climate, rather than my own island. The great thing with mind-mapping is that you can easily continue to explore each element into deeper and deeper detail, as appropriate.

Let's stick to the private island for a moment. What is the purpose of this island? How will I primarily use the island? Scuba diving, sailing, deep-sea fishing, traveling to other interesting islands, having a working sugar cane plantation, a place to work on my tan? While I identified three places, where else in the world might my island be located? How big must my island be to accommodate the deep-sea harbor and airstrip? Or does a heli-pad make more sense? What style will the main house and outlying houses be like? Etc.

Your Turn! You've Just Won a $200 Million Lottery!

As fast as you can, brainstorm what you would do with your $200 million. Don't worry about practicality—you've got $200 million! You can do anything! Your goal is to identify at least five major areas and ten spinoffs that clarify more details. After you've captured some of your options, step away for ten minutes and then come back and complete your mind-mapping. While you were away from your chart doing something else, invariably several additional ideas will have popped into your mind. Go fantasize with your $200 million!

Figure 5-2   Mind-mapping my $200 million lottery winnings.

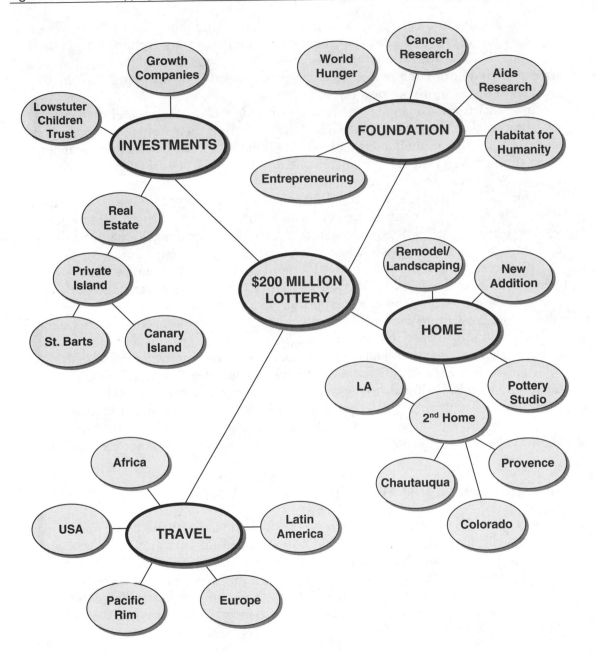

Mind-map your choices for your $200 million lottery winnings.

$200 MILLION
LOTTERY
WINNINGS

Mind-Mapping Career Options

Now it is your turn to begin fantasizing about your career options by creating your own mind-map.

Step 1:   Get a large piece of paper; a flip-chart sheet works great. If you don't have a large sheet, tape four 8 1/2-by-11-inch sheets together so you can really let loose.

Step 2:   Draw a circle in the middle of the paper and print "My Career, Inc." Consider yourself to be a company. Your products and service offerings are your talents, experiences, wisdom, drive, and commitment. Draw upon all the insights you gained in your professional/personal life and the work you have done to date in these worksheets: your strengths/developmental needs; that which you liked best/liked least; your career achievements; your core personal values; your passions; the elements that make up your authentic, genuine self, to name a few.

Step 3:   At the top of your sheet create a "purpose statement." In 25 words or fewer, write down the essence of "Why does My Career, Inc. exist?" For instance, since my firm, Robertson Lowstuter, provides executive development consulting, my purpose statement might be the following: "As an executive coach, I enable individuals, teams, and organizations to significantly enhance their authenticity, performance, and profitability." Your statement should be broad enough for you to really brainstorm far-reaching possibilities while giving you some parameters within which to play.

Step 4:   Ask yourself out loud the question, "What are all the different products and services My Career, Inc. can potentially offer?" Regardless of my ultimate career outcome, what are all my career options? Whatever your fantasy is, put it down on the paper, spinning out circles of options without regard to whether they are practical. Your goal is at least five primary career options; for example, land a corporate role, write a book, start a consulting business, buy a business, launch a franchise, be a college professor, start an incubator business, invest in real estate, manage investments, sail around the world, retire, try out for the senior golf tour, or be a permanent volunteer for Habitat for Humanity. Whatever.

Step 5:   Refer back to your purpose statement at the top of the sheet. Out loud ask yourself, "What else? What are other products and services My Career, Inc. can potentially offer?" Because many of us have not thought deeply or often enough about what we are capable of, your goal is at least four additional career options.

Step 6:   Ask out loud, "Who could benefit from the breadth of My Career, Inc.'s products and services?" Open up and expand your thinking. Consider (and write down on your chart) individuals and companies. For-profit and nonprofit organizations? Start-ups and Fortune 500 companies?

Step 7:   Ask out loud "What are all the ways that My Career, Inc.'s products and services could go to market?" Consider (and write down on your chart) a number of ways you might promote your products or services—for example, direct mail, networking, e-commerce, customer/colleague evangelism, introductory trials, free/low-cost seminars to introduce your capabilities, or newsletters (e-mail/U.S. Postal Service), to name a few.

Step 8:   Stand up, step back, and evaluate the progress you've made so far on your mind-mapping. I recommend that you set it aside and come back to it a little later. By that I mean a few minutes, hours, or even overnight. Don't put this aside for weeks, as you will lose most of your momentum and creativity around the good thinking you've done so far. As a break from mind-mapping, you might wish to answer the questions outlined in the next section.

When Exploring Career Options, Ask Yourself a Few Questions

If you have ever considered a radical departure from your current type of position, company, or industry, you should consider answering some practical questions.

1. What do you really want in your career? In your life?
2. What are your alternative career options? Describe the title, function, and industry.
3. What might be your roles within these options?
4. What appeals to you when you see yourself in these roles?
5 . What motivates you to want to do this?
6. What are the positive aspects of this job?
7. What are the negative aspects of this job?
8. Who do you know who might be an expert in this area?
9. What might you learn from this expert to be successful?
10. In your opinion, what skills, capabilities, and commitment do you have to succeed in these roles or industries?
11. In the opinion of others, what skills, capabilities, and commitment do you have to succeed in these roles or industries?
12. What skills, abilities, or contacts do you need to strengthen?
13. To be fully equipped to function in these roles, what is required?
14. How would you establish credibility?
15. What are you willing to do to be successful? By when?
16. How will you know when you've acquired the necessary skills for these roles?
17. What do you gain by pursuing this dream?
18. What do you lose by pursing this dream?

19. What do you gain by *not* pursuing this dream?
20. What do you lose by *not* pursuing this dream?
21. How much of a market is there for your services?
22. To what extent will you be able to capture business?
23. How will you create a sufficient distinction for you to succeed?
24. If you were someone else, would you invest in you? Why? Why not?

Traditional or Alternative Career Paths

Since I come from the business world, I define a traditional career path as being employed in a publicly traded or privately held corporation. I consider alternative career paths as all the other career venues, such as nonprofit, academia, consulting, or entrepreneuring.

Having helped clients launch hundreds of alternative careers since founding Robertson Lowstuter, we know that there is honor in all work and in all roles. There is not a best or preferred career path. What is perfect and right for you might not fit me at all, and vice versa.

By way of example, I started my career in organizational consulting at Ernst & Ernst (somewhat of an alternative path) and then followed a traditional career path by going into organizational development and effectiveness in a corporate role when I was employed by The Ansul Company, Chemetron, and Fiat Allis for a number of years. Since 1981 I have been following an alternative career path providing executive development coaching and consulting to diverse clients. My son, Nathan, is in global supply chain and operations at Honeywell International following a more traditional career path in the corporate world. My daughter, Cammen, is likewise on an alternative career path with two jobs: managing the marketing and public relations for Colorado Free University and as a significant collaborator with RL on our materials and workshops, including this book. Examples abound of people leaving the corporate world to pursue alternative careers. One of our clients had an enviable track record as a senior executive with significant P&L responsibility when she announced that she wanted to give back to society. She joined STRIVE–Chicago in a leadership capacity to help unemployable urban adults gain the skills to successfully enter mainstream business. She's now in Wilmington, Delaware, operating in a philanthropic capacity to help senior adults enhance their lives. Rather than continue his 30-plus-year R&D career in a health care company another client, launched an MBA-style curriculum for a Chicago-area medical school designed to equip newly minted physicians to be more effective in managing costs and running their practices. Another client was the 53-year old president of a $3.5 billion pharmaceutical company who took advantage of his company's generous retirement policy and announced his intentions to retire early.

His plan: relocate to the Southwest and provide strategic leadership to an area university and a handful of other nonprofits to help them optimize their charters.

The examples of people leaving corporate roles and pursuing alternative paths abound. To the uninformed, it appears easier to move from traditional careers to alternative ones than it does to move from alternative careers to traditional ones. In either case, it is less a function of what direction you are headed and more a function of answering three key questions:

1. What do you have to offer?
   - What unique value and set of experiences do you bring?
   - What can you do that someone else cannot do?
   - How will hiring you help the company accelerate its mission and long-range goals?
2. Why are you pursuing this venue?
   - How realistic are you regarding your ability to significantly contribute?
   - How sound is your reasoning? Are you making the right decisions for the right reasons?
   - What was missing in your other roles that you hope will be present?
3. How will you effectively brand and package yourself?
   - What adaptive shifts are necessary to be successful, and how will you reinvent yourself in this new context?
   - What skills are directly applicable to this role and venue? Which ones are not?
   - What are the top five challenges that you would face in this new arena that you haven't faced before, and what will you do about them?

Exploring Traditional and Alternative Career Options

Not all alternative career paths are entrepreneurial, though many are. Increasing numbers of executives, fed up with the internal organizational political struggles, are actively exploring alternative venues, specifically being an entrepreneur. To that end, Chapter 6, "Entrepreneuring — To Be or Not To Be?," focuses on alternative careers. We'll cover entrepreneurial myths and realities and common characteristics of successful entrepreneurs. Additionally, we'll identify a number of resources for you can access. Accordingly, you will be drawing upon the insights you have gleaned thus far from the exercises you have finished.

ENTREPRENEURING—TO BE OR NOT TO BE?

Career Options

The one constant that I am always struck by is how many career options people have. Granted, you may have been in one job or employed in one industry for many years, but that does not dictate your being stuck there. In much the same way you could have gone to different schools, majored in different things, made different choices in your early career roles but now choose to pursue different paths. While you might not dramatically shift your career, the mere fact that you have explored diverse options opens up your horizon. The following are a few options from the myriad number of things you could do.

Traditional Career Path—Corporate World

- Publicly traded corporations
- Privately held companies
- Small to midsized organizations

Alternative Career Path

- Buy a business
- Entrepreneuring: start-up or early-stage companies
- Consulting
- Franchising
- Academia
- Not-for-profit/philanthropic organizations

Interested in Becoming an Entrepreneur?

The entrepreneurial route is another avenue for career changers—namely, buying or building a business. If you are interested in becoming an entrepreneur and exploring what it would take to launch your own business, then we suggest you begin by becoming immersed in the entrepreneur's world. Begin to keenly observe what is suboptimal or missing in your business and what, if spun off, could represent a business. Speculate what product line extensions might be available to existing businesses if they only considered them. Nothing will serve you quite as well as talking with both entrepreneurs who have been successful and those with notable failures under their belt. My belief is that you learn as much or more from failure as you do from success.

Entrepreneurial Reality

According to The Entrepreneur's Source, a leading franchise consulting firm:

- 75 percent of the adult population has that grain of sand to control their own destiny.
- Only 5 percent of them are ready, willing, and able to buy or build a business.

Based on Robertson Lowstuter's research, we have discovered the startling statistics that:

- 50 percent of all start-up businesses fail within the first year.
- 70 percent of all start-up businesses fail within five years.

Starting a New Business—Pros and Cons

Managing the paradox: that's what is required when you contemplate starting a business. It is common to experience a number of conflicting emotions. On one hand, you are excited and hopeful. On the other hand, you are terrified and worried. That's the paradox—the "yes, and" of our emotions. You might be thinking, "I want to launch my own business, *and* I don't want to risk all my worldly possessions." I might add that both sets of emotions are worth noting and exploring their deeper meaning while learning from them. Clearly, there are some pros and cons to entrepreneuring:

Pros

- Few constraints regarding product/service offerings.
- Greater independence of thought and action.
- Can often start with a clean slate of ideas and business plan.
- Usually less expensive to launch than buying an existing business.

Cons

- Very high failure rate in the first three years.
- May take years to be profitable, if ever.
- Financing may be tough to secure.
- Incredible drain of personal time and energy.
- High probability of straining personal/family relationships.

Buying an Existing Business—Pros and Cons

Buying an existing business is analogous to buying a used house versus designing and building one from scratch. The advantage is that the business exists, though you don't always know the hidden issues, like a cracked foundation covered up by newly installed carpeting.

Pros

- Generally requires less time and energy to get going versus a pure start-up.
- Lots of freedom to create the business the way you want.
- May have a proven record and process to follow.
- If business is/has been profitable, financing terms will be more favorable.

Cons

- Often takes one to three years of diligent searching to find the right business.
- No guarantee of success.
- May take longer to be profitable than anticipated, if ever, especially if overpaid for the business.
- Could inherit considerable unseen number of problems and liabilities, including customer dissatisfaction, staff conflict, inertia, and incompetencies.

Being Awarded a Franchise—Pros and Cons

Franchising might be a viable career alternative for you to seriously explore if you have the entrepreneurial itch but do not already have a specific product or service offering in mind. Unless you have been down the entrepreneurial path previously, getting guidance is absolutely essential if you want to be successful. You want and need a mentor to accelerate your business's growth and profitability. This is one of the roles that a franchisor plays for you. As you know, you learn from the franchisor what to do and what to avoid. For the privilege of having a knowledgeable guide, you will pay a franchise fee and ongoing royalties for the life of the franchise agreement. In general, the franchisor breaks even on the franchise fee, given all the training and materials you receive. Accordingly, franchisors make their money (and are successful) when they make their franchisees successful. It can be a great synergistic relationship for both parties, provided everyone lives up to the letter and spirit of the franchise agreement.

Pros

- Quality of franchisor products and services usually high.
- Lots of preopening training and launch support.
- Franchisor strongly invested in your success.
- Financing may be relatively easy to secure, as business might be prequalified for loans from the SBA (Small Business Administration) or other sources.

Cons

- Franchisee is not able to operate totally independently or able to introduce creative venues without permission.
- Franchises are required to pay ongoing royalties/minimum marketing fees.
- Terms of franchise agreement may be more restrictive than person is comfortable with, including length of franchise.
- Only awarded franchise; never really own the business.

Learn More About Franchising

A ton of data is available on the Internet regarding entrepreneuring and franchising. Contact the International Franchise Association (IFA) for free information about the myths and realities of franchising: www.ifa-university.com. To identify franchise opportunities and resources, go to such sites as: www.americasbestfranchises.com, www.franchise.org, www.franchisegator.com, www.franchisesearch.com, www.franchise-solutions.com, or www.entrepreneur.com.

Contact franchise consultants or brokers to learn more about how they help people assess the viability of franchising, as well as help them find the optimal franchise. The Entrepreneur's Source and FranNet are certainly top resources; they can be found at www.entrepreneurssource.com and www.frannet.com.

Entrepreneuring—A Viable Career Option?

While you might be intrigued, or even enthralled, with the idea of being an entrepreneur, it is incumbent upon you to objectively and very carefully evaluate your reasons. You want to ensure that you are doing the right thing for the right reason. Doing the right thing for the wrong reason is pursuing the entrepreneur path because of some ego trip. If you want to be an entrepreneur to fulfill self-gratification or if you think you'll have more free time, then I contend that following this path fundamentally may not be right for you. It is fraught with peril and a way to become disheartened or, worse, lose your life's savings.

 Just because you *might* be successful as an entrepreneur is no reason why you *should* become one.

Reasons Given for Wanting to Be an Entrepreneur

Over the years, our clients have revealed that they want to be an entrepreneur because they:

- Have a great business concept and a strategy to execute it.
- Are passionate about a service or product and want to market and sell it.
- Know that they can contribute better and more fully utilize their creativity and drive outside of a corporation than inside.
- Were too intense and focused on generating results and didn't consistently get along well with others.
- Needed to be the one to direct their own efforts versus having a boss.
- Wanted to involve their family members in the business.
- Were committed to creating a legacy for future generations.
- Wanted to earn what the marketplace allowed—not what a company's salary grade dictated.
- Wanted to retire at an early age, after selling the entrepreneurial venture.

The main question we always ask and help clients discover is this: Is entrepreneuring right for you? Launching an entrepreneurial venture is not for the faint of heart. While 75 percent of our clients actively explore entrepreneuring, only about 25 percent consummate it. Why the fallout? Many people discover that they are better suited operationally and interpersonally to be in a larger organization. They might have higher affiliation needs than being a sole practitioner can provide. Other clients realize that since they were uncomfortable networking for a corporate job, they would be incredibly uncomfortable in prospecting and selling as an entrepreneur. These clients learn that uncovering leads for a corporate role or for a consulting engagement draws upon the same networking skill set.

 Everyone has the capability of successfully operating in a number of different business venues, including entrepreneuring. Though entrepreneuring is not for everyone.

Do You Have What It Takes?

An entrepreneur is

- A person who sees problems and hassles as unrealized business opportunities and who then creates the products, services, and systems to generate the desired outcome.
- One who sees the business potential beyond what is readily apparent or beyond the reach of currently available resources.
- A visionary who turns a creative "what if?" into a sustainable and viable business.
- An eternal optimist who is willing to risk his or her time, energy, and money in pursuit of a dream.

Major Characteristics of an Entrepreneur

Remember the exercise of identifying your top 10 core personal values? As we delve deeper into the realm of entrepreneuring, you might wish to revisit your top values in Chapter 5, "Career Strategies and Options," and see how these might correlate to being an entrepreneur. I liken referring back and forth to previous exercises as part of your careering reality check. The last thing you want to do is leap off into a career option that is not right for you.

OK, let's look further at some of the reasons and characteristics of entrepreneurs. You might be a strong entrepreneurial candidate if you are committed to being your own boss, provided your motivation is more than merely getting out from under someone else telling you what to do. The following traits or background conditions are common to many successful entrepreneurs. *Note*: Not all persons who have the following traits make successful entrepreneurs, and not all successful entrepreneurs have all these traits. Nonetheless, you may wish to evaluate yourself in light of these dimensions and your core personal values.

Optimism	Positive expectancy
Objectivity	Interpersonal skills
Authenticity	Creativity
Ability to execute	Focus/self-discipline
Compelling vision	Leadership
Competitiveness	Emotional maturity
Self-management skills	Commitment
Drive	Courage
Boldness	Confidence
Enthusiasm	Ability to take risks
Business acumen	Ability to solve problems
Practical/pragmatic	Decisiveness
Perseverance	Accountable

Entrepreneurial Characteristic Profile

If you'd like to take RL's *Entrepreneurial Characteristic Profile* please contact us via our web site, www.robertsonlowstuter.com. This profile will help you assess how strong your entrepreneurial orientation might be.

Please note that if your score is not at the highest level, it does not mean that you wouldn't succeed as an entrepreneur. Listen to your heart and gut, as well as your head. Being an entrepreneur is a balance of logic and passion. It might mean that your background, education, or training does not fit the "standard" profile of your classical entrepreneur. A low score represents an opportunity for you to examine the suitability of launching your own business and areas that you might consider strengthening. In much the same way that a high score does not guarantee entrepreneurial success, a low score does not predict failure. In fact, we have had clients who scored high on this profile, yet their spouses were dead set against putting their personal assets at risk. Wisely, these clients did not proceed down the entrepreneurial path.

Interpersonal Skills and Work Traits

The following words have been used to describe many entrepreneurs: scrappy, confrontational, creative, driven, independent-minded, tough to manage, maverick, socially bold, overly confident, opinionated, possessing a can-do attitude, bright, articulate, courageous, visionary, determined, having a tendency to be a workaholic, and not overly influenced by others.

Entrepreneurs come in all sizes and shapes and have diverse employment backgrounds. Entrepreneurs are innovators and change agents. They clearly and routinely challenge the status quo within their organizations. Because they are typically so much more confrontative, entrepreneurs often "blow-up" relationships, and it is common for them to have been fired more than once. Entrepreneurs generally have occupied roles in which they have been on the leading edge of concepts, approaches, or technologies, even if their organization wasn't ready, willing, or able to accept their contributions or ideas.

Because entrepreneurs are so creative and have a global perspective, they have a pronounced tendency to be somewhat disorganized, which is the one trait they need help with: administering the details.

Successful entrepreneurs are usually not seen as highly collaborative, prone to consensus decision-making, or necessarily willing to accommodate their style to fit someone else's personality. The entrepreneur is more likely going to exert some energy convincing someone of the merits of his or her approach, so others may feel their opinions and feelings are overlooked or ignored.

Motivations

Entrepreneurs think primarily of gaining and servicing customers versus being focused on building a large organization to fuel their egos. Entrepreneurs "fall in love" too quickly with new things or people, new product ideas, new employees, new manufacturing ideas, and new financial systems.

The successful entrepreneur is constantly looking for purpose and the bottom line in business and social encounters. Shallow issues bore entrepreneurial-type people, as they tend to be reluctant social mixers when there is no clear agenda. Entrepreneurs typically are driven achievers with a low need for affiliation with others and a moderate need for power.

WORKSHEET 25

Why Do You Want to Be an Entrepreneur?

While it's relevant to understand what the common traits of entrepreneurs are, what is important is to get a handle on why you are exploring being an entrepreneur. So, I invite you to ask yourself the following questions:

- What are you passionate about and would love to do?

- What unmet career needs do you have?

- What career options do you have?

- What have you done that is aligned with this?

- What glaring need do you want to change, improve, or address?

- What market research have you done to determine if there is a need?

- What have you done regarding creating a prototype or business plan to take advantage of this glaring unmet need?

- What personal assets are you willing to invest in your business?

WORKSHEET 26

What Are You Going to Do?

- What four personal capabilities do you possess that you can leverage in an entrepreneurial venue?

- As an entrepreneur, what product or services might you offer? Immediate term, spinoffs, or longer term?

- In what ways will you truly differentiate your product or service from others?

WORKSHEET 27

Who Are Your Customers?

- Who are your prime targets?

- What is your secondary audience?

- What logical service or product line extensions might there be, and what do your target customers *need* and *want*? Can they pay your asking price?

- What are the pros/cons of doing business with your audience?

WORKSHEET 28

Where Will the Business Come From?

- What is your value-proposition to attract investors and/or customers?

- What segment of the business should be rolled out first?

- What does your S.W.O.T. analysis reveal regarding product and market viability?

- What self-limiting beliefs do you have that might distract you, slow you down, or derail you?

- What are those drivers/accelerants that you can engage in to guarantee success?

WORKSHEET 29

How Will You Be Successful?

- How will you market your product or service?

- To whom might you turn for credible and knowledgeable information or assistance?

- What experiences do you have in successfully conceiving of and launching a business or products?

- What is it about your business model or plan that would appeal to investors?

- What financial resources are you committed to utilizing?

As an Entrepreneur, Do I Need a Résumé?

Even if you are focused on being an entrepreneur, or buying or building a business, you would benefit from the process of creating a results-oriented résumé. Minimally, your customers, investors, referral sources, and others will want to know about your expertise. How you have contributed to past employers is a reflection of how you might be able to contribute to others in the future. So, while you should *not* send your résumé along as part of your business plan, you might develop a biographical summary that is extracted from your fact-based résumé.

As previously stated, a well-crafted résumé is a powerful advanced marketing tool. As an entrepreneur, you'll soon discover the lifeblood of any venture is marketing—how well do people know and trust your ability to deliver?

Resources for Buying, Building, and Launching Your Business

All of the successful entrepreneurs we know have routinely sought assistance, advice, and counsel. Such support comes in all different forms and venues. In addition to the few resources listed in this section, I recommend that you network with entrepreneurs in your geographic area or industry and ask them if they would recommend any programs or resource materials that would help you in your quest. Also, ask them if they would share some of their wisdom. Unless you are vying to be a direct competitor, many entrepreneurs would be glad to give you input. You might ask them:

- What did you do particularly well in the launch of your business?
- Knowing what you now know, what would you do differently?
- Given what I've told you about my entrepreneurial plans, what advice would you give me?
- Who else would you recommend I talk with?

In addition, the following are great sources of information and guidance:

1. *Small Business Administration (SBA)*. The SBA offers free workshops on most of the nuances of how to find, finance, launch, and build a business. SCORE (Service Corps of Retired Executives) is a service arm of the SBA and usually charges a small fee. SCORE consultants are seasoned pros in most, if not all, of the entrepreneurial dimensions that you'll need to know. This includes legal, finance, operations, marketing, and logistics, to name a few.
2. *University marketing or entrepreneurial students*. One of our clients had an innovative business idea and wanted to leverage his time and capabilities. He contacted his former marketing professor at the University of Chicago

and explored the viability of exchanging class credits for the experience of researching and justifying the business launch. While our client hoped that three graduate students would express interest in this project, he quickly became deluged with more than 12 students wanting the experience. This project was mutually beneficial and saved an estimated 6 months of precious start-up time.

3. *Consultants.* Of course, there are any number of advisors who specialize in small businesses and who have the commitment and time to partner with you. These might include a franchise broker, certified public accountant (CPA), attorney, valuation specialist, financial planner, and wealth manager.

4. *Board of Advisors.* Invite 8 to 10 accomplished executives to be part of your Board of Advisors. (Given the increased liability Board of Directors have, your selected people would probably appreciate only being identified as an "advisor" with little or no legal exposure.)

   For instance, your Board of Advisors could
   - Evaluate your readiness to be an entrepreneur.
   - Fine-tune your optimal entrepreneurial path and business venue.
   - Calibrate your business plan, focus, and target customers.
   - Identify sources to gain financing and objectively assess the viability of having business partners.
   - Counsel how to successfully launch, market, and manage your business.
   - Help you ready your business for sale by sourcing and utilizing business valuation consultants to competitively position and price your business.

5. *Financing.* Without adequate money, your entrepreneurial dream is dead. I'm sure you've heard the phrase, "CFIMITYM" ("Cash Flow Is More Important Than Your Mother!"). While you might have a phenomenal concept, have a fantastic product, and deliver a terrific service, if you do not have good cash flow, you'll soon be out of business. This is where OPM (other people's money) comes into play. Private-equity firms, venture capitalists, individual investors, banks, family members, and, of course, self-funding are all sound sources of financing.

   As there are so many variables that will determine the optimal funding vehicle for you, I will not attempt to cover every nuance. In general, the more money you receive from others, the less company ownership you get to retain. An interesting middle ground for you to consider might be angel investors. "Angels" are successful businesspeople who are committed to helping credible business plans get the financing and assistance in launching. Unlike venture capitalists, angel investors typically do not take a majority ownership stake in the business. If you are interested in learning more about angel investing, then perform an Internet search for "Angel Investors." You can then access lots of great information on what these investors look for, as well as articles and listings of angel networks in your area. It's been my experience that angel investors and the angel investment groups will gladly hear your business plan pitch, provided you are fully prepared and your concept is appropriate for them or the group.

6. *Entrepreneurial tools.* You may wish to consider purchasing some tools (online, on CD-ROM, or in hard-copy format) to help you distinguish your business venture. One of the best software programs we and our clients have used is *Palo Alto Business Plan* software. There are at least two versions of the program, depending on the depth of the details you need, financial spreadsheet templates, and how much you want to spend.

    Additionally, the Internet has an almost limitless supply of resource material for someone wanting to learn about and access all things entrepreneurial. One such online source is *Entrepreneur Magazine* (www.entrepreneur.com), a service that has been around for years that now has an extensive Internet capability. Through its many free articles (and services for purchase), you can acquire the information and the tools you need to start, develop, and succeed in your own part-time or full-time business.

7. *Professional and trade associations.* Being active in the associations that align with your product or service might be a good way to gain visibility for yourself and your business. Plus you will be able to evaluate your competition. Take the time and invest money for memberships. Perhaps you can go to several meetings as a guest before you decide to join. Before spending a lot of money for groups or associations, evaluate which organizations and resources best serve your needs. Let common sense prevail. If you are not learning or excited about these venues, drop them and explore others.

8. *Community colleges and adult classes in area high schools.* These are usually a great source of valuable information for budding entrepreneurs. Learn about the pros and cons of being an entrepreneur, including many of the nuances of owning and operating your own business. Become educated about operations, financing, marketing, and so on. Most free universities (noncredited community education institutions), community colleges, and high schools have short, inexpensive, practical courses for people exploring business ownership.

My Two-Cents' Worth

If you are on the fence as to whether you should explore entrepreneuring, you might not have the suitable drive or commitment to make such a venture successful. While I have seen reluctant entrepreneurs be successful in spite of themselves, it is quite rare.

Perseverance, passion, and focus are keys to getting to first base as a business owner. As I type this on a beautiful Sunday afternoon when many of my compatriots are out on the golf course, I admit that there is fine line between creating a thriving business and working hard for the demanding, unsympathetic boss who happens to be sitting in your chair. While being an entrepreneur demands that you sacrifice more than if you were a corporate citizen, often the personal satisfaction is far greater and the politics are of your own making. I know that I feel that way!

STEP 3
CREDENTIAL BUILDING

CHAPTER 7

YOUR RÉSUMÉ: THE KILLER APP

Do You Really Need a Résumé?

Without a doubt, you need a résumé. Yet the topic almost always creates controversy, as people have such divergent views on the subject. A well-crafted résumé is in harmony with your talents, with what prospective employers want and need, and, most importantly, with your career strategy. All three of these elements need to be aligned and in balance.

You are a mosaic of your talents, experiences, accomplishments, intellectual agility, conceptual ability, leadership capability, organizational savvy, humanity, compassion, drive, authenticity, and a thousand other nuances. How can one even begin to capture all of this in an interview without having a plan (i.e., a results-oriented résumé) clearly in place?

 Your goal is to develop a powerful résumé that compels people to contact you.

What Do Employers Really Want? Results, Results, Results!

Employers want to hire, develop, promote, and reward people who can contribute to the achievement of the company's goals, including its growth and profitability.

The best way to convey potential future contribution is to document past accomplishments in the most compelling way possible. Accordingly, you need to quickly demonstrate that you are the kind of person who can make things happen and achieve results. For each job, use action verbs to create brief, "sound bite" statements of your accomplishments, of the *results* that you delivered . . . not just a recitation of your responsibilities. A well-constructed résumé will help you highlight specific examples of significant achievements.

 A results-driven résumé raises the bar for your competition and differentiates you from others.

Résumé Reality Check

You have less than 10 seconds to hook the person scanning your résumé. That's the average amount of time spent on it before it is determined if you should go in the "A" pile for more in-depth evaluation or the "B" pile for moderate interest. The "C" pile is a nice way of saying that there is a high probability that your résumé will get trashed.

Realistically, 10 seconds for your fate to be determined by an overwhelmed researcher at an executive search firm is not much time. That's the bad news. The good news is that your credentials more often will be thrown into the "A" pile when you create a powerful, result-oriented résumé and an equally compelling marketing letter. Through this process you will stand out and clearly differentiate yourself from others competing for the same position. How do I know this? Time and time again our clients receive accolades about their marketing materials (résumé and cover letters) from their references, search firms, and networking contacts with whom they are interacting.

Scannable Résumés: Tips and Techniques

The format that I recommend in this chapter is 100 percent scannable. Scannable not only in the sense of a *person* scanning your résumé looking for key words that reflect your accomplishments and technical capabilities, but also a *scanning device*. High-visibility companies that receive a high volume of unsolicited résumés and many, though not all, retained search firms use computers to scan ("read") résumés, using optical character recognition (OCR) software. Scanning helps employers and search firms manage large numbers of résumés by categorizing a person's résumé any number of ways. To ensure your résumé catches the software's attention, do the following:

1. Use trigger words that make it easy for the search firm researcher and/or software to identify your specific skills and background. For example, the résumé of a Chief Marketing Officer (CMO) would probably have trigger words such as,

Senior Vice President–Marketing, CMO, brand, channel strategy, product development and management, ROI, account penetration, accelerated sales and profits, to name a few.

2. Employ common section headings, such as Career Summary, Business Experience, Education, Patents and Publications, Outside Boards, and the like. Even though the ideal scannable résumé only uses short "sound bite" phrases, crisply worded sentences will do just fine.

   I suspect that the vast majority of opportunities that you will be introduced to will not require your résumé to be scanned. Nonetheless, I still recommend that you occasionally review the position specifications for your "ideal job" from search firms or employers to determine that your résumé is still scannable.

   The main categories that will be scanned are the following:
   - Industry niches (aerospace, healthcare, biotech, etc.)
   - Roles held (CEO, CIO, CFO, CAO, GC, CHRO, etc.).
   - Educational degrees (PhD, MBA, BS, etc. and the college, universities, or any other advanced non-degreed executive education, such as Harvard's Advanced Executive Education Program).
   - Specialized training (Six Sigma, Kaizan, Benchmarking, Scorecarding, SAP, etc.).
   - An interesting and relevant background (served in applied branch of the government or military, lived and worked in an expatriate role internationally).

3. Use key words that identify specific skills and experience relevant to your role and organizational level. The fact that you might have done production planning as an entry-level engineer enroute to your current role as VP of Operations is interesting, but it's not appropriate to put on your résumé today. It's implicit that you would have had some entry level role as this. I know it's obvious, but use language and concepts that reflect your current level and at least one level up from where you are now, including the Board.

4. Keep your scannable résumé plain, simple, and straightforward. Cute, slick, and manipulative images went out of vogue in the 1980s *and* that look does not scan very easily anyway. You might be able to get away with being more innovative if you are in advertising or graphic arts. Remember, however, your résumé needs to project the elegant simplicity of an effective executive, not how technically creative you are.

5. Avoid italics, underlining, small print, script, condensed type, brackets ({ }), borders, shading, newspaper columns, vertical or horizontal lines, compressed lines, and decorative graphics. Capital letters and common abbreviations (KY, BA, MBA, GPA, CPA) will scan. Virtually all systems can scan boldface. However, caps and boldface should be used in headings and subheadings and not for emphasis, as they can be difficult to read or give exaggerated prominence to certain words and take away from others.

We Take Our Accomplishments for Granted

Everyone takes for granted the results they've achieved throughout their careers. It's not surprising that you will have taken your accomplishments for granted or that you have not thought through the nuances of how you have greatly contributed to others. However, now is the time to focus on how you want to be portrayed and the breadth of your achievements.

As you can imagine, your goal is to develop a well-rounded résumé that reports on what you have done (results) while reflecting what you can do (capabilities). Therefore, it is important that you identify and prepare an extensive list of at least 30 accomplishments or areas of significant responsibility and involvement. This translates roughly into at least five meaningful results per each position held. Now, don't get excited. It's doubtful that you'll use every results "bullet." As you know, it is always easier to edit statements than it is to create them. Also, you'll concentrate on the most recent parts of your career; you'll not have much need for a lot of detail for jobs held beyond 15 years.

However, developing a lengthy list of results will do a number of things for you. You will:

- Sharpen your awareness of the areas in which you possess skills and abilities.
- Be intimately familiar with the span of your accountability, the scope of your responsibility, and the accuracy of your accomplishments.
- Exude confidence and competency. A well-developed, results-driven résumé is a huge confidence builder. It demonstrates that you have made a difference. And, isn't that ultimately what people want to do? To make a difference. Be significant.
- Attract others to you. Prospective employers want to be around executives who know themselves and are bold, confident, courageous, authentic, and capable.
- Be prepared for interviews as you have thought through the tough questions about every aspect of who you are, what you're capable of, and the results you've achieved.
- Have a résumé when you need it. If you do not have one, chances are that you'll feel pressure to throw one together at some point, and it may not represent you in the most powerful manner.
- Highlight your innate and developed skills. For instance, if you have capabilities and accomplishments in your:
  Intellectual agility, then emphasize how you were able to quickly unravel some long-standing, complex problem that significantly contributed to the P&L.
  Conceptual ability, then highlight how you conceived of, created, or led a team that introduced some innovation that produced incremental sales or eliminated operating costs.

Leadership capability, then speak to how you might have developed, upgraded, or built a results-driven team. Perhaps you created the compelling vision and led the team that turned around the organization.

Jostling Your Memory

I know that you are probably raring to get started on creating your own résumé, if you haven't already. My intention is to help you craft a powerful résumé that generates enthusiasm about you and creates an irresistible groundswell for others wanting to meet you. The following exercise will help trigger your thoughts on the major things you have achieved. I invite you to circle all the action verbs that resonate with you. Next, ponder and reflect on each action verb for a few moments. In a cryptic manner, jot down those items that come to mind of things you have accomplished.

Please turn to the next page and complete the Worksheet 30, "Action Verbs = Accomplishment Triggers." Have fun as you remember some of the great things you have done in your career.

WORKSHEET 30

Action Verbs = Accomplishment Triggers

The following is a list of common action verbs that may be helpful in triggering your memory about the accomplishments you achieved. You can even use them in writing your accomplishment statements. CIRCLE those that relate to what you have done. After you have circled all those that are relevant, go back and HIGHLIGHT YOUR TOP 10 ACTION VERBS to help you develop your accomplishment statements.

Accomplished	Enlarged	Performed	Strengthened
Achieved	Established	Planned	Stressed
Administered	Examined	Presented	Stretched
Analyzed	Expanded	Presided	Structured
Approved	Founded	Processed	Succeeded
Arranged	Generated	Produced	Superseded
Completed	Guided	Provided	Terminated
Conceived	Headed	Purchased	Traced
Conducted	Implemented	Recommended	Tracked
Consolidated	Improved	Recruited	Traded
Contracted	Improvised	Redesigned	Trained
Controlled	Increased	Reduced	Transferred
Converted	Indexed	Reorganized	Transformed
Coordinated	Innovated	Researched	Translated
Created	Installed	Reshaped	Trimmed
Cut	Instituted	Revised	Tripled
Delivered	Introduced	Scheduled	Uncovered
Demonstrated	Invented	Serviced	Unified
Designed	Investigated	Set-up	Unraveled
Developed	Launched	Simplified	Utilized
Devised	Led	Sold	Vacated
Directed	Managed	Solved	Verified
Disapproved	Moderated	Sorted	Widened
Distributed	Negotiated	Sparked	Withdrew
Doubled	Operated	Staffed	Won
Earned	Organized	Started	Worked
Eliminated	Originated	Streamlined	Wrote

Your Turn—Use Action Verbs to Create Results Statements

Instructions: Use the action verbs you circled from the previous exercise and those written in the blanks that follow to trigger your memory of significant achievements you and your team realized. You might also refer back to some of your insights that you captured in the exercises in Chapter 5, "Career Strategies and Options." These musings will provide additional dimensions for you to consider as you develop your tightly worded accomplishment bullets or sound bites. As you complete this exercise, note that this is merely the beginning not the end of your developing results statements.

What You Did		The Result ($, %, #)
_____	increased	_____
_____	improved	_____
_____	enhanced	_____
_____	eliminated	_____
_____	readied	_____
_____	reduced	_____
_____	avoided	_____
_____	led to	_____
_____	protected	_____
_____	enabled	_____

Build Your Accomplishment Statements

1. Identify all your jobs and your relevant responsibilities. Indicate the years involved. Keep in mind, the last 10 to 15 years of employment are generally the most relevant.
2. Utilizing the previous worksheet, brainstorm the creation of your accomplishments. Jot down your achievements, as fast as they come to mind. Do not worry about how well they are written, go for a long list. If you prefer, use an index card for each accomplishment.
3. After you have exhausted all possibilities, go back and identify time, location, and company for each result mentioned. This is the start of your fine-tuning process.
4. Next, assign an A, B, or C priority to every contribution. "A" priorities are those that have contributed a great deal to the company, perhaps required a lot of people, or were very difficult to achieve. "B" priorities are important, though they did not contribute quite as much monetarily. "C" priorities represent those activities that were necessary, though not critical.

5. Fine-tune your accomplishments according to the following guidelines:
   - Make them brief, crisp, and specific, highlighting the financial impact in terms of dollars, numbers, or percentage contribution ($, #, or %), whenever possible.
   - They should indicate to the reader how they made life easier, saved money, improved productivity, resolved problems, or attained something for the first time.
   - Lead off your accomplishment statements with a quantified result, whenever possible, beginning with an action verb.
     ◦ Saved $175 million by leading global profit improvement initiatives, spanning eight countries and 2,500 employees.
     ◦ Increased incremental revenues $160 million through the introduction of 15 new products and line extensions.

     However, you might lead off with an interesting process or activity for emphasis and end with the quantified result, such as:
     ◦ Introduced Lean Manufacturing and Six Sigma throughout the company, globally, thereby reducing cycle time 35% and enhancing annual profits $75 million.

6. Describe any opportunities you saw and the recommendations you suggested that would have made your organization more successful or effective had one of them been implemented.

   It does not matter if you were not able to execute the program; great projects often get put on hold for a wide variety of reasons. What does matter is that you recognized some opportunities or problems and acted to solve them. Companies are looking for imaginative and agile problem solvers and people who are committed to continuous improvement.

   To make your data collection easier and your credentials more reflective of what you have done, please consider results falling into three categories:

- *Actual Results.* Bona fide achievements based on your efforts. This is the most preferred result statement, as it is documentable and verifiable.
- *Estimated Results.* Those results which are in the process of becoming. For instance, we might reference the launch of a new product, knowing that it is expected to yield much more significant returns in its third year. So, perhaps the projected *third-year* sales should be highlighted, as it is more reflective of your true accomplishment.
- *Potential Results.* Often, results are not realized because strategies are not fully executed due to intervening political, timing, or capitalization issues. To that end, what would have the result been if the program was fully executed? That is the potential result. I would caution you from having too many results being Estimated or Potential, as it may reflect that you haven't really accomplished much of anything.

Your Accomplishments ... "So What?"

One of my favorite, yet most obnoxious, questions is "So what?" When you have identified an accomplishment, I encourage you to probe deeper. Recruiters and prospective employers certainly will! The most effective résumés will present accomplishment sound bites that capture the essence of what you have done and its powerful impact on the P&L. With résumé in hand, I invite you to ask yourself a series of "so what?" questions:

"What has been the positive impact on your ability to achieve your annual and/or strategic goals?"

"How have you enabled others to realize significant gains?"

"What have you done that has benefited your customers or suppliers, making them more profitable?"

Countless résumés cross my desk and very few of them are truly results-driven. Oh, I'm sure that these résumés represent people who have achieved significant results and are rightfully proud of their contributions. However, rarely do the résumés accurately and completely reflect what the person has done or can do.

In fact, the other day I was helping a friend of mine power up his résumé. It was too long, with virtually no white space to make paragraphs stand out, and filled with jargon and abbreviations that made my head spin. To top it off, he constantly used language that was highly specific to his position, company, and industry. I was completely turned off by my friend's "pride and joy"—his *magnum opus*. While I was convinced that my friend had, indeed, accomplished a lot in his career, you could have fooled me. After rereading his resume for the third time trying to get a handle on how to help him fine-tune the language, I was reminded of a quip concerning a playwright and his producer. The playwright proudly boasted that he had put lots of passion and fire into his work. Not impressed with the playwright's declaration, the producer wrote back and wryly observed that what was actually needed was less fire in his work and more of his work in the fire! That's what we ultimately did with my friend's ramblings—put more of his work in the fire to produce a better outcome.

"So What?" in Real Life

The following are some highlights of a first attempt at capturing "so whats?" in a résumé from an actual RL client. At first reading, if you thought that this resume is solid and results-oriented, you're right. However, there are a number of implied results that have not been effectively teased to the surface or considered. The client's name and the names of his organizations have been deleted to protect the person's identity. His results statements are in bold for ease of reading; use my questions (in italics) as a means of sharpening your skill in asking "so what?" questions for yourself. (Not to worry, by the way; his final résumé was greatly improved, and he was emboldened by the clarity of his contributions.)

Executive Vice President

- **Provided the strategic direction and had full P&L responsibility for this privately held $70 million automotive performance parts company. Reported to the President and Board of Directors.** *What was your distribution channel? (dealers, direct, . . .) How many employees? What was your operating budget?*
- **Increased sales 17% or $11 million, despite less than 6% overall industry growth.** *Great, nicely captured. Succinct as is.*
- **Hired assertive new management to oversee manufacturing and materials functions resulting in 15% increased productivity and improved shipping performance.** *How did assertiveness positively manifest itself? What was the financial impact of improved shipping performance? What was the dollar amount of new business? $ amount of lost business that you recaptured? The dollar amount of threatened business that you protected?*
- **Reduced $800,000 of excess and obsolete inventory over a six-month period through collaborative team efforts.** *Great! Now what about the financial impact over a 12- to 18-month period? In what other areas did this collaborative effort show up, and what was the financial impact? What is the aggregate amount in total? How many more inventory turns did you realize? What financial impact did this have on the cost of capital? How many more sales were realized as a result of freed-up space that was probably converted to manufacturing?*

Group President

- **Restructured the global service center repair organization and developed a new high performance management team.** *Why did you restructure the service organization? What was the P&L of the way the center was running previously compared to now? Financial impact on customers? What was the financial result after the reorg? Increased sales, profits, customer satisfaction, and repeat business? What was the impact of the "high-performance team?" What was the negative impact of the executive team prior to it becoming a "high-performance team?"*

- **Championed a "customer first" philosophy for the Aftermarket division, driving on-time delivery to 93% and focusing managers on the imperative of meeting customer's expectations on every order/job.** *What is the P&L impact of the 93 percent versus what it was previously? Ninety-three percent represents what percentage improvement? What other areas of improvement were positively impacted as a result of the managers now being focused on meeting customers' expectations? (i.e., now addressing inventory turns, obsolete inventory, accounts receivables, scrap/rework expenses, productivity, increased availability of capital due to faster turnaround time on order processing, etc.)?*

- **Led innovative inventory management and receivables initiatives reducing working capital 15%.** *Excellent . . . what made it innovative? What was the financial impact of these initiatives? Impact on DSOs? What processes/systems did you put in place to prevent the loss from happening again? What financial impact has there been since you left? What other residual gain did you and/or the organization realize from the management discipline that you clearly brought?*

- **Developed a comprehensive plan to increase EBITDA from $2.0 to $8.5 million, involving innovative sales initiatives, 20% in reduced personnel costs, and facility consolidation.** *Did the plan achieve these numbers? If so, then you need to say, " . . . plan that increased EBITDA. . . ." FYI: "to increase" alludes to the fact that your intention was to increase XYZ, but it did not necessarily do so. What was innovative about these sales initiatives? What increases in incremental sales did you realize? What percent does this incremental sales increase represent? What operating cost reductions/eliminations/avoidance were realized?*

 Operate under the assumption that every unnecessary word in your résumé will cost you $500 off your base pay!

Secrets of Powerful Résumés

Virtually everything you do or have done in your career has a bottom-line impact in some form or another, whether you realize it or not. As you develop your results, I invite you to focus on your role and *responsibilities* and the projects or situations in which you were engaged. Hopefully, you took action to rectify those situations that needed addressing and you produced a meaningful result.

R + S + A = R (Responsibilities + Situation + Action = Results)

Reflect on your own résumé. How clearly have you stated the *what* and the *so what*, in terms of outcomes ($, #, % impact)? How well have you eliminated all the unnecessary words?

Imagine yourself in an interview with a naturally inquisitive recruiter. Of course, she'll be asking you a number of questions to learn more about you, your capabilities, your operating philosophy, and, of course, your current or former organization's culture. If you have left your organization, you'll obviously be answering these questions in the past tense. By the way, lest you think these are unfair questions for a recruiter to ask, think again. If I was a recruiter, I would definitely be asking the following:

- "What are your responsibilities?"
- "What are the most important projects you are engaged in (or were engaged in), and why do you rate them such? What is the estimated first-year PL impact, in terms of dollars, numbers, or percentage contribution? Third-year impact?"
- "How do these projects and your role serve the greater organizational good? What's the impact on the organization, employees, vendors and distributors, customers, and society? What is the estimated ROI?"
- "What do your customers *need* and *want* from you and your team? How well have you delivered against these? What's the P&L impact for others?"
- "What are the conditions that led you and others to feel these projects were important?"
- "If nothing was done in those cases where something was derailing, if left unchecked, what would be the P&L impact?"
- "How has your work helped another entity (inside or outside your company) operate more effectively?"

Example of R + S + A = R in Action

The following is an example of each element in the R + S + A = R formula:

Responsibility: P&L general management.
Situation: Production scheduling was haphazard and not very efficient. Also, it seemed that some days there were idle machines and people, and the very next day the plant could be paying overtime!
Action: The operations team analyzed the situation by evaluating sales orders, special customer demands, and manufacturing capacity and needs. They talked to machine operators, customers, supervisors, and internal Six Sigma black belt experts. The team recommended and introduced an innovative yet simple scheduling system.
Result: Reduced operating costs more than $21 million annually. Leveled off production spikes that enabled production analysts to be more proactive regarding

procurement, staffing requirements, and inventory turns. Allowed Kaizan continuous improvement mentality and programs to be readily accepted. Reduced product manufacturing cycle time 28% which sped up production throughput. Increased inventory turns from three times a year to more than seven times, eliminating $18.7 million in materials and cost-of-carrying capital. Also, eliminated $2.5 million in annual overtime labor costs expenses, for a total profit increase of $21.2 million.

Stating the Result in the Résumé

The following is how the result might look:

- Reduced operating costs more than $21 million by implementing a fully integrated production scheduling process. Introduced Six Sigma that sped up manufacturing 28%, increased inventory turns from three to seven, and eliminated discretionary overtime.

The following are additional examples of solid results sound bites that both reflect *what* the person did and its *result*:

- Generated $36 million in incremental sales, an increase of 59% over prior year by prioritizing sales targets and emphasizing higher-margin proprietary products.
- Co-led the M&A team that directed the due diligence, purchase, and integration of two key acquisitions that added $48 million in annual revenue, effectively doubling the size of the company.
- Improved annual sales $34 million by developing and launching 28 new products in three years.
- Instituted Lean Manufacturing methods that increased pilot plant yields from 78% to 91% and lowered production costs $14 million annually.
- Renegotiated corporate logistical service contracts from transportation carriers, reducing annual rates 23%, or more than $4.5 million.
- Established a finance and accounting Shared Services organization. Reduced headcount, implemented financial controls, and decreased DSO, collectively decreasing the cash burn rate 40% or $5.8 million annually.

What a Résumé Is—and What It Should Do

A résumé

1. *Is an advanced marketing tool.* Looking for that ideal job can be a bit taxing on the nerves. It's no wonder that we rise to the defense when someone criticizes our

résumé—after all, it does represent us, doesn't it? It does, but only partially, much like a photograph captures only a portion of who we really are.

2. *Considers the motivation of the résumé screener.* Is it to screen you in or to screen you out? Screen you out, of course. Wouldn't it make sense that the more ramblings you engage in, the greater the probability you'll strike out? Now, to be fair, it could be argued that the more information you provide the greater the likelihood that you'll find some common ground and hook the scanner.' Tis true. But generally, résumé scanners will give up and reject your résumé long before they discover the common ground. Of the thousands of résumés I've seen over the years, the poorest examples of a person's capabilities (and the ones that have irritated me the most) have always been tell-all résumés.

My recommendation is to create a résumé that succinctly reveals the major initiatives and their results while illustrating the nuances of your inherent skills and capabilities (your mosaic).

3. *Should be results-oriented.* As a senior executive, you've probably forgotten much of what you have accomplished or taken many of the results you've generated for granted. *A results-oriented résumé is always more powerful and impressive than one which highlights only responsibilities.* Obviously, the more impressive the résumé, the greater the likelihood of your being considered for an opportunity that might be right for you.

4. *Portrays what you can do by what you have done.* A résumé documents what you have done (highlighting past achievements) and is written to reflect what you can do in a new role (alluding to your capabilities). A well-written résumé is a must. If it is not well crafted, you run the risk of being seen as a poor communicator.

5. *Should have broad appeal.* The language and the examples used should not be specifically written to a particular function, industry, or geography, so as to preclude the possibility of an opportunity outside of your present or previous industry. For example, a talented CIO should be able to effectively cross over from the chemical industry to the food or consumer products industries without too much difficulty.

6. *Needs to avoid the obvious.* Keep it simple and straightforward. Less narrative is more powerful. It is more easily understood and has a higher likelihood of being read. *Less is more.*

7. *Cannot engage in puffery.* Your résumé has to be accurate, accurate, accurate! If you were part of a team effort, don't indicate that you "led" the project if you didn't. Say instead "Co-led." There is a distinct difference between honest, creative wording and false elaboration. Puffery is easily spotted by seasoned executives and skilled recruiters. If you get caught with your data down, your credibility may be irreparably damaged, and now everything on your résumé is suspect. Do not risk

a golden opportunity for the sake of portraying something you are shaky on. When in doubt about a statistic, leave it off or verify it with someone in your former company. And walk your references through how you calculated the results.

Also, be extremely careful not to disclose proprietary, company confidential information that is not in the public domain. This is especially true if you are currently or formerly employed by a privately held organization. Even results at the division level of publicly traded companies need to be considered confidential. When in doubt, ask your references what is the acceptable line that you don't want to cross. There is a balance to maintain between revealing too much data and not being results-oriented enough.

8. *Avoids using jargon and abbreviations.* Only résumé writers like jargon. The rest of us hate it. In my opinion, the most powerful résumés are those that everyone clearly understands. They are written simply and straightforwardly—without jargon and without pretense.

9. *Should be visually attractive and easy to read.* Most of us are in love with what we have accomplished. Hence, we loathe to leave anything out, lest we miss a key screening item. *A résumé's appearance is equally important as its content.* A densely packed résumé might tell a prospective employer or search firm everything there is to know about you, but there is a high probably that it will be immediately tossed. It is simply too difficult and time-consuming to read. On the other hand, you might have an attractive-looking résumé with plenty of white space, but there are no quantified accomplishments and it belabors the obvious on some things. Résumés with no substance or ones that are too dense are rarely given consideration.

10. *Must be easily scanned.* Your résumé must contain key words that hook the person scanning résumés. Relevant words and phrases will pull these scanners into your experiences and contributions. This same language will trigger the electronic scanners used by search firms sorting through résumés that fit a given search or when they are looking for "best athletes."

Clearly, it is to your advantage to have your résumé land in the "A" high-priority stack first, since there are no guarantees that résumés in the other piles will ever be read. Make a list of 15 to 20 key words or phrases for your role and industry. Incorporate them into the executive summary or general text of your résumé for scanning.

11. *Is not a tell-all document.* A well-developed résumé is a powerful, highly telegraphic marketing tool which will sell you in advance of your being able to personally tell your story in an interview. The text is crisp, punchy, and succinct. It is designed to prompt the résumé scanner into contacting you for a

preliminary phone screen, then a face-to-face interview. Prune out many of the extraneous pieces of your old or current résumé to speak the language and address the concerns of the hiring authority. A résumé *per se* never obtained a job for anyone—by itself.

Your résumé should not be longer than three pages; two pages are preferred. Experienced individuals, like yourself (15-plus years of experience) will mostly have a two-page résumé. Two pages provide an opportunity to identify a number of your accomplishments and it also creates a sense of substance, depth, and capability.

There is no advantage to a one page résumé as it cuts out too much of your background and accomplishments, which may be full and rich with relevant experiences.

12. *May include an addendum.* If you have a tremendously rich background, spanning academia and the corporate world, you can always include some of that information in an addendum. The addendum is helpful in capturing great information like patents, publications, conferences, speaking engagements, as well as some of the older or less pertinent data, so it does not get lost on the "cutting room floor."

Caution: If you have written a résumé to impress someone with your immense vocabulary, you run the risk of turning off the vast majority of your intended audience. When I begin to read a jargon-filled résumé (outside of the scientific, technical, or military field), my response is invariably, "Give me a break!" And, I often trash it soon thereafter.

Critical Parts of a Résumé

While your résumé needs to reflect the unique aspects of your background and career focus, the following are the categories/headings common to most résumés:

1. Contact Information
2. Executive Summary
3. Business Experience
4. Accomplishments/Responsibilities
5. Education
6. Professional Associations/Affiliations
7. Patents, Publications, Awards, Recognition
8. Military

Let's look at each of these in turn.

1. Contact Information

This section is pretty straightforward. As people need to reach you, include name, address, home office and cell telephone numbers, and e-mail address. Center all the information with your name **in all capital letters** and all other contact data in upper- and lowercase type style. If you are still employed, you may wish to use your cell phone number instead of your office number. For home coverage, it's a toss-up, in my opinion. Some executives prefer to bring another telephone line into the house to eliminate inaccurate phone messages or phone competition in your house with teenagers or your spouse/partner. Others executives prefer to just use their cell phones: It's simple, it may be attached to your hip, and you can readily return calls. Don't assume that the persistent interviewer will track you down at home during evening hours. The point being, make yourself available and easy to reach.

Never, ever, assume someone is going to be as committed to your search success as you are. Don't wait for others to call you back. *You* take responsibility for connecting. *You* call them back.

2. Executive Summary

Composed of 50 to 70 words, the Executive Summary allows the résumé scanner to quickly determine if the résumé represents enough of a fit to continue scanning. Its goal is to boldly telegraph your qualities and strengths. The following Executive Summary is a snapshot of your:

- Functional areas of expertise
- Significant technical strengths or skills
- Relevant personal qualities
- Industries served
- Results realized

The following is Michele Cannon's Executive Summary:

Accomplished executive with a record of accelerated sales and profit growth, business turnaround management, and enhanced shareholder value. Operate effectively in fast-paced environments, building and managing world-class teams that focus on profit improvements. Skilled in leadership in diverse domestic and international markets encompassing start-up and early-stage businesses and mergers and acquisitions.

In most cases, we recommend *against* having an objective statement, as it is either too limiting and restrictive or too broad and general to have any real meaning. You also run the risk of eliminating the possibility of being considered for several career options because the résumé scanner pigeon-holed you. Instead, plan on using your cover letters to isolate career options while utilizing an Executive Summary on your résumé.

3. Business Experience

Identify organizations in reverse chronological order, starting with the most recent employer first. If you are unemployed, indicate start date and exit date or "to Present." Many employers support their exiting executives by allowing them to indicate "to present" on their résumé during the time of their notice period prior to beginning separation pay. Do not mislead; rather, wait for the right time to indicate your status of "looking with the full knowledge and support of the company." However, if your exit is well-known, then, of course, indicate the year only (not month and year) in which you exited your organization.

If your career spans more than 25 years, you may want to consider collapsing the work (and the names of your employers) longer than 15 years ago under the title **"EARLIER BUSINESS EXPERIENCE,"** located just before the **"EDUCATION"** section. If you use this summary listing of previous employers, be sure to write a solid summary paragraph (no more than eight lines) that reflects the work you have had or the titles and the type of companies. (I recommend that you refer to the résumé examples highlighted later in this chapter to see what I mean.) While significant gaps of employment should be identified, minor gaps can be minimized by using only "years" of employment, instead of "months and years." This résumé format is acceptable for a résumé, in that it is not intended to be a legal document or signed application. We recommend that if this is the case, you clarify any such gaps in the interview so you do not get caught with your data down!

Do not falsify any information. Obviously, you need to volunteer information that clarifies the situation, both past and present. If you have some significant issues concerning how to portray this on your résumé or how to verbalize it, seek the opinion of a respected business colleague.

When you are employed at a division or strategic business unit of a much larger, well-known organization, it is recommended that the major corporation be identified first (in all caps) followed by the division's name (in upper- and lowercase). For example: **ACME FINISHING** (insert 4 spaces here) **Powder Coatings Division**. On the other hand, lead off with the division or subsidiary's name if your division was once a well known stand-alone, independent company and it was acquired by a lesser known company.

As you indicate the breadth and scope of your responsibilities make sure that information such as revenues, number of employees, etc. is reflective of your division or subsidiary, and not the corporation at large.

4. Responsibilities/Accomplishments

As previously indicated, organizations hire individuals who can demonstrate they can both handle the responsibilities of the assigned job and produce significant results. To that end, it is essential to have a results-oriented résumé that has a number of quantified accomplishments.

Caution: A résumé can be so skewed toward accomplishments that it becomes hard to read, as it is too busy with facts and figures. The biggest sin: that it's mind-numbing. A boring résumé is distracting and not effective. Ironically, rather than illustrating the ability to get things done, your résumé may indicate a preoccupation with "things" or that you are trying too hard to prove yourself.

5. Education

List the highest degree first. Identify the degree, field of study, college or university, and year of graduation. List both your graduate degree and your undergraduate degree. Unless your college graduation date reveals that you are older than 60, include your dates. Why? By leaving off the year of your graduation you run the risk of recruiters and employers thinking that you are older than you really are. By the way, regardless of how proud you might be of your prep school, I would only list it if other "captains of industry" might have attended it in their youth. Otherwise, don't list your high school education.

6. Professional Associations/Affiliations

List only those technical or managerial associations that are appropriate to your organizational level or functions area. Do not reference groups that you have long outgrown or societies that may mistakenly communicate a niche expertise that is too limiting. For instance, if you were a member of the American Society of Young Chemical Engineers early in your career, and now you are the COO, you may wish not to include this association, unless you occupy a significant leadership role. Some associations may infer that your expertise (or how you view yourself) is much lower or more limited than it really is.

Avoid listing those affiliations that isolate your age, race, sex, marital status, or religion, unless such listing would engender a distinct marketplace advantage. While community organizations are very worthwhile, for the most part, they are usually inappropriate to list on the résumé. Exceptions to this are when your involvement is part of your company role (public relations, for example) or if it reflects a significant leadership or board capacity. Nonetheless, please be careful here, as you don't want to create the impression that you spend a lot of your employer's time on your personal organizations.

7. Patents, Publications, Awards, Recognition

If you have a limited number of items of recognition, it is probably best to highlight them in the résumé. However, if you have a significant number of patents, publications, or awards, then it might be more appropriate to develop an extra sheet labeled, "**ADDENDUM.**" This information is more important and highly acceptable for people with technical, scientific, medical, research, or academic backgrounds and goals than for general managers.

8. Military

Identifying military experience with your rank is certainly appropriate. On the other hand, if you are marketing yourself as a leader and your highest rank was Pfc (you might have been a late bloomer!), you may wish to reconsider telling people your rank.

Personal Data—Not Recommended

My recommendation is this: In this era of political correctness, it is best *not* to include any personal data. Most people exclude it on the grounds it is not "legally" necessary to provide personal, non-job-related data. Some companies we know will immediately reject résumés that include personal data. Now, I think that is a little extreme, but it's their prerogative. Generally, personal data hurts more than it helps.

Instead of revealing personal information on your résumé, save some interesting facts about yourself for ice-breaking or background conversation when you are in the interview. Many people have fascinating hobbies and interests and are rightfully proud of their skill in these areas. Be aware, however, of trying so hard to develop rapport that you end up sharing mutual hobby "war stories." The danger is that you and the interviewer could run out of the allotted interview time and not explore how you fit and could contribute to the organization. Tragically, we have heard of a number of talented executives who lose their perspective by straying too far afield from their interviewing objective by talking about areas of mutual interest. The unintended result is that they lost the opportunity to be seriously considered for the perfect job.

The goal of your resume is to get you the interview. Your goal in the interview is twofold: highlight how you can contribute to the company *and* "peel back the layers" of the company so you know if you want to proceed further.

If you still want to highlight your personal interests and hobbies, just be careful. Keep things conservative. While you may feel that you are reflecting your community involvement and personal commitment to society, the résumé scanner may see it differently. She may wonder how much of your community efforts are performed on company time, utilizing company resources.

Hobbies such as scuba diving, flying, sailing, skydiving, race car driving, sword swallowing, tightrope walking, and juggling with operating chainsaws may all reflect your courage and independence, but they may also highlight an unwise risk orientation, and an unnecessary hospitalization liability for the employer. Plus, most executives may question your judgment for putting such things on your résumé. Now, don't jump to the conclusion that if that's how they'd react to some personal data, then perhaps this may not be the kind of organization you want to work for. "Better safe than sorry" is my motto. When in doubt, just leave it out. You can always reveal that you just completed a three-city tour of displaying your prized collection of popsicle sticks *after* you've taken the job.

What's the Best Résumé Format?

Every form of a résumé has a purpose and a place. I prefer a reverse chronological résumé format in the vast majority of cases. You need to know when to use each one and under what conditions. While there are numerous looks one can create for a résumé, there are fundamentally six types.

- Reverse chronological
- Combination (chronological and functional)
- Functional
- Biographical letter (the "no résumé" résumé)
- "Handbill résumé"
- "Tell-all" résumé

We'll look at each of these more closely.

Reverse Chronological Résumé

The Reverse Chronological Résumé is the most preferred and the most common type seen. This style displays your business career in reverse chronological order, beginning with the most current company/job first. This format quickly allows the reader to know what you are doing now and where you are most-recently experienced. The assumption is that the most recent experience is also the most significant and revealing of your responsibilities, accomplishments, skills, and abilities. The bulk of what follows in this chapter is devoted to helping you create a powerful reverse chronological résumé.

Combination (Chronological and Functional) Résumé

The Combination Résumé is most often used to identify a number of promotions within the same company (perhaps even within the same function). In this format the titles are listed in reverse chronological order (with dates that include years only), followed by the major responsibilities of the most recent position(s), which are most representative of the breadth of the job and the talents of the person.

Functional Résumé

You may wish to consider a Functional Résumé if your previous experience is clearly more significant than your most recent experience or if you have worked in quite a number of different companies and you are interested in minimizing your job hopping. A functional résumé highlights disciplines and results achieved first, so the résumé scanner would, hopefully, focus on your results rather than the number of positions you've held.

A functional résumé is also helpful if you want to minimize advanced age, unstable work record, history of hospitalization, or major periods of unemployment. (Raising a family is seen as completely acceptable, and many companies look very favorably upon men or women who interrupt their careers for this significant and tremendously challenging responsibility.)

However, the downside of a functional résumé is that it may trigger suspicion that you might be hiding something, such as age or a number of terminations. Being upfront, straightforward, and nonapologetic is usually the best course of action.

Biographical Letter: The "No-Résumé" Résumé

A well-written Biographical Letter or marketing letter has some strong advocates. In essence, this no-résumé résumé is a mini biography. If you are an executive being considered for board seats, you absolutely need a well-crafted biography that highlights your contributions. This means that you will start with a solid results-oriented résumé and prune it to a powerful biography. This "letter bio" works well if you are addressing known issues in a specific target company.

My issue is that job searchers grab hold of this philosophy blindly and use their bio letter universally, especially with mass mailings. Playing hide-and-seek with your credentials does not work well with companies you know nothing about. On the other hand, if you do know details about a company you are in a much better position in which to tailor your bio letter. For instance, let's say you've previously been the EVP of Supply Chain for a multibillion-dollar global manufacturer. You've done the research and you know that the XYZ Company is in dire need of a streamlined supply management system, as it was reported that the company is losing $400,000 a month. Well, great.

You can tailor your marketing cover letter to address specific issues XYZ Company most likely would have.

However, you might be committed to networking with a broad range of people, such as executive recruiters or the CEO in a number of target organizations in diverse industries. If that's the case, a slightly more general marketing letter that emphasizes your skills and results with an accompanying résumé may be more appropriate. Since you typically have one shot to capture a prospective employer's attention, a results-oriented résumé will be more powerful than a letter bio format.

Handbill Résumé

Handbill Résumés are handy when you're at a networking event in which you are encouraged to freely pass your "paper" around. A handbill is a one-page summary of your career focus, background, skills, achievements, and target organizations or industries. If you have ever been to such a meeting, you know that it can be a frenzy of networking. Hence, your handbill needs to be crisp and succinct and provide an intriguing glimpse into your talents and accomplishments. It is meant to introduce you only—not to replace your use of the full résumé. Accordingly, it is designed to highlight your credentials in a sound bite format, somewhat different than your powerful, results-oriented résumé.

Tell-All Résumé

I refer to the Tell-All Résumé as the "blah, blah, blah" résumé. Often beginning in early childhood with every award or activity, this chronological résumé is often 10 to 15 pages or more filled with mind-numbing blather. Not even the proudest parent would be able to stay awake through such drivel. It never ceases to amaze me that there are still some career advisors out there in this fast-paced world who recommend this Tell-All Résumé as a form of full disclosure.

Some people espouse a tell-all approach because they want you to reveal more than what you normally would. They favor no limit to the number of pages your résumé might take. *Tell me everything. Don't hold back. Give me all.*

You're an executive; let me ask you, do you prefer a brief executive summary preceding a detailed 15-page report, or do you prefer to wade through the whole report with the essential data embedded in the narrative? Of course, you want the executive summary distillation of the report! There are some who advocate a no-limit philosophy, with the resulting résumés filled with self-indulgent ramblings only a mother would love. In one popular book, the author proudly displayed a 10-page résumé with overly wide margins and loose grammar. Not my style—and not what I would recommend for you.

Great caution should be used if you are determined to use a tell-all résumé. Ask yourself the following:

- "What need am I filling by creating a 10 to 15 page résumé?"
- "What is the possible negative impact of having a 10-page résumé?"

A while back, we were coaching an executive in transition, and he had an equally strong academic and industrial R&D background. He had a 15-page résumé, filled with every paper written, patents filed, conferences attended, speaking engagements, and educational courses taken during and after he was awarded his PhD. Even for a traditional academic curriculum vitae (CV), it was too much. After much haranguing about the length of his résumé, he finally revealed that he wanted to create a 20-plus-page résumé solely because his old mentor bragged about his 20-page CV. To accommodate the possibility of going back into academia, we crafted a two-page results-oriented résumé with separate addendums for patents, publications, and speaking engagements, respectively. He was quite pleased with the result. Nonetheless, before launching his campaign, he asked his old mentor, still at the university, to evaluate it and give him comments. His former professor was effusive. He complained that he was sick of his cumbersome CV and wanted our client to give him some pointers on how to streamline it. Needless to say, our client was thrilled with his résumé after that call.

So, which résumé format is best for you? Obviously, the one that generates the calls for interviews and equips you to powerfully communicate your capabilities. However, because of the number of factors involved, there is no one right format. Your decision will be based on your credentials, career goals, and personal considerations. However, as previously stated, I prefer a Reverse Chronological Résumé. It is much easier to read and to understand the key contributions: also, it is the most straightforward.

Accordingly, the majority of the résumé samples included in the back of this section are Reverse Chronological. However, Bill Robbins has a **Functional Résumé** and Mike Commons, George Pratt, Donna Samuels, and Sam Donovan all have Combination Résumés, which have more than one job/job title combined because of the similar job activities. Whatever your choice, keep the layout crisp and highly telegraphic.

Reverse Chronological Résumé Format

FULL NAME
Street Address
City, State Zip Code
(XXX) XXX-XXXX
E-mail Address

EXECUTIVE SUMMARY

This is a summary of your experience, knowledge, and abilities. It highlights for the reader who you are, what you are capable of doing, and the industries in which you have contributed.

BUSINESS EXPERIENCE

CURRENT EMPLOYER   Year Started to Present

Describe your current employer, including the size of the business, number of employees, and the type of product or service they provide. When in doubt, turn to your company's Web site and note how it describes itself.

Job Title   Year Started–Present

In two or three sentences, briefly describe your job responsibilities. Be sure to use the present tense and incorporate action verbs. If you have been in a high-visibility role in which your departure has been well publicized, then identify the year of your departure. You might consider indicating "to Present" if you are still transitioning responsibilities in your former role or are in a full-time consulting capacity with your former organization. Regardless of how you posture your departure date it is incumbent on you to candidly inform others of your status.

- Starting with an action word, describe in one or two sentences an accomplishment from your present job. Also, leave a blank line between your "bullet" paragraphs and also indent your accomplishments, as they will stand out better with more white space.

- When listing your accomplishments, you can describe problems you have solved, money you have saved, or new procedures you have developed.

- You can also highlight frequently performed tasks and special skills or list projects you have completed. RL's rule of thumb: Keep your narrative bullets to under four lines. More than that and you run the risk of losing the scanner's attention.

Full Name   Page Two

Job Title   Year Started–Year Ended

In two or three sentences, briefly describe your job responsibilities in your previous position. Be sure to incorporate action verbs and use the past tense.

- List accomplishments from this position using varied action words.

- You will use three to five accomplishments for each position you describe.

PREVIOUS EMPLOYER   Year Started–Year Ended

Describe your previous employer; include the size of the business, number of employees, and type of product or service they provide.

Job Title

In two or three sentences, briefly describe your job responsibilities in your previous position. Be sure to incorporate action verbs and use the past tense.

- List accomplishments from this position using action verbs.

EARLIER BUSINESS EXPERIENCE

After you have listed titles/accomplishments for approximately 10 to 15 years of your most recent experiences, summarize your remaining experience in a short paragraph. Include titles held, employers, and dates of employment.

EDUCATION

MBA	Major	Graduate School	Date Graduated
BS	Major	Undergraduate	Date Graduated

PROFESSIONAL AFFILIATIONS

List professional organizations to which you belong. Include any offices you have held. Identify any business board seats that you hold.

Résumé Preparation Hints—Let's Do Some Work Together

Following are some points to keep in mind when preparing a résumé:

- Begin to pull together all the relevant data on your background—the companies you've worked for, their revenue sizes, their exact names, your titles, areas of accountability, and accomplishments. Complete all sections thoroughly. How well you complete the exercises here will have a direct influence on the quality and clarity of your résumé.
- The more details you provide, the more powerful a résumé you will create. Now, obviously there is a balance to be struck in developing the details in your résumé. Too many facts and figures can be as distracting as too little data is disappointing.
- Reread the résumé model carefully and review the résumé samples that follow. Fill in all the information requested in each section. Look up any missing information. You may ask a friend or former colleague for details to complete this section. Missing information will weaken your résumé and, ultimately, your ability to interview convincingly.
- Have your résumé printed on heavy linen paper. We recommend 24-lb. in brilliant white. Save your pastel bond paper for home art projects with the kids. Check all data, company names, and spellings for accuracy. Errors of this nature are your responsibility, not your typist's. Errors send a strong message that you may not be a very disciplined or accurate person.
- Have others read your résumé for both clarity and typos. You should reread your résumé *backwards, one word at a time* to catch spelling errors. Also, call all of your telephone numbers to ensure their accuracy. It's easy to unintentionally invert or reverse critical telephone numbers. Have someone else call your numbers—and not from memory—to verify accuracy.

Résumé Samples*

Reverse Chronological Résumés

Michele D. Cannon	General Management
Gary L. Eisensplat	General Management
Calvin Q. Cost	General Management
J. Michael Commons	Sales and Marketing
Lou Da Jorge	CFO
Sandra A. Neil	CIO
Keith C. Lane	Human Resources

Combination Résumés (Reverse Chronological and Functional Résumés)

Stephanie B. Able	Marketing
Peter R. Anton, PhD	Technology
Amid Suhee, PhD	R&D

Functional Résumés

Vera K. Pang	General Counsel
William W. Robbins	Manufacturing

Biography Letter: The "No-Résumé" Résumé

Juan D. J. Castaneda	General Management

"Handbill Résumé"

Michele D. Cannon	General Management

Tell-All Résumé

None given. I'm sparing you the boredom and agony of a "blah, blah, blah" résumé example.

---

*Although these résumés are based on real clients, actual names of people, organizations, and locations are fictitious and concealed.

Reverse Chronological Résumés

Michele D. Cannon	General Management
Gary L. Eisensplat	General Management
Calvin Q. Cost	General Management
J. Michael Commons	Sales and Marketing
Lou Da Jorge	CFO
Sandra A. Neil	CIO
Keith C. Lane	Human Resources

MICHELE D. CANNON

1693 Elm Street, Antwirl, CA 86732

(415) 585- 2290 Home   (925) 317-1451 Cell

m_cannon@rr.ca.com

CAREER SUMMARY

Experienced executive with a record of accelerated sales and profit growth, business turnaround management, and enhanced shareholder value. Operate effectively in fast-paced environments, building and managing world-class teams that focus on profit improvement. Skilled in leadership in diverse domestic and international markets for start-up and early-stage businesses.

BUSINESS EXPERIENCE

ACME INTERNATIONAL   A Colorant Partners' Subsidiary   2000–2006
President Services Group   2002–2006
Executive Vice President   2000–2002

Complete P&L responsibility for this $2.6 billion global chemicals business. Directed strategy, sales, marketing, operations, finance, HR, and IT. Managed an $800 million SG&A budget and 2,500 employees. Colorant Partners acquired Acme in 2006.

- Doubled sales to $2.6 billion in three years through organic growth and acquisitions, achieving $238 million in pretax earnings.

- Successfully acquired and integrated five companies, with combined annual revenues of $850 million. Increased operating profits from $86 million to over $150 million run rate in 18 months.

- Replaced $300 million in lost sales with $450 million in new accounts and concurrently retained 98% of the base book of business. Accomplished this through strategic selling and the execution of rigorous account management.

- Personally negotiated and led the team that secured a $500 million client contract, the single largest customer in Acme's history.

- Accelerated availability of $300 million of finished goods by streamlining production processes, consolidating plants, and introducing Six Sigma and cellular manufacturing.

PILLAR AMERICAS   A Pillar A.G. Company   1993–2000
President and CEO

P&L general management responsibility for $485 million distributor of concrete curing forms and licensing businesses for this $900 million global manufacturer. Participated on Senior Management Committee in Switzerland for global business issues.

- Restructured and turned around this underperforming organization, focusing on customer service, dealer support, and improved operating efficiencies.

- Grew sales $125 million in a flat market, increased market share more than 22%, while significantly improving pretax profit.

- Increased ROI from 10% to 33% through a highly effective asset management program. Eliminated $55 million in obsolete and low-margin products that no longer met North American customer or market needs.

PINDER ADVANCED SCIENCE CORPORATION   1983–1993
President Scientific Products Industrial Division   1989–1993
Vice President and General Manager Scientific Products   1987–1989

P&L responsibility for a $300 million scientific products distribution business. Directed sales, marketing, planning, operations, finance, and HR. Managed a $24 million SG&A budget and 1,000 employees.

- Grew sales $85 million while maximizing operating earnings growth at a 13% compounded annual rate.

- Increased Return-on-Managed-Capital from 24% to 56% over three years through a revamped asset management process.

- Implemented a strategic vendor management partnership that improved pricing and margins while simplifying technical support to customers.

Vice President International Operations   1983–1987

While based at Vevey, Switzerland, directed business planning and development for this Pinder–Eagle joint venture. Developed international business plan for joint venture in complementary products, with market potential of $500 million annually.

- Identified key markets for penetration in UK, France, Germany, Italy, and Canada. Set up and launched business operations in every country served.

- Sourced three acquisition candidates valued at $50 million and led the due diligence process. Two companies were acquired, contributing $30 million in annual revenues.

EARLIER BUSINESS EXPERIENCE

Progressed rapidly through numerous general management, product management, sales, and marketing management positions with STRATEGIC ALLIANCE (1980–1983), a global manufacturer of branded consumer products.

EDUCATION/PROFESSIONAL AFFILIATIONS

BBS   Finance   University of Michigan   School of Business   1980

Harvard University   Graduate School of Business Executive Management   1988
President Antwirl School Board
Treasurer Board of Directors Blue Note Technology, LLC

GARY L. EISENSPLAT

4313 Surrey Lane South, Pasadena, CA 91030

(310) 976-5438   eisensplat.gary@aol.com

CAREER SUMMARY

P&L general management executive with significant operating responsibility. Experienced in sales, marketing, manufacturing, distribution, and services. Skilled in developing and executing short-/long-range profit plans and strategic initiatives. Customer-focused leader with a record of results in diverse industries. Excellent problem solving, communications, and interpersonal skills.

BUSINESS EXPERIENCE

OMNI CABLE, INC.   1989–Present
President and Chief Executive Officer

Responsible for P&L general management and strategic direction of this $100 million distributor, manufacturer, and services provider of computer networking services and products. Customers are in health care, finance, manufacturing, education, and retail industries. Direct a staff of 200.

- More than doubled the size of the company and improved earnings 70% while aggressively reinvesting in the business for future growth.

- Created a performance-based culture, and repositioned the company from a pure distributor to a value-added provider of high-technology products and services. Improved market capitalization an estimated 150%.

- Reduced operating costs $2.5 million by eliminating two unprofitable locations and by consolidating two production facilities. Productivity increased 37%.

- Launched ISO 9000 international quality standards program which positioned self-manufactured cable assembly products for aggressive sales, growth.

- Identified and evaluated 10 acquisition candidates ranging from $15 million to $50 million, including due diligence and deal structure development. Two businesses valued at $45 million were acquired.

- Recognized as "Partner of the Year" in 1996 by a Fortune 500 manufacturer for best sales and service to customers. Won two national excellence awards in consecutive years for breakthrough network design and implementation.

HEALTHCARE SUPPLY CORPORATION   1974–1989
Vice President—National Accounts   1986–1989

Provided the strategic direction and business development of $1.4 billion in sales to national integrated health-care networks (IHN) throughout the United States.

- Increased sales $500 million, or 55%, representing 71% of division's total volume.

- Generated $175 million in incremental sales by creating new contractual approaches in medical/surgical, foodservice, and housekeeping divisions.

- Personally led negotiations on major sales contracts in excess of $50 million. Additional profits of $29 million were gained as a result of direct intervention.

- Developed and implemented a pricing management system that improved profitability $10 million annually.

Vice President—Midwest Area   1984–1986

Total P&L responsibility for a $172 million business, including sales, marketing, operations, and manufacturing/assembly with more than 300 employees in 5 locations.

- Increased sales 20%, or $70 million, and operating earnings 24%, on average each year, through margin improvements and expense reductions.

- Consolidated and reorganized three distribution facilities, reducing operating costs in excess of $1 million annually.

Vice President—Sales and Marketing   1982–1984

Directed sales and marketing for a start-up entrepreneurial venture with projected annualized sales of $150 million. Additionally, provided marketing support for the export of health-care products in the Far East, Middle East, and Latin America.

- Averted $5 million in annual operating costs through numerous on-site customer discussions that led to the dissolution of this design/build health-care concept.

Director of Corporate Hospital Systems   1981–1982

Led the development and marketing of state-of-the-art computer order-entry systems interfacing with the entire $3 billion Healthcare Supply Corporation with 27 divisions and more than 4,000 hospital customers.

- Generated $100 million in new sales through these value-added systems.

PREVIOUS BUSINESS EXPERIENCE   1969–1981

Held increasingly responsible sales, line, and staff management positions with Healthcare Supply Corporation (1974–1981), the American Cobalt Corporation (1973–1974), and Scott Douglass Company (1969–1973).

EDUCATION/PROFESSIONAL AFFILIATIONS

| MBA | Finance | Indiana University | 1971 |
| BS | Marketing | Northwestern University | 1969 |

The Executive Committee (TEC)

St. Jude Children's Research Hospital

CALVIN Q. COST

2800 Carter Place
San Francisco, CA 94105
Home: (463) 091-6273   Cell: (463) 760-0001
cqcost@yahoo.com

EXECUTIVE PROFILE

Senior executive with significant P&L responsibility. Strategic leader skilled in building, developing, and leading teams that accelerate sales and profit growth, enhance productivity, and exploit hidden business opportunities. Operate effectively in fast-paced, challenging turnaround environments.

EXPERIENCE

HOLDINGS, LLC.   2000–Present
Senior Vice President Network Services (NS)

Complete P&L general management responsibility for $1 billion service and parts business. Direct strategy, operations, and customer-centric support centers. Manage a budget of $220 million and 5,500 associates, 25 call centers, and 120-plus million customer interactions.

- Provided strategy, led development, and executed a corporate-wide customer agenda that included service standards and complaint management for Holdings.

- Drove $184 million in profit improvements across multiple business sectors, sales channels, and customer segments by implementing rate-based productivity initiatives, consolidating facilities, integrating organization-wide processes, and implementing new technologies.

- Doubled operating profits to $670 million for the Network Services Contracts Aftermarket by successfully implementing multiyear sales, expense, and productivity improvements.

USA-TECH CORPORATION/Communication Services (CS)   1996–2000
Vice President Planning and Administration   1999–2000

Developed and led the strategic and annual planning for $5 billion business. Provided counsel, tracked, and analyzed performance of all CS sales channels to maximize effectiveness, optimize resource utilization, and minimize competitive losses.

- Generated $160 million in incremental sales by converting savy product/ service collection associates into front-line sales representatives, thereby significantly accelerating sales.

- Led merger integration teams that leveraged performance benchmarking, improving sales and call center close rates, revenue per order (RPO), and revenue per call.

CALVIN Q. COST   Page Two

Vice President Sales and Operations   1996–1999

P&L responsibility for 1,600-employee call center sales and operations for this $3.3 billion global provider of communications services. Developed and executed sales channel strategies that maximized revenue and satisfaction of 1 million customers throughout a five-state region. Directed a $130 million operating budget.

- Generated $75 million in incremental profits by increasing overall employee productivity 25% in six months.

- Developed the strategy that increased sales $115 million by implementing call center sales effectiveness programs. Leveraged channel strategy and consultative sales that significantly enhanced customer satisfaction.

- Created an innovative direct sales force that increased sales effectiveness 40% and revenue 70% in nine months, contributing $125 million in incremental sales.

BACKSTREET CORPORATION A Paver Company   1991–1996
Senior Vice President Operations   1993–1996

Had P&L responsibility for all operations for this $300 million international provider of asphalt paving services. Provided the company's strategic direction and managed a $130 million operating budget with 1,500 employees in six facilities in North and Central America.

- Member of Paver's Board, representing BackStreet Corporation's 45% equity investment in Market Decisions, Inc., a strategic partnership. Was principal contact for strategic technology alliances and national account sales contract review board.

- Conceived and executed strategies that increased profits $40 million by improving productivity 50%, trimming headcount 40%, and eliminating $26 million in operating expenses. Consolidated operations, delayered and realigned management, and outsourced noncore activities.

- Reduced operating costs more than $10 million and improved data quality in excess of 25% by implementing data processing efficiencies, negotiating favorable contract amendments, and repositioning service capabilities.

Vice President Real Estate and Administration   1991–1993

Responsible for real estate and administrative strategies and solutions, including leasing and asset management of 1.5 million-square-foot national portfolio. Administrative responsibilities

CALVIN Q. COST   Page Three

included purchasing, management of several property/departmental budgets, and key strategic alliances.

- Designed and gained approval for 400,000-square-foot headquarters relocation and consolidation, which generated a $10 million gain on sale, and a $4.2 million annual expense reduction. Returned $25 million in working capital for reinvestment in core business initiatives.

- Saved $10 million annually by consolidating divisional occupancies, sharing administrative services, and leveraging virtual/just-in-time office concepts.

EDUCATION/AFFILIATIONS

MBA   Business   Pepperdine University   1988
BS   Finance and Entrepreneurial Studies   UCLA   1984

Member Executive Leadership Council

Member Link Unlimited Board of Directors

Member Dominican University Graduate School of Business

Advisory Board

Member Hispanic Network—Holdings, LLC

J. MICHAEL COMMONS

207 Arbor Court, Princeton, NJ 08540

(Office) 609.903.5412   (Home) 609.727.3900

jmichael.commons@aol.com

CAREER SUMMARY

An experienced Sales and Marketing executive skilled in developing and executing winning strategies to consistently achieve sales, profitability, and market penetration objectives. A creative problem solver, with exceptional analytical and project management skills. Strong leadership and communication skills, with a proven facility to build and maintain productive business and customer relationships throughout the world.

BUSINESS EXPERIENCE

BROWN & BRASS COMPANY   1985–Present

A $600 million leading global producer and distributor of specialty food products and additives.

Senior Vice President Sales and Marketing   1998–Present

Vice President Sales   1996–1998

Provide the strategic direction and manage sales, marketing, distribution, and customer and technical service for two divisions totaling $480 million. Divisions encompass multiple channel distribution through five sales regions. Manage a $250 million budget and staff of 1001.

- Increased operating profit 5%, or $61 million by restructuring sales, marketing, and service that eliminated sales force/dealer conflicts. Incorporated a global Business Area strategy that improved customer and dealer satisfaction survey scores 35%.

- Grew market share 50% in one year through branding, value repositioning, product rationalization, and distribution channel strategy implementation.

- Directed outside marketing and sales consultants that improved the alignment and productivity of sales representatives and resulted in doubling annual sales growth to 8%, with corresponding increases in profitability.

- Recipient of the company's Award for Outstanding Sales Results in 1998 and 1999 for sales and profit target overachievement.

- Reduced order cycle time from 60 to 45 days. Led a supply chain enhancement task force that focused on improving, order entry.

- Improved sales representative effectiveness by partnering with Human Resources to develop and implement a training protocol, "Brown & Brass University," enhancing technical, interpersonal, and selling skills.

Area Sales Director, Northeast Region   1993–1996

Responsible for driving sales and profitability in a 7-state $13 million region through 10 sales executives and more than 20 multichannel distributors.

J. MICHAEL COMMONS   Page Two

- Transformed a previously complacent sales organization that achieved only 40% of its sales goals to a motivated team in which 70% overachieved annual sales and marketing objectives.

- Increased sales 15% and profits 45% while transitioning to a direct sales operation, simultaneously overseeing the phaseout of nonperforming dealers.

- Developed and implemented a "Strategic Territory Management" sales executive training program in New York City, Boston, and Philadelphia, leading to the successful conversion of key accounts from the competition.

- Recognized for sales and operational performance excellence by being the first recipient of the *President's Award*, the company's highest honor.

Senior Sales Executive   1998–2001
Sales Executive   1994–1998

Developed and managed one of the company's key territories (Mid-Atlantic).

- Overachieved territory sales targets each year. Implemented a key account practice, sponsored junior sales representatives through a sales protégé program, and improved customer satisfaction.

- Increased average annual sales 18% through account targeting, creative marketing, value-added selling techniques, and sales process/contact management control.

- Received the 1992 *President's Council Award* as company's top sales performer.

SELMAN ASSOCIATES   1992–1994
Sales Representative

Responsible for the marketing, sales, and service of food products to larger national accounts. Selman Associates was a distributor of Brown & Brass in Philadelphia.

- Grew sales from 167% to $600,000 within two years. Responsible for a significant business turnaround through increased penetration at key accounts.

EDUCATION

MBA	Marketing	Temple University	1994
BS	Business	University of Denver	1985

SANDRA A. NEIL
725 Prospect Lane
St. Paul, MN 55474
Cell: 651-456-4402
sandra456neil@yahoo.com

INFORMATION TECHNOLOGY EXECUTIVE

An innovative, profit-driven leader with a proven record of exceeding business goals and delivering impressive operating and financial results. Widely known and highly regarded by IT and business professionals. Possess excellent balance of business acumen and technological knowledge. Skilled leader who effectively aligns groups and resources around organizational goals.

EXPERIENCE

TECHNOLOGY CONSULTANTS   2003 to Present
Senior Vice President

Provide IT management consulting and related services to midsized corporations. Scope of practice includes information and technology assessments, strategies planning, business and marketing strategies, project portfolio management, technology and distribution strategies.

LAKEWOOD CORPORATION   1998–2003
Chief Information Officer and Senior Vice President   1999–2003

CIO for this $500 million residential construction business, one of the nation's largest independent builders. Responsible for e-Commerce and the acquisition, development, operation, and maintenance of information systems within the corporation and its subsidiaries. Managed a staff of 3000 and an operating budget of $22 million.

- Halved overall technology budget $23 million while improving quality processes without jeopardizing critical services. Accomplished reduction through process re-engineering and contract renegotiations.

- Eliminated $1.6 million (or 18%) in system development costs by instituting Six Sigma that achieved record QA metrics while accelerating completions and staff reductions.

- Directed the development of e-Commerce capability that will process an estimated $125 million in its second year.
  - Instrumental in company's recognition for technology and IT team awards.
  - Named in the Top 100 CIOs by *CIO* magazine for 2001 and 2002.
  - Awarded "Innovator of the Year" within the hardware industry in 1999.
  - Listed by *Information Week* in the Top 200 IT companies.

SANDRA A. NEIL

- Subject matter expert on e-Commerce and information technology for *Wall Street Journal, Crain's Business, National Home Center News, DIY Retailing, Industry Week, CIO Magazine, Stores,* and *BusinessWeek.*

Vice President Electronic Business   1998–1999

Responsible for EDI systems, electronic commerce on the Web, and e-business development.

- Authored the corporation's first e-business strategy and secured its approval by senior executives within the organization within four months.

- Increased sales $13 million annually by designing a B2B commerce system.

- Designed and implemented an Internet custom catalog selected as the procurement software of choice for Lucent Technology, Universal Film, and Honda Motors. The process decreased catalog distribution pre-press production costs 60 percent.

- Developed a building site manager's extranet (*Siteleaders.com*) that reduced direct communications costs by $1.2 million and provided site managers with instantaneous project tracking, inventory management, and technology information.

HIGH PERFORMANCE GASKETS, INC.   1980–1998
Director of Electronic Commerce & Sales Force Automation   1996–1998
Senior Project Manager   1980–1996

Managed EDI systems, electronic commerce on the Web, and the design, deployment, and support of 150 field sales force automation systems for the world's largest automotive gaskets manufacturer.

- Installed a sales force automation system that analyzed sales representatives' calls and customer buying trends, reducing costs per call 50%, from $120 to $60.

- Published white papers to industry groups on the utilization of the Internet for electronic commerce. Pioneered Web-based automotive industry applications that featured integration of catalog items with the Internet.

EDUCATION

MBA	Kellogg School of Management	Northwestern University	1980
	BS Mathematics	University of Chicago	1978
	Advanced Executive Management Program	Harvard University	1989

LOU Da JORGE

930 Beckwith Lane
Steamboat Springs, CO 77076
970-234-5825 Office   970-123-4560 Home
loudajorge @ aol.com

EXECUTIVE OVERVIEW

Financial executive experienced in transportation, warehousing and distribution, commercial printing, manufacturing, and service industries. Proven record of significant contributions in strategic and operational planning, contract profitability, capital management, financial systems, treasury, and acquisition analysis/integration. Build and lead highly motivated teams that improve operating efficiency, profitability, and cash flow.

PROFESSIONAL BACKGROUND

TRUCKS INTERNATIONAL, INC.   1999–Present
Chief Financial Officer

Provide the strategic direction and manage finance and IT for this $1.5 billion industry-leading, international manufacturer of specialized trucks and transportation services.

- Played a key role in the financial restructuring of the bankrupt, $4.5 billion publicly traded parent company. Developed a five-year business plan that helped secure more than $1.2 billion in critical exit financing.

- As an integral part of the restructuring, co-led business plan presentations to the investment community, including senior bank lenders, bondholders, and potential equity investors.

- Strategized and guided the implementation of technology improvements in each of the five regions to save an estimated $18 million annually.

M&A HOLDINGS, INC.   1997–1999
Chief Financial Officer

Accountable for the turnaround of a troubled finance group for this private equity and investment management organization. Analyzed and evaluated acquisition target companies. Managed acquisitions from due diligence to closing.

- Prepared long-range financial plan, securing $112 million of committed funds. This was the required equity investment to build a $500 million business "roll-up" of diversified marketing services companies.

- Led the due diligence and acquisition of a $5 million sports and event marketing company, the first entry into this market space.

- Managed the due diligence of two potential advertising agency acquisitions with combined revenues of $83 million.

- Brought credibility to a dysfunctional finance and accounting organization. Created reliable financial reporting and planning systems while cutting $400,000 in audit and consulting fees.

- Successfully negotiated extensions of $110 million in credit agreements, enabling the business to remain in operation and invest for growth.

SOFTWARE COMPANY   1994–1997

Senior Vice President Operations and Finance

P&L general management responsibility for this data/content management software company targeted to grow to $100 million. Provided strategic direction to the database publishing group, finance, design services, marketing communication services, and facilities. Managed a team of 150 and an operating budget of $22 million.

- Codeveloped and presented the strategy that secured $10 million in additional funding for needed product development.

- Reduced operating costs $11 million by consolidating two divisions, eliminating two noncore business units, and creating a customer-driven focus for the R&D group.

- Saved $2.6 million by leveraging existing assets upon introducing an inter-group capital planning process.

PACKAGING, INC.   1989–1994

Chief Financial Officer Board Member

Led finance, accounting, and treasury for this high-growth, $200 million privately held manufacturer and distributor of packaging, promotional pieces, and diverse printed material. Managed financial analysis and reporting, MIS, budgeting and planning, and credit and collections.

- Turned around an underperforming financial group by staffing with talented professionals and aggressively developing those high-potential employees who remained.

- To keep pace with doubling company revenues, significantly upgraded the accounting systems and MIS. Upgrades enabled the processing of 230% more invoices, 200% more freight bills, and 46% more vendor invoices with no additional costs.

- Renegotiated credit facilities with more favorable terms while reducing interest rates by five percentage points.

- Averted a $373,000 increase in benefit costs by renegotiating medical plan premiums and coverage, and by implementing a creative two-tier employee cost-sharing program.

MADISON GRAPHICS GROUP Madison Corporation—UK   1987–1989

Corporate Controller

Reported to the President of this fast-paced, $790 million commercial printer with 15 manufacturing plants employing 4,500. Responsible for all accounting, financial reporting, operational and capital budgeting, forecasting, credit, and financial analysis functions.

- Successfully integrated four acquisitions with sales of $660 million annually. Created the financial organization, implemented procedures and controls, and reduced head count 35%.

LOU Da JORGE   Page Three

- Played a key role in renegotiating contracts with two major accounts representing $112 million annually. Saved these significant revenue sources by turning around and reestablishing the customer relationships.

- As the most senior financial executive, played a significant role in the sale of the company. Codeveloped the offering memorandum, prepared financial analyses and forecasts, and co-led the due diligence team.

CORUNDUM & SONS COMPANY   1980–1987
Director of Internal Audit   1985–1987
Manager Financial Analysis and Corporate Development   1984–1985

Developed and executed comprehensive audit strategies and policies, encompassing all 32 domestic and international facilities. Reported to the EVP/CFO.

- Improved overall departmental productivity and audit coverage 41% and saved an estimated 15% in external audit fees.

- Led the on-site audit team for a $125 million business unit in the UK.

- Streamlined the audit process in a joint business relationship, which significantly reduced outside fees paid to a Big Six public accounting firm.

- As Manager Financial Analysis, codeveloped and evaluated business plans for three prospective joint ventures, and directed all valuations for 10 potential acquisition candidates with combined sales of $300 million.

EARLIER BUSINESS EXPERIENCE

At CORUNDUM, was Senior Financial Analyst (1982–1984) and also Internal Auditor (1980–1982). Served as Senior Auditor at ARTHUR YOUNG & COMPANY (1977–1980).

EDUCATION / CERTIFICATION

| MBA | Financial Management | University of Chicago | 1983 |
| BBA | Accountancy | University of Notre Dame | 1977 |

Certified Public Accountant—Illinois   1978

KEITH C. LANE
148 Wheeling Circle
Pittsburgh, PA 18458
412.404.5780 Office
412.935.4846 Cell
kjlane123@aol.com

GENESIS CORPORATION   1996–Present

Vice President Human Resources and Administration   **Small Business Services**

Chief Human Resources Officer providing strategic HR leadership for Genesis's $1.5 billion high-tech communications division serving 1 million customers. Responsible for cultural transformation, leadership development, executive coaching, communications, staffing, employee relations, and compensation and benefits. Direct 60 professionals and an operating budget of up to $8.5 million.

- Achieved $150 million in incremental revenue by rebuilding the management team that created a proactive, consultative market approach that incorporated highly effective market segmentation, target marketing, and account management strategies.

- Generated $50 million in operating cost savings through the 1997 reorganization and consolidation of business units with combined annual revenue of $4.6 billion.

- Transformed the human resources function into a world-class team that consistently overachieved targets. Streamlined HR operations, rebuilt the staff, and cut $3.5 million from the HR operating budget.

- Appointed to Genesis CEO's senior leadership task force to investigate and recommend strategies to maximize business opportunities and to counter significant competitive threats.

- Representing HR, drove the comprehensive company-wide rollout of a new brand strategy, "In a World of Change, People Make the Difference." External advertising and employee communications efforts were launched during this time of heightened competition.

- Sponsored a leadership development program and curriculum that was implemented across all of Genesis's domestic business units. More than 5,500 employees will participate in this training.

ARC INTERNATIONAL   1990–1996

Vice President Human Resources   **Asia-Pacific**   1995–1996

Provided strategic human resources leadership for 10 business units for ARC International's high-growth $800 million region with 11,000 employees in 25 countries.

- Represented international regions on a restructuring initiative across ARC's $5.5 billion business. Annual HR savings exceeded $23 million.

- Directed the strategies, design, and installation of world-class human resource programs, including performance management systems, compensation and incentive programs, and HR planning efforts.

Vice President HR & Development Asia-Pacific, Latin America   1993–1995
ARC International/ARC Japan, India, Africa

While in residence in Sydney, Australia, led human resources for these businesses with combined annual sales of $325 million and 13,000 employees in 42 countries. Directed a team of 100 HR professionals and managed a $6 million operating budget.

- Led HR due diligence efforts for six acquisitions whose combined revenues exceeded $200 million. As Regional Board Member, established the standards for effective integration and growth.

- Supported business expansion and cross-border initiatives, including the largest acquisition in Asia-Pacific, spanning 25 companies in 15 countries.

Vice President Human Resources   1992–1993
Director Human Resources   1990–1992

Chief human resources executive responsible for ARC's $300 million domestic marketing research division with 4,400 employees.

- Directed organizational streamlining, outsourcing, and reengineering, which eliminated $18 million in operating expenses while increasing overall productivity, more than 50%.

- Developed a comprehensive employee relations strategy that influenced the creation of the first business plan.

- Upgraded talent across all regions. Initiated performance management, human resource planning, executive development, and reward systems.

HOUSE STORES, INC.   1982 to 1990
Regional Human Resources Manager   1988–1990
Manager Executive Recruitment and Placement   1982–1988

Directed human resources team of 50 in an eight-state region with 8,000 employees, including 40 store locations, two distribution facilities, and the regional office. Key contributor in rebuilding the HR function.

EDUCATION/AWARDS

Advanced Executive Program—University of Pittsburgh

Graduate School of Management   Carnegie Mellon University   1997–1998

BS   Administrative Sciences   Allegheny College   1982

ARC International Award—1993, 1994, 1995

House Chairman's Award—1989

Society for Advancement of Management—1987 National Manager of the Year

Combination (Reverse Chronological and Functional)

Stephanie B. Able	Marketing
Peter R. Anton, PhD	Technology
Amid Suhee, PhD	R&D

STEPHANIE B. ABLE
319 Lakeview Court
Freeport, SC 98376
(478) 321-5576
lbeable3196@aol.com

CAREER SUMMARY

Capable executive with significant record of sales and marketing, operations, strategic planning, and business development achievements. Demonstrated success in providing leadership to cross-functional teams that achieve record sales and profits. Able to function effectively in turnaround, growth, established, or entrepreneurial environments.

RESULTS ACHIEVED

P&L General Management

- Successfully integrated two acquisitions representing $485 million in total revenues, both in under nine months.

- Generated $76 million in incremental annual profits by streamlining facilities 50% and by collapsing numerous operating systems. Selected and directed 30-person multidisciplinary teams to manage the integration.

- Facilitated the acquisition of a $30 million Canadian home-care business and led its profitable growth to $150 million. Strategy became the model for business launches in France, Japan, and Great Britain.

Sales

- Expanded sales in a service niche 565% to $80 million after crafting the comprehensive business plan for the company's major division.

- Increased sales $90 million by refocusing sales on the highest growth opportunities, while introducing innovative new services.

Marketing

- Conceived telemarketing that identified $25+ million in new product opportunities and achieved an 800% ROI within six months.

- Initiated a UK consulting engagement that resulted in a British Telecom Communications joint venture. Elected to the Board.

- Co-led due diligence on an innovative Web-based developer of medical Internet technologies that resulted in a $85 million strategic alliance.

STEPHANIE B. ABLE Page Two

Business Development

- Developed strong relationships with senior level managed care executives and multiple market expansion opportunities.

- Consummated several "at risk" contracts covering 380 million covered lives and representing $1.5 billion in annualized revenues.

- Represented the corporation in numerous conferences and industry meetings as both presenter and spokesperson. Presented White Papers at conferences in Barcelona, Helsinki, Paris, Hong Kong, Jerusalem, and Sidney.

BUSINESS EXPERIENCE

ZEBRA-TREK CORPORATION 1997–Present
A $700 million health-care company that develops, produces, and markets technologically advanced, user-friendly medical devices and software.

Vice President Marketing
Responsible for expanding the company's core product market share and profits, increasing the impact and profitability of new products and building integrated marketing strategies across divisions and strategic partnerships.

HEALTH MANAGEMENT SERVICES, INC. 1996–1997
A privately held (venture capital-backed) disease management company specializing in the care and case management of Alzheimer's patients.

Vice President Managed Care and Business Development
Established a managed care presence through "carve-out" contracting, orchestrating utilization of the company's resources during implementation, and profitably fine-tuning risk products.

MARKE INTERNATIONAL, INC. 1989–1996
A $2.5 billion global health-care company providing physician practice management and disease management services.

Vice President Planning Home Infusion Services Division 1994–1996

Responsible for mergers and acquisitions, planning, and the execution of strategic business alliances for this $500 million, 4,000-employee health-care services division.

STEPHANIE B. ABLE   Page Three

Vice President Mid-Atlantic Area   1992–1994

P&L general management responsibility for $80 million region with 360 employees in eight regional home care operations. Directed sales, marketing, operations, clinical services, strategic market development, finance, and human resources. Managed a $68 million operating budget.

HEALTHCARE INTERNATIONAL   1977–1992
A $10 billion worldwide manufacturer and distributor of diverse health-care industry products.

Vice President Strategic Planning   1989–1992
Directed corporate strategy development, new business development, long-term business portfolio management, and merger/acquisition activities.

Director Sales and Marketing Pharmaceutical Division   1988–1989
Director Marketing   1986–1988
Market Manager   1977–1986

Managed sales and marketing for an entrepreneurial venture involving a new product licensed from a health-care firm in England. As Director of Marketing, developed and managed strategic, operating, and advertising budgets for $120 million worth of surgical products within 5 unique segments.

EDUCATION/AFFILIATIONS

MBA	Management	Pepperdine University	1996
BA	Business Economics	University of California at Santa Barbara	1977

PETER R. ANTON, PhD

470 Mountain View Drive

Chicago, IL 60601

Office/Cell 312-850-8790

peter@anton.com

EXECUTIVE PROFILE

Technology executive with proven record of delivering exceptional results in Silicon Valley start-ups and "most admired" Fortune 1000 corporations. Excel in building and leading focused, highly creative technology teams that think beyond preconceived boundaries to create solutions that deliver major financial impact. Reputation as a pioneer in computer graphics.

TECHNICAL/BUSINESS EXPERIENCE

CON-AIRE INDUSTRIES   2001–present

Recognized as *America's Most Admired Company* in the silicon wafer computer industry by *Fortune* magazine in 2003, Con-Aire is a $1.8 billion provider of products and solutions for the high-tech military, industrial, and manufacturing industries.

Executive Vice President and Chief Technology Officer

Responsible for directing the corporate Technology Center and influencing the development of products and processes that advance corporate brands, revenue, and profitability.

- Top graded the organization while significantly strengthening core competencies resulting in major contributions in materials, ergonomics, new product concepts, and profitable go-to-market channels.

- Developed key technologies and innovations for award-winning products projected to contribute incremental sales of $90 million and potential savings of $40 million over five years. These innovations are currently protected by 40 U.S. and 85 foreign patents and filings.

TAIG GLOBAL RESEARCH   1990–2001

Corporate R&D function for Taig's $13 billion diversified businesses.

Senior Vice President Manufacturing and Business Process Lab   1996–2001

Provided the strategic direction for the advancement of manufacturing technologies to help achieve Taig's business goals. Managed a high-powered global team of 150 with an operating budget of $25 million.

- Crafted a compelling vision and expanded the lab's technology focus from purely manufacturing to include high-value industrial and financial services. Broader business involvement drove the unit's staff growth from 85 in U.S. to 150 globally.

PETER R. ANTON, PhD   Page Two

- Generated $200 million in net income with Taig and its partners by incubating a business process team that analyzed value creation opportunities while managing risk. The team grew from four in the U.S. to an aggregate of 30 in India, China, and the U.S.

- Leveraged and enhanced medical imaging technologies that justified and supported the start-up of two service businesses that now have combined annual sales of $500 million.

- Led the launch of an R&D facility in China that now employs 200 scientists and engineers, while supporting the start-up of the R&D site in India that has grown to 1,700 professionals.

Vice President Manufacturing Research Center   1990–1996

Managed engineers and scientists developing advanced mathematical algorithms for sophisticated design, manufacturing, and inspection processes.

- Directed R&D effort that provided vital manufacturing and inspection technologies to enable production of the revolutionary composite fan blade for the GE90 aircraft engine. Presented the results to GE's board of directors. To date, engine orders valued at more than $2.5 billion have been taken for the Boeing 777 aircraft.

- Generated $10 million in operating savings by pioneering a highly successful "PhD's on the Factory Floor" program that had R&D staff augment Six Sigma efforts in diverse manufacturing and service settings.

ACADEMIC TEACHING/RESEARCH EXPERIENCE   1983–1990
UCLA   1977–1990
Professor of Advanced Applied Research   1977–1985/1988–1990

Taught graduate-level classes in electrical engineering and software development. Directed teams of graduate PhDs in leading-edge research for metallurgical properties for aerospace and automotive applications. Was chief university liaison with R&D business community.

Vice President Engineering Sanar Company   1985–1988

As "Professor in Residence" on loan from UCLA, worked with Silicon Valley software start-up firm that developed and marketed unique mechanical analysis and optimization technology. Created the engineering organization from three founders to more than 26 full-time and contract consultants.

- Responsible for building the product development organization and producing leading-edge software products during fast-paced, highly demanding start-up phase and growth.

PETER R. ANTON, PhD   Page Three

- Produced the first release of the mechanical analysis and optimization software. Developed product specifications, development processes, and computer facilities.

- Built the team and technology platform that ultimately generated annualized sales of more than $25 million in 1995 when Sanar was purchased for $180 million.

EDUCATION AND TRAINING

PhD	Electrical Engineering	Rensselaer Polytechnic Institute	1983
MS	Architectural Science	Cornell University	1977
BS	Architecture	Pennsylvania State University	1975

Certified Six Sigma Green Belt; Design for Six Sigma Tollgate Process

PROFESSIONAL/COMMUNITY SERVICE

Vice-Chair, Advanced Manufacturing Research Consortium

AMID, SUHEE, PhD
123 Lake Shore Drive
San Diego, CA 91045-1115
619-649-0776
drtsuhee@comcast.net

CAREER PROFILE

Accomplished technology manager, communicator, facilitator, and mentor. Experienced in fostering development of unique product platforms and enhancing profitability by applying technical "reality checks." Strong university/industrial collaborations to spearhead company exploratory research programs. Excellent interpersonal and organizational skills, highly intuitive and practical problem solver with a collaborative leadership style.

EDUCATION

PhD	Organic Chemistry	Stanford University	1970
MS	Organic Chemistry	UCLA	1966
BS	Organic Chemistry	Hiram College	1963
	Certificate in Management	USC	1973

INDUSTRIAL EXPERIENCE

HEALTHCARE CORPORATION   1985 to 2003

University Technology Liaison
Office of the Chief Technical Office   2002–2003

Senior Director Research
Materials Science and Engineering   2001–2003

Vice President
Medical Materials Technology Center   1998–2001

Senior Scientist and Director
Medical Materials Technology Center   1991–1998

Research Scientist
Materials and Membranes Tech Center   1985–1991

AMID. SUHEE, PhD   Page Two

EARLIER EXPERIENCE

Employed at Da Borg as Manager, Analytical Chemistry (1979–1985). Worked as Manager, Contract Research (1978–1979) and Technical Manager, Spectroscopy Group (1975–1978) at Chrysler Chemical Company. Contract research in Drug Detection and NMR Spectroscopy at Bee Memorial Institute (1971–1975).

LECTURING EXPERIENCE

Stanford University	Hurlburt Lecturer	1997
University of Winnipeg	Visiting Lecturer	1979
Academy Institute	Instructor	1974–1975
Ohio University	Chemistry Instructor	1973–1974
Ohio Wesleyan University	Visiting Assistant Professor	1969–1971

SELECTED INDUSTRIAL ACCOMPLISHMENTS

Product Concepts

- Reduced production costs $39 million annually of disposable component of a blood pathogen inactivation product platform.

- Led development of a low-cost, high-volume drug delivery system with NPV estimated at $80 million for one application

- Generated $100 million in first-year sales through innovative packaging design and manufacturing expertise in support of a new business venture in "Neutraceuticals."

- Developed a family of low-cost, chlorine-free replacements for Healthcare's $6 billion PVC-based medical fluids management product platform that were capable of being manufactured in existing facilities.

Technical Support

- Defended $8 billion potential implantable heart assist device business by guiding the purchase and integration of elastomeric polymer technology central to the device function.

- Protected $2.5 billion global Renal division by determining within seven days the cause of a major product failure. Settlement exposure, if left unchecked, was conservatively estimated to exceed $1 billion.

AMID. SUHEE, PhD   Page Three

Innovation

- Established $2.5M, five-year program of incubator grants and early career investigator fellowships in nanotechnology at Stanford University and started a collaborative business development program in biotechnology with selected universities.

- Won a $2.4 million three-year National Institute of Science and Technology grant for development of improved biological filters.

- Led a program that reversed diabetes in test animals for six months by creation of a membrane-based isolation system for implanted foreign islet cells.

PROFESSIONAL MEMBERSHIPS

American Chemical Society   Society for Applied Spectroscopy

Society for Biomaterials   Society of Plastics Engineers

Functional Résumés

Vera K. Pang	General Counsel
William W. Robbins	Manufacturing

VERA K. PANG
1716 North Wells Street
San Francisco, CA 37365
Home: (925) 349-8745
Office: (415) 367-9832
Cell: (415) 345-0983
vernonk.papiere@yahoo.com

CAREER PROFILE

Broadly experienced U.S. and international corporate generalist and litigation specialist. Excels in providing winning, cost-effective business solutions with speed, impact, and versatility. Superb litigation avoidance and resolution record. Inspirational leader, mentor, and change agent who builds focused, disciplined, and motivated teams. Help shape business growth and performance while managing legal and business risks.

Corporate

- Transformed an underperforming legal function into a high-response department recognized as the company's best. On or under budget eight consecutive years. No attorney turnover in past five years. Consistently achieved company-wide 95% client satisfaction ratings.

- Managed an in-house attorney hourly rate at 25% below national company averages, saving the company millions of dollars in outside counsel fees.

- Trained staff to explain complex legal issues in lay terms and to provide business-friendly and culturally sensitive real-time solutions. Redrafted contracts to be readily translated, "plain-language" documents, enabling the company's globalization initiative and achieving 99% acceptance of all contracts submitted.

- Engineered a creative, Web-based contracting process to eliminate scores of "legalese" forms and move a 110-year old company into the 21st century.

- Served as Compliance Officer, chairing the Compliance Oversight and Review Board. Created the company's first corporate compliance program, overseeing responsibilities for investigating and fairly resolving reports of alleged ethical, antitrust, and Foreign Corrupt Practices Act issues.

- Managed Board of Trustee governance issues to ensure Sarbanes-Oxley compliance.

- Successfully concluded union negotiations resulting in collective bargaining agreement that allowed restructuring of the company's workforce.

- Thoroughly knowledgeable in product standards development processes in the U.S., Europe, and Japan.

VERA K. PANG   Page Two

Litigation (U.S. and International)

- Successfully defended numerous products liability and business cases throughout the U.S.

- Successfully managed international product liability litigation in France; three Canadian class action suits, including a $1 billion claim; and various labor law matters in the UK, Italy, Japan, Hong Kong, and Taiwan.

- Developed successful litigation strategies and tactics to defend over 150 toxic tort (asbestos) personal injury cases in California, Oregon, Washington, Utah, and Illinois. More than 100 asbestos cases dismissed prior to trial or at the close of plaintiff's case.

Global

- Oversaw all legal aspects of the company's global expansion in Europe, China, and South America. Established 14 local subsidiaries and 3 representative liaison offices.

- Negotiated first Chinese government-sanctioned joint venture agreement between U.S. certification organization and Chinese organization. This ensured local service to China export customers and secured future Chinese import product certification.

- Knowledgeable in U.S. regulatory requirements and EU "New Approach" Notified Body directives with which U.S. and EU manufacturers must comply to sell products globally.

- Retained and provided general oversight to a world-class network of international counsel. Developed and negotiated independent contractor relationships in the U.S. and abroad.
- Routinely handled trade sanction matters. Successfully negotiated disputes with the U.S. Department of Treasury's Office of Foreign Assets Control.

Mergers and Acquisitions (US and International)

- Negotiated and closed strategic Japanese ($35 million) acquisition and merger. Acquired companies in Denmark ($7 million), Italy ($3.5 million), and UK ($1.5 million).

- Negotiated and closed three underperforming U.S. acquisitions with combined worth of valued at $12 million in California, Illinois, and Indiana.

Intellectual Property and Branding

- Registered and maintained the company's global intellectual property involving 93 certification, service, and trademarks in 62 jurisdictions.

VERA K. PANG   Page Three

- Managed international anticounterfeiting operations (100 seizures/raids that yielded counterfeit goods valued at $15 million in 2003).

- Participated in a nationally covered press conference with representatives of Immigration and Customs Enforcement (division of Office of Homeland Security) and the Chairman of CPSC.

ACME COMPONENTS CORPORATION	1996–2005
Vice President, General Counsel	2001–2005
General Counsel	1999–2001
Assistant General Counsel	1996–1999

Member of senior management team. Managed the legal liability and business risks for this leading components manufacturer and distributor. Collaborated on key company growth initiatives. Directed a 24-person staff (10 attorneys, 8 paralegals). Managed a $6 million budget.

BADABING, BADABONG, & BOYD	1978–1996
Equity Partner — Litigation Department	1984–1996
Associate	1978–1984

- Broad litigation experience specializing in consumer and products liability, insurance coverage, CERCLA, accountant's malpractice, injunction proceedings, class actions, and general commercial matters. Represented mid- and large-cap publicly traded and privately held companies. Extensive, highly successful motions practice.

- Tried cases in state and federal courts. Prepared and argued appeals in the California Supreme Court and 7th Circuit Court of appeals.

EARLIER EXPERIENCE

Employed by State of California as **Law Clerk** (1976–1978) for Honorable John J. Jones, California Appellate Court (ret.). From 1974 to 1976, served as **Law Clerk** for the Criminal Appeals Division, Madison County (CA) State's Attorney Office.

EDUCATION

JD	The Law School University of Chicago	1976
BA	Occidental College, Los Angeles, CA	1973
	Magna Cum Laude Phi Beta Kappa	

WILLIAM W. ROBBINS
Three Wilkshire Court
Cincinnati, Ohio 80045
(513) 450-9832

Experienced general manager with a demonstrated record in manufacturing, maintenance, engineering, and facilities. Skilled in production enhancements, operational troubleshooting, preventive maintenance systems, and team building. Able to contribute equally well in turnaround situations with mature products or with emerging technologies and new products.

RESPONSIBILITIES AND RESULTS

Manufacturing and Operations

- Increased profits more than $60 million annually through the development and implementation of a highly effective QC effort, which reduced the number of defective parts by 95%.

- Accelerated replacement parts sales $19 million annually by establishing a reliable order processing and follow-up system. The time to deliver parts dropped from an average of over 75 days to under 30 days.

- Saved $35 million through executing an online MRP system for inventory control. Eliminated stock shortages, reduced special production runs, and secured favorable price concessions from raw material suppliers.

- Negotiated the interest free use of a special milling machine for 12 months, saving $912,000 in annual labor and outside machining costs. Productivity increases are estimated to increase 75%, yielding more than a $30 million annual gain.

Engineering and Maintenance

- Eliminated $28 million in operational costs by developing a fully integrated, online preventive maintenance program that reduced operational downtime 23% and improved productivity 12%. Annual profits increased $18 million.

- Generated $117 million in annual savings through three acquisitions by consolidating operations, rationalizing duplicate functions, and by implementing management controls, cross-training, and innovative productivity improvements.

- Redesigned manufacturing process equipment that eliminated the need for $8 million in capital expenditures while improving overall productivity 15%.

WILLIAM W. ROBBINS   Page Two

BUSINESS EXPERIENCE

THERMO-MAINLINER, INC.   TML Division   1987–Present
Executive Vice President—Manufacturing and Operations

Have P&L responsibility for this $630 million TML Division manufacturing and distributing of precision widgets. Responsible for the turnaround of this suboptimized business. Direct production, supply chain, finance, HR, sales and marketing, material handling, and maintenance. Develop strategic and operating plans and manage 3,200 employees. Report to the Group President

POPULAR PRODUCTS, INC.   1981–1986
Senior Vice President—Engineering and Maintenance

Provided the strategic direction to maintenance, facilities, and engineering. Managed process and productivity improvements, safety and health, operator training, and vendor selection. Directed a workforce of 1,500 and a $90 million capital budget.

THE MONTEHALL COMPANY   1978–1981
Vice President—Engineering and Technical Services

Built and directed a highly skilled technical group providing hands-on consulting support to plants throughout the United States in operational troubleshooting, maintenance, equipment development, engineering, and process improvements. Managed a $10 million operating budget.

EDUCATION / PERSONAL

| MBA | Lake Forest | Graduate School of Management | 1978 |
| BS | Industrial Engineering | University of Illinois | 1976 |

PROFESSIONAL AFFILIATIONS

American Institute of Packaging Companies
The Packaging Institute

Biographical Letter: "No Résumé" Résumé

William D. J. Castenada   General Management

Bill Castenada is a global executive and senior general manager with 20-plus years of experience in the United States as well as in all major Latin American/Caribbean, Asian, and European countries. He recently founded **Castenada Consulting,** a strategic marketing practice with a focus on the Americas.

Prior to founding his consulting company, Bill was **Vice President and General Manager** for the **Reed Sugar Company** in the Caribbean, a $470 million/27 country business, which he led out of San Juan, Puerto Rico. Under his leadership, Reed Sugar's regional volume grew by 30% while share price rose 21 points in the five largest markets. This was accomplished through strategic alliances with key, nationally recognized customers, an aggressive product launch schedule, which doubled Reed's regional brand portfolio, and a strategic refocusing on growth markets.

Before his Caribbean assignment, Bill was **Managing Director** for Reed's $1 billion operations in Chicago, Indiana, Northern Ohio, upstate New York, and Pennsylvania. In the face of tremendous competition, Bill's team grew volume 5% annually while increasing profits at an 8% rate. This was accomplished through a combination of operational improvements, business restructuring, and marketing initiatives targeting youth and multiethnic consumers.

Prior to joining the Reed Sugar Company, Bill was **Vice President and General Manager, Latin America and Asia/Pacific** for the **Specialty Foods Company.** He pioneered Specialty Foods' entry into the Latin American food ingredient and consumer products markets. He created a $50 million business through the use of distributors; JV partners in Mexico and Argentina; acquisitions in Chile, Argentina, and Colombia; and entirely new entities including manufacturing facilities in Brazil and Argentina. He also was responsible for expanding Specialty Foods' business into India, China, and Southeast Asia. This initiative resulted in a $35 million enterprise with offices in Mumbai (Bombay), Shanghai, Bangkok, Sydney, Singapore, and Hong Kong.

Bill has also held a number of manufacturing, quality, and logistics positions including head of **Global Facilities Planning** for one division of the **Edible Chemical Company** and head of production, engineering, and distribution for another division.

He is a past guest lecturer at the University of Southern Florida on creating and building strategic alliances in Latin America. He has also been a regular speaker and an advisor to the Duke University's Graduate School of Management faculty on industrial issues in the Caribbean. He recently spoke to the International Economic Trade Club of Chicago on marketing in Latin America.

Bill holds an MBA in marketing and general management from Northwestern and has participated in advanced management programs at Harvard Business School. He also holds an MS in Biochemistry from the University of Chicago and a BS in Chemistry from the University of Illinois at Chicago.

As a native Chilean, Bill is bilingual in Spanish and English.

Bill Castenada b.castenada@castenadaconsultinggroup.edu (825) 509-9376

"Handbill Résumé"

Michele D. Cannon   General Management

MICHELE D. CANNON
1693 Elm Street Antwirl, CA
415-585-2290 (Home)   925-317-1451 (Office)
m_cannon@rr.ca.com

PRESIDENT, CEO, COO

Broadly experienced in P&L general management, accelerating sales and profit growth, business turnaround, and enhanced shareholder value. Strong leadership capabilities in diverse domestic and international markets for start-up, early stage, and turnaround businesses.

INDUSTRY EXPERIENCE

Global Manufacturing and Distribution
Chemicals, Industrial, and Scientific Products
Branded and Private Label Consumer Products

- Doubled sales to $2.6 billion in three years through organic growth and acquisitions, achieving $238 million in pretax earnings.

- Successfully acquired and integrated five companies, with combined annual revenues of $850 million. Increased operating profits from $86 million to over $150 million run rate in 18 months.

- Replaced $300 million in lost sales with $450 million in new accounts and concurrently retained 98% of the base book of business. Accomplished this through strategic selling and the execution of rigorous account management.

- Personally negotiated and led the team that secured a $500 million client contract, the single largest customer in Acme's history.

ACME INTERNATIONAL   A Colorant Partners' Subsidiary   2000–2006
A $2.6 billion global chemicals business. Managed an $800 million SG&A budget and 2,500 employees. Colorant acquired Acme in 2006.

President Services Group   2002–2006
Executive Vice President   2000–2002

PILLAR AMERICAS   A Pillar A. G. Company   1993–2000
President and CEO

P&L general management responsibility for $485 million distributor of concrete curing forms and licensing business for a $900 million global manufacturer.

EDUCATION

BBS   Finance   University of Michigan   1980
Harvard University   Graduate School of Business   Executive Management   1988

Tell-All Résumé

Come on, now. I couldn't be so insensitive as to include a tell-all résumé with 10 or more pages of blah, blah!

CHAPTER 8

CREATE COMPELLING MARKETING LETTERS THAT EVOKE ACTION

You only have three to five seconds to hook the person scanning your letter. These letters are clearly part of your branding and a vehicle for marketing you in advance of your being able to do so in person. The better the marketing, the greater probability of someone picking up the phone or e-mailing you to meet or discuss open opportunities . . . or provide a contact name as a lead.

All good marketing messages have a clear and compelling call to action. This is what you want. You want an individual to think, "Wow! This person has achieved a lot. If she is able to generate a fraction of what she has contributed to her previous employer here, I'd be thrilled. I hope I can still reach her today."

Each time you transmit your résumé, send it with a powerful, easy-to-read cover letter that reinforces and markets your credentials, accomplishments, and the value you can add to the organization.

A well-written marketing letter, along with your results-oriented résumé, is a key ingredient in prompting a person to call you for a conversation and an interview. Directed at decision makers, letters connect you with the people most likely to grant you interviews.

Attributes of Effective Marketing Letters

Marketing letters have the following qualities:

1. *Use short sentences that are crisp, succinct, and punchy.* They are more powerful, and they are easier to read. Shorter sentences have the ability to create a greater sense of urgency. Shorter paragraphs have a more powerful impact than long ones.
2. *Are directed to a specific individual, not merely an office holder.* Most executive search firms' Web sites identify the partners-in-charge of an industry group. This is the person to whom you wish to e-mail your marketing letter and résumé. If you are

responding to an advertisement, identify this person. While the salutation, "To Whom It May Concern" is still grammatically correct, it will have much more impact if you use the hiring authority's name. If a name is not revealed on a classified advertisement or on an online Web site, investigate it. Research the appropriate contact at the company. Even though the probability of connecting through an advertisement or by a blind contact at an organization is under 3 percent, I still recommend that through research you identify the person to whom this position reports. Once you have a name, call first to make a connection so that when you do send your résumé in, you can personalize the letter.

3. *Employ different language than in your résumé.* Highlight specific information about your credentials, responsibilities, accomplishments, and potential benefits to the reader's organization. If you are targeting a specific organization, research the company's greatest challenges and tailor your letter, appropriately mentioning your capabilities. If you are sending your *résumé* out in a widespread broadcast mailing, then your marketing letter can be somewhat generic.

Address what all organizations want. They want to increase their revenues, improve their margins, introduce innovative products and services, and, most of all, serve their customers well.

4. *Request specific action to be taken by the search firm or organization.* This is the call to action that you want the résumé readers/scanners to respond to.

5. *State the action you plan to take with the individual in the organization.* Simply put, you might be informing the reader that you will be calling them. *Do not indicate that you'll be calling* if you're not planning to or are unable to do so on a timely basis. Some people convince themselves that they will absolutely call the hundreds of individuals to whom they have sent letters. Practically speaking, you will most likely be able to call back only about 25 people in a week. (This 25 is in addition to your normal networking calls of 20 a day. We'll talk more about networking in Chapter 12.)

6. *Are professional, yet warm and inviting.* Write like you most likely would speak. As I write this I shudder to think the license this statement might evoke. What I am saying is this: Don't try to impress anyone with your immense vocabulary or your ability to use a thesaurus. A good rule of thumb for all elements of your career search process is to ask someone you trust to give you honest feedback. This includes any written materials (résumé, letters, etc.) and your overall search strategy.

Marketing Letter Format

The following format outlines the key points to be made in a cover letter:

1. Introduction
2. Objective
3. Strengths, qualifications, and accomplishments
4. Next steps: requesting an interview, information, or advice.

Personal Contact Letters

Ideally, you will have spoken to your personal contacts before you send them your e-mail and résumé. However, there are any number of valid reasons for sending an e-mail message first indicating that you will be following up with a phone call. Personal letters are just that—personal. It's preferred that you make the personal connection first then lead into the body of the letter, the text of which will be almost identical to the text in the other letters outlined herein. The following is an example to a personal contact:

Letter To:
Personal Contact

Dear _____:

It was great to touch base with you recently concerning my career search. Thank you for your interest. As we discussed, personal networking is certainly the most effective means of creating the level of visibility that ultimately leads to interviews and later offers. Your help is greatly appreciated.

To recap, I am seeking a senior P&L role as CEO or COO of a growth-oriented company. I am skilled in developing strategies that generate significant top-line growth while enhancing margins.

Most recently, I have been responsible for the accelerated sales growth and P&L of a $2.6 billion chemicals business. My background includes leadership of turnarounds, organic growth, and acquisitions. In each situation I have dramatically improved the profits and cash flow of these businesses, significantly enhancing their value multifold.

Highlights of my accomplishments include:

- Turning the company around by reorganizing, revitalizing, and upgrading leadership talent throughout the organization.
- Doubling sales to $2.6 billion through organic growth and a key acquisition.
- Halting $300 million in customer erosion, while protecting 88+% of current business base and securing $450 million in higher margin business.

After reviewing my credentials, I would appreciate hearing about names of search firms, companies, and/or individuals you feel it would be appropriate for me to contact.

I look forward to touching base with you again to keep you posted on the progress of my search. Thanks again for your help.

Personal regards,

Michele D. Cannon

Enclosure

Private Equity Firm/Investment Banking Letters

Increasingly, senior executives are actively exploring alternatives to the traditional corporate career route—namely, the alluring, high-stakes world of private equity (PE) and/or investment banking.

Given the focus and mind-set of this target audience, it is important for you to straightforwardly communicate how you would be able to turn around and accelerate the growth and profitability of a PE firm's portfolio company. While this capability is important and highly desirable for a corporate role, the perspective of PE firms is how quickly can this company be restored to profitability and flipped for the highest multiple of the EBITDA. If I could generalize, most corporations look to grow and keep their businesses, reaping the rewards over many years. Most PE firms look to gain profitability and sell the business as quickly as it makes sense to gain the optimal return.

Please note that Michele Cannon's letter to a private equity firm is slightly different than the letter she is sending to a target organization for a traditional corporate role.

Letter To:
Private Equity Firm

Dear _____:

Are you seeking an accomplished P&L executive for one of your portfolio companies?

As the enclosed résumé reflects, I am a executive with more than 20 years of leadership and general management success in chemicals, industrial products, and health care companies. I am seeking a senior general management role as CEO or COO of a growth-oriented company. My strengths are in developing strategies that generate significant top-line growth while enhancing margins.

Most recently, I have been responsible for the accelerated sales growth and P&L of a $2.6 billion chemicals business. My background includes leadership of turnarounds, organic growth, and acquisitions. In each situation I have dramatically improved the profits and cash flow of these businesses, significantly enhancing their value multifold.

Highlights of my accomplishments include:

- Turning the company around by reorganizing, revitalizing, and upgrading leadership talent throughout the organization.
- Doubling sales to $2.6 billion through organic growth and a key acquisition.
- Halting $300 million in customer erosion, while protecting 88+% of current business base and securing $450 million in higher margin business.

If you are intrigued by how I might contribute to your organization's growth and profitability, I'd welcome a call or an e-mail.

Thank you for your consideration. I look forward to meeting with you soon.

Sincerely,

Michele D. Cannon

Enclosure

Search Firm Letters

Search firm account executives are busy. In addition to the critical need to develop business and complete the assignments that they currently have, they are overwhelmed by the requests from talented executives, like yourself, wanting to meet "for purposes of introduction." All search firms balance their desire to meet people with the pressing need to source and interview executives for open positions. While you might be an incredibly successful executive with an international reputation, if you are not a fit for an ongoing search, you may not be able to open the door until there's a breather in their schedule. Since this is such a sensitive topic, I'll address this nuance in more detail in Chapter 13, "Executive Search Firms: Your Success Partners."

Letters to search firms are very similar to those you would send to private equity firms.

The letter following is an example of such a letter.

Dear _____:

If you are conducting a search for a (position title), you may find my credentials of interest. Enclosed is a résumé for your consideration.

Highlights of my experience and accomplishments include:

> [*List two to four key attention getting points that closely relate to the job being sought. Items from résumé may apply if reworded.*]

After you review my attached résumé, I look forward to exploring with you how my background might contribute to the growth and profitability of your _____ [group, department, company technical effort]. Thank you for your consideration. I look forward to your call.

Sincerely,

Accordingly Michele Cannon's letter to search firms might look like the following:

Letter To:
Retained Search Firm

Dear _____:

If you are conducting a search for an accomplished P&L executive for one of your clients, you may find my background of interest.

As the enclosed résumé reflects, I am a executive with more than 20 years of leadership and general management success in chemicals, industrial products, and health care companies. I am seeking a senior general management role as CEO or COO of a growth-oriented company. My strengths are in developing strategies that generate significant top-line growth while enhancing margins.

Most recently, I have been responsible for the accelerated sales growth and P&L of a $2.6 billion chemicals business. My background includes leadership of turnarounds, organic growth, and acquisitions. In each situation I have dramatically improved the profits and cash flow of these businesses, significantly enhancing their value multifold.

Highlights of my accomplishments include:

- Turning the company around by reorganizing, revitalizing, and upgrading leadership talent throughout the organization.
- Doubling sales to $2.6 billion through organic growth and a key acquisition.
- Halting $300 million in customer erosion, while protecting 88^+% of current business base and securing $450 million in higher margin business.

If you are intrigued by how I might contribute to your client's organizational growth and profitability, I'd welcome a call or an e-mail.

Thank you for your consideration. I look forward to meeting with you soon.

Sincerely,

Michele D. Cannon

Enclosure

Follow-Up Letter To:
Retained Search Firm

Dear _____:

I appreciate your continuing interest and support of me, even though we haven't yet connected with an active search assignment. As promised, I am keeping you updated on my situation, as it might be useful to you as things develop on your end.

If you recall, it has been a few months since I first wrote to you concerning my intentions for a senior P&L, general management role. Since launching my search, I have had initial exploratory interviews with a number of companies and have been slated quite a few times by search firms for additional discussions. While I am pleased and flattered with the level of activity, it is still early in my campaign, and I am intent on making the best possible career match.

If you have an active or pending search for which I might fit, it may be mutually advantageous for us to meet within the next several weeks.

My primary objective remains a challenging CEO or COO position. I am flexible regarding location and employment terms.

Your help and support will be sincerely appreciated and remembered.

Sincerely,

Michele D. Cannon

Target Organization Mailings

Before the widespread use of e-mail and posting on the Internet, in general, we used to advocate sending your credentials to selected organizations on a "cold call" or unsolicited basis. Unfortunately, because so many executives were flooding the marketplace, target organizations rarely accessed the thousands of résumés collecting dust in their files. These days, we do not recommend mailing to organizations, as the return yield is so incredibly low. If you want to target companies and explore the viability of opportunities in a given organization, fine.

Do you want to know the optimal way to make the connection and open the right doors in your target organization? It is networking. If you want to move from cold calling/letter writing to warm introductions, then network. This process of networking into your target organizations is explained in more detail in Chapter 12.

Letter To:
Target Organization

Dear _____:

If you are conducting a search for an accomplished P&L executive for your organization, you may find my background of interest.

As the enclosed résumé reflects, I am a executive with more than 20 years of leadership and general management success in chemicals, industrial products, and health care companies. I am seeking a senior general management role in a growth-oriented company. My strengths are in developing strategies that generate significant top-line growth while enhancing margins.

Most recently, I have been responsible for the accelerated sales growth and P&L of a $2.6 billion chemicals business. My background includes leadership of turnarounds, organic growth, and acquisitions. In each situation I have dramatically improved the profits and cash flow of these businesses, significantly enhancing their value multifold.

Highlights of my accomplishments include:

- Turning the company around by reorganizing, revitalizing, and upgrading leadership talent throughout the organization.
- Doubling sales to $2.6 billion through organic growth and a key acquisition.
- Halting $300 million in customer erosion, while protecting 88+% of current business base and securing $450 million in higher margin business.

If you are intrigued by how I might contribute to your organization's growth and profitability, I'd welcome a call or an e-mail.

Thank you for your consideration. I look forward to meeting with you soon.

Sincerely,

Michele D. Cannon

Enclosure

Letter To:
Advertisements/Internet/Classified Ads

Dear _____:

In response to your recent advertisement for _____ [title] in the
_____ [Internet site (or paper's name)], please find attached my résumé
for your consideration.

As the enclosed résumé reflects, I am a executive with more than 20 years of leadership
and general management success in chemicals, industrial products, and health care companies. I am seeking a senior general management role in a growth-oriented company.
My strengths are in developing strategies that generate significant top-line growth while
enhancing margins.

Most recently, I have been responsible for the accelerated sales growth and P&L of a
$2.6 billion chemicals business. My background includes leadership of turnarounds,
organic growth, and acquisitions. In each situation I have dramatically improved the
profits and cash flow of these businesses, significantly enhancing their value multifold.

Highlights of my accomplishments include:

- Turning the company around by reorganizing, revitalizing, and upgrading
  leadership talent throughout the organization.
- Doubling sales to $2.6 billion through organic growth and a key acquisition.
- Halting $300 million in customer erosion, while protecting 88$^+$% of current
  business base and securing $450 million in higher margin business.

If you are intrigued by how I might contribute to your organization's growth and
profitability, I'd welcome a call or an e-mail.

Thank you for your consideration. I look forward to meeting with you soon.

Sincerely,

Michele D. Cannon

Enclosure

Note: "To Whom It May Concern" is acceptable and is preferred salutation to "Dear
Sir or Madam" in a blind ad if you have searched and are unable to find a contact name.

Letter To:
Advertisement/Internet/Classified Ads
(Second Response Mailed within a Few Weeks)

Dear _____:

A few weeks ago I responded to your ad for a senior executive with significant P&L experience in _____ [Internet site or paper]. I can well appreciate that you have been inundated with responses and have not been able to get back to every person. Nonetheless, I would like to indicate my continued interest.

To recap, I am an executive with more than 20 years of leadership and general management success in chemicals, industrial products, and health care companies. I am seeking a senior general management role in a growth-oriented company. My strengths are in developing strategies that generate significant top-line growth while enhancing margins.

Most recently, I have been responsible for the accelerated sales growth and P&L of a $2.6 billion chemicals business. My background includes leadership of turnarounds, organic growth, and acquisitions. In each situation I have dramatically improved the profits and cash flow of these businesses, significantly enhancing their value multifold.

Highlights of my accomplishments include:

- Turning the company around by reorganizing, revitalizing, and upgrading leadership talent throughout the organization.
- Doubling sales to $2.6 billion through organic growth and a key acquisition.
- Halting $300 million in customer erosion, while protecting 88^+% of current business base and securing $450 million in higher margin business.

I would appreciate the opportunity to discuss how I might contribute to the growth and profitability of your organization. Thank you for your consideration. I look forward to hearing from you.

Sincerely,

Michele D. Cannon

Enclosure

Interview Thank-You Letters

It is proper protocol that you write individual thank-you letters to each and every person with whom you interviewed. In much the same way that every interview is different, so should every thank-you letter emphasize different points.

Note: It is a common practice for the hiring manager or for Human Resources to request every thank-you letter that candidates write to the interviewers. I know that I did when I managed this process when I was in my corporate roles.

Well-crafted letters give you one more opportunity to articulate your interest, ask a probing question, or clarify something that you might want to emphasize or restate.

FYI—Virtually 100 percent of executive job seekers send their thank-you notes back to the company via e-mail. Given that, you might wish to consider handwriting such a note on high quality, embossed note cards. It is much more personalized, and you will definitely stand out from your competition.

Letter To:
Interview Thank You

Dear _____:

Thank you for the recent interview. It was a pleasure to discuss employment opportunities with you for the position of _____. As I indicated, I am interested in pursuing matters further and welcome the opportunity to do so. My proven track record fits what you are looking for at _____, and I am confident that we could be of mutual benefit.

I was particularly intrigued by the strategy you have in place for the organization's continued growth and expansion [tailor these comments with the particulars you discovered]. Your commitment to pulling a world-class group of top talent is exciting and one in which I would perform well. Additionally, I was impressed by your authentic leadership style. Your executive team clearly enjoys working for you and seems to thrive in this challenging environment.

As promised, I will track down and send to you under separate cover a copy of the article, "The Hard Side of Change Management" from the *Harvard Business Review*. Given your bias on measuring the P&L impact of such initiatives, I'm sure you'll appreciate the focus on performance metrics. I hope you will enjoy it as much as I have.

As agreed, I will call you in several days to see how we might proceed. Thank you again for your consideration.

Sincerely,

Michele D. Cannon

Note: Add value and distinguish yourself from your competition by providing an insightful article or some thought-provoking research. Sending an article in a separate e-mail provides you another opportunity to be visible.

Letter To:
Interview Thank You

Dear _____:

I would like to thank you for the opportunity to interview at XYZ Corporation recently. Everyone I met made me feel quite welcome. I understand what you meant when you explained that XYZ was a large company with a "family feeling."

After hearing about your plans for the future and your current departmental needs, I feel that I am ideally suited to help your team achieve its goals. I am pleased that you feel the same.

Highlights of my background and your requirements match well.

Your Needs:	My Capabilities:
• Develop strategy for turnaround.	Turned the company around by reorganizing, revitalizing, and upgrading leadership talent throughout the organization.
• Improve overall profitability.	Doubled sales to $2.6 billion through organic growth and a key acquisition, while significantly enhancing aggregate profitability.
• Enhance customer relationships.	Halted $300 million in customer erosion, while protecting $88^+\%$ of current business base and securing $450 million in higher margin business. Achieved this by developing a close partnership, aligning customer needs, improving on-time performance, and dedicating responsive technical and customer service personnel.

_____, I am enthusiastic about the possibility of joining the XYZ organization and contributing to its growth and profitability. I look forward to speaking with you soon to discuss next steps.

Sincerely,

Michele D. Cannon

Answering Rejection Letters

While you should save your reject letters, the majority of executives searching for jobs never respond to them. However, if you are highly committed to being known to a given target organization, an option is to answer back *and* to network your way in. We'll talk about networking in Chapter 12, but let's stay focused on answering rejection letters, shall we?

It may be appropriate for you to recontact some of the firms that sent you rejection letters. Now, don't misunderstand me. I'm not talking about contacting every single organization that sent you a rejection letter, rather only your top 5 percent.

If the rejection letter is from one of your top organizations, recontact the person to whom you originally wrote and thank him or her for getting back to you (whether him- or herself or through a Human Resource person). That's right, thank them! Few firms today take the time to respond to résumés and contacts. Let the person know that you appreciate his or her thoughtfulness. Indicate that the executive's thoughtfulness reconfirms your high evaluation of the company when you selected them as an organization you would like very much to work for. Following up on rejections will distinguish you from your competition, as few people take the time to do so. However, don't get carried away by responding to too many companies or, more to the point, get your hopes up or spend a lot of time on this very, very low-yield activity. My perspective: Ironing your shirts for the next day is probably more important than responding to rejection letters.

Nonetheless, if the rejection letter said that there are no current openings but your information would be kept on file for future needs, you can still ask for a meeting. Request the opportunity to meet personally, "for purposes of introduction, information, or advice." Such a brief introductory meeting might be valuable in the event that a future need arises. If that happens, they will already know of your abilities and can call you.

Your first goal in these calls is to establish a warm, professional, and comfortable telephone or e-mail connection with someone who can potentially hire you. Even if this is all you achieve this time, you have done well for a first contact.

Your second goal is to meet the manager briefly, for purposes of introduction, so that you are no longer a faceless name on a résumé. This distinguishes you from the thousands of job searchers who depend primarily and solely on their résumé to get them a job.

Don't be overly concerned with being rejected again in the follow-up calls. Your goal in these networking calls is not to get a job per se, but rather gather some additional advice or contact and to develop a large "No" list. All too often we do not initiate a follow-up call because it is uncomfortable and we want the call to be perfect. Do not worry about perfection; your aim is to create visibility and exposure for yourself in these introductory calls.

Follow-Up Letter To:
Target Organization—After Being Rejected

Dear _____:

Thank you for the consideration that you gave my credentials. Your company is one of the top five companies that I have selected as an ideal place to work, given my skills and interests. I appreciate your committing to contact me as an appropriate fit develops.

I am disappointed that there were no opportunities for me at this time. Nonetheless, I feel my marketing and sales background can significantly contribute to _____'s long-range plans at some point.

Thank you for maintaining my candidacy as a priority. I hope that you will keep my résumé in your top desk drawer as the growth plans of _____ materialize. I would like to be considered in your core group of key executives that will "make it happen."

As agreed, I will periodically keep you posted on the progress of my job search and to see when we might meet for the purpose of an introduction.

Sincerely,

Michele D. Cannon

Rejection After Being Interviewed

For the job seeker, rejection is a fact of life. As you well know, or might suspect, being hired is a numbers game. Accordingly, rejection is the hard reality that all job seekers have to manage. In fact, my belief is that executives actively searching to make a move will experience more rejection in a few months than they may experience through several years of being employed. Simply put, every time you make a networking call, every letter that you send, and every interview that you conduct are fraught with the potential for rejection.

Let's specifically look at the rationale that companies might have for rejecting you. The rationale seems to fall into one of two camps.

Camp #1: Skills Don't Match

Your qualifications did not match what the organization was seeking. An example might be that you have only domestic experience and the company needs/wants an experienced *global* executive. While you might argue that you are a quick study and can learn the nuance of the Asian and Latin American business cultures, you simply don't have these credentials. When this happens, rejection may not hit you as hard because it should be more obvious that you don't exactly fit the position specifications.

Camp #2: Lack of Fit

As I have alluded to before, executives exit their organizations because of the lack of personal fit, chemistry, or endorsement—and they are hired because of the abundance of personal fit, chemistry, and widespread endorsement. Because fit is so very important, you don't want to talk the organization into hiring you if they are reluctant. *Au contraire*, you might protest. However, it is vital that the organization want to hire you as much as you want to be hired. If you are the one who is more committed, your relationship will be unbalanced. The following is an actual letter that a client of mine used to try and shift a CEO's perspective.

Follow-Up Letter To:
Target Organization—After Being Rejected for
Being Too Strong/Experienced

Dear _____:

I heard back through the search firm that you were going to continue the search for the COO position at the ABC Company. The feedback I got was your concern about me being "overqualified" or "bigger" than the position. I quickly accepted that response, as I somewhat expected it, and moved on. Then, it kept gnawing in the back of my head for a few days. Let me try something out on you.

I believe your concern is that I'll come on board and then leave in a short period for a new position—that my phone will ring and I'll be out the door to a larger role in another organization. I certainly cannot promise you five years, but I'm not sure anyone can. My track record speaks for itself on stability; if I make a commitment, I keep it. When I went to Acme International in 1999, the president that recruited me left ten days later. Shortly thereafter, the new company's organization dramatically changed as the new German-based president asserted himself significantly more than expected. Both of these were big inflection points where I could have easily gone back to my previous company with no issue. But I didn't. I stayed and fought through the changes and on to success.

_____, from our discussions, you indicated that your issue is deeply rooted in the lack of strength in your executive team, especially issues of accountability, silos, and cross-functional synergies. One of the things I do very well, and my background supports this claim, is to grow and develop teams that produce results. I'm also a good judge of talent and a strong recruiter. This combination has served me well in accelerating the growth and profitability of every firm in which I have worked.

What if I came in with the intent of partnering with you to upgrade and improve the overall organization? I can't promise that I'll retire from the company, but I can promise I'll be there until we get the job done. If I'm having fun, making an impact, and growing the business, I would not have a reason to leave. My core value is that I want to make a long-lasting impact on the people, culture, attitude, and success of the employees, shareholders, and customers.

What are your thoughts? Are you interested in having a further discussion on how we could make this work? Would you like to get together for lunch or dinner to discuss it further? Give me a call at 925-317-1451 or drop me an e-mail at the address above.

Best regards,

Michele D. Cannon

Letter For:
Follow-Up on Rejection for a Being a Nonfit

Dear _____:

Thank you for the favorable and positive consideration that you provided me during my interviews at _____. I felt truly welcome, and everyone I met was extremely gracious and professional.

I am sorry that this was not the opportunity for me; however, I feel my track record of P&L accomplishments can significantly contribute to your organization's long-range plans at some point.

Thank you for committing to maintain my candidacy as a priority. I look forward to your keeping my résumé in your top desk drawer as new growth plans materialize. I would like to be considered in your core group of good people that will "make it happen."

As promised, I will keep you posted on the progress of my job search from time to time, and periodically review my future possibilities at _____.

Best regards,

Michele D. Cannon

Letter That:
Follows a Too-Low Offer
(After you have already spoken to your possible boss)

Dear _____:

Thank you for the opportunity to meet and revisit the specifics of _____'s offer and the advantages in joining your company. I appreciated your observations concerning the dynamics of a smaller manufacturing organization and how it might support some of my longer-range goals. The possibilities are exciting, and I am even more interested in joining your team.

As we discussed, there are several distinct benefits to bringing a more senior manager, like myself, on board. I offer an experienced leadership management approach, balanced with a keen sense of cost-effective innovations.

I am confident that you can see how the breadth and depth of my background can contribute to your immediate needs, as well as represent a sound investment for your future growth.

_____, I am enthusiastic about the opportunity to join _____ and would like to creatively explore how we can reach a mutually agreeable compensation arrangement.

While money is important, it is not the only career consideration, as we both acknowledged. My interest is in remaining whole, salarywise, over a year's period of time. I would like for us to discuss some compensation package that might include additional stock grants, options, and life insurance and credit for pension calculation.

Let's continue to discuss how we might come to a mutually satisfactory and rewarding employment decision. Thank you for your consideration.

Personal regards,

Michele D. Cannon

Your Announcement Letter—Marketing Yourself and Your Company

After a few weeks in your new job, I recommend that you create and send out an announcement letter to your personal contacts and those people in the search firms and private equity firms with whom you want to maintain relations. Depending on your strategy (and your organization's predilection for visibility), you might send out a press release announcing your hire.

Obviously, with close friends, you'll probably want to contact them straightaway. For the rest of your professional colleagues, I recommend that you wait until you know that your role and your relationship with your boss is legit and something that will hopefully stand the test of time. By legit, I mean the role, the relationships, and the company situation are as they were described. Why? Because over the years, we have the occasional horror story in which that seemingly considerate, collaborative boss turned out to a brutal Attila the Hun whose emotional outbursts were legendary. Or, the almost unbelievable tale of the long-service direct report who was very supportive of one of our client's being hired as the COO, only to become a manipulative saboteur who threatened to quit and take all the key accounts with him if our client wasn't fired immediately. And the insecure owner of an entrepreneurial enterprise actually did just that on this client's third day!

A sample announcement letter follows on the next page.

Letter That Announces:
New Position Accepted

Dear _____:

I wanted to get back to you and say "Thank You" for all of your help, care, and support over these last few months. As you know, I have conducted a selective campaign of existing job opportunities, during which time I explored not only the private sector but consulting and equity situations as well.

With these priorities in mind, I have recently accepted a position as President and CEO of Omni Corporation headquartered in Denver. Omni is a $5 billion global manufacturer and distributor of high-tech electronic components for the aerospace and automotive industries. We are in 37 countries and have more than 8,000 employees. If you wish, you can also visit www.omniglobalcorp.com to learn more about this dynamic global organization.

In this P&L role, I will be responsible for:

- Building and integrating a global sales and marketing team.
- Aggressively driving product development and management.
- Establishing preferred vendor relationships with key customers throughout Europe, Africa, the Middle East, and Pan-Asia.

_____, I genuinely appreciate your consideration and response to my initial contact and look forward to a continuing professional relationship in the future. If I can help you in any way, please do not hesitate to call. My new contact information is listed below.

Thanks again.

Personal regards,

Michele D. Cannon
President and CEO
Omni Corporation
8734 Palm Boulevard
Denver, CO 80206
303.608.9356
E-mail: m.cannon@omniglobalcorp.com

CHAPTER 9

YOUR VERBAL RÉSUMÉ™— MARKETING SOUND BITES THAT GRAB 'EM

Marketing 101

The first lesson in marketing is to grab the attention of the audience and have a compelling message that moves people to act. Think back to marketing messages that have grabbed your attention. They are usually short, somewhat dramatic, and powerfully intriguing. They typically identify a persistent problem that is common to most people and offer a proven solution. If you've ever been drawn into an infomercial, you know what I mean. The premise of effective marketing is that once "hooked," you want to know more. Implicitly, you are asking the marketer to "Tell me more." Layer by layer. Piece by piece. Bit by bit. So, it should be with your Verbal Résumé, your marketing sound bite.

Your Verbal Résumé—A Marketing Sound Bite

Obviously, your written résumé is a vital part of your job search campaign. It covers your entire career, highlighting important aspects of your responsibilities, accomplishments, and abilities while using language that reflects your capabilities to contribute.

Your Verbal Résumé is a 15-second to 3-minute, tightly worded, brief and punchy presentation that concisely presents a clear and interesting summary of you—your brand. It parallels your written résumé, and it also highlights your key qualifications and how you can contribute. Think of your Verbal Résumé as an advertising commercial, quickly gaining the listener's attention and with enough interesting benefits to make it worth the person's while to continue to listen.

Just as your written résumé was scripted and clarified, your Verbal Résumé is also written out and refined until you have an attention-getting and distinctive sound bite. In much the same way that the Hippocratic Oath extols that physicians knowingly commit no harm, the "Verbal Résumé Oath" invites job seekers to not unwittingly put interviewers to sleep. I remember an interview early in my career in which I had bored the interviewer to death. He asked me about myself, and I took him at his word. After 100,000 well-chosen words, he had a faraway, glazed look about him. I was hoping he was in a pensive, reflective state; although I'm sure he was merely asleep with his eyes open. Ironically, he was a whole lot more patient with me than I am now with people who are not aware of their mind-numbing impact.

> Your goal is to refine and rehearse your *Verbal Résumé* until you are comfortable and confident with your interesting, relevant, and action-oriented career synopsis.

Practice, practice, practice delivering your Verbal Résumé in a nonhurried, flexible manner within 15 seconds, 30 seconds, 60 seconds, or up to 3 minutes depending on the setting and your sense of what is needed. Consider your 15-second delivery your "cocktail party, meet-and-greet handshake speech." You give people 15 seconds of the top layer of who you are and the arena in which you contribute. Your 3-minute summary is more appropriate in an interview or if someone asks, "Tell me more!" Whatever the length of your Verbal Résumé, your goal is to deliver it in such a confident style that it feels natural and genuine, compelling people to inquire further. Being fully authentic is the goal. When you practice, boldly deliver it, rather than merely recite your Verbal Résumé. You'll be more credible and more interesting. Practice it with your close friends or family. Practice with yourself in the car or in your friendly bathroom mirror. Practice with a loud, booming voice, as if you are on a Broadway stage playing to a packed house. Practice with a stage whisper. Practice with no energy. Practice with great enthusiasm. Practice your Verbal Résumé in punchy 15-second, 30-second, and 60-second sound bites for when you want to leave a powerful and confident voice mail message. These are your "elevator speeches"—something that can be quickly and succinctly delivered in just a few sentences. Ultimately, your goal is to be as comfortable with your background story as you are with an endearing childhood story that you delight in the accurate retelling.

Your Elevator Speeches

Depending on the circumstances in which you network, you'll want to have sound bites of different lengths. These mini-bios are referred to as elevator speeches because there you only have a few seconds of uninterrupted conversation before someone else enters the elevator and breaks your connection with your networking contact. The following are examples of 15-second, 30-second, and 60-second elevator speeches that I might use to describe Robertson Lowstuter. You'll note that for increasingly longer sound bites, I've just added another layer of data.

15-Second Elevator Speech

My name is Clyde Lowstuter. I head up Robertson Lowstuter, an executive development consulting and coaching firm. We work with individuals, teams, and organizations, equipping them to accelerate their performance and profitability. Our clients range from the Fortune 50, to early-stage companies.

30-Second Elevator Speech

My name is Clyde Lowstuter. I head up Robertson Lowstuter, an executive development consulting and coaching firm. We work with individuals, teams, and organizations, equipping them to accelerate their performance and profitability. Our clients range from the Fortune 50 to early-stage companies. RL has a proven track record of creating synergies in teams and facilitating strategy development for revenue gains, product launches, and operational improvements.

60-Second Elevator Speech

My name is Clyde Lowstuter. I head up Robertson Lowstuter, an executive development consulting and coaching firm. We work with individuals, teams, and organizations, equipping them to accelerate their performance and profitability. Our clients range from the Fortune 50 to early-stage companies. RL has a proven track record of creating synergies in teams and facilitating strategy development for revenue gains, product launches, and operational improvements. Specifically, the services we provide encompass executive coaching, high-performance team building, change leadership, entrepreneuring, and career transition for executives. Through the RL Leadership Institute we also create and load innovative workshops, including the Leadership Mastery Series and Coaching Competencies for Leaders. My background includes leadership development and organization development for global manufacturing and service firms. I have a BA in Psychology and an MA in Labor and Industrial Relations with an emphasis in organizational psychology. Additionally, I have been awarded the MCC, Master Certified Coach, designation from the International Coaching Federation. Less than one percent of all coaches worldwide have their MCC.

Now it's your turn to develop your series of three elevator speeches. Turn to the next worksheet and create your own. I recommend that you craft your 60-second sound bite first, and then just prune it back for the other ones.

 Many experienced job searchers keep copies of their *Verbal Résumé* near all their phones as visual support. They find that these copies help their self-confidence and reduce worry about what to say next on the phone.

WORKSHEET 31

Your Elevator Speeches

- 60-Second Elevator Speech

- 30-Second Elevator Speech

- 15-Second Elevator Speech

Elements of Your Verbal Résumé

I've broken down each element of the Verbal Résumé so that you can craft and deliver one with confidence.

1. Introduce Your Verbal Résumé

If at all possible, get the prospective employer or recruiter sharing first in the interview, so you have a context for your comments. Chapter 16, "Power Interviewing" identifies three stages of the interview and provides a number of practical tips and suggested language on effectively managing the interview. Smoothly introducing your Verbal Résumé requires a little bit of finesse. Ideally, you have already asked the other person some questions, and she has given you an overview of the company's history, strategic vision, and current challenges.

You might find the following helpful as a way of introducing your Verbal Résumé.

Thank you for the overview on your company. It was insightful. I wonder if it might be helpful if I were to summarize my background and capabilities and highlight some of the ways in which I've contributed to the growth and profitability of my companies. Would that be appropriate?

What are they going to say, "No, I don't want to learn about you in this interview?" Universally, your focus is very much appreciated and will meet with an immediate approval. Proceed immediately to deliver your Verbal Résumé, which should include the following elements.

2. Career Focus

In a sentence or two, concisely focus your primary career orientation. As you feel comfortable, you might expand your career focus a bit—something similar to your résumé's executive or career summary. If you are a CFO, you might begin by saying the following:

I'm a CFO, broadly experienced in manufacturing, service, supply chain, and service industries. I have a demonstrated record of significant contributions in strategic and operational planning, contract negotiations, capital management, financial systems, and acquisition analysis/integration. Additionally, I am effective in building and leading highly motivated teams that improve operating efficiency, profitability, and cash flow. I am looking for a similar challenging position.

If you are a line executive, you might say:

I am an accomplished senior executive with significant experience in P&L management, operations, engineering, sales, and marketing. I have a proven record of accelerated sales, profit growth, and business turnarounds.

Or, if you are changing career focus, you might say something like this:

While I have not been employed full-time in the nonprofit sector, I have led many aspects of my company's foundation and have sat on the boards of four charitable organizations.

3.   Born and Raised

In a single sentence, briefly outline where you were born and raised. Do not go into detail. The purpose is to focus yourself geographically, domestically or internationally. Plus, if you and your interviewer were both born in Turin, Italy, there's a high probability that it would create instant rapport.

4.   Education and Special Training or Skills

Briefly state your degrees, major subjects, and school names in about five seconds. Do not elaborate on your college experiences or choices. It is not necessary to fit this information chronologically into your presentation. Quickly cover the information here so that you can concentrate on your experience. For example:

I have my Bachelor's in Psychology from University of Kansas and my MBA from Cornell University.

You may also wish to cover special credentials or relevant special nondegree or non-college training such as seminars or workshops. Be careful to only include those items that are relevant to this interview, as this can take up valuable time in your three- to four-minute limit:

In addition to my formal education, I have completed the Senior Executive's Leadership Course at Wharton and am a certified instructor for Outward Bound, specializing in executive team building and helping senior executives operate more effectively.

5.   Work History and Significant Accomplishments

Unlike your written résumé, your Verbal Résumé starts at the beginning of your work career and proceeds chronologically up to the present, without mentioning every position change and dates.

The reason for reversing this procedure is to quickly skip through your early years so that you can finish your presentation by talking about your most recent work experience.

Of the time remaining, spend 80 percent of the time on the last five to eight years of your career. If your earlier experience is more important to the position you are seeking than your last five to eight years, then, of course, you should shift your emphasis accordingly.

Begin with your early position or positions in summary fashion and move up to the current time, listing companies, titles, key responsibilities, and accomplishments. A good rule of thumb for accomplishments is do not provide more than about four results for your entire Verbal Résumé. If you provide more, you will probably get bogged down in detail and your delivery will lengthen unnecessarily. The accomplishments you select should be significant and provide a clear link to the needs of the particular job opportunities in the organization in which you are interviewing.

Pay particular attention to your transitions from company to company. They should be reasonable and believable. Refer to new skills, responsibilities, or experiences that each new job provided. Keep track of your time. Two to three minutes go by quickly, so diligently watch your tendency to provide more data than is needed when the interviewer reinforces you with a positive comment or an affirming smile.

Keep in mind, this is not a time for you to wax philosophic, demonstrate your command of the language, and dazzle 'em with 100,000 well-chosen words, like I did once. In fact, if you are off on a tangent, there is a high probability of being interrupted and never being able to get back to your Verbal Résumé.

6.   Reason for Leaving and Current Status

Until you discuss your reason for leaving your current employer, the entire interview remains under a cloud. *If you do not bring up your reason for leaving, the interviewer will.* When the interviewer raises the issue, you run the risk of it being asked in an investigatory manner, which may sound as though there is some suspicion about your circumstances.

If you bring it up, the issue of your departure is presented voluntarily, and you are able to use language which clearly reinforces your candidacy. The result is usually quick recognition of the realities of economic, political, interpersonal, or organizational events. Once expressed, you have the freedom to continue the interview, further exploring your abilities and the company's needs. Plus, your credibility is greatly enhanced in the eyes of the interviewer. The employer knows that if you confidently reveal this potentially damaging information, most everything else you say probably is also believable.

Also, since many résumés indicate that you were still employed at the time the résumé was written, this section allows you to clear up what has happened since you wrote your résumé and your current status.

Conclude this section by offering a concise statement about what has attracted you to this particular company or position (if possible) and an inquiry of the interviewer to see if they would like you to expand further on any of the areas you have summarized.

The following example illustrates how Michele Cannon introduced her reasons for leaving her current employer:

> *While I've had a very challenging senior management career with Acme International, it has recently been acquired by Colorant Partners. Unfortunately, the combined companies are being*

consolidated and duplicate functions are reorganized. As such, Colorant's CCO will assume operational leadership for the merged companies and my position has been eliminated. Obviously, there was no need for two senior executives at this level. So, I am seeking other similar challenging executive positions with the full knowledge and support of my organization.

While it is disappointing to end my career with Acme, I'm excited about the opportunities out there with fine global manufacturers like yours.

Before preparing your Verbal Résumé, review the following examples of introductory summaries utilized by two other job seekers. The speaking times of these examples are approximately 2 minutes and 55 seconds. Read this example out loud with a watch so you can experience an optimal delivery speed.

At no point should your uninterrupted Verbal Résumé be longer than four minutes. You'll have time for greater elaboration later, but not now in this capsule summary of your credentials.

Verbal Résumé Examples

The following are two solid examples of crisp Verbal Résumés that their respective own-ers found helpful in keeping them focused and on track. The first example is in a narrative format, with the second one presented in a bulleted format. While these Verbal Résumés are from actual executive clients of ours, their names and their company names have been altered to maintain privacy.

Narrative Example—Sally Jones

"I am a seasoned R&D executive with 23 years of business development and general management experience in the field of applied organic chemistry for specialized industrial application.

I was born and raised in Philadelphia. I went to Pitt and received a BS in Chemistry and got my PhD in Organic Chemistry from UCLA.

I began working at American Laboratories as an R&D technician in the Diagnostics Division. Over the next several years I have held positions of increasing responsibility in applied research and quality control.

As I got more involved in business, leading teams that created breakthrough results, I decided to seek an MBA in addition to my PhD. I enrolled at the University of Chicago, participating in the evening program while I continued to work. After six years with American Labs, I was contacted by a start-up company founded by some former American colleagues. I joined this company as the head of R&D and Applications. Immediately after joining, the company was acquired by Price Industrials Corporation, a $5 billion global conglomerate specializing in chemicals, plastics, and moldable metals products.

I remained with the company, which became a division of the diagnostics business, for eight years in a variety of increasingly challenging leadership positions including the head of marketing and business development. Ultimately, I was promoted as head of R&D for all of Price Industrials, which included three major business groups. As a result of this expanded role, I've gotten more involved in business development and general management. I have certainly gained valuable experience in strategy development, mergers and acquisitions, technology licensing, and business portfolio management. While it's a far cry from the lab bench, I enjoyed the diversity of my work immensely.

As you may be aware, this year Price Industrials began a major restructuring and downsizing that impacted more than 4,000 employees in multiple businesses. Part of this restructuring involved splitting up my function and integrating it with all the other businesses, which was my personal recommendation.

While I was offered another significant position as head of global operations, I chose not to accept the job as it did not fit my career goals.

I had a great run at Price. I worked with some outstanding people and was given some excellent opportunities to gain valuable experience and hone my leadership skills. I am now looking forward to continuing my career in a challenging new opportunity and am interested in learning more about your company in this interview. Are there any particular parts of my background you would like me to expand further?"

Bulleted Format—"Sir" Anthony

- High-energy Scot, married 29 years, two adult children.
- Family heritage of papermaking converting and printing from 1760.
- Educated in Business in Scotland. A self-starter with a high sense of urgency and ability to effectively build teams and execute strategic plans. Interested in the packaging industry.
- Started as an industrial engineer, became a supervisor of 65 people at an early age and then production manager. The company was acquired by Trickle Creek Corp of USA in 1984; became General Manager and grew business 600% through new product innovation in six years, raising the ROS (Return On Sales) from a loss to 17% positive profit.
- Trickle Creek moved us to the United States in 1990 for me to become president of a $130 million decorative-covering business. Built a strong management team and moved the business from number 3 to 1 in the market, raising ROS from 4 to 15%. I was part of the leveraged buyout of a $700 million piece of Trickle Creek, including my business with investors from New York. Later, we sold this business to Maxer International.
- Returned with Maxer to the UK in 1998 to turn around a $271 million printing business, strategically changing the company to a full-service print outsourcing company and then selling it in 2001.
- I returned back to the U.S. with Maxer in 2001 to be President of their healthcare packaging $300 million global business with plants in Singapore, France, UK, Brazil, Puerto Rico, U.S., and Mexico. Built a strong team and by reducing complexity, cutting cost, focusing on customer needs, and retaining a $40 million customer raised ROS from 6 to 9% after major selling price reductions.
- Led the sale of Healthcare Flexibles and concluded this in October 2003. Maxer International has asked me to return to the UK to run their $700 million European Glass business; however, my wife and I have decided to remain in the United States. I now seek a new leadership role.
- I enjoy travel and love the outdoors: sailing, skiing, shooting, hiking, and gardening.
- Lived in the United States for the past 11 years.

WORKSHEET 32

My Verbal Résumé

Using the preceding guidelines, write out your own Verbal Résumé.

CHAPTER 10

YOUR REFERENCES ARE LIKE GOLD

References Are Overblown . . . or Are They?

No one intentionally provides a poor reference. However, a well-intended, though poorly prepared reference may do more harm than good. If the vast majority of people provide only those names of people that will speak glowingly of themselves, you might ask yourself, "What's the value of references?" Good question. While the reference process is far from foolproof, it does offer prospective employers some measure of comfort that the person is who he or she represents. In this time of heightened competition for jobs, there is an increasing falsification of employment, degrees obtained, schools attended, and results achieved. Some employers require significant background checks, including academic credentials verification, credit reports, and occasionally, FBI clearances. You have to judge whether you want to be considered for an opportunity enough to undergo this level of in-depth scrutiny. Perhaps you can legitimize this level of scrutiny, if you are applying for a job that requires a high-level security clearance.

Sorry, No Comment—Company Policy

To compound the difficulty of references, many companies have a policy of "no comment"; that is, they do not provide or allow employees to act as references. When employees receive calls referencing a former colleague, policy often instructs people to refer all such calls to Human Resources where a caller will be provided only basic information concerning former employees: dates of employment, job titles, and, in some cases, salary history. The reality is that regardless of policy, most search firms and prospective employers require that you be referenced at your most recent employer. So, what to do? Merely find a colleague who knows you well and will speak on your behalf.

You can have a great background, the best résumé in the world, and interview superbly well, but if your references aren't golden, your candidacy is dead.

Who Should Be Your References?

You may wish to consider the following as business references:

- Current or former bosses in your company or previous companies
- Board members in your most recent company and/or previous companies
- Executive peers and colleagues or business friends
- Major clients, vendors, or consultants who have seen you in action
- Subordinates who can describe your managerial style

Manage Your References to Produce the Outcome You Desire

Determine the key points you want to be mentioned by your references. For example, if you are a "General Manager with significant P&L responsibility" and are ready for advancement to President and CEO, you will need people to speak to your effective leadership capabilities, ability to develop and realize strategies, and sound interpersonal skills, among other things. So before you select people solely based on your friendship, *identify the four major things you want most to be said in support of your career focus and options.* Then select those colleagues who are credible and knowledgeable of these elements.

WORKSHEET 33

Four Things You Want from Your References

Identify the four major dimensions or traits you want your references to highlight. These traits should be general enough to portray the breadth and depth of your strengths, abilities, and experience yet not too specific as to not apply in most situations.

1.

2.

3.

4.

It is now time to select your references. From among the four categories just identified in the previous worksheet, select 10 people who will give you the best reference. Then narrow the list to your strongest six references. Now it's time to prepare people to be your references on Worksheet 34, "My Potential References."

WORKSHEET 34

My Potential References

1. Name: _____   Title: _____

   Company: _____   Phone: _____

   E-mail: _____

2. Name: _____   Title: _____

   Company: _____   Phone: _____

   E-mail: _____

3. Name: _____   Title: _____

   Company: _____   Phone: _____

   E-mail: _____

4. Name: _____   Title: _____

   Company: _____   Phone: _____

   E-mail: _____

5. Name: _____   Title: _____

   Company: _____   Phone: _____

   E-mail: _____

6. Name: _____   Title: _____

   Company: _____   Phone: _____

   E-mail: _____

7. Name: _____   Title: _____

   Company: _____   Phone: _____

   E-mail: _____

8. Name: _____   Title: _____

   Company: _____   Phone: _____

   E-mail: _____

9. Name: _____   Title: _____

   Company: _____   Phone: _____

   E-mail: _____

10. Name: _____   Title: _____

   Company: _____   Phone: _____

   E-mail: _____

9 Ways to Prepare Your References

Do not assume what your references will say. Speak to them face-to-face (if possible) and be sure you know how they will respond to questions before you give out their names. Search firms and prospective employers do check references, regardless of stated policies. Your references can be of great help to you, and they can also hurt your chances if they give a poor or lukewarm reference.

There are formal and informal references. Formal references are those colleagues that you have identified on your reference list. Informal references are people that recruiters know and, perhaps, unbeknownst to you, they are contacted. Informal references are fair game when and if you indicate that you are searching with your company's knowledge and support.

You have some control over the formal references you provide and very little control over your informal references because you do not always know what colleagues a recruiter may know and call. One way to minimize informal referencing—or "out-of-control" referencing—is to ask the recruiter if he or she is desirous of contacting others, not on your formal list. When others are identified, take the initiative and meet with them to prepare and ready them to answer questions about your past performance.

1. Arrange for a meeting, at which time ask if they would be willing to be your reference. Review with each reference from Worksheet 37, "Questions Your References May Be Asked."
2. Tell your references about the kind of job you are seeking. Ask if they are comfortable recommending you for such a position. *Give them a copy of your résumé and review it with them to familiarize them with the data.* This provides an opportunity for you to clarify your accomplishments or answer any questions they might have.
3. Suggest that you would appreciate their especially strong recommendation in three or four key areas. See your list on Worksheet 33, "Four Things You Want from Your References." Ask, "If I outline these areas, would you be willing to try to work them into your recommendation?" Then outline several specific areas of strengths or areas in which your competence is key to success in gaining job offers.
4. Ask about weaknesses. "One of the questions I keep getting asked about is my strengths and weaknesses. I'm sure that you will be asked about my weaknesses or development needs, as well. May I ask if there is anything that I should be aware of that might come up in response to a question on developmental needs so that you and I, at least, are consistent?"
5. With former bosses, clarify reasons for leaving. Tell them what you are saying, and ask if they are comfortable saying that as well.

In Steps 4 and 5, if you disagree with your references:

 a. Listen carefully.

 b. Don't argue.

 c. Offer more favorable wording. For more information on how to speak about weaknesses, refer back to the Worksheet 15, "My Developmental Needs" in Chapter 5, "Career Strategies and Options."

 d. Ask if the person would be comfortable using more favorable wording.

 e. Thank the person.

 f. If you feel the reference the person would provide would be negative, you may ask another close, former business associate to make a reference check on you to verify the quality of the reference.

6. At the close of your reference discussion, ask your reference if it would be okay if you sent him or her a copy of your reference summary, highlighting the points you two have discussed. Suggest that it might be helpful as a reminder. Then write up a reference summary using the format in Worksheet 35, and send it to your references with your "Thank You" note. Prepare an original, separate summary for each reference. Don't worry, the reference summaries will look very similar, so don't feel that you are creating a lot of extra work for yourself; you're not.

7. Tell your references that you will let them know to whom you give their names, so they will not be surprised when they are called.

8. Also, gain their commitment to call you if they are contacted. This enables you to more fully manage the referencing process (because it keeps everyone in the communications loop), and it also allows you to legitimately keep the pressure on prospective employers to press for reference checking. Presumably, this will be to your advantage because if a company checks you out early, given the strength of your references, you might very well "knock out" the other candidates under consideration for the job for which you're interviewing.

9. Ask if it would be okay to periodically recontact your references to keep them posted of your career search. And then do so.

Listen deeply to the responses of potential references when asked if they would be comfortable speaking about your skills, capabilities, and personality. If you sense hesitancy or discomfort, address it whenever possible or do not use them as "faint praise is damning praise."

Prepare Your Reference Summary

Turn to the sample reference summary on the next page written by our fictitious client, Michele Cannon, to a reference after they met.

You can see that having an agreed-upon Reference Summary as a written endorsement is a great way to keep your references' comments fresh. This is especially important if your search campaign becomes prolonged. Your references want to speak positively about you, but with a lengthy search, the specifics become a bit hazy without a well-crafted reference summary.

Forward a summary to each of your references *only after* you've had an in-depth reference discussion with them. If you send them your reference summary ahead of your discussion, people will feel that you are using a canned approach. Quite frankly, you run the risk of offending them. As such, they won't be very committed to helping you craft the language specific to them.

Note: Your reference summary is to be given only to your references—*not* a prospective employer.

MICHELE D. CANNON

1693 Elm Street   Antwirl, CA 86732

H 415-585-2290   C 925-317-1451

m_cannon@rr.ca.com

REFERENCE SUMMARY

CAREER FOCUS

Michele is looking for a senior P&L general management position, perhaps CEO or COO for a mid-sized manufacturing or service company committed to growth.

SUMMARY OF STRENGTHS

Leadership: Michele is a seasoned global business leader who is able to create a compelling vision, develop the best in people, and achieve results. She has practical strengths in strategy development, turnarounds, organic growth, and successful acquisition integrations.

Sales and Marketing: She has a demonstrated track record of accelerating sales and profit improvements, market share increases, protecting and enhancing customer relations, and strengthening distribution networks, globally.

DEVELOPMENTAL NEEDS

Michele is a quick decision maker, and she might be seen as overly demanding and impatient. However, she understands this and has learned to be more patient with slower-moving staff to make sure that they fully understand her ideas while still holding them accountable for results. This has produced stellar results.

REASON FOR LEAVING

Colorants Partners acquired Acme International in mid-2006, and the COO of the parent company has been promoted to take over Michele's role. As such, there is no room for two general managers of the Acme International business. Accordingly, Michele is looking for new opportunities with Colorant's full knowledge and support.

WORKSHEET 35

My Reference Summary

Career Focus

Summary of Strengths

Developmental Needs

Reason for Leaving

Prepare Your Reference Sheet

Now that you have selected your references and spoken to them, you are ready to prepare a handout of your references to be used in your campaign. You need to include each of your references' name, title, company, phone number, and e-mail address. Consider the following:

- You do not need street addresses. Your references will be called or e-mailed, not sent correspondence to answer. City and state information will alert the recruiter to the appropriate time zones and will be helpful, although not necessary.
- Use business or home phone as your reference wishes. If your references will take calls in the evening, include the residence number as well.
- If one of your references is retired, put "formerly" before his or her title. If one of your references is unemployed, you may want to consider the emotional state in which he or she is in before using this individual as a reference. If your potential reference is likely to be upset because of being unemployed and may damage you, you may wish to reconsider including him or her as a reference at this stage of your interviewing. If pressed by an employer to include your unemployed reference, you might want to work with your friend to help him or her get emotionally settled down and prepared for the reference call. Nonetheless, you should refer to this reference as "formerly [former title]."

To help manage the reference checking process, we recommend that you develop the context for each reference by identifying several key points about your relationship. Write a brief, crisp sentence or two that tells (1) how the person knows you and (2) those things that this person is able to best describe about you. This minimally directs recruiters and prospective employers to some extent.

These brief descriptions help to "precondition" the reference checker to focus on those areas that you and your references have already agreed are your strong points and those you want to emphasize.

Action

Now take the following steps:

1. Study the sample page of business references on the next page to spark some ideas for your own reference list.
2. Complete Worksheet 36, "My References," incorporating your own language.

Remember, list five to seven people who can speak with specific knowledge of your job performance abilities—and your capabilities going forward. *State how they know you and the key characteristics they are best qualified to describe.*

MICHELE D. CANNON

1693 Elm Street   Antwirl, CA 86732

H 415-585-2290   C 925-317-1451

m_cannon@rr.ca.com

BUSINESS AND PERSONAL REFERENCES

SAMUEL C. SHEFIELD

Chairman   Acme International   San Francisco, CA

415-555-1890   fc_shefield@acme.intl.com

I reported to Sam for seven years in my two roles at Acme International. He can attest to my leadership capabilities, strategic agility, and track record of accelerating sales and margins, as well as successfully integrating key acquisitions.

BRADLEY N. RUBEN

CEO   Landover Express   Salt Lake City, Utah

Chairman of the Audit Committee – Board of Directors – Acme International

801-958-3402   bradley.rubin@landoverexpress.com

Brad is on the Board at Acme and has known me since 1999 when I came on board. He saw first hand my skills as I strategized and led the turnaround of Acme and its record setting growth. He can effectively address how I developed and managed relationships with my executive staff and customers on a global basis.

FREDERICK P. HUDSON

President & CEO   Creative Design,   San Francisco, CA

(415) 535-1827   frederickh@creativedesign.com

Rick runs an advertising and marketing firm that specializes in corporate marketing services I have hired and directed on numerous occasions. He and others have seen me effectively balance a results-oriented approach with a distinctive flair for helping spark innovative marketing campaigns that generate significant product sales and profits.

SUSAN P. WATNEY

Senior Vice President   HR   Acme International   San Franciso, CA

415-555-1890   sp_watney@acme.intl.com

Susan is both a business and personal reference. She has known me for 15 years in positions of increasing responsibility. Susan had been reporting to me for four years when I became President Services Group. Together, we crafted the organizational and talent acquisition strategy and rebuilt the executive team.

HUGH PACKARD

Executive Vice President   Operations   San Francsico, CA

415-555-1890   h_packard@acme.intl.com

Hugh is one of the most talented manufacturing and operations executives I have ever had the privilege to partner with. Hugh can share his insights as to how I created a compelling vision and aligned the organization's capital and human resources.

WORKSHEET 36
My References

Name: _____ Title: _____

Company: _____ (_____) _____

E-mail: _____

Job characteristics this person would best support:

Name: _____ Title: _____

Company: _____ (_____) _____

E-mail: _____

Job characteristics this person would best support:

Name: _____ Title: _____

Company: _____ (_____) _____

E-mail: _____

Job characteristics this person would best support:

Name: _____ Title: _____

Company: _____ (_____) _____

E-mail: _____

Job characteristics this person would best support:

Name: _____ Title: _____

Company: _____ (_____) _____

E-mail: _____

Job characteristics this person would best support:

Name: _____ Title: _____

Company: _____ (_____) _____

E-mail: _____

Job characteristics this person would best support:

How to Present Your References

Do not put references on your résumé. Also, do not waste several lines on your résumé indicating "References available on request." That's belaboring the obvious. List them on your letterhead stationery with all the appropriate contact information, as Michele Cannon's Business References sheet illustrated.

If you would like to include a *personal reference* make sure that person is in a very senior role and occupies a position of high visibility and credibility.

Any reference, professional or personal, should be intellectually agile, able to easily anticipate the flow of the reference call, and reveal a balanced, positive summary of who you are and what you can do. This means that he or she knows how to answer questions well, will say good things about you, and will be relevant in your business context.

Caution is the better part of valor. Do not ever take for granted that your references are fully prepared to support you in your targeted job. Your references may only view you from a narrow perspective. It's your job to broaden their view of you through discussions of the key points in your reference summary and career goals, and by reminding them of your accomplishments. Remember, I do not recommend that you share your reference summary with any reference before chatting with him or her first. By having the discussion with your references first, you may indeed tweak the content of the reference summary from person to person. Plus, you want each reference to feel that he or she is directly contributing to your reference summary.

Only share your references in the following circumstances:

1. When asked and you have interest in exploring a given opportunity further.
2. At the close of an interview. If you have a strong interest in the position, volunteer to provide a list of references.
3. As a follow-up technique to remain highly visible during a competitive interviewing time period.

Do not include your reference list when you mail your résumé initially to a search firm or prospective employer. If you are asked to provide a complete list of references by a recruiter or your potential boss before you interview, I suggest that you identify only three people as a means to get the process started.

If they keep pressing for all your references, you might indicate your reluctance to provide a complete list of references at this time, as it is still early in the interview process. Further, state that your references are extremely busy, and while they are more than willing to talk about you, they only want to be called, if an offer is pending. Ultimately, it is up to you to manage the use of your references. If overused in situations where you are not a finalist for a job you run the risk of your references becoming less enthusiastic and responsive when you need them the most.

Evaluate the power dynamics between you and the management team, your potential boss, and the search firm as a valuable source of data for your ultimate decision making. Note how you feel toward him or her. Are your feelings positive or negative? Are you feeling diminished, pushed around, and manipulated? Your feelings may reflect how the company operates and how it treats its employees. On the other hand, you might merely be overly sensitive to providing your references early, given that your set of expectations are different than someone else's.

If you do reveal references, you need to get back to these people and indicate your strategy and ask for their support on this opportunity.

Do not wear out your references by having them support you for a job you do not want.

References Are Priceless and Should Be Handled With Care

Countless people let their guards down in the face of reference requests. In my opinion, they are revealing their precious references way too easily. It is increasingly common for executive search firms to conduct full-blown references on you before presenting you to their client. It's understandable that search firms cannot risk waiting until the final round of interviews to learn that you have shaky references. You can mitigate some of a recruiter's apprehension by indicating that you'd be happy to share additional names (beyond the three references previously provided) when you are further along in the process and under serious consideration.

Do Letters of Reference Really Work?

Executives rarely, if ever, use them unless they are legally mandated to do so. To that end, using a reference letter may raise more alarms than help. As in the case for personal references, you may use a letter of reference only if the person is internationally known, is next to impossible to reach, or wants a letter to serve as a preliminary reference, until you are a serious candidate.

The practical reality is this: Never let a letter of reference take the place of a recruiter talking with your references personally. They will be contacted anyway. Most employers don't ask for or use letters of reference, so don't push your references for a letter of support. They will support you more readily and help your campaign more over the phone than by putting something down on paper.

How to Offset Poor or Damaging References

I sometimes ask our clients, "If you think your boss will give you a poor reference, would you use him or her?" Not surprising, the immediate response is always a resounding "No!" However, it is a trick question. First, don't *assume* the reference is poor. Don't speculate; instead, know what kind of reference your former boss might provide.

Remember when I wrote earlier about asking the person if he or she would be comfortable being a reference? Help possibly poor references save face by asking how comfortable they'd be—not whether they'd be a reference. Most references don't really want to hurt you. They may just be hesitant about saying something negative, and as such, it may sound like lack of real support.

During your face-to-face meeting with your reference, offset a potentially damaging referral by rephrasing some of the comments. Negative comments like "He is too impatient" could be more neutrally worded as, "He has a high sense of urgency." Before any reference meeting, reread your reference summary, which highlights what you want your references to emphasize, especially strengths, weaknesses (referred to as overplayed strengths), and reason for leaving. Anticipate your reference's most typical comments and be prepared to volunteer some weaknesses or developmental areas if there is any hesitation on the reference's part.

When References Are Clearly "Bad News"

1. Work out a nondamaging way of talking about the problem. (Mention position elimination during consolidation versus your boss taking advantage of a merger to terminate you for poor performance.)
2. Raise the issue yourself with a potential employer, telling it your way. (When looking, I indicated that I was zapped because I "was zigging and my boss was zagging." If asked to elaborate, I had a number of scenarios I could address, such as differences in operating philosophies and interpersonal styles.)
3. Provide another reference with a different point of view on the subject and with whom you got along well. (One of our clients operated in a matrixed organization and reported to four company presidents. The most senior company president was continually embroiled in shouting matches with our client. Rather than use this president as his reference, our client wisely chose a board member and one of the other company presidents as his company references.)

Minimize Potentially Weak References

If you are fairly certain that your boss will provide only a moderately strong reference, you may purposefully exclude him or her from your reference list, hoping that an informal reference call will not be made.

As we have previously indicated, your references fall into two categories: formal (those that are provided) and informal (those that you do not provide and the recruiter ferrets out). Excluding some people as references, such as your most recent boss, represents a potential red flag to an astute interviewer. Expect the question, *Why didn't you include your immediate manager as a reference, given that you are looking with his full knowledge and support?* Good question. (You probably don't want to indicate that you discovered that he was a pathological liar and a political sleezeball. Unless you deliberately want to sabotage this opportunity, keep the whole truth to yourself.)

While in the interview, you can minimize a potentially weak reference from a former colleague or boss by indicating something like the following:

> *I excluded my boss because given her heavy travel schedule and the way we worked independently from one another, she does not have as much knowledge of my results as the people I served. You are certainly welcome to call her, as long as you keep in mind that she doesn't know me as well as the other references on my list.*

WORKSHEET 37

Questions Your References May Be Asked

Note: To more fully prepare your references for a search recruiter's or prospective employer's call, you might wish to provide this list of questions to them.

What position did (*your name*) hold?

How long was (*your name*) with the company?

Why is (*your name*) leaving (or has left) the organization?

What responsibilities did (*your name*) have?

What were (*your name*)'s most significant accomplishments?

How long did (*your name*) work in that position? (months/years)

How long was (*your name*) under your supervision? (if relevant) (months/years)

Describe (*your name*)'s strengths:

Describe (*your name*)'s developmental needs:

How would you describe (*your name*)'s performance? (*your name*)'s team's performance?

Provide an example of (*your name*)'s self-initiative:

Describe (*your name*)'s attitude toward the job:

How would you evaluate (*your name*)'s relationship with peers?

Would you consider (*your name*) for rehire? Why? Why not?

References can make or break a final deal. To that end, select them very carefully. Understand fully and be comfortable with the level of support they will provide to you. Take the time to meet and discuss what things you'd like them to emphasize. Always brief them ahead of any potential reference call. Ask them if they would call you after each reference to debrief for any additional intelligence to leverage your candidacy. Additionally, be alert for ways you might add value to your references.

STEP 4
THE SEARCH PROCESS

CHAPTER 11

WHERE ARE THE JOBS, ANYWAY?

Driving Down Multiple Paths

I view this small chapter as creating the context for your search activity. It's a portal, if you will, through which you will dive deeper and explore further the nuances of the four main avenues of job getting:

Networking	Chapter 12
Search firms	Chapter 13
Target organizations	Chapter 14
Internet/advertisements	Chapter 15

Based on our executive clients in career transition, the following illustrates the average percentages by which executives land a new job, by job source.

Networking	80 percent connect
Search firms mailings	15 percent connect
Target organizations mailings	3 percent connect
Internet/advertisements	2 percent connect

All these search venues are viable. Because you cannot predict when and by what avenue you are going to connect and land that great job, it is incumbent on you to explore all four job-hunting paths, though in proportion to the probability of success. To be able to conduct a well-rounded, effective career search, you must become intimately familiar with the various job-hunting strategies outlined here and become skilled in the use of each one.

 Two things you cannot control: timing and luck. You never know exactly how and when you are going to land that perfect job.

So often, as soon as we have figured out how our clients are going to get connected, things change. Because we know that anything is possible, we operate largely with the mindset of executives creating opportunities that align with their personal/professional aspirations and career path. Most of our clients have what we call a "ricochet search," as they successfully bounce from one surprising connection to another until they land. By way of example, I recently heard from one of our clients who relocated from Chicago to Pittsburgh to network more effectively in his old hometown where he and family desired to be. In a coffee shop in downtown Pittsburgh one morning he overheard two people lamenting their lack of luck finding a technical sales executive. My friend approached these two and introduced himself as a perfect fit and, quite possibly, the answer to their dilemma. Within two weeks, he was hired. Talk about serendipitous networking!

The Hidden Job Market

Unlike a bona fide job opening, the hidden job market deals in the realm of possibilities and potential, not certainties. Career opportunities are not readily apparent in the hidden job market. Opportunities emerge, like my friend in Pittsburgh discovered, largely out of your own efforts. You uncover these hidden possibilities by diligently networking with your personal contacts and by asking penetrating questions that reveal needs that you can fill. Often, these needs hadn't yet been identified at the conscious level until you began probing.

It might surprise you that the majority of all executive jobs are found in the hidden market through networking or by connecting into target organizations. Yet many people spend the majority of their time in lower-yielding activities such as surfing the many Internet job Web sites, responding to ads, and writing cold-call letters to companies with no intention of follow-up. Why, you ask? Because effectively conducting a campaign in the hidden job market is often more difficult and requires more persistence than some people's commitment. Not more skill or talent; just more guts, discipline, and personal commitment.

To learn more about the Hidden Marketplace, refer to the following chapters:

Chapter 12, "Power Networking—Unlocking the Secrets to Career Success"
Chapter 14, "Target Organizations—Who, What, Where, and Why?"

The Visible Job Market

The visible job market almost explains itself. When an employer places an ad online or in a newspaper or retains an executive search firm, you know that the company is hiring. The opportunities are now in the public domain. As such, they are considered "visible."

The vast majority of executive job seekers scan selected Web sites—such as Monster, 6FigureJobs, and CareerBuilder—subscribe to one or more of the dozens of for-fee search engines, or read the want ads in major newspapers, such as the *Wall Street Journal*, the *New York Times*, and the *Los Angeles Times*. Far too many job seekers restrict their search campaigns to these passive mail campaigns. While seemingly active, firing off your résumé to search firms or your target organizations or responding to advertisements are actually low-yield strategies. My friends in the executive search community estimate that no more than 15 percent of all executive hires are filled through executive search firms. For executives, no more than 3 percent of hires are filled through writing directly to target organizations. Only 2 percent of hires come from responding to advertisements (online or in papers) or through for-fee job listings subscription services.

If you are uncomfortable with mastering networking, you'll probably have a pronounced tendency to rely heavily on these low-yield techniques and blame the economy for your lack of job-hunting success. The lack of success opening up bona fide opportunities might undermine your confidence and cause you to continue to use these more passive ways of connecting, versus actively networking. Imagine the competition for those visible jobs.

To put it another way, if you restrict yourself to responding only to want ads, you are going to miss many of the jobs waiting to be filled. Your challenge is to effectively balance your efforts in both the hidden job market and the visible job market.

To learn more about the visible marketplace, refer to the following chapters:

Chapter 13, "Executive Search Firms—Your Success Partners"
Chapter 15, "Into the Vortex—The Internet (Plus Traditional Classified Advertisements)"

Improve Your Networking Skills, Enhance Your Leadership Skills

We have found that there is a direct correlation between an executive's networking mastery and his or her demonstrated leadership competence. An effective networker is comfortable, emboldened, confident, and enthusiastic about taking the initiative to connect with others. Often these contacts may be more senior to us in organizational title, rank, or compensation. The extent to which we hold back from reaching out to these "organizationally superior" colleagues is the extent to which we will probably have a tendency to hold back from developing strong rapport with them in our leadership capacity once we are employed.

Stretch Yourself . . . Get the Job You Deserve

The bottom line for me is that you should consider what success you want to have. While you cannot control timing and luck, you can certainly enhance your probability of accelerating your connection by spending a disproportionate amount of time on the high-yield search venues—namely, networking.

Lest you think that the only avenue I am recommending is networking, I'm not. One of RL's recent graduates pointed out that he connected through an Internet advertisement. While Tim had solid networking skills, he also surfed employment search engines for relevant opportunities.

Table 11-1 reflects our experience regarding career searches. While your situation may be different and your success may vary, these are guidelines, not absolutes.

Table 11-1

Avenue	% of Jobs Obtained	Your Job Hunting Goals
Hidden Marketplace		
Personal networking	80	Contact 15–20 people daily
Target organizations	3	Network into 20–30 target firms
Visible Marketplace		
Ads: Internet ads/classified ads/ blind ads/open ads	2	Contact 4–5 firms per week
Retainer search firms	15	E-mail to 500+ firms

Career Search—By Level, By Avenue

Many people ask us what is the expected probability of success by organization level for the various career search avenues (personal networking, search firms, target organizations, and advertisements). While all avenues work and should be utilized, Table 11-2 reflects our experience of people getting connected.

Table 11-2

	Personal Networking	Search Firms	Target Organizations	Advertisements
Executive	Extremely high	Moderately high	Low	Very Low
Managerial	Moderately high	Moderate	Low	Moderate
Professional– Technical	High	Moderate	Low	Moderately high
Administrative– Secretarial	Moderately high	Moderate	Very low	High

For more practical networking tips and techniques, please refer to Chapter 12, "Power Networking—Unlocking the Secrets to Career Success."

POWER NETWORKING— UNLOCKING THE SECRETS TO CAREER SUCCESS

Effective networking is key to a successful job search. If you recall, I mentioned that approximately 80 percent of executive positions are filled by people successfully networking. Regardless of your position or organizational level, the success of your campaign is directly related to your comfort and success in networking. It's not surprising that you may feel a lot of pressure around how to effectively network without exploiting your personal relationships.

A Little Help from Your Friends

A little help from your friends goes a long way when you are networking. Think about how you got your last few jobs. Did you answer an ad? Did you network into a retained executive search firm? Were you referred to a company by a friend, relative, or neighbor? If you were referred, you were really tapping into the hidden job market through networking. Even if you wrote directly to a company but you met the decision maker via a colleague, you also connected through networking.

My recommendation: Don't write letters to your personal contacts initially—this seems too impersonal, and it often backfires. If at all possible, call them first, reconnect, *then* e-mail them and attach your résumé. I know it's terrible to admit, but whenever I get an unsolicited letter from a distant acquaintance I haven't heard from in years asking for help, I am often ambivalent. (What? I wasn't worth a call?) The lesson for me was this: If you want help from others, personally connect with them. Don't just e-mail them asking for leads. Yes, I well understand how efficient e-mailing is, but I suspect the yield of high-quality contacts will be low through such a detached outreach.

Based on our general rule of thumb (that's violated all the time, by the way), if you successfully interview with 12 different organizations, you'll generate at least one offer of employment. *Since your objective is to produce three offers, your goal is have serious discussions with, minimally, 36 companies over the course of your campaign.* That means you may need to make 360 highly effective networking calls to reach this level . . . with no guarantees, of course.

Get Grounded in Your Empowering Beliefs!

Following are some tips to consider when you are networking:

- Focus on your past powerful networking experiences and visualize success.
- Recontextualize any disempowering beliefs about networking.
- Keep in mind that how your world looks is related to the meaning you attach to people, events, and things, especially your thoughts and feelings about networking.
- Believe that you are talented and have a tremendous amount to offer.
- Realize that everyone has been where you are and is willing to help; provided you approach the person well and add value.
- Keep in mind that you're not asking for a job—you are networking for professional advice, information, and leads (into search firms, target organizations, and other professionals in your chosen career field).

Individuals do not plan to fail, they fail to plan.

Sipri Cuthbert

Don't Just Hope for Success, Get Prepared!

Following are some tips:

- Understand the conditions in the market and in your field, including the challenges and opportunities for yourself.
- Establish your career objective, including its many diverse nuances.
- Conduct an in-depth evaluation of your strengths/developmental needs, skills, accomplishments, passions, drivers, core beliefs and values, and interests.
- Be confident in your differentiated "brand" and specific ways in which you can contribute to the growth and profitability of an organization.
- Develop a compelling results-oriented résumé and high-impact marketing letters. And, learn the details of your résumé, backwards and forwards.
- Be cognizant of your empowering and disempowering beliefs and how those influence your boldness, confidence, and how you network.

- Create "best practices" habits, manage your time, set daily networking goals for yourself, and track your progress. Use the Internet judiciously—it sucks time up if you're not careful!
- Develop "elevator speeches" (15-second, 60-second, 3-minute marketing sound bites), and have a specific objective for each call to a contact.
- Develop an exhaustive list of everyone you know, personally and professionally, in your current and every past job. Initially, your goal is quantity, not quality. Next, prioritize your names on an A, B, C basis with the A's being most important, best known, and well-networked themselves. Now you have a quality list of your top priority networking contacts. Your ultimate goal is to develop a list of at least 150 names that are A contacts.
- Identify your top 50 target organizations and prioritize them on an A, B, C basis as well. Select the top 20 A's, and ask your network contacts if they know anyone in this high-priority grouping.
- Practice your 15-second, 30-second "elevator speech," and 3-minute Verbal Résumé until you can confidently deliver these anytime, anywhere, to anyone.
- Prepare and practice phone "scripts" until you sound bold and confident and are able to successfully secure leads and overcome objections.

The Magnificent Seven: Networking Essentials

The seven things you absolutely must do with your personal network contacts:

1. Make a connection and develop rapport.
2. Inform the contact of your status.
3. Ask for information, advice, or referrals.
4. Request a meeting in person, as appropriate.
5. Legitimize sending your résumé and periodically reconnecting.
6. Give back; add value.
7. Follow up immediately on the qualified leads provided.

Let's look at each of these individually.

1. Make a Connection, Develop Rapport, and State Your Purpose

Whenever possible, make a connection in the first sentence. Such connections might be people that you have prequalified, such as a mutual professional or personal friend. Perhaps you are both alumni from the same university, an executive recruiter referred you, or you are/have been a Robertson Lowstuter client, to illustrate a few examples.

After establishing rapport, crisply and concisely state the purpose for your call or visit. As a means of creating the context of the conversation, deliver your 15-second elevator speech. If you recall, this should include excerpts from your résumé's career summary and one or two sentences on your distinctive skills, strengths, and achievements. For example:

> *A former colleague of yours, Gary Eisenplat, says "Hi" and recommended that I contact you for networking purposes. Gary and I were close friends when he and I were both at ABC Company, a $300 million global office furniture manufacturer.*

2. Inform People of Your Status

Briefly inform people of your situation, provide them a career focus, and highlight several things about what you have done and can do and the kind of job you are seeking.

For example:

> *As you may be aware, ABC Company recently went through a reorganization centralizing its operations, and my position was eliminated. Gary left in the second wave of downsizings, and I am leaving in the third wave. In my capacity as Senior Vice President of Sales and Marketing, I am skilled in accelerating sales, creating profitable alliances with distributors, and launching new products that positively impact the P&L.*
>
> *While I might have had the opportunity to remain in the organization in a lesser capacity, I was not interested in putting my career on hold for three to five years. As such, I am looking with the full knowledge and support of the company for a challenging senior sales and marketing management position.*

3. Ask for Information, Advice, or Referrals

After you have established a connection and validated the reasons for your call, ask the contact for information, advice, or referrals. Just a word about networking with your friends and their contacts. Do not put contacts on the spot by asking them if they know of any openings. You are not asking your contacts for jobs—rather, for information, advice, or referrals of people they would contact if *they* were to make a career move. If they freeze up in the conversation, it's likely they felt you were asking them directly for a job or that you were presumptuous in the way you asked for names of companies or contacts. If your contacts stiffen up, immediately apologize and indicate that you are not asking for a job. Rather, you are asking for the following:

- Information
- Advice
- Referrals

Depending on your objectives, the following highlights the kinds of things you might explore during your networking connections.

Network for Information

- Industry information (current trends, challenges, problems, opportunities)
- Target company information (restructurings, culture, changes in executives)
- Networking groups
- Professional associations
- Top recruiters in your industry or profession

Network for Advice

- Career advice (career or industry "changers")
- Possible career alternatives (entrepreneuring, large versus small companies)
- Résumé and marketing materials
- Alternative approaches to reach key targets
- Reaffirmation or determination of career direction
- Possible target organizations
- Effective career search techniques
- Entrepreneuring dos and don'ts

Network for Personal Referrals

- Executive search firm recruiters
- Private equity firm contacts
- Company executives or board members
- Target companies
- Executives within your profession
- Contacts regarding career strategy
- Persons knowledgeable of your target industry or companies
- Other power networkers

Your goal in networking is not to secure a job directly from one of your contacts but rather to create *visibility* for yourself and your campaign. You connect with others to see if they have appropriate contacts or information or advice they'd be willing to share. If you are able to maintain that perspective, the pressure to perform perfectly in your networking is diminished. Plus, others don't feel that you are hitting them up for a job.

When soliciting your networking contacts follow this sequence of garnering referrals:

- *Executive search firms.* Ask your contacts if they have any experience with executive search firms that they would recommend. If they do not have any direct experience, ask if they know of others who have had good experiences with retained search firms. Obviously, get their names, e-mail addresses, and telephone numbers.

Additionally, you may wish to secure the name of the head of human resources or staffing in your contact's company. Upon contacting the Vice President of Human Resources, ask if he or she would give you names of the search firms the company uses, based on your referral from your contact. For every contact you make, diligently follow the recommended seven-step process: Make the connection; inform of status; ask for help; request a meeting in person, if appropriate; legitimize sending your résumé and periodically reconnecting; give back/add value; and immediately follow up on the names of people provided.

- *Target organizations.* Ask if they can suggest some good companies in your geographic area or industry that you can send your résumé to so these companies will know of your availability as future needs arise.

    Second, have your personal contact respond to *your list of target organizations.* Show them your list or read to them your top 20 companies. These companies represent your highest priorities and the ones in which you want to network. Ideally, your networking contacts will provide names of other senior executives in your target companies, or people who may know people who have connections into these companies.

- *Personal leads.* Ask your contacts if they can give you the names of several friends *they* would call if *they* were looking to change jobs. Have a goal of securing three to five additional names per contact person.

- *Employment opportunities.* Ask your contacts if they will remain alert to employment opportunities and let you know if they hear of a lead. (You might provide two or three additional résumés, which they might give to someone if they think it might help.) Caution: Never lose control of your campaign. Do not rely upon others to blindly distribute your résumé no matter how gracious or well-intentioned they are.

Always follow up with friends who volunteered to send résumés out on your behalf. If they volunteer to create a mailing for you, it is best for you to have your friends write the letter and for you to do the mailing. You then have the ability to recontact these people.

4. Request a Meeting in Person

Face-to-face meetings are most always more effective than mere phone conversations. It always surprises me how many people multitask when on the phone, whether answering e-mails, printing out a document—whatever. Why are we surprised when contacts draw blanks when asked for information, advice, or leads? We shouldn't be. These multitasking folks are distracted, and you are the interruption. Here's an idea. If practical, ask for a personal meeting, indicating that you guarantee that you will not take more than 15 minutes of their time. It's tough for a contact to multitask when someone is in front of them. Only a handful of people on the planet are that rude!

5. Legitimize Sending Your Résumé and Periodically Reconnecting

As you close your conversation, thank them for their time and the assistance they extended. I recommend that you get the OK to both send your résumé as well as to periodically follow up to inform this contact of your search's progress and to ask him or her for help if you have additional questions. Nail down logistics. Get the correct spelling of this contact's name and e-mail address. Confirm your follow-up with an appreciative e-mail, reaffirm your agenda to periodically reconnect, and attach your résumé.

Most people will readily agree to the strategy of reconnecting at another time, if only to get you off the phone. However, it is a great opportunity for you to have a more productive conversation sometime in the near future if you are able to create linkage to a third-party who knows you both well and if you are able to demonstrate success in your search. Be patient and understanding. Create that image of success by being focused, confident, enthusiastic, open, socially bold, and forthright in your dealing with others.

6. Give Back and Add Value

A critical aspect of networking is giving back to those who have graciously given to you. Seek to add value. Ask the person with whom you have just been networking what you might do for him or her. More often than not, the person will say, "Nothing." Be creative about giving back. One way is to send something of value, perhaps a small book that has meant something to you and is likely to resonant with the other person. I occasionally like to send *The Four Agreements: A Practical Guide to Personal Freedom* by Don Miguel Ruiz, which helps people broaden their perspective around attaining personal freedom.

Also, create an article file. As a means of distinguishing yourself from others, I recommend that you assemble a file of powerful and insightful articles that are timely and relevant for the role for which you might be interviewing. Regardless of your industry or functional expertise, you cannot go wrong with articles on leadership, high-performance team traits, succession planning, strategic planning, team development, change leadership, and the like. Given the crush of normal business and the volume of business material that needs to be digested, many executives are not as well-read as they might otherwise wish. To that end, you may wish to ask leading questions that would naturally transition you into talking about a particular management tenet or experience that was researched and reported on in a given magazine or book. It is easy, then, to legitimize sending your networking contact (or the search firm recruiter or the prospective employer) a reprint of that article a week or so after your thank-you note. Why send the article separately from your interview thank-you note? A second note provides you a second point of contact with the prospective employer. Because the majority of job seekers rarely go to that amount of trouble, by definition, you will stand out as more of a value-add than your competition.

Great sources for articles include, but are certainly not limited to, the *Harvard Business Review, Fast Company, Fortune, Forbes,* the *Economist,* the *Wall Street Journal,* and scores of other fine business or technology magazines and journals. (Please note that all articles will be copyrighted, so you will need to pay for any reprints.) However, such a thoughtful touch might be well worth the positive impact it has on others. It's not uncommon to receive a call from your contact thanking you for the article, accompanied by some additional leads. Plus, sending an article is an easy way to give back and add value.

7. Follow Up Immediately on Leads That You Want to Pursue

As soon as you can, always contact those A priority leads, that have been provided to you. These people are the individuals whose names your personal friends have given you. This is not cold calling. It is simply following up with people who will be happy to talk with you on the basis of your mutual friend's suggestion.

If you manage yourself well while networking, you will be delightfully surprised by the extent to which others will help without your prodding. Your personal contacts will continue to keep you in mind as they begin to ask others about leads they know of that might help you. As such, your chances of finding a job this way are truly greater than other methods, although you must use all methods in your job search campaign.

Putting It All Together

The following is an example of a complete networking call. You'll have an opportunity to do likewise in the next worksheet.

Hello, my name is Michele Cannon. George Smith referred me to you, as he thought that you would be open to a networking call. I am the former President of the Services Group of Acme Manufacturing where I had complete P&L responsibility for a $2.6 billion global chemicals business.

As you may be aware, Colorant Partners acquired Acme in 2006 and their COO recently assumed my role in the midst of subsequent restructuring. As such, I am now seeking a similar senior P&L role.

While you might not have any appropriate opportunities in your organization, at this time, I am interested in becoming known to (*ORGANIZATION'S NAME*), as well as tapping into your contacts into search firms and target organizations. George indicated that you are a master networker and you'd know a number of people I should meet, given our respective interests and skills.

As I am just now beginning to conduct a job search, I'd love to get to know you and your company better.

Could we set up a brief meeting to network or is now a more appropriate time? What is your e-mail, so I might confirm this appointment?

Thanks very much. I look forward to meeting soon.

WORKSHEET 38

Network Introduction

Using the preceding example, write out your own networking overview, briefly introducing yourself, your capabilities, and the reason for calling.

Developing Your Networking Contact List

Think expansively. Include a broad number of contacts. Have a new perspective. Think of all the people you've influenced over the years. It's huge, even though you might not fully realize it. One of the biggest roadblocks in networking is undervaluing the impact you've had on others. If you depreciate yourself, you won't feel confident contacting colleagues. Another roadblock is pre-judging others as not being at your level, which inhibits you including them on your network list. You probably have judged some people as too senior (as they don't really know you and they'd never return your calls anyway), others as too junior (they wouldn't know anyone at your level), and still others, like relatives, as not relevant because they don't operate in your world.

However, it's critical that you develop a large list of names of people for you to potentially contact. Begin by printing out your address book. Brainstorm additional contacts, writing down names as fast as they come to mind. Include business colleagues, acquaintances, and personal friends. List everyone you can think of who might know about other business professionals and companies or hear of a job opening. Include your holiday mailing lists. Don't worry about being perfect—or even close. You'll sort these names out later. Don't stop. Keep writing. As you might imagine, your contact list will only expand; you will never run out of names if you do this well.

For your networking leads, capture the contact information per your A, B, and C ranking. To keep yourself organized, I recommend you master Microsoft Outlook, if you have it and/or explore using a contact software program. Two such programs that salespeople and master networkers use are ACT! and GoldMine available online or at any retailer selling management software programs or virtually any software programs are sold. While I'm sure there are other fine programs out there, these are the two I am most familiar with and recommend. The following are some categories from which you can draw your contact names.

Professional

- Current and former managers, coworkers, former subordinates
- Clients and customers
- Vendors and consultants
- Search firms
- Professional associations
- Highly visible notables in your industry

Personal

- Friends, relatives, and neighbors
- Schools (high school, college, grad school)

WORKSHEET 39

My Personal Contacts

Without considering if a person would be an A, B, or C priority contact, write down the names of business colleagues or personal friends as fast as you can. Your list is "written on paper"—not carved in granite. You can always delete a name after you've captured the data the first time. Your goal is a list of 150 names before you prioritize them as A, B, or C. I recommend capturing these names electronically; such a list is easier to work with later.

- Religious affiliations
- Sports/hobbies
- Clubs (health, golf, tennis, social)
- Community organizations (Chambers of Commerce, Rotary Club, Lions Club, etc.)
- Children (families from school, extracurricular activities, etc.)

When a contact does give you a networking lead, ask the following:

- "What is the best way for me to connect with this person?"
- "Would it be best if you called on my behalf, or shall I just mention your name?"

When such leads result in an interview or a good contact, get back to your contacts and thank them. It may result in additional leads.

Get Jazzed—Kill Your Fear

While we have many clients who are great at interviewing, a few are stymied when it comes to networking. They are intimidated to pick up the phone and initiate a call. These people are comfortable networking only with their closest friends. Tragically, since these clients only relied on their closest friends, their friends bore the burden of the job-hunters' overreliance on them. Once these overly dependent clients found the support from their contacts waning, seemingly overnight the lines went cold. Calls were not returned, or there were significant delays in callbacks. The solution: Think back to a time in which you were successful making an important pre-sentation and a lot was on the line. Yes, you might have been nervous, but you stepped through the fear into a powerful presentation. See yourself making powerful, affirming networking calls. Stand up. Be enthusiastic. Get jazzed.

 People take their cues from you. If you confidently believe that you can contribute significantly to an organization's growth and profitability, then others will believe it, as well. You get what you create in life and, also, in your career search.

"I'm Uncomfortable with Networking!"

This lament is common from executives who have historically not done an effective job building widespread organizational endorsement and advocacy for themselves. These people are solid performers. They contribute mightily to their companies. People think the world of them and would do anything to help them. However, too often these proud, accomplished executives resist networking. Their reluctance manifests itself in only calling their closest friends to abject fear of initiating a call. They are caught up in being overly concerned that others might think the worst of them. Unfortunately, many such executives project their own shame, misplaced pride, and fear onto others. Their awkwardness reinforces the feeling that the displaced job seeker is really beat up and clearly not on top of his or her game. Given that, can you blame contacts for not providing their best contacts for a person to call? No, of course not.

The following are but a few other phrases that we hear. See if any resonate with you. I also invite you to write down any other objections on the following worksheet that you occasionally hear rattling around in your head.

WORKSHEET 40

My Objections to Networking

Check which networking objections you have.

___ I do not want to impose on my friends.

___ I do not want to ask others for a job.

___ If I ask people for a job or to hire me, I will be rejected.

___ No one likes rejection, so why make contact.

___ I'm self-reliant. I don't ask for help; never have, never will!

___ I'm embarrassed. I don't know what to say.

___ I can sell stuff, just not myself.

___ I tried it once; it doesn't work.

___ I ran out of people to call.

___ No one helped me the last time I was out of work, so why bother this time?

___ Calling people when you're out of work is tacky!

Write down other objections that come to mind:

Flip Your Objections—The 30 Day Challenge

Given all that you know about networking, how does *not* networking serve you in getting the job you always wanted?   To shift your beliefs about networking, revisit Chapter 3, "Recontextualize: It'll Rock Your World!" All I am asking is that you diligently apply the networking strategies and wholeheartedly (and with positive expectancy and joy) work this process for 30 days. If the number of leads you create doesn't significantly increase, then you can go back to the way you've always conducted your search. You have nothing to lose and everything to gain! Trust me. As you risk and expand your comfort zone, you'll find that you can, indeed, master networking.

Stand Up and Take No Prisoners!

As I write this, my thoughts center on one of my clients, named Tom. Tom was a highly competent operations executive and well-known in his industry. Despite his significant visibility and credibility, Tom was hesitant to network and to rely on others. Asking for help was not part of his DNA. Tom prided himself on being independent and resourceful. People asked *him* for help, not the other way around. Even though Tom knew he had great credentials and capabilities and was effective face-to-face, he unwittingly sabotaged his efforts to network.

After observing him in action and tape-recording a few calls, I knew that he needed to modify his approach. I asked him when he felt most powerful and confident. Tom indicated that in his previous job he often stood up and gestured when talking on the phone and in meetings. I suggested that he stand up and mirror his confident behavior. He experimented with this idea and was immediately successful and more confident. This change in physical posturing strengthened his voice projection. He also significantly enhanced his skills in presenting his background. He was much more natural and more conversational.

With these initial successes, Tom's confidence soared as he overcame his networking jitters. He also learned a valuable lesson: People were delighted when they were able to give back to him. He shortly became as effective in networking as he was in operational turnarounds.

Overcome Stage Fright

Without exception, the telephone will be the primary means of personal contact concerning career opportunities, regardless of how you become introduced to the organization. If your background generated interest and there is a possible fit, you will receive a call. Prospective employers and search firms generally call before they send an e-mail, and certainly before a "snail mail" letter. Telephones are extremely potent search tools. While the telephone can be your greatest ally, it can also stop you dead in your tracks before you get to first base if you're not prepared.

Presenting yourself professionally and clearly over the telephone is a critical marketing skill that must be learned by serious job seekers. Before looking at the techniques and skills needed to make the presentation, let's first address the fact that many of us have serious reservations about using the phone to generate leads and interviews. With this is mind, the following are some tips to empower you even further.

Tape-Record Practice Calls

Ask several friends if they would be willing to be taped-recorded so you might enhance the effectiveness of your networking skills. Locate a good quality tape recorder and a recorder hookup any speciality electronics retailer that allows you to record both sides of this practice conversation. Your friends know that you will be recording, so you have consent.

My recommendation is that you record a few practice networking calls employing your networking techniques, including the checklist and scripts. Tape three to four exchanges. Then stop the taping, rewind and listen to how well you did. The first time you listen to it, you might think that you did OK or that you poorly represented yourself. That's normal. Play through your taped conversations again. You'll be amazed at the things you missed the first time listening. Note any cues that you might have missed. Be particularly mindful of those opportunities in which you could have spoken up or made a point, but didn't. Write down all of these for your learning, fine-tuning, and mastery. Consider your first time through as Round 1. Begin Round 2 with another series of tape recordings with another friend and critique these conversations, as you did in Round 1. After you complete Round 2, consider doing Round 3 with yet another friend. Repeat this process periodically to master your telephone networking. This is a powerful, yet simple process to significantly enhance your skills and build your confidence.

Stay Relaxed

Remember to stay relaxed on the telephone. Be focused on the other person's agenda, not on yours. Listen deeply to both what is being said, as well as to the possible meaning and messages embedded in the conversation. Be insatiably curious, ask penetrating questions that follow what the other person is saying. Take notes only on the conversation's most salient points. My rule of thumb is this: The more notes you take, the greater the likelihood of you missing important cues. The more you are scratching on your paper, the less engaged you are with the other person. Now, that being said, there will be some facts or details you'll need to write down, such as directions, names of people, dates of company visits, and so forth. Also, you might pick up some ideas for your article file, either to add to it or send one of the reprints that might be appropriate to this contact's situation. Do not be afraid to have a person repeat a name, the spelling of a company, or an address. These facts are crucial to your job search.

To effectively market yourself on the phone, you need to be willing to

- Be committed to mastering this career search process, including communicating your message clearly, concisely, credibly, and powerfully.
- Be open to the idea that you can be highly successful marketing yourself.
- Carefully prepare to do well on the phone.
- Practice raising your comfort level about using the telephone.

Why, Oh Why, Must I Do All This Networking?

First, this process is an investment in yourself. If you are not going to invest in yourself, enhancing your skills, why should others? Second, you want to get the best job you can with the most attractive compensation package you can for this role, right? Third, and most importantly, by mastering networking and all aspects of the career search process, you will absolutely, positively distinguish yourself from the competition. You want to go the extra mile by being better prepared. Don't worry about being too slick or smooth. Focus on being well-grounded in all of your material and by relating to others as your natural, authentic self. You will be seen as "slick and slippery" if you attempt to manipulate or force others to do your bidding. People resent being sold. Rather, they want to be shown the way and then they, themselves, will make their decisions.

 Contrary to what your mother said, you *do* want to stand out from the crowd.

Tips for Networking Meetings

Manage Your Expectations

- Do not expect to receive real "job leads."
- Don't think you'll meet decision makers there; you'll only meet your competitors.
- Be cautious of personal referrals disguised as "name dropping."
- Don't get caught up in the frenzy of volunteering your best contacts; you don't know how others will represent you or themselves.

Establish Your Objective

- Supply more general information than contact leads until you determine the lay of the land and how solid contacts/leads are shared and managed.
- Identify a least one person you want to follow up with and meet. Establish that connection and an appointment.
- Network on a one-on-one basis, getting to know that person.
- Make sure that you balance attending pure networking meetings with professional association-type meetings in which you gain value from the topic presented and where there is an opportunity to network.

Look for Promising Networking Candidates

- Seek out anyone who has worked in one of your target companies in the last five years.
- Network with anyone in or closely aligned to your profession.
- Network with anyone who works in your target industry.
- Look for anyone who has high energy, appears sharp, is connected, and is savvy as to how to effectively network and appropriately share valuable information.

Networking Call Checklist: Getting Prepared

- Be prepared with an agenda for the type of help you want: personal advice, information, and referrals.
- Remember, if you come across prepared, confident, polished, and poised, there's a high probably you'll get the appointment—and additional contacts.
- Introduce yourself, linking yourself to a personal referral that builds endorsement from a mutual acquaintance.
- Establish credibility by highlighting your career focus and a key accomplishment.
- Request a personal meeting, per your agenda.
- Set the meeting and determine logistics; confirm with an e-mail, and attach your résumé.

In the sections that follow, sample scripts are provided for different networking scenarios.

Request for Network Meeting (Script for Executive Assistants)

Partner with every assistant that you encounter. They're pros and should command your respect. Fancy footwork or pretending that you're merely returning the executive's call will immediately damage your credibility. Bring the executive assistant into your networking strategy and ask for help in getting an appointment.

For example:

> *[Name of Assistant], I'm Michele Cannon. Clyde Lowstuter who is a friend of your boss, suggested that I call to network with [Ken, the boss]. I am the former President of Acme Services Group, a $2.6 billion global chemicals company. As my skills are in accelerating revenues and profitability through organic growth and acquisitions, Clyde thought that Ken and I might have some things in common.*
>
> *I would appreciate the opportunity to meet with Ken for 30 minutes and get his advice on the private equity community, relative to my search. When might he be available to meet or talk with me? [Assistant], thank you for your help arranging an appointment with [Boss].*

Request for Networking Meeting (Script for Industry Colleague)

Good morning, John. My name is Michele Cannon. I was referred to you by Clyde Lowstuter. I understand you and he have been friends for more than 10 years. I am the former President of Acme Services Group, a $2.6 billion global chemicals company. As my skills are in accelerating revenues and profitability through organic growth and acquisitions, Clyde thought you and I might have some things in common.

I am currently conducting a career search for a CEO or COO role, preferably in the chemicals, health-care, or industrial products industries. Clyde and I met recently, and after he had the opportunity to get to know me, my professional accomplishments, and career interests, he felt our meeting maybe of mutual benefit. I would appreciate the opportunity to meet with you for 30 minutes and solicit your personal advice and input relative to my search. Might you be available to meet? [Schedule the meeting.]

Request for Network Meeting (Script for Target Company)

The following is an example of a meeting request to a colleague, Fred James, in the ABC Company, one of your target organizations:

Good morning, Fred. My name is Michele Cannon. I was referred to you by Clyde Lowstuter. I understand you and he worked together at Fiat-Allis a number of years ago. I am the former President of Acme Services Group, a $2.6 billion global chemicals company. As my skills are in accelerating revenues through organic growth and acquisitions, Clyde thought you and I might have some things in common, especially the aspect of living and working internationally.

During my meeting with Clyde, he became aware of my potential interest in working for ABC Company. ABC has an outstanding quality reputation and seems to be committed to growth through global expansion. Clyde thought you would be willing to meet with me and share your experiences in working for ABC Company—it's culture, business philosophies, and leadership styles. Would you be available to meet? [Agree on the logistics for the meeting.]

Handling Objections

Following are some objections to your networking request that you might encounter:

Objection 1. *"I am not hiring now, and I do not know anyone who is. Why don't you send me your résumé, and I will get it to Human Resources."*

Response. *"I appreciate your willingness to do that for me; however, that is not why I called. I am really interested in obtaining your advice and input regarding my career search. In addition, once we meet and you have personal knowledge of my experience and interests, you may suggest I contact others you know who could be of help. Would it be possible to meet for 15 minutes?"*

Objection 2. *"I am very busy over the next few weeks. Call me back next month."*

Response. *"Thank you. I appreciate how busy you must be. Based on my schedule, I was not suggesting we meet until _____ [two to three weeks out]. How is your schedule the week of_____ ? [Schedule a date.] In the interim, I'll send you some information on myself. Would that be all right? "[Schedule your follow-up call in your planner and, later, make the call.]"*

Networking "Math"—Exponential Growth Made Simple

It is really incredible how quickly your networking list can build. Indeed, if you start with 20 names and if you secure two names from every contact provided you, within six levels you will have generated more than 2,500 names!
For example:

Start with 20 people in your network.   20
#1 Contact 20 people and get 2 referrals each.   @ = 40; + 20 = 60
#2 Contact those 40 and get 2 referrals each.   @ = 80; + 60 = 140
#3 Contact those 80 and get 2 referrals each.   @ = 160; + 140 = 300
#4 Contact those 160 and get 2 referrals each.   @ = 320; + 300 = 620
#5 Contact those 320 and get 2 referrals each.   @ = 640; + 620 = 1260
#6 Contact these 640 and get 2 referrals each.   @ = 1280; + 1260 = 2540!!

And on and on . . . Your network can grow exponentially—if you master networking!

12 Guidelines You Have Probably Forgotten

1. While the Internet is a phenomenal resource and e-mail is a great tool, you still need to touch base with search firms, networking contacts, and potential employers via the telephone. The telephone can be one of your best means of covering the job market. It is so fast you can get in touch with virtually anyone, anywhere in just a few minutes. Consider the following:
   - How long would it normally take you to meet 10 to 15 prospective employers if you talked in their offices or wrote them a letter? You can reach 10 to 15 employers *every day* just by picking up the telephone and dialing.
   - You can gather information and leads faster and easier by using the telephone because there's no waiting for people to respond back to your e-mail.

Making a phone call can be 10 times more effective than writing a letter or sending an e-mail.

2. Avoid lengthy telephone interviews if at all possible. At least 50 percent of the data you would give in a face-to-face interview is lost because you cannot pick it up over the telephone. Not only can you *not* read body language over the telephone, but you cannot project your own either. Also, since hearing is the only sense channel being used, *how* you sound is very often more important than *what* you say. Over the phone, your vocal self will be distorted. Excitement and enthusiasm may be misinterpreted as nervousness or tension. Practice developing a well-modulated voice.

3. A prospective employer forms an impression by the sound of your voice and the questions you ask. Whether you are a man or a woman, if your voice pitch, tends to shift to a higher register when you are excited or nervous, practice speaking more from your diaphragm, accessing a slightly lower voice pitch or tonality. A higher registry often connotes nervousness and insecurity. A deeper, more relaxed voice connotes more power, confidence, and boldness. Additionally, you can also learn a lot about a possible employer by how you are treated on the phone.

4. Your main objective in making personal contact is to get the employer or search firm account executive interested in meeting you. If an employer or recruiter calls you regarding a position in which you are clearly not interested, gracefully decline consideration and provide leads of other people, if appropriate. Generally, it is beneficial to also be known as a value-added resource for search firms or prospective employers.

5. If called, do not reveal more than your Verbal Résumé (see Chapter 9, "Your Verbal Résumé—Marketing Sound Bites That Grab 'Em".) without getting some information in return on the organization and the position opening. If there is some mutual interest, press for a face-to-face interview.

6. If you feel that you are being dragged into a full-blown interview over the telephone and you want a face-to-face discussion, you need to regain control. One technique is to say something like the following:

Since it sounds like we have some mutual interest in exploring this further, let's establish a convenient interview time. While we have covered some excellent ground over the telephone, I feel a face-to-face discussion would enable us to get to know each other and the situation better. Don't you agree?

7. Many job seekers feel that executive assistants are their adversaries, not their allies. Indeed, many assistants operate as though their jobs are the gatekeepers

of their boss's schedule. Think of the assistant as your partner in getting you introduced to his boss, your target executive. Invite him or her into your confidence. Don't demand, be rude, or think the assistant is beneath you. If you are overly pushy, you will lose every time. I can guarantee you that you'll never get in. On the other hand, if you bring him or her into your confidence and give him or her the power to decide about your background, you'll most likely win an audience with the boss. Indicate that given your ability to accelerate top line revenue gains while significantly increasing margins (such as Michele Cannon did) the assistant's boss would definitely appreciate knowing of your availability. When talking to the executive's assistant, ask his/her name and use it. Be confident, positive, and polite. As a general rule, use your former title (". . . the former President of $2.6 million global chemicals manufacturer that competes with your biggest customer. My expertise is in significantly improving company performance and profitability. I'd like to talk with your boss about my capabilities. I know she is busy, as I am. Based on the company's desire for gross sales and improved top and bottom line growth, she might find it of value to see me.")

8. Be prepared to answer some reasonable questions, for instance, "How does your background relate to this industry, company, or open position?" Do enough research for every networking meeting and interview that you can sufficiently intrigue your contact with your observations or penetrating questions. Again, avoid a full interview over the telephone, if at all possible. Remember: sound bites, short pithy comments.

9. The executive typically will attempt to reject an interview gesture. Since executives are busy people, you expect to hear, "We have no appropriate openings now. What do you really want to see me about?" Come back with a simple statement indicating that your main interest is to meet for purposes of personal advice, information, or referrals in your target industry, if and when something develops. Or, you are interested in learning about the private equity world in which they operate, for instance.

 Have bite-size expectations. Don't expect to hit a home run on your first contact with a person with whom you network.

10. If denied an interview, politely indicate your disappointment and ask for names of individuals who might be approached.

11. Become more comfortable on the phone by doing the following:
    - You can call colleagues to get a better idea of the types of questions retained recruiters ask executives like yourself. You might even ask, "What are some of the tough questions your company asks?" Keep a list, periodically review it, and modify it as new ideas emerge.
    - Leave the most daunting of your ideal prospects for last, and call them when you feel comfortable on the phone. Practice your telephone presence with friends or others whom you know are also looking for a job until you are able to talk comfortably.
    - Making a lot of calls as you look for a job is as easy or difficult as you make it. If you believe it will be easy or difficult, you are right. What you believe is what you get. Confidence and self-esteem are what will get you through these tough times. The right job is out there, if you have the patience and perseverance to find it.

12. Make it a game. After all, getting a job is a matter of probability, no matter how you look at it. It's timing and luck. At the executive level, the people that you'll be contacting may not directly come out and say, "No, I'm not going to help." Rather, the "No people" will be gracious, even sympathetic, and wish you well, but they'll not open any doors for you. How many no's does it take before you can come up with a yes? Provided you are effectively networking, we have learned that *if you get one yes for every 10 no's, you'll do just fine!* A yes is really all that matters. Keep your perspective and embrace your no's, as you are that much closer to a yes.

Use your personal contacts to leverage an introduction into as many retained search firms as you can within 60 days of your mailings. That's the best window of opportunity.

Final Networking Tips

- Plan your activities.
- Establish a tracking and follow-up system.
- Document your discussions.
- Track your referral sources.
- Always set up a follow-up activity for a networking contact before you move on to the next one.

- Always follow up and acknowledge thanks.
- Offer to help others—build relationships and add value (provide leads, send articles that would enhance the executive's capability or knowledge, etc.).
- Regularly review your effectiveness against your goals.
- Practice, practice, practice—and stay organized.
- Remain confident, enthusiastic, powerful, bold, and authentic.

Summary

As you have seen in this chapter, you *can* raise your networking comfort level. By beginning at the relatively low-risk "research" communication stage and by developing a comfort level at each successive stage through repetition, you will become more confident, bold, and self-assured in the use of the telephone.

It is critical that you learn how to talk comfortably to an executive recruiter and a company's representative about yourself and your abilities as a valuable resource for a firm's future needs.

Using the telephone as an integral part of the campaign is a powerful marketing approach designed to specifically improve your success in securing an appropriate job for you in the least possible time.

 Some people believe that practice makes perfect. Not so. *Perfect* practice makes perfect. Commit to mastering networking—perfectly.

Preparation is the key to building self-confidence in networking. It is the result of courageously experimenting, learning from mistakes, visualizing success, and never giving up.

Successful networking is not an accident, nor is it luck. As Earl Nightingale once said, "Luck is preparedness meeting opportunity."

I say, "The harder I work, the luckier I get."

CHAPTER 13

EXECUTIVE SEARCH FIRMS— YOUR SUCCESS PARTNERS

Retained Executive Search Firms

The executive search business is a noble business filled with hopes, dreams, trust, and faith. Client companies put their trust in search firms to find the very best talent available who, they hope, will significantly enhance their organization's future. Executive recruiters are change agents in the purest sense, in that they have the ability to dramatically change their client's organization—its culture, vision, and direction by the executives they introduce and that hired. Candidates, likewise, hope that the boss, team, and organizational dynamics will be a good fit for them and trust that the executive recruiter has critically and accurately evaluated these company factors—balanced against their own technical, interpersonal, leadership, and personality fit. Everyone wants a hire to fit and be successful; the company, the search firm, and especially, the executive being hired.

Executive search firms handle searches for jobs at the level you want to be considered—$250,000+. Based on conversations with my search firm colleagues, an estimated 15 percent of all the senior-level jobs are filled through this process. These firms are paid on a retainer basis to locate a qualified executive for a particular position. They receive their fee regardless of whether they are successful in their search.

Universal Truths/Reality

1. Retained search firms do not work for you; they work for the organization that retained them. If you fit, great!

2. When you are the perfect fit, the search firms will be your advocate and partner with you to be successful.

As a rule, retained executive search firms are the *only* search firms you should be targeting. Your job is to uncover and network into the best and most talented recruiters. While many search firm executives are talented executives in their own right, the truth of the matter is that not all recruiters are alike. Notwithstanding the differences in their capabilities, executive recruiters have access to C-suite opportunities.

Contingency search firms, on the other hand, rarely have access to senior-level searches as they, generally, do not have contacts into top management. With rare exception, contingency search firms flood the marketplace with executives' résumés without regard to the fit or whether there is a legitimate search. Many contingency firms don't particularly care if their actions tarnish your reputation, as they are paid a fee contingent on you being hired. They are hoping that they can lay claim that they introduced you to the hiring organization first and get paid. That's why I say many contingency recruiters are incented to indiscriminately blast your résumé into organizations. They feel that the first one in wins. Fortunately, it is not always so.

While contingent recruiters do have connections into many organizations, they rarely have connections at the organizational level suitable for you. Hence, the problem. Periodically, clients will find themselves in compromising situations where they are being seriously considered for viable opportunities, but a contingency search firm is clamoring for a fee if our client is hired. There have been circumstances where the client is hired and has to pay a portion of the unauthorized fee. Worse is when a great offer is withdrawn because the company doesn't want to pay the fee or get into legal wrangles.

If you do mistakenly send your résumé to a contingency firm, try to get your résumé back. Formally declare (in writing) that you do not wish to be represented by the firm and that you consider yourself not to be obligated in any manner.

I don't mean to sound harsh or negative toward contingency search firms as there are a number of highly reputable firms out there. I have a good friend who owns a contingency firm that is a credit to the industry, adds tremendous value to his clients, and is incredibly successful. However for most executives, contingency firms, as a whole, pose more problems than benefits.

Strategies for Dealing with Search Firms

1. *Never pay a fee!* The fee for these services should always be paid by the employer. If you are asked to sign an agreement or pay a portion of the employer's fee up front, walk away. If you feel you must use a firm that has a contract, have a qualified attorney take a look at it.
2. Increasingly, there are firms that advertise that they have open opportunities, yet when you respond, you discover that it was merely a ploy to sell you résumé evaluation/writing services. I recommend that you stay away from these résumé

mills or firms advocating mass mailing in the tens of thousands as the preferred job-hunting method. Such firms have a vested interest in scaring you into investing $2.50 to $3.50 a letter, spending $10,000 or more on a mass-mailing campaign that will yield less than 3 percent, on average.

3. While you might be an "A-level" executive, if you are a "B-fit" for a current search, you may not ever get a call. Should your background match the needs of an ongoing search assignment, the search firm will usually contact you by telephone or e-mail. Letter responses are generally used to inform you that there is no current client assignment matching your background. Many of the larger and better-known firms receive such a volume of mail from individuals announcing their availability that they use postcards and form e-mail or paper letters to respond. Or, you may not hear back at all. Don't take it personally if you do not hear back. It's not uncommon for high-visibility search firms to receive up to 5,000 unsolicited résumés a month. Direct-mail responses to search firms generating a hire is about 1 percent—akin to the responses from other forms of unsolicited direct mail. If you are uptight about not receiving a response back, consider what *you* do with unsolicited mail. You toss it. When was the last time you wrote back to a chimney sweep company thanking them for announcing their availability? Never, I bet. So don't be judgmental of search firms.

4. Use your personal contacts to network into 8 to 12 search firms daily. However, unless you have a personal lead into a search firm account executive, do not telephone to follow up on your mailing. It is seen generally as an annoyance to the recruiter. Also, do not walk in and expect an interview, regardless of how accomplished you are. Think how you'd respond to an unsolicited walk-in or call from a salesperson.

5. If asked about income, tell the recruiter straightaway the value of your total compensation (base, bonus, and options/stock, if appropriate). Do not try to defer revealing salary data, as the search firms are only trying to identify the level of suitable jobs. Certainly, you can indicate that you are open and flexible with regard to total compensation and how/when it gets configured.

6. Retained search firms do not send unsolicited résumés to a company. Contingency firms, on the other hand, certainly send résumés unsolicited to companies, which, can eliminate you from consideration if there is a fee dispute. Resend your résumé or bios to retained search firms again within six months if you are still in the market. Do not take the salary minimums listed by a search firm too literally; merely use them as a general guide.

7. If an executive search firm (or a company) asks you to travel some distance to meet with them and you incur expenses, these expenses should be reimbursed. Your appropriate response should be this: "How do you want me to handle these expenses? Do you want to have your travel agency send me prepaid e-tickets, or

should I just put this and other travel-related expenses on my credit card and bill you after the trip?" You may wish to reconsider traveling for an interview if the recruiter balks at reimbursing you for normal expenses, as is the custom. Perhaps the search is not yet mature enough to warrant a trip at this time or it is a contingency firm in disguise. At any rate, you would be well advised to probe a bit and determine the reason for the hesitancy.

8. The recruiter, as a professional, must respect the confidentiality of your situation. Nonetheless, if you are currently employed, you need to identify the search firms with whom your company engages and eliminate them from any mailings or networking. While you might have a great professional relationship with a recruiter your company uses, don't compromise his or her integrity and responsibility to your organization. Ultimately, your judgment and integrity may be questioned. Bottom line: Use caution; protect yourself against an overzealous recruiter squealing on you. Protests to the contrary, it does happen. As such, indicate in your marketing letter that you are "conducting a discreet and confidential search." If you have any doubts, do not venture out.

Even in the best of circumstances, there is always a remote possibility of a slipup, so you need to assess the risk of exposure. I had a friend be summarily terminated because a recruiter informed on him. This ambitious partner wanted to get in the good graces of a prospective company president, so he improperly shared this confidential information. To be fair, my friend naively did a mass mailing to the major search firms in the Midwest without deleting the search firms his company employed. So, he got caught with his data down.

What About Mailing My Résumé to Search Firms?

Good question. There are three schools of thought:

School 1:   *E-mail your résumé.* Send your résumé to thousands of search firms, nationally, regardless of whether you know them. Your goal is to blast your résumé out into the marketplace only to retained executive search firms. The more, the better. Even if they only get 1/2 to 1 percent acknowledgment, many job seekers welcome the visibility in the search community. Indeed, most search firms are receptive to mailings because such mailings impressively swell their databases, and the "needle in the haystack" may come along via a mailing. However, when asked what percent of the jobs are filled from their databank of thousands of unsolicited résumés, search firms report "that less than 8 percent of all their searches are filled through such mailings or their database." Nonetheless, 8 percent is 8 percent and may be worth the effort.

School 2:   *Network only.* The attention you receive when you effectively network into a search firm partner is far greater than when you merely cold-call or send only a mailing. Search firms will tell you that they will flag the file of a high-potential executive and not purge it at the 6-month or 12-month mark. Therefore, if you network into a search partner using the name of an "A" player that the firm wants to continue to court, you will invariably get an audience. It stands to reason; high flyers hang out with high flyers.

School 3:   *E-mailing and networking.* I advocate this combination of networking into search firms, in conjunction with targeted e-mailings to them. As a résumé markets you in advance of your being in an interview, I recommend you follow up on your mailings and connect with key recruiters via your senior networking contacts. This one-two punch seems to be the most effective door opener.

We often get asked, "Should I send my résumé *only* to the large national retainer search firms?" The answer is "No." There is something to be said for contacting a broad array of retained firms. *National, regional, and boutique search firms are all ones that you should target.* If you do not have any idea how to sort out these firms, be generous and include those executive search firms you have never heard of. Why? Your goal is to create widespread visibility and exposure for yourself. If you restrict your contacts to those firms you know have jobs, your contact list will indeed be short.

How many of your résumés should you mail out—10, 100, 500, 5,000 or more? The answer is—it depends. It depends on a number of factors, including your job and level in the organization. If you are a senior executive open to relocating anywhere in the world and your compensation is in excess of $400,000, you probably will zero in on retainer search firms, nationally handling engagements above $150,000. That is about 100 or so firms. By the way, there is *no* search firm directory that I know of that lists firms who only handle assignments $400,000 and above. Quite frankly, it would be impractical for search firms to restrict their searches to only assignments that large.

The reality is that even the major search firms have a minimum salary level to which they reasonably adhere. My advice: Send your résumé to all the retained executive search firms (conducting general searches) in your geographical target areas, regardless of their stated minimum salary level. For the rest of the country, I recommend that you send your résumé to only those search firms that indicate they specialize in your industry or function. (For instance, *Technology* is a relevant search parameter if you are in R&D.) As you select those niched search firms, indicate a relatively high salary minimum so as not to have a mailing of thousands. You don't want more than 500 firms for your e-mailing, maximum, because you will not be able to easily initiate networking follow-up calls.

Additionally, you may wish to consider e-mailing your unsolicited, out-of-the-area résumés to no more than 100 search firms at a time. Why? So you might follow up through networking. E-mailing to thousands of retained executive search firms is largely a waste of your time, even though some people will advocate that you track down every search firm on the planet and send out tens of thousands of résumés. We whole-heartedly disagree with this blanket, mass-mailing approach, as it is impossible to network into and follow up with more than a handful of the key firms. Besides, if you fall significantly above (or below) the minimum stated range of searches in which the firm might be involved, your résumé runs the risk of summarily being discarded.

Use your personal contacts to leverage an introduction into as many retained search firms as you can within 60 days of your mailings. That's the best window of opportunity.

Interviewing with Recruiters

During the initial phone contact and even during the first interview, the identity of the client firm who has a bona fide opportunity may not be divulged. Nevertheless, sufficient information will usually be given to enable you to get a rough idea as to a possible fit (i.e., size, industry, geographic location, etc.).

If you are able to identify the name of the organization with whom you are interviewing, great! You now have the ability to conduct some research and network with others who may know something about the company. Electronically or through a visit to a well-equipped library, conduct in-depth research on the company, its organizational structure, diverse business units, the Board of Directors, sales and profitability, and any significant issues that it identifies in the annual report. Contact your stockbroker (for publicly traded companies) for analyst reports. One of our clients in Grand Rapids, Michigan was considering an opportunity as EVP for a division of a publicly traded, Houston-based, company. I snagged an analyst report from my broker that indicated that the parent company was exploring possible sale or spin-off of this division. Armed with this prized nugget of data our client not only surprised the CEO with this level of detail but was also able to secure a sizable number of shares and options that he might not have been able to secure without this valuable, closely held knowledge.

Once the recruiter shares the identity of the client, ensure that the account executive gives you full particulars regarding the qualifications and performance expectations that are guiding the selection of qualified candidates. Armed with this information, you can then do a side-by-side comparison of the requirements versus your experience and capabilities. If there is a qualifications area where you feel you may be lacking, you need to create a credible response to counter the objection.

Regardless of whether the company's identity is revealed, you should ask questions about the company, its products or services, corporate culture, the greatest challenges and opportunities—growth or turnaround, the industry, company revenue, and status—private or public, profitable or not, and so on. It's OK to push a bit for some data. In fact, when I was in corporate and did senior executive recruiting, I used to deliberately hold back relevant information to see how assertive candidates were about asking for what they needed.

If you were interviewing for a role in my company I'd ask diverse questions to determine how:

- Technically competent you are.
- Appropriately assertive you are.
- Transparent you are and how your authenticity is manifested.
- Well-developed is your judgment and how sound is your logic.
- Skillful are your interpersonal skills.
- Fluidly you respond to and adapt to my operating style and, by inference, how effective you would be in building relationships with others in this organization.
- Effective is your leadership presence and capabilities.
- Persuasive you can be with others.
- Reasonable are your requests.

My philosophy in interviewing is that "as you give information about yourself, you should get information about the company and opportunity." Obviously, the more information you can glean from the recruiter about the client company, the better. It's tough to interview without a context.

You're the Needle They've Been Searching For!

Snap judgments are often a recruiter's stock and trade; they've had a lot of experience assessing people. You want to make it easy for them to put you into the slate of final candidates that see the client. I recommend that you do all the normal things such as get in shape, be impeccably dressed, be rested, be authentic and enthusiastic. In addition, always, always, always ask for the position specifications that have been developed by the recruiter. You ask for two fundamental reasons: first, so you have a context for your interviews, and second, having the specs enables you to tailor your background to the position specifications developed by the recruiter.

The following example is the actual comparison of the position specifications for a CFO's role and the background of one of our clients. My client graciously allowed me to use his response to the listed qualifications and traits. He found this approach to be highly effective in the interviewing process. He expanded his comparison from one of the letters found in Chapter 8, "Create Powerful Marketing Letters That Evoke Action." The company specifications are **underlined and in bold typeface**. To maintain confidentiality of my client and his previous organizations, I have disguised company names, product lines, and industries.

A strong understanding of or high interest in the operational dynamics of the business in addition to the financial dynamics.
Although I have spent my entire career in financial roles, at Siroc I was also responsible for operations. This experience provided me with a more complete understanding of, and appreciation for, the total environment in which a business functions. It is my strong personal belief that CFOs create greater value when they are in tune with the activities of the business itself.

Able to communicate the financial impact of alternative strategies to the rest of the organization. Demonstrated strategic thinker about competitive strategy, business models, and financial management. Experience with financial ratios and metrics that lead to shareholder value and with the business levers that affect them.
Strategic planning was a very important part of my job as CFO of Waldial Education Services. Since it generated 30 percent of the revenue and 75 percent of the EBITDA of the total enterprise, our business plan was a critical component of the parent company's exit from Chapter 11 bankruptcy. I played a key role in the development of that long-range strategic plan.

In addition, Waldial products and services are bid business. Bids, if won, require substantial capital expenditures for support infrastructure. Pricing strategies are critical as contracts renew every three to five years. I designed, and my team implemented, a unique discounted cash flow-based bid model, including metrics, to analyze the financial impact of each dollar of capital expended under Waldial Education Services' $175 million annual capital budget.

The competencies to scale or replicate the business in a growth mode.
At Zra International I restructured the financial and IT functions, which enabled the company to expand into new markets and double in size. They were transformed into departments that were seen as facilitators to obtaining new business where they had previously been seen as impediments.

<u>Strong leadership skills marked by collaborative team-orientation and apolitical style; open and inclusive. The ability to recruit, retain, coach, and mentor top-quality staff. The ability to assess the talent on board and attract exceptional new people as needed</u>.
I have built and restructured both financial and IT functions several times in the past. But more importantly, I have built functions that have been seen by others as becoming collaborative entities that are supportive to the operations and sales functions. I am also a mentor, in that most of the people who work for me appreciate the challenging, learning experience that I can provide. I accomplish this while taking full responsibility for my departments' actions.

<u>Management experience in a national/international business with multiple operating units and extensive real estate holdings and high relationship orientation</u>.
Waldial generated, in Canada, C$200 million of its C$1.5 billion of total revenue. It had five operating regions and more than 500 facilities of which about one-third were owned. The business is heavily relationship driven as there are more than 1,250 customers and 1,500 contracts.

<u>Preferably background and experience in more than one business model. The competencies to work in difficult times, and a track record of collaboration to bring about business improvement</u>.
I have worked in commercial printing, database publishing, manufacturing, distribution, transportation, and even private equity. These companies have ranged from large public companies to family-owned and operated businesses. They have had U.S., Canadian, and UK parents. One was capitalized with all equity, while the parent of another was in Chapter 11 bankruptcy for more than two years while I was with the company and implemented a new ERP system for the purpose of process improvement.

<u>Familiarity with Information Systems management, with an emphasis on information flows and using information systems as an enabler for business decisions</u>.
I have been responsible for IT at several companies. At Waldial Education Services, after moving all computer systems to Santa Fe from Canada in December of 1999 at the height of Y2K, my team then implemented a major JD Edwards ERP conversion across the company. We also had the foresight to develop and implement the operating software, which now provides the backbone for field operations to run the business (e.g., safety, routing, etc.).

Wasn't this comparison an easy way for this recruiter to select him for further consideration? I invite you to spend a few minutes each time you receive a position specification from a recruiter and match your achievements and capabilities with the needs/wants of the job and company.

Registering with Search Firms Online

Virtually all of the major search firms will have you complete a Personal History Form (PHF) that enables your résumé to be registered within their system. *Note:* Even though you may have sent them your résumé via e-mail, you still need to register online. Don't wait for a firm's researcher to enter your credentials into their database; take the initiative yourself by submitting it directly.

PHF's Tips and Traps

"Why are you searching now?"

A great question. No employer wants to hire a person who is still beat up from leaving or is troublesome and difficult to deal with. Ironically, the answer to this question will never fit into the space allotted on the Personal History Form (PHF), so you need to master the shortest sound bite possible. "Downsizing" will suffice versus trying to elaborate with something like, "the recent strategic alliance produced the expected duplication of functions and executives. While I had the opportunity to remain, albeit in a less responsible job, I elected not to put my career on hold for three to five years. So I am looking with the full knowledge and support of my company." I'm sure you get the picture.

"What is your salary history?" "What are your salary requirements?"

Regarding questions concerning compensation, I recommend that you fill in the blank for your current or most recent job with something like "Will discuss"—nothing more. People will naturally try to get you to declare your current or recent compensation, as well as the compensation you require going forward. As the makeup of an executive's compensation package is so complex, merely indicating a number may not serve you well. You might be proud of the level of your compensation in a large organization and might be more than willing to take significantly less base pay for an equity stake in a start-up or early-stage company, for example. In my opinion, these two questions are best answered in person, not on a PHF. Now, having said all that, I recognize that with online PHF you may not have the luxury of indicating that you are "flexible" or "will discuss." You may have to insert an actual number.

Completely fill in the Personal History Form

By the way, I recommend that you download to your computer and/or print out a search firm's PHF and take your time answering the questions before you complete the form online. You don't want to risk having your PHF prematurely transmitted with incomplete information because you can't maneuver easily within a search firm's Web site. By completing one search firm's PHF, you will have captured the majority of data needed on other firms' forms.

- *Carefully review the blank PHF before answering any questions.* This will enable you to determine the layout of the online application, as they are all different. Some forms ask you to fill in boxes; others ask for information below (or above) the lines. Unless you have scanned the format, you may not catch this subtlety. While it may look nice, you've just communicated to the employer that you overlook details and do not always follow instructions.

  While I'm sure that you'll be able to attach your résumé to the PHF to help amplify the requested information, never type in "See résumé" as a substitute for completing the online form.

- *When in doubt about some question, leave it blank.* You can always answer it later. If the information will not harm you, as you feel it is best explained in person or if it is of a highly confidential nature, indicate "Will discuss." If anything, it might be intriguing enough for a curious recruiter to call you if your background is sufficiently appealing. Questions that might make you uncomfortable may be deemed to be perfectly appropriate to the recruiter. Don't have a hair trigger about something that is minor in the grand scheme of things. When in doubt, leave it blank or indicate you considered the question, responding with a dash "–."

- *Follow directions carefully.* Accuracy and following directions are important. It's not uncommon for a search firm to imbed an assessment element in the PHF. Such a practice would not be unexpected for a boutique search firm that specializes in industry segments where precision, accuracy, attention to detail, thoroughness, and ability to handle ambiguity are important. Ergo, how well you complete the PHF is one indication of how closely aligned you might be to those traits the search firm deems valuable.

CHAPTER 14

TARGET ORGANIZATIONS— WHO, WHAT, WHERE, AND WHY?

Five Steps in Identifying Your Target Organizations

Target those companies where you are best known and capable of quickly contributing. Certainly, you will be considering such things as, type of industry, kind of products/service offerings, manufacturing processes, forms of distribution, marketing channels, company size, geographic location (domestic, international, or global), operating styles, corporate culture, and general reputation, to name a few.

By way of an example, think of a target. The bulls-eye is in the center, with a series of concentric circles emanating away from it. Accordingly, your highest-priority target organizations would be those in the bulls-eye. Organizations further out from the bulls-eye are deemed, by you, to have lesser priority. Developing your target organization list of 20 to 50 companies is similar. Your "A" priority list of companies is very specific and very focused, and is composed of "core companies." You broaden your list of companies by adding to it organizations related to your primary career focus.

Determining your target organizations:

1. Identify the Standard Industrial Classification (SIC) codes for your current organization (and all previous companies). SIC codes are found in many of the resource directories online or in your area library. These might be your "A" priority organizations if you want to stay in the niche you currently are in or have been in.
2. Identify the major competitors of your current organization (and all previous companies) and the SIC codes for all of their operating units. These might, also, be your "A" priority organizations, unless you have noncompete restrictive covenants from your prior employer.
3. Identify companies (and their SIC codes) in related industries or related product lines. These might be considered your "B" priority organizations.

4. Identify companies (and their SIC codes) with related manufacturing processes, technologies, or related distribution channels. Likewise, these companies might be considered your "B" priority organizations.

5. Identify companies (and their SIC codes) in your preferred geographic region through the use of selected free or subscription services on the Internet. If you haven't been to your local library lately, check it out. Libraries have a number of amazing resources and talented people trained and willing to assist you. Depending on the importance geography plays in your career search campaign, the priorities might range from "I will not relocate!" to "I am open to relocating anywhere, worldwide." If you are looking locally, your goal is to create widespread visibility for your availability, regardless of the industry.

To illustrate, let's develop a list of target organizations for our fictitious job changer, Michele Cannon.

MICHELE D. CANNON

Background Profile:
President Acme International—Chemicals and Coatings products.

1. Michele identified the SIC codes for Acme International and all of its subsidiaries:

    2851 (paints), 3479 (coatings), 2816 (inorganic pigments), 2869 (industrial organic chemicals).

2. For each of Acme International's SIC codes, Michele identified its major competitors and the SIC codes for all of their operating units. Competitors' SIC Codes are
    2891 (adhesives and sealants), 5162 (plastic materials), 5169 (chemicals and allied products), 5198 (paints and varnishes—wholesale), 5231 (paint, glass, and wallpaper stores).

3. Michele identified companies and their SIC codes in related industries or product lines. For instance, DuPont is not a direct competitor to Acme's niche, they are in the broad industry category of chemicals—inorganic and organic. Likewise, most companies in the 2850 and 2860 series of the SIC codes would be potential target organizations, as they are all chemicals related.

4. Michele identified companies (and their SIC codes) with related manufacturing technologies or distribution channels. Michele's familiarity with high-speed chemical product handling, packaging, and distribution can likewise be applied in many other fields.

5. Michele also identified companies (and their SIC codes) in her preferred geographic region of Chicago through the use of several free and subscription Web sites. Additionally, Michele also paid a valuable visit to her area library, which educated her further on additional directories to source online.

6. Part of Michele's research included perusing the Web sites and news releases of her top target organizations (through Hoovers.com, *The* Wall Street *Journal,* and *The New York Times,* to name three sources).

Explanation of SIC Code Numbers

When you are researching businesses, the SIC (Standard Industrial Classification) code is one of the most valuable tools available. Knowing how the SIC codes categorize industries enables you to zero in on your desired organizational niche. Indeed, you'll be utilizing SIC codes regardless of whether you are referencing a hard-bound directory or using the Internet. The following explanation of the SIC code system is intended to help you understand how you can cross-reference industry sectors more effectively.

The U.S. government developed the SIC code system in conjunction with the private business sector. Prior to its development, no system was available that comprehensively captured U.S. industry. Describing our economy by defining its types of activities, the SIC code is a universal system of comparison through which we can study today's businesses.

SICs are an integral part of any business study. Marketers and advertisers rely on them to pinpoint the kinds of businesses they want to reach. When economists study business segments, they use SICs to identify and compare industries—especially when they are analyzing changes or trends in business and the economy. Job hunters use SICs to identify appropriate or interesting prospective employers. Finally, SIC codes are used for hard-copy and computer-assisted searches in business and research everywhere.

SIC codes divide all economic activity into 10 major divisions. These business segments are represented by the first two digits in the SIC code:

Agriculture/Forestry/Fishing	01–09	Wholesale Trade	50–51
Mining	10–14	Retail Trade	52–59
Construction	15–17	Finance, Insurance, and	
Manufacturing	20–39	Real Estate Services	60–67
Transportation,		Business Services	70–89
Communication, and		Health/Social Services and	
Public Utilities	40–49	Public Administration	91–97

Each line of business is placed within one of these 10 divisions and is assigned a code. A four-digit SIC code is the most widely used, but some systems define businesses to six or seven digits.

The first two digits describe the general line of business. The third and fourth digits further pinpoint the business activity. For instance:

22	Manufacturing—Textile mill products
227	Manufacturing—Floor coverings
2272	Manufacturing—Tufted carpets, rugs

Virtually anyone who touches the business world will find the SIC system invaluable in locating the right kinds of businesses. Through your online or library research, you'll be able to find the SIC alphabetical and numeric code descriptions.

At any library, I'd advise you to ask if there is a charge to printout any databases or save to a CD. Sometimes there is a charge for the retrieval of such information. Before you blindly pay for a lengthy database printout, ask to examine a sample run. Then you can determine if it meets your specific needs. The ideal format of your target organizations should include corporate headquarters addresses and contact information, company officers, and revenue size (if not private). Better to be cautious than to be surprised and disappointed if you pay for something that doesn't help you in your search.

Guidelines for Contacting Organizations

Even though mailing your résumé to target organizations statistically will yield a low response, there are some proven guidelines for doing so if you want to pursue this venue. The key is to mail in smaller batches of no more than 50, followed by highly assertive networking. You don't want to contact more than 50 companies because you won't be able to follow up expeditiously. To that end, I recommend that you choose your top 20 to 50 target organizations. Let's say you're the Chief Marketing Officer (CMO) and you want to work at Pixar. So, with each networking contact, you ask that person if he or she knows anyone at Pixar or if he or she knows anyone who might know anyone at Pixar. That's how to go after target organizations when you are networking.

Call key decision makers in your target firms. If you are focused on the "C-Suite" the person you want to talk to would probably be the CEO or group president, depending on the size of the organization. If you might report to a C-Suite officer, then the appropriate functional head is probably your target.

If at all possible, talk to executives at least two levels up from where you would report. Why? If you contact the individual to whom you would report, you might pose too much of a threat and, also, that person may not have the same broad-based exposure to organizational needs as a more senior executive.

Unless you are a human resources professional, avoid sending your résumé initially to the human resources department. Human resource staffs are trained to screen out résumés. Your goal is to create a lot of visibility with a broad-based mailing and an aggressive follow-up telephone campaign, employing your network contacts. Consider 10 calls a day to or about your target organizations to be a good stretch goal, given all the other networking calls you'll be making. Instead of viewing these as "cold calls," maintain the perspective that considers these to be marketing calls to organizations predisposed to your background and experiences.

The following are some guidelines and examples when contacting organizations.

1. Quickly introduce yourself, your area of expertise, and your referral source (if appropriate), and your reason for calling.

   Charlie, my name is Michele Cannon. I was formerly the President of Acme Services Group, a $2.6 billion global chemicals company. I met you several months ago at the Institute's meeting when you spoke. Your remarks resonated with me, as I also believe in many of the same issues.

   As you may have heard, Acme was acquired by Colorant Partners and recently reorganized. While I could have stayed at Acme in a senior strategic role, I elected to exit. To that end, I am beginning to search for a senior P&L position in the industry with my old company's full knowledge and support. As I put together a list of the companies I wanted to work with, your company was one of the top five.

2. If the company previously sent you a rejection letter:

   Recently I sent you a letter with my résumé informing you of my intentions, which you graciously forwarded to Human Resources. They got back to me, indicating that while there are no current openings, they would keep my résumé on file for future opportunities, as they were intrigued with my background. I appreciate their willingness to do that beyond a standard form letter. Nonetheless, I would appreciate the opportunity to meet you in person, senior executive to senior executive, to network.

3. Indicate the reason why their organization is a target. It is advantageous for you to identify why you have targeted a given company and what value you feel you can bring to the firm. Include some of your skills, abilities, or accomplishments that may fit the company's needs.

   I selected your company as a prospective employer for three reasons. You are a highly visible company with a reputation for having (1) quality products, (2) excellent customer relations, and (3) a commitment to expect the best from your employees. I feel I possess many of those same qualities that have helped your company grow, namely, a results-producing focus, team orientation, strong leadership capabilities, and excellent interpersonal skills.

4. Ask for the opportunity to meet for purposes of introduction so that, should a need arise, they will already know of your abilities. It is also an opportunity to network! Suggest a date in the next few weeks when it might be possible to meet briefly.

   While I recognize that you do not have any bona fide openings, I would still like to meet for purposes of introduction. In your recent speech, you indicated that your company is always on the lookout for new ideas and the right people to develop new products, save money, and enhance customer relations.

   I can make a difference. Two things I know with great certainty: All successful businesses are highly adaptive to change and how to make money for my organizations.

   I believe the time to learn about the availability of new technology and new people is before a bona fide need exists. To that end, I would like to meet and introduce myself. And a company requires an individual with my background in the future, you will have already known about me. Can we meet sometime within the next couple of weeks?

5. Don't accept a "No" answer too readily. Respond with phrases such as:

   I understand that your schedule is full; however, my skills are excellent, and I know that I can be a valuable part of your succession plan. I can be brief and would very much appreciate a few moments of your time.

6. If you don't get an interview with your target company, respond with something like the following:

Well, I understand. I do appreciate your consideration. I would like to check back with you periodically to see if your schedule frees up in a month or so. Would that be all right?

May I also send another résumé for your center desk drawer in the event that you should encounter a need within the near future? Thanks.

7. Write a thank-you letter. After all, you have introduced yourself, told the person what you are interested in, described your qualifications, and asked for an interview.
8. Write a follow-up date on your calendar, describing the nature of your next contact. Then, when the time arises, make the call!

Resource Directories—Internet and the Public Library

I recommend that you quickly master a number of sources for general business information, job leads, and in-depth profiles on the management of your target organizations. Accordingly, your two most important main sources are the Internet and the public library, as I have already mentioned.

Rather than spend a lot of time here on the Internet, see Chapter 15, "Into the Vortex—Internet Career Searching (Plus Traditional Classified Advertisements)." Remember the library. As a kid it was filled with wonder and great things to read and see. As adults, somewhat jaded by the lightning-fast access to data via the Internet, we've often overlooked the resources the library has waiting for us. Let's take a walk down memory lane. Your area library has books and brochures that contain useful career information, especially if you are exploring the viability of entrepreneuring. Out-of-town newspapers at the library may be a source of employment in nearby areas. Industrial directories list employers in your geographic area that might have a need for your services.

Librarians are delighted to assist you in finding the materials you need. Research librarians can help you identify some excellent resources that you might not be able to have access to or be aware of otherwise. Ask for help in locating job sources and job search information. Most libraries have more online subscription service Web sites than you'd want to pay for yourself. The following is a list of basic library resources that will provide you with a good source of employers who may be able to use your skills:

Library Checklist

Financial/Business Directories

- Career Search
- EDGAR (SEC filings)

- *Hoover's*
- *Standard & Poor's Register*
- *Value Line*

Manufacturing Directories

- *Billion Dollar Directory* (and corporate families)
- *Corporate 1000*
- *Directory of Corporate Affiliations*
- *International Directory of Corporate Affiliations*
- *Million Dollar Directory* (Volumes I, II, III)
- *Moody's Index*
- State Directory of Manufacturers

Papers/Periodicals

- *The New York Times*
- *The Wall Street Journal*
- *Chronicles of Higher Education*
- *Crain's Chicago/Cleveland Business*
- *Federal Career Opportunities*
- *Federal Jobs Digest*
- National daily and major metropolitan Sunday papers

Service Directories

- *Directory of Consultants and Consulting Organizations*
- *Directory of Executive Recruiters (U.S. and International editions)*
- *Dun's Directory of Service Companies*

Technology/R&D Directories

- *Directory of American Research and Technology*

Venture Capital Directories

- *Pratt's Guide to Venture Capital Sources*
- *Venture's Guide to International Venture Capital*

Miscellaneous

- Annual reports
- *Encyclopedia of Associations*
- *Directories in Print*
- Trade publications

Get to Your Target Organizations Through Networking

On average, 3 percent of all executives successfully connect with their target organizations via direct mailings (e-mails or snail mail). That's not a very high percentage for you to spend a tremendous amount of time and effort on. Indeed, one of my clients recently challenged me on why anyone then should ever contact organizations directly. My response was twofold: First, people *do* occasionally connect through the process of e-mailing their credentials directly. Second, you significantly raise the odds of standing out when you follow up on your e-mails via networking. (This is where the percentages can increase from 3 percent success—through direct mailing—to 80 percent success—through focused networking). The reality is that when you network in your given industry, provided you don't have a restrictive noncompete covenant, organizations will be most receptive to your experiences, accomplishments, and capabilities. In most cases, your competitors will see you as an attractive candidate.

CHAPTER 15

INTO THE VORTEX—INTERNET CAREER SEARCHING—(PLUS TRADITIONAL CLASSIFIED ADVERTISEMENTS)

The Internet—Friend or Foe?

The Internet. It's your best resource and your biggest time waster. It's great for sending and receiving instant messages. It's a boon for conducting research and accessing job search engines. However, the Internet's advantages also can represent your greatest stumbling block if left unchecked. You have instant access to so much fascinating information on the Internet that you can find yourself instantly distracted if you aren't disciplined. On more than one occasion, I have found myself sucked into its vortex. So has every one of our clients at one time or another. The Internet. It's fast. It's evolving at a frenzied pace. But is it your best approach to open the right doors that lead to the right job?

Why Use the Internet?

The Internet provides ready access to the following:

- Local, national, and international career opportunities
- Changing markct conditions with companies advertising online
- Research, breaking news, or position listings
- Unlimited reach to specific company's job sites
- Internet networking
- Articles of interest to send to networking contacts and interviewers as a value-added

The Stats—Good News, Bad News

Based on our experience, the likelihood of an executive landing an opportunity through the Internet or classified advertisements is very low. Currently, it's less than 2 percent. I suspect as time marches on, and as more search firms increasingly rely on the Internet and other forms of technology, this percentage might increase slightly. Nevertheless, the Internet is an incredibly valuable search tool and one that you should aim to master.

I'll address the particulars of searching through classified advertisements at the end of this chapter.

The Internet Job Market and the Lottery

It is estimated that there are more than

- 130,000 employers in 20 countries generating more than a million job postings annually.
- 1.6 million "eyeball" visits each day.
- 35 million active résumés online.
- 25 million job opportunities posted per quarter.

That means that there are millions of millions of job seekers looking for an opportunity to change jobs. The reality is that your chances of successfully connecting through the Internet, for example, are slim as the competition is staggering:

- Your résumé on the Internet: 1 of 35-plus million résumés
- Odds of winning the Illinois Lottery: 1 in 10.2 million

The odds of your winning the Illinois Lottery are 3.5 times greater than your landing a job through the Internet!

As mind-boggling as the odds are, a talented executive client of ours with a great background in software development and e-commerce had three job offers found through the various search engines. While not all the jobs for him were fully appropriate, it illustrated that bona fide executive roles are posted. Based on his experience, I gave him a dollar and told him to buy me a lottery ticket! I'm still waiting to collect my winnings.

It's All About Focus

Before you jump into the Web, it's advisable that you have a specific objective in mind and that you stay focused, lest you get lost and distracted.

Another good friend of ours is a very capable IT consultant. He shared with us the highly practical approach he uses. He limits his time on the Internet. He sets an alarm. He knows specifically what he wants to retrieve from the Web. He said that he plays a game with himself: he thinks of himself as a special agent on a Mission Impossible assignment. The rules: focus on the mission, get in, retrieve the data, and get out. No extra moseying around. He's got networking to do and interviews to conduct.

Consider the Internet a valuable tool, just one of many, and not the main focus of your search efforts.

Effective Internet Search Strategies

Our Internet "jackpot winner" has some sage advice for your Internet use:

- When in search of opportunities:
  - Know what positions interest you.
  - Find cheap or free sites where you can effectively search for opportunities. There is a listing of our favorite sites on RL's Web site, under Career Resource Links.
  - Have technology work for you by using e-mail alerts or search agents that notify you of opportunities that are close to your specifications.
  - Answer Internet job postings the same day.
  - Apply to all postings that come close to your expectations and for which you are qualified. A quick 30-minute conversation, if selected, would help you determine your options.
  - Don't consider positions in geographical locations where you would not consider living.
  - Do not allow Internet browsing/job searching to get in the way of regular networking.
  - Maintain the privacy of your résumé; do not post it publicly as there is a high probability of your being taken advantage of by scam artists. Your résumé could also be blasted throughout the marketplace without your consent by unscrupulous persons hoping that your credentials hook some organization. Plus, the rise of identity theft should make you wary of blindly trusting others.
- When researching and networking:
  - Utilize free Internet research capabilities.
  - Target the Web sites of companies for latest news updates.
  - Join networking groups or professional associations that have significant electronic capabilities and databases.

Benefits of a Resource Site Like LinkedIn.com

Use the Internet to network with people who know others, which will eventually lead you to opportunities. I'm a firm believer that we truly live in a small world and that we are only several people away from connecting with almost anyone on the planet.

There are a number of remarkable, free, Internet networking services, such as LinkedIn (www.LinkedIn.com). These networking sites bring new meaning to the concept of "six degrees of separation." Such services enable you to search and electronically network for many diverse products and services, especially jobs and people. These sites identify who you or your contacts know at a given company, which could conceivably lead you to an introduction to the hiring authorities. Here are benefits:

- You can connect to an unlimited network of people, including finding past work colleagues and friends with whom you might have lost contact.
- You can search for companies, people, or current job listings for a particular company, location, and position specifications. In many cases you will be able to identify the best persons to help you connect with your targeted person. Plus, you can decide if you want to be visible, connect with them, or not.
- You can identify key officers and board members that are currently or were affiliated with a certain company.
- Anytime you make updates to your account, notices are sent to your contacts automatically. So, it's a great way to maintain your visibility without having to reach out to everyone individually.

Search Engines and Employment Sites

Times are a-changin' and so is the landscape of search engines and job sites. It's like being at a smorgasbord with all your favorite foods. Very enticing. Very overwhelming. So many choices; so little time. As of this writing there are 840,000 sites catering to the executive job seeker, and they are growing exponentially every day. It stands to reason that it would be a huge waste of time to research all 840,00 sites for your online campaign. What to do? Network. Ask search firm recruiters and respected colleagues what search engines/Web sites they have found particularly helpful. Visit a few sites. Remember though, that some Web sites might have yielded tremendous results for one person, but might just be totally dry for you.

Spend no more than 10 percent of your job search energy on the Internet. A mistake that many make is spending more than 70 percent of their efforts on the Internet and only 5 percent networking. Use the Internet. Don't let the Internet "use you." Now that my lecture on the evils of the Internet is over, this section lists a few sites in which our clients have had success.

For the latest online job site resources, go to www.RobertsonLowstuter.com and click on Career Resources links. In addition, here are but a few of the better job search sites as of this writing:

Job Search Sites

6Figure Jobs	www.6figurejobs.com
CareerBuilder *	www.careerbuilder.com
Executive site	www.execglobalnet.com
IT site	www.dice.com
Indeed	www.indeed.com
Monster	www.monster.com
Resource sites	www.resume.magic.com
Simply Hired	www.simplyhired.com

*The Wall Street Journal and other major metropolitan papers utilize areerBuilder as their job search Web site.

Subscription Sites That Charge a Fee

BlueSteps	www.BlueSteps.com
CustomDataBanks	www.custom databanks.com
ExecutiveTrumpet	www.executivetrumpet.com
ExecuNet	www.execunet.com
Directory of Executive Recruiters	www.kennedyinfo.com
NetShare	www.netshare.com
TheLadders	www.theladders.com

Fee or No Fee—That's a Great Question!

Like so many other things in life—there's a balance to be struck. Fee or no fee to access a database and search engines? I recommend that you explore the free services first to test out the viability of these sites. If I were you, I'd also ask my network what subscription sites they have found most helpful. Test drive a service with a limited trial subscription first before signing up with extended services that you may not need.

For example, CustomDataBanks provides you with contact information and helpful descriptions of almost 16,000 search firms (about half of them are retained executive search firms). Additional for-fee databases include 7,500-plus rapidly growing companies and approximately 2,400 private equity firms with 7,500 key contacts. The fee for the Search-Select enables you access the majority of the retained executive search firms in the U.S.

through Kennedy's Directory of Executive Recruiters. It is another great paid Web access database that identifies more than 7,000 large and boutique retained executive search firms and 15,000 recruiters, indexed by 80-plus job functions and 120-plus industries. As of this writing, the fees range from approximately $400 to $650 for annual subscriptions.

I don't know about you. But in my case, I always look at things rather simplistically. If by spending $500 on a database I can shave a month off of my career search, then it's a no-brainer. I'll be ahead tens of thousands of dollars for that modest investment.

Note: As many libraries already have paid subscriptions to some of the fee-based Web sites, you might call or visit to find out what local services have free access. Ask them about CareerSearch, a 1.5 million company Web access database which provides privately held and publicly traded company descriptions, addresses, key contacts, and e-mail addresses. It has powerful search capabilities by industry, SIC code, location, and key words to fine-tune your research.

Executive Search Firm Sites

Virtually every retained executive search firm has its own Web site where you can inquire about current searches and post your résumé, often after completing an online personal history form. It is advantageous for you to post your résumé—then follow up and network into each firm. An overall "Guide to Internet Recruiting Sites" can be found at www.recruitersnetwork.com/sites.

Major Search Firms:

The following is a list some of the top retained executive search firms.

Battalia Winston International	www.battaliawinston.com
Boyden	www.boyden.com
Christian & Timbers	www.ctnet.com
DHR International	www.dhrintl.net
Egon Zehnder International	www.egonzehnder.com
Edward E. Kelley & Partners	wwwewkp.com (formerly A.T. Kearney)
Heidrick & Struggles	www.heidrick.com
Highland Partners	www.highlandpartners.com
IIC Partners	www.iicpartners.com
Korn/Ferry International	www.kornferry.com
Lucas Group	www.lucasgroup.com
Ray & Berndtson	www.rayberndtson.com
Russell Reynolds	www.russellreynolds.com

Signium International	www.signium.com
Slayton Search Partners	www.slaytonintl.com
Spencer Stuart	www.spencerstuart.com
Stanton Chase Intl	www.stantonchase.com
Whitehead Mann	www.wmann.com

Boutique or Regional Search Firms:

By way of example, Chicago, like every major city, has a number of senior-level boutique or regional firms that you may want to consider such as:

Blackshaw, Olmstead, Lynch, Koenig, Kreutz	www.bolksearch.com
Came Sweeney	www.camesweeney.com
Clarey, Andrews, Klein	www.clarey-a-klein.com
Crist Associates	www.cristassociates.com
Ken Clark International	www.kenclark.com
O'Hara International	www.oharainc.com
Patrick Delaney & Associates	www.pdelaney.us
Ronald Dukes & Associates	www.rdukesassociates.com
The Hollins Group	www.thehollinsgroup.com

Niche Search Firms:

Many executive search firms have niches, as opposed to functional or industry specialization. For example, one such niche is occupied by firms conducting searches predominantly for minority candidates. Given that I live and work in the Chicago area, here is a sampling of Chicago minority firms.

David Gomez & Associates	www.dgai.com
White, Roberts, Stratton	www.wrssearch.com
Carrington & Carrington	www.ccltd.com

Remember that location is not the only consideration for including search firms in your mailing and networking list. Because of long standing personal relationships, a search firm located in Philadelphia could have a search engagement with a company in La Jolla, California. Indeed, the president of one Chicago-based boutique firm indicated that in one year, 70 percent of his business was out of town. Bottom-line: identify and network into top players in your industry niche through, large, boutique regional firms nationwide or internationally, if that is your focus or one of your options.

Search Agents or E-mail Alerts

Many job search sites and nonrecruiter Web sites, have e-mail alert capabilities, paid for or free. From one site to the next, these e-mail alerts are referred to as "search agents," "job alerts," "e-mail alerts," and so on. For ease of referencing them, I'll only refer to them as search agents. Such search agents are useful for identifying your selection criteria and e-mailing the results of this criteria to your e-mail inbox daily. Once the e-mails are received, it takes no more than 30 minutes to browse through all of these e-mail alerts and make decisions on what to pursue.

Often you can establish up to five e-mail alerts per site. Some sites allow more than five search agents; others allow fewer. Nonetheless, these alerts are either sent separately each time there is an opportunity that matches your parameters or the site will bundle them and send them in one e-mail to you, per your preference.

Sites, such as www.simplyhired.com, or www.indeed.com each search through 50-plus career-related sites, such as Monster and CareerBuilder, so that you don't have to access each site separately.

Setting Up Your Search Agent Account

The process for signing up for Search Agents is easy and is as follows:

1. Begin by going to www.monster.com, for instance. Click on My Monster. If you don't have an account, go through the registration form carefully. Be attentive to ensure that you are not signing up for anything that will cost you.
2. Once you are signed up, click on My Account/My Monster. About halfway down the page, under Job Search Agents, click on Create Search Agent. Your selection criteria are as follows:
   - Job Location
   - Job Category
   - How often you would like to have these e-mail alerts sent to you?
   - Part-time, Full-time, etc.
   - Keyword. This is the most important element of the search agent criteria. See the next section. Indicate specific search agent title.

Congratulations! You have just signed up for a search agent that will automatically alert you to relevant opportunities according to your parameters. Keep in mind, you can modify your search agent criteria if you are receiving too many or too few responses.

Keywords for Searching Online—What's the Trick?

Every Internet job search site, such as Monster.com, is built on top of a search engine. This search engine determines what results to display back to you based on your selection criteria, none of which is more important than the keyword.

Note: Typing "VP" as the keyword may not return positions specified as "vice president." You might have to create a separate agent with the keyword phrase "vice president." Similarly, typing "CEO" for the keyword may not return positions specified as "Chief Executive Officer." Test your agent by running it online before you finalize what keyword to use. Just be alert to the fact that different sites allow different selection criteria.

For example, say Michele Cannon is desirous of being employed at a midsize manufacturing company with aspirations to expand internationally. Ideally, she'd like to be the CEO or COO of a private equity firm's portfolio company, whereby she could have a sizable equity stake.

The key words in Michele Cannon's search agent listings for her perfect job, then, should minimally include the following: CEO, Chief Executive Officer, COO, Chief Operating Officer, General Manager, global P&L responsibility, and private equity firms. Key industry segment terms might include chemicals, coatings, healthcare, and industrial products.

Network Smarts—Some Cautions

- Don't fall prey to the mistaken belief that if you pay for it, it's better, by definition. However, when in doubt about the value of a for-fee service, determine if you can have a limited-cost, trial subscription.
- When creating your account online and posting your résumé, make sure you are clear about the decisions you make.
  - Do you want your résumé public or private? (I recommend keeping it private and not posting it on any Web site.)
  - Looking for consulting positions? (I recommend that you avoid saying "yes" to this temptation, even if you are contemplating consulting. There is a high probability that you will be scammed with some bogus con. If you want consulting, you keep control over where and how your contacts are utilized.)
  - If you publicly post your résumé, you will invariably get contacted by a few people misrepresenting themselves and opportunities. Be very wary and very careful before you leap into something you have not keenly evaluated.

Maintaining Your Online Accounts

- Keep a list of what accounts you've created and on what sites.
- Update or tweak these account every two weeks. Recruiters look for recently updated accounts, or résumés, even though nothing significantly changed in your profile.
- Some sites provide stats on how many times your résumé has been searched for and looked at. Reset these stats if you make changes.
- Remember the purpose of the search agents/e-mail alerts is to get someone to read your résumé and contact you for a job.

 Job sites are *not* designed to find the ideal candidate. It is clearly a case of quantity over quality.

Résumé Blasters—Convenience That Can Kill You

Many of us effectively use services for convenience. Having a lawn or maid service are examples. Rarely do we do our own plumbing, electrical, cabinetry, dry walling, asphalt resealing, reroofing, appliance or carpeting installation, and a hundred other tasks requiring specialized knowledge or skills. Therein lies the danger. We are accustomed to utilizing services that promote convenience.

Résumé blasters is a Web service that does provide convenience, yet may do irreparable harm to your search. As you respond to an online ad or post your specifications on a search engine employing a search agent, some Web sites will blast your résumé to thousands of contingency recruiters, employers, and any site that posts an opportunity that is even remotely close to your search agent parameters. This blanketing in the marketplace is similar to the indiscriminate approach that most contingency recruiters use. It's akin to throwing Jell-O at the wall; if you throw enough, some of it will stick. In my opinion, it's a dangerous practice for you, an executive, in which to engage. When blasting your credentials, you do not have any control over where your résumé is going. You are being represented by a service that also sends out the gamut of résumés (administrative, professional, supervisory, and possibly hourly résumés). You run the risk of having your credentials and identity being manipulated or misused. Simply put, you do not want to be associated with such a service.

One of our clients mistakenly sent his résumé to such a site that looked very promising and geared toward executives. This firm blasted Bob's résumé out into cyberspace without regard to whether there were any positions available. Coincidently, it was sent to an organization Bob was targeting about the same time he was contacted by a recruiter firm retained to conduct the search. Ultimately, Bob was hired. The résumé blaster demanded a sizable fee from the company. The company refused to pay a fee for this unsolicited résumé. This unscrupulous firm then sought to get the $35,000 fee from Bob. Bob refused to pay. The résumé blaster sued him. After much agonizing deliberation and escalating attorney fees, Bob settled for $8,000 out of his own pocket! The moral of this tale of woe: be very, very careful about engaging resume blasters and non-retained executive search firms. Read the fine print twice, and have your attorney review any such online contract before you sign on. You should always contact the Association of Executive Search Consultants (AESC) at www.aesc.com for its opinion about a firm/Web site claiming to be a retained search firm. When in doubt, walk away.

 Résumé scanners only search for *key words* in your résumé. They are not experts. Their role is to screen out versus screen in.

Newspaper/Classified Ads—Prehistoric or Viable Source?

As we have been discussing, an increasing number of executive positions are being advertised on the Internet. Correspondingly, the percentage of executive roles showing up in the classified pages of *The Wall Street Journal* or *The New York Times*, to name two papers, is dramatically decreasing. Do you remember me saying in Chapter 11 that we estimate that only 2 percent of all the executive jobs are filled through listings on the Internet or in the classifieds? Further, the majority of these executive positions are now disproportionately filled through the Net, not the classifieds. The point being, even if you were to conduct a national campaign, there is little need for you to track down all the major metropolitan newspapers, given the access to ads through the Internet. To that end, I'm only going to highlight the relevant considerations when managing the nuances of responding to advertisements.

- While *The Wall Street Journal* and all major metropolitan newspapers will have advertisements for executive positions, from time to time, many of them utilize Career Builder as an electronic source for such listings. To that end, I'd recommend that you access Career Builder first, before attempting to track down open executive positions in regional newspaper listings.

Responding to Classified Newspaper Ads

Fundamentally, there are two kinds of advertisements for your consideration: "Blind Ads" and "Open Ads." Blind ads are classified ads in which the search firm or company seeking executives is not known. Typically, the only way to answer the ad is to respond to a P.O. Box number. Conversely, open ads have the organization clearly identified, often with the name of the individual to whom qualified executives should respond.

Blind Ads Tips

1. Wait three days after the ad's appearance before sending your letter and résumé to the box number in care of the paper in which the ad appeared. As the majority of all responses will be sent the same or next day of the ad's appearance, by waiting three days your résumé will not have as much competition for the reader's attention. (However, for e-mail job postings, respond the same day!)
2. Scan or type in all the relevant ads on your computer for electronic tracking, or do it manually, as you like. If you are headed down the manual route, get a three-ring binder and tape a copy of the ad to a sheet of paper to allow for note taking. Do not tape more than three ads per page. This will be part of your filing system. To effectively stay on top of all your activity, it is advisable to *review your files daily*.
3. Indicate the date of
   - The ad's appearance (and newspaper)
   - When your letter and résumé were sent
   - Three weeks after the ad's appearance to allow for a second mailing
4. If you are worried about confidentiality and do not want your résumé to be received by a certain company, place your résumé in an envelope marked with the name of the firm you wish to avoid. Most newspapers running blind ads will honor your request. Use wording such as, "If Box XYZ is Company ABC, please destroy the contents of this envelope."
5. Responses to blind ads continue to be forwarded from the paper to the hiring company usually for a period of 30 days by the newspaper. If you send out a second résumé response within this four-week window of opportunity, your letter and résumé will stand out above the competition.

   Conversely, if you do not respond within this four-week window, your résumé and second letter may be discarded. For effective language that could be used in a second mailer, please refer to the letter examples in Chapter 8, "Create Powerful Letters That Evoke Action."

Open Ads Tips

1. When the organization is identified, we recommend that you get online or call the company and ask for the name of the person who heads up the department or function in which you most likely would work. If possible, probe the decision maker regarding position demands and company needs. Minimally, you want to make a positive connection.
2. Send your résumé and letter to the department head, not the person in the ad. Your letter should be warm and slightly informal, given that you connected with the person.
3. It is also recommended that you enter the position's particulars in your electronic database or tape a copy of the ad in your three-ring notebook, if you are using a manual system.
4. Send a second mailing within four weeks or, better still, follow up with a telephone call to the decision maker and discuss your capabilities again or ascertain the status of the search. Examples of marketing letters can be found in Chapter 8.

How to Respond to Ads That Want Salary Information

While the preferred procedure is *not* to provide the data, there is a risk either way you go. If you respond and the salary is too high or too low, you can be ruled out by a résumé scanner for being over- or underqualified without really reading your qualifications. On the other hand, there is a risk that you will be rejected by a clerk who is screening résumés using the arbitrary ruling that people will be rejected if they do not send salary information with their résumés. Either way, it is a roll of the dice. My bias is to *not* include your salary demands, or current salary/history as it may take away the one reason why a recruiter may call you.

Companies request salary data for a number of reasons. Generally, they may be looking for a fast means to sort out résumés or sometimes they want to see if the salary range for the job is in the ballpark. Whatever the reason, if you ignore the request, you can always handle it later when you call to follow up, or, for a blind ad, when you write in 20 days.

Following is some sample language about compensation for your consideration:

My compensation requirements are open and flexible for a position that has advancement potential, challenge, and provides an opportunity to contribute directly to profits.

or

I am seeking a position with an overall compensation package including benefits and incentive in the low $_____'s.

or

My current salary is $_____, and I am seeking a salary that ranges from $X to $Y, depending on the opportunity for growth and equity participation.

Industry- and Function-Specific Web Sites

Every function and industry has its own Web site, specific to its niche. Every professional association or trade group, regardless of size, has now or will soon have its own Web site. These sites are valuable for tracking down publications citing trends or identifying association board members for networking purposes. I recommend that you check out the Web site that is most appropriate for you.

Company Web Sites

My bias: Don't waste your time perusing the employment offerings on the Web sites of your target companies. You are much higher than anything that will probably be posted. You are better off employing search agents to scour the major employment Web sites versus you spending hours in pursuing company Web sites, no matter how productive it might make you feel.

Generally, corporate Web sites are not very helpful in assisting job seekers who are exploring employment opportunities at their companies. However, company sites may effectively highlight the organization's product line and often key management, including the board of directors.

Books on Searching the Internet

In addition to asking your networking contacts what books and resources they'd recommend, I suggest that you evaluate the latest books at Amazon.com, Barnes & Noble, Borders, Walden Books, and of course, other major and independent booksellers. You might even contact a knowledgeable reference librarian for a recommendation. As of this writing, I searched on Amazon.com and scrolled through 256 recent titles. Given that there are so many new books on Internet job searching, I hesitate to recommend any one specifically. My advice: Just be sure that the books have been published or updated within the last year, as the Internet is so rapidly changing.

The Internet. It represents the greatest advancement and tool for those "In Search of the Perfect Job." My wish for you is that you quickly master it and find what you need to conduct a highly effective search campaign. Happy surfing!

STEP 5
SELLING YOURSELF

CHAPTER 16

POWER INTERVIEWING—
BEAT OUT YOUR COMPETITION

What Would Robert Redford Do?

I have to confess. Whenever I get stuck, I mean, really stuck, I ask myself, "What would Robert Redford do?" I don't know Robert Redford, personally, though I'm sure he's a wonderful person. While I'm not sure how he truly is off-screen, I have a sense of how I want him to be.

In virtually all of his movies, Robert Redford plays pretty cool characters. He doesn't seem to get ruffled or become emotional. He exudes quiet confidence, boldness, integrity, and charisma. On and off the screen, he appears fully authentic and genuine. When he speaks it is with deep self-assuredness, humility, authority, and wisdom. This is how I want to be living my life.

Once I get a glimpse into what Robert Redford would do in my exact situation, I feel more grounded and certain. I also feel relieved, for I know that as I tap into my own and Robert's collective wisdom, I will produce a pretty awesome outcome. How could I not? I have now become my persona of Robert Redford: confident, authentic, articulate, wise, and calm.

Now, you might think this mental posturing is a little extreme; it's not. I am just turning up the dial a bit more than we're used to. You use this technique all the time, albeit perhaps at the unconscious level. You've thought back to a time in which an old boss effectively defused a potential conflict particularly well. You model some of her behavior and attitude. You admire the graciousness of someone else under tremendous pressure, and you wonder how he is able to remain optimistic and positive in the face of great adversity. The next time you act in the same way you might even have remembered where you got the inspiration to do so.

In this context, I invite you to think about your ideal role model, living or dead, real or imagined. This is a person with whom you resonate. With whom you identify. Your role model would always be able to recover when he misspoke, flubbed a sentence, or failed to behave as powerfully as he truly is. Your role model exhibits and reflects your core beliefs and behavior. Once you have identified your role model, write down his or her positive, powerful attributes (core attitudes, thoughts, feelings, and behavior) you admire and respect.

Why do this? What is the benefit? Do I really have to do all this? Let me answer these questions in reverse order: No, you do not have to identify your role model, though you get to. The benefit: You will show up more confident, authentic, innovative, and powerful. Why do this? When you are preparing for or are in the midst of an important interview, it's critical for you to be as bold, confident, and enthusiastic as you can be. If you can mentally capture what your "Robert Redford" might do or say to a given question, then you have significantly increased your chances of successfully nailing the interview. Additionally, since your ideal role model would powerfully distinguish himself or herself in the interview, so will you. Expanding on this theme, let's look at it from a slightly more detailed perspective.

Visualize Success—Create Personal Power

Visualize success . . . see yourself answering the tough questions successfully and confidently. If you saw yourself being successful, what would you be thinking as you entered the interviewer's office? If you knew, beyond a shadow of doubt, that you had the power to manage this interview exactly as you wanted it, how would you act?

Identify an individual that you know personally or suspect would have terrific interpersonal skills and interview superbly well. Have you identified that person? Can you visualize that person, physically, in your mind? Good. Let's have that person go on one of your interviews. Visualize your person getting ready, driving to your next interview, greeting the receptionist, being ushered into the interviewer's office, commenting on the surroundings, asking several initial leading questions to establish rapport, volunteering information, fielding tough questions, making observations about the company's growth, and effectively probing further into sensitive areas concerning organizational politics.

Feel the reactions of your person when he is asked a particularly difficult question and he confidently responds, "I'm sorry. I've never been asked that question before. While I'd like to think more about this question, what comes immediately to mind is _____." Visualize the interviewer and your person continuing to comfortably converse, exchanging information on a mutual "I talk . . . you talk" basis. Sense the interview drawing to a comfortable close. Visualize your person beginning to summarize the interview, thanking the interviewer for the opportunity to learn more about the company, expressing a mutual fit, appropriately asking for feedback and the "next step," and see your person exiting the building.

Now repeat this interview process, only with yourself in place of your person. Don't strive to have your words and actions be identical to your role model; rather, be confident and relaxed as you greet the interviewer. Ask and answer penetrating questions in a friendly conversational tone. See yourself handling with ease those questions that have always derailed you previously. Experience yourself as poised, confident, gracious, genuine, interpersonally warm, and technically competent.

Visualize the interviewer becoming enthusiastic about your candidacy and asking about your availability for a second round of interviews. Visualize yourself comfortably managing the interview's summary and close, asking for and giving appropriate feedback, and exiting the interview.

When our clients visualize their ideal role model and walk themselves through a preinterview "meditative state," they report back to us that their interviews went far better than any interviews previously. Most comment that it felt as if they were interviewing with an old friend. *"Déjà vu* all over again!" is how several clients described interviews after their modeling and visualization process. Like they had been there before . . . for indeed they had!

WORKSHEET 41

Visualize Successful Interviewing

- Given your visualization exercise, describe how your body feels right now.

- Describe your mental state as you were visualizing a successful interview.

- Describe your emotional state right now.

- Where did you get in trouble in your previous interviews, and what can you do to prevent its reoccurrence?

The Top Three Questions Asked by All Interviewers

The interview is the key to being hired. Your networking, marketing letters, or résumé may get you the interview, but you will get hired because of the solid job you do in the interview.

Ultimately, the employer is interested in the answers to three fundamental questions.

1. *Can you do the job*? Do you have the technical background, training, education, capabilities, and experiences to perform the work, short-term as well as long-term? Do you have a track record of results that match the opportunity? Do you have the knowledge, intellectual horsepower, and political savvy to do the job?

2. *Will you fit in*? Do you have well-developed interpersonal and organizational skills? Are these skills sufficient to interact well with the team? Do you exhibit an operating style and a level of flexibility that would accommodate changes? To what extent are you able to gain the widespread endorsement and advocacy of others? Will you get along well with my boss and peers? How well will you get along with the Board? How well will you get along with your peers and your subordinate staff? Will I be applauded or embarrassed for hiring you?

3. *Do you want the job*? How enthusiastic are you? How well prepared are you for the interview? How engaged are you? What do you know about the company, the competition, or end users? Did you ask to receive company literature before the interview? What did you discover about the company, its competitors, and its industry from the Internet research you conducted? How well did you challenge the interviewer through observations, comments, and questions? How did you communicate your desire to contribute to the business?

Given roughly the same level of technical competency, the employer will hire the person that she likes the best. If you both meet the minimum requirements, it is just common sense to go for the person who might be more personable on the job. It is true that "people hire people they like."

> The people hired are not always the best at doing the job, rather they are the best at getting the job.

No Mulligans Allowed! Prepare for the Interview

12 Commonsense Approaches That People Surprisingly Ignore

1. *Do your research*. Get online and find out about the company you are interviewing. Do the same level of research on its competition and its industry. Become conversant on any significant emerging technologies or socioeconomic or legislative trends that might impact the company. Take a trip to the local library, and ask the librarian for reference directories in which you can find additional information about the company, its competitors, its vendors, and its industry.

2. *Request company literature from the interviewer*. This might include annual reports, employee newsletters, promotional material, or product brochures that would help you prepare for the interview.

3. *Ask your network about the company*. It is always helpful if you get some advance "lay of the land" prior to the interview. You are interested in getting people's impressions of the corporate culture and personality of the company. As you know, every organization has its own unique culture. Minimally, you want to ensure that your personality is reasonably compatible with the company's. Remember my Wisconsin experience where I zigged and my boss zagged? I felt that I was an "A" player, but a "C" fit in that relationship. Your goal is to be an "A" player and an "A" fit.

4. *Anticipate, prepare, and practice, practice, practice*. It is essential that you *anticipate* questions that may be asked of you, *prepare* solid responses that are truthful and credible, and *practice* responding in a relaxed, confident, and authentic manner. Practice, practice, practice answering the interview questions throughout Chapters 16, 17, and 18. Read them out loud in front of a mirror, or have someone else ask you the questions. Practice in the car. In the shower. Anywhere and everywhere. Don't forget to smile, speak up, enunciate clearly, and practice using gestures until your "delivery" is and looks natural and genuine. You should become so skilled at interviewing that you can "plan out your spontaneity" in the interview.

5. *Maintain your perspective!* Don't lust after the job. You have a lot to offer. Remember, there is the potential for mutual benefit. The company will gain more (in terms of sales or profits) from hiring you than you gain from compensation being employed. If the company is exceedingly reluctant to hire you, and you are anxious about it, cool your jets. Interviewing is like dating. If you are more in love than the object of your affection is with you, your relationship is out of balance. It's not healthy and you risk being

taken advantage of or, minimally, you subordinate your own wonderful capabilities and judgments for fear of being rejected. We've seen many a talented executive involuntarily exit their companies because the advocacy for them was not present. Therefore, the relationship is out of balance.

If the interview process is excruciatingly laborious, note how you feel about it. Chances are this is highly reflective of the company's culture: careful, cautious, conservative, risk-averse, consensus-driven. If people are trying to make a perfect decision (versus an excellent decision), it may be indicative that something is a bit broken in the company. Indeed, people may be punished for making mistakes, hence, the glacial speed of hiring accomplished executives.

6. *Be engaged. Ask probing, penetrating questions.* Effective interviewing is a two-way street. A candidate who does not ask challenging questions runs the risk of being seen as weak, indecisive, or uninterested. Chances are, you may not be seen as being very engaged. As an employer, I want to see a high level of interest, aliveness, energy, and creativity displayed in the interview. Passive people are passive for any number of reasons: They might be intimidated by those in authority or the role for which they are interviewing. Or they might just be painfully shy, quiet, reflective, and analytical, which is often interpreted as being passive and nonengaged. Quiet, analytical people can still be enthusiastic and engaged. On the other hand, if everyone in an organization had a highly creative style, it might be the most fun and creative environment in which to work. The problem is that it would be chaos. Bottom line: Get grounded in your behavioral style; show up in all your many personality facets. Crank up your enthusiasm, your aliveness, and your creativity.

7. *You have rights as an interviewee.* You have the *right* to be treated with dignity and respect in the interview. If you feel a lot of tension in the interview, feel intimidated, find it impossible to turn it around to your advantage, you have the *right* to push back. Indeed, you should. Caution: You need to assess if you are way over- or underqualified for the job. If that is the case, the interviewer may be frustrated or angry at you for wasting his time. In other words, pay close attention to the interviewer's needs, and assess what you are doing, if anything, to evoke this kind of reaction on the interviewer's part.

We had one client, Karen, report that when she voiced her observation and feelings, the interviewer sighed and indicated that he was pulled out of a critical meeting to meet with her and he was totally distracted by a crisis out of state. Karen graciously insisted that he go attend to his crisis and that she welcomed the opportunity to continue the interview by phone when things settled down. The company executive was deeply grateful for her sensitivity and greatly impressed by her ability to see beyond the obvious. While Karen did have an incredible phone interview, subsequently, she elected not to pursue the opportunity.

When there is obvious stress or strain, assume 100 percent of the responsibility for it. Determine if you are not answering questions well or whether it is the interviewer's style of questioning that is throwing you off. You also should ponder how reflective this behavior is of the corporate culture. Calmly observe that you feel a great deal of tension. Ask the interviewer what seems to be the underlying issue to this. Often the intimidation tactics will immediately stop; the interviewer may acknowledge that he or she is conducting a stress interview to ascertain how well the person reacted under pressure. If you are being greatly inconvenienced by an unusual interview schedule, you have the *right* to ask for some accommodation to your own schedule. It is common for busy executives to have a full interviewing slate, with little room to shift one set of interviews in favor of another. By not accommodating every urgent request to interview, you create the impression that you are a talent in great demand, that you are busy as well, and that you have great worth so they should have a higher sense of urgency about your candidacy.

8. *Listen to your intuition.* When interviewing, your gut instincts reveal significant pieces of information that should be considered.

Most people do not seriously evaluate the data they collect from their intuitive "selves." They believe that how they are intuitively reacting to a person or a job opportunity is not a valid source of information. Years ago I took a job because I fell in love. I fell in love with the role, the title, the base salary, the bonus potential, the stock options, the double matching 401K plan, the profit-sharing/pension plan, the hiring bonus, the reporting relationship, access to the company plane, etc. When several top executives wondered why this role was being filled, I had the answer at the ready. I was so enamored by the role and opportunity that I did not pause and ask them why they thought the role was superfluous. Disappointingly, this was a highly toxic environment, and in this role/culture I was a "D" fit. I let my guard down. I should have listened to my gut that said, "Run as fast and as far away from this company as you can." Three months into this job, I went to my boss and asked him to explain again why he created the role. After 20 minutes of his enthusiastic explanations, I remember myself saying to him that, "Neither in my lifetime nor in yours would this role ever succeed in this culture." It was quite a learning experience, to say the least.

You might discover that you will be tempted to accept the first decent opportunity that comes along. Given the uncertainty of the future, it is very easy to rationalize yourself into a position while blindly ignoring your gut instincts that might very well be saying, "Whoa!"

9. *Dress appropriately.* Common sense prevails. You want to stand out from the crowd in a positive manner. Hair should be conservative. If you have a beard or mustache, it should be neatly trimmed or shaved off for the interview. You can always grow it back after you have been hired. Men should aim for a clean-cut appearance.

   Napoleon Hill once said, "You become what you think about." Fine clothing, which fits comfortably and flatters, helps instill confidence. If you think confident thoughts, so shall you behave. Women should wear a business suit, an attractive dress, or a skirt/blouse with a minimum amount of jewelry. Gentlemen and ladies, please, either zero or only the barest hint of cologne or perfume. You don't want to trigger an asthmatic attack on the part of the interviewer, as I had with one candidate I was interviewing. Men should preferably wear a suit, or a nice sports jacket, at least. In some areas of the country, it would seem out of place to wear a suit or a sports jacket, so you need to use your own judgment. When in doubt or even in the case of everyone else wearing casual business attire, overdress slightly. You are trying to make a positive impression.

   Remember: You never get a second chance to make a good first impression.

10. *Arrive early.* If you arrive at the reception station, less than 10 minutes ahead of time for an interview you're late! Being punctual is very important to a prospective employer. It gives him or her an idea of how responsible and reliable you are. If you come too early, you may have to wait for the employer, and it could be awkward. And it may interrupt the interviewer's schedule.

11. *Be cordial.* Take your mother's advice: Always be nice to everyone you meet. Anyone and everyone can have a positive (or negative) influence on the person who is conducting the interview. Many employees know that a position is open and people will be coming in for interviews. They also can spot strangers, and how you carry yourself will form an impression. If it is a good impression and it is passed on to the interviewer, it can only work in your favor. When I interview people, I always enlist the administrative staff to give me feedback on their impressions of the candidates. One of our clients, the president of a hospital system in Chicago, was recounting how the lead candidate for the job of Senior Vice President of Human Resources blew up his candidacy. He was impatient, rude, and discourteous to an elderly volunteer at the receptionist desk, who mentioned it to the president at the end of the day. The president mentioned that this qualified candidate's discourteous behavior tipped the scales against him. Clearly, his opinion of his own inflated self-importance did him in.

12. *Overweight?* Begin a conservative exercise and weight loss program. Like it or not, physically fit people appear more "together." The employer may unfairly assume that if you are undisciplined regarding your physical being, you probably are also somewhat undisciplined on the job. I know that when I'm in better shape, I feel more confident and that enthusiasm is contagious.

Stages of the Interview

Each interview is composed of three stages or phases, whether it is with an executive search firm or a prospective employer.

Stage I: Rapport Building
Stage II: Discover Needs/Create Linkages
Stage III: Summary and Close

Stage I: Rapport Building

While you've researched the company and are prepared for the interview, it is appropriate to both develop rapport quickly and get the interviewer to talk about the organization conversationally so you have a context for the interview. This way, you can vary your responses specifically to the unique demands of the interview. I liken this process to playing cards with the interviewer, who always lays all of her cards face up. This is a great way for you to pick and choose which topics you want to address in your comments.

Keep in mind that your goal is to manage the interview, not to dominate it or control it. An extremely effective way is to ask several strategic questions immediately upon sitting down as a means to quickly develop rapport and focus. That's done by employing the past, future, or present perspectives, as well as volunteering information about yourself in your *Verbal Résumé*.

A. Past, Future, and Present Perspective

Past: "Thank you for the opportunity to interview. I have always been impressed with your organization, and even more so after I took the liberty of doing some research on the company. Your growth rate over the past five years is impressive. What were the main things you would attribute to the company's success?" (After the interviewer has provided the context for what has led up to today, ask about the future organizational plans.)
Future: "Thank you for that historical perspective. While you've grown rapidly in the past, how do you plan to continue that growth in the face of changing technology and increasing competition?" (Asking about the organization's plans for success in the future provides clues as to the leadership capabilities, strategic agility, and compelling vision. After you've probed a bit further into their future plans, ask about the present situation.)
Present: "Given where you have come from and your ambitious plans for the future, how well equipped are you now, in the company and in your department, to meet these challenges today? What attracted you to my background?" (Uncovering valuable

information about the organization's historical past, its strategies for the future, and the condition of present talent and performance expectations enable you to create leverage in the interview and for the position.)

B. *Verbal Résumé*

After the interviewer has shared with you some things about the organization, it's your turn to share. Remember, limit your Verbal Résumé to three minutes with your goal being to create a context for the interview and deepen your rapport. Your lead-in could sound something like this, "Thank you for sharing about your organization. Would you like to hear a summary of my background and the results achieved?" At that point you can highlight your track record in the context of information provided by the interviewer.

Stage II: Discover Needs/Create Linkages

You will be spending the majority of your time in Stage II, the "body" of the interview. You'll note that many of the questions in Chapter 17, "230 Tough Interview Questions" are commonly asked in the give-and-take during the interview. The more you prepare for interviews, the more confident, comfortable, and knowledgeable you'll be.

Discover Needs

This is the time in which you will have an opportunity to uncover needs, discover possibilities, and create linkages. One of the most powerful interviewing approaches is to create a "consultant's perspective." Imagine that you've been hired by the organization with whom you are interviewing to provide top-quality advice on how to address the challenges in the open position's job description. As a consultant, you will listen, observe, ask probing questions, respectfully challenge both premises and statements made, and reflect on things you have seen and learned in the organization.

As an interviewee, you may think of yourself as not having as much power as the interviewer. You may even unconsciously grant more power and credibility to the company representative than to yourself, a senior executive as a potential employee. However, this is a time for a mutual exchange of ideas and information to see if there is a fit. Remember, you have as much to give any company as they have to offer. Indeed, the company's benefit will be a multiple of your total compensation. So, don't capitulate by not asking penetrating questions. Robert Redford wouldn't.

Create Linkages

Linkages enable you to ask questions or respond to issues in ways that allow you to effectively transition from one topic to another. For instance, if you ask a question of the company decision maker, presumably she will respond with some information. You can either ask another question, use that information to "bridge" to a new topic of discussion, provide supportive information from your own background, or make an observation that encourages the interviewer to continue the discussion. For example, you might ask that given her comment about the need for added executive bench strength, what has the company done regarding succession planning, leadership development, or team-building initiatives? Your question and her answer allow you to create a linkage to your extensive background of building high-performance teams. Interview linkage enables you to operate on a mutual "give-and-get" basis, which will feel more balanced and which the interviewer will appreciate.

The optimal interview balance is one in which the interviewer speaks 60 percent of the time. This will be easily achieved if you are insatiably curious and skilled at asking penetrating questions. Your 40 percent is spent probing, following up on statements made, and creating linkages. If you're talking, you're not learning.

Stage III. Summary and Close

Managing the interview well means you know where you are and where you want to be in the interview at all times. Given that, it is appropriate to create some closure to the interview and to get some idea as to how you are fitting into the candidate pool. It is recommended that you do the following:

1. Briefly summarize the interview, acknowledge your interest, and express your appreciation for the opportunity to interview.

    Sally, we have covered some very good points in our interview, especially the critical need to get the executive team aligned, which is one of my strengths. I sincerely appreciate the time you spent with me and the care with which you outlined the position. I am very interested and enthusiastic about this opportunity.

2. Acknowledge a mutual fit or nonfit, if appropriate.

    Based on what you and your colleagues have described, it appears as if there is a very good fit. I am particularly pleased with how well you and I seem to work together and the values we seem to have in common.

    [Pause. Let the other person respond.]

3. Ask for feedback as to how the interviewer sees the fit.

How do you see the fit with my background, skills, and abilities?

[Pause. Let the other person respond.]

4. Ask for any objections or roadblocks to you being considered further.

What objections might you have to considering me for this position?

[Pause. Let the other person respond.]

If there are areas of concerns, wait for the other person to respond. It is not uncommon to feel awkward at first asking for feedback in the interview. However, *the absolute best time to handle lingering objections is right now, in the interview.* Not surprisingly, most objections are misunderstandings, not true career deficiencies. Confidently address these major objections before cordially and confidently asking for the job by confirming your interest.

5. Always end your interest confirmation with the words: "What is the next step?" Listen to what occurs next. You may learn extremely valuable information on the timetable of the decision and the status of other candidates.

6. While you don't want to be seen as presumptuous, commit to a timetable to get back together for a second round of interviews, perhaps at the board level, a psychological appraisal, reference checks, etc.

... that ought to put us about the 20th of the month for the next step. Great! If we have not confirmed our schedules by then, I will give you a call to see how plans are developing. Would that be all right?

7. Invariably, the whole interviewing/candidate selection process usually takes a lot longer than you'd like. If you can ascertain where others are in the interview sequence, endeavor to put yourself last or near the bottom of the list of those being considered. Why? The law of recency applies. Last in, most recently (and most vividly) remembered. Besides, if you interview first or too early, you will educate the interviewer and unintentionally give your competitors an edge.

Let's drop in on our friend, Michele Cannon, to summarize a successful interview:

Thank you for the opportunity to meet you and your team. I sincerely appreciate you making this possible. I thought we covered some very interesting things both about the company's long-range growth plans, your departmental needs, and how my background seems to relate with your sales and marketing strategies.

There appears to be a "fit" from my perspective; what do you think? Great! What might the next step include? What do you think our time frame should be to get back together again? Given that you are going to be out of town for the next two weeks, are there some other people in the organization I can interview with while you are out? This might be one way to keep up the momentum. Would that be possible?

Excellent. I look forward to hearing from you this week. Since I have a number of business appointments, as well, I will reach out to you if we haven't connected by Friday. I look forward to our next meeting.

During and After the Interview

During the Interview

1. *Make your grandmother proud.* Smile, have a firm handshake, stand erect, sit up straight, maintain eye contact (especially with difficult questions), enunciate, speak clearly, answer questions concisely and directly, and do not ramble. Further, ask questions, create linkages from one topic to another, be enthusiastic, do not take criticism or pointed questions personally, legitimize objections, add value, and keep visualizing success.

   Don't take notes, unless absolutely essential. If you are relaxed and focused, you'll remember 95 percent of everything that is relevant. Keep in mind, I am advocating that you ask probing, penetrating questions that will, hopefully, reveal some interesting data. If you are taking extensive notes, not only will you miss a ton of body language cues, but you'll probably make the interviewer nervous. After all, how might those notes be used? I have seen extensive note-taking have a decided dampening affect on interviews that otherwise might have been quite revealing. When I am in sales calls I rarely take notes. Rather, I am super-focused on the person, what he might be saying and avoiding addressing. By being intently other-focused, I am more easily able to effortlessly pick up on subtle nuances. It never ceases to amaze me how the slightly raised eyebrow or the minute shift in posture often reflects a topic of discomfort and, hence, an area to gently probe further.

   Be genuine and let the positive aspects of your personality show through. If you have a sense of humor, reveal it; do not force it, and by all means, never tell jokes.

   Remember, interviewing is a two-way process with the opportunity for you and the company to be of mutual benefit. If you have trouble remembering names, repeat the person's name several times immediately after meeting the person and several times throughout the course of the interview. The exchange of business cards immediately is an effective way to reinforce your remembering a person's name and title. Also, you now have the appropriate contact information for your follow-up later.

2. *Ask for feedback ... and the job.* When you feel the interview is coming to an end, tell the interviewer how much you have enjoyed the meeting and acknowledge

that you feel there is a fit. State that you would like to take the next step. Ask the employer if he or she feels the same. Offer a firm handshake. Smile. Ask them how soon a decision will be made. Ask if you haven't heard by that date, if you can, call and check. Employers like directness handled with tact and diplomacy. Ask for the job if you want it.

3. *What to do about a poor interview.* If you feel that you answered a question poorly, don't beat yourself up. Lighten up. You might wish to acknowledge (in the form of poking fun at yourself), "Well, I certainly went off on a tangent didn't I? Let me respond more crisply." Then do so! Poor interviews are more a result of your being nervous and unprepared versus your being unqualified. Chemistry and interpersonal fit will have a huge impact on how well you perform. Relax. Don't push too hard, trying to make a good impression. The more grounded you are in your own authenticity, the more credible, confident, and powerful you will be. When I'm in an important meeting and I'm nervous, I always picture the interviewer as my respected colleague and friend. I invite you to try this technique of projecting familiarity with what you want to have happen.

After the Interview

1. *Interview critique.* After the interview, make notes on how you felt about the interview, using the Interview Critique Sheet at the end of Chapter 17. This worksheet will help you identify key topics discussed with each interviewer, your background fit, and additional questions that may have surfaced. Assess what you did well and what you can improve upon. Identify the questions that tripped you up, and craft a response for future interviews.

2. *Thank-you letters.* Follow up with separate and distinctive thank-you letters to all the people with whom you interviewed. Make sure that each of these letters are a bit different, tailoring them to each interviewer and discussion. When I was recruiting for a position, I would always ask to have any thank-you letters forwarded to me. Upon consolidating these letters, I would note the extent to which the candidate tailored his or her comments. If the letters were largely the same, the person would get low marks for creativity and initiative.

   You may want to bring up any unresolved issues for the interviewer and how your skills and abilities match the company's needs. Remind each person what a good employee you would be, and bring up any new information that you have come across since your last meeting. For examples of thank-you letters after interviewing, please refer back to Chapter 8, "Create Powerful Marketing Letters That Evoke Action." Hard-copy thank you letters, in the form of a classy note card, is always appropriate. E-mail thank yous when the timing is critical, for global counterparts whom you might have met when they were in town, or for those executives who would clearly favor this style of communication.

Don't forget to select a reprint from your article file that you had previously assembled, sending it along a week or two after your initial thank-you letter. A note accompanying said article is another opportunity to personalize your ongoing contact. If you recall, particulars on creating an article file is highlighted in Chapter 12, "Power Networking—Unlocking the Secrets to Career Success."

3. *Follow-up phone call.* Several days after the round of interviewing and after your letters have been mailed, you may wish to follow through with a call back to the decision maker and the respective human resource representative to see if there is any additional feedback or questions they might have.

Thank that person once again for the interview. Inquire if the next step has been established, as you are fitting other meetings into your schedule. If you have additional questions, about the job, the organization, the department . . . whatever, now is the time to ask them.

At the end of the discussion, let the prospective employer know that you are actively interviewing. If you are now, or will be soon, considering other offers, inform her of that as well. No bluffing, by the way. Don't say that you have offers pending when you do not. Quite frankly, it's too easy to call your bluff. You run the risk of being left empty-handed and further behind than you were before. I tried bluffing a bit once when I was looking for a job, and he called my bluff. The search firm told me good luck in my new role and to keep him posted.

It is perfectly acceptable to telegraph the situation, such as the following:

> *I have been actively interviewing with other companies, and things are coming to a head. I may need to make a decision in a few weeks. As I would really like to work with ABC Company, what else needs to be done to move this process along? When will you be making a decision on this role? When might I expect to hear from you?*

4. *Keep networking and interviewing.* By all means, do so! Following an exciting set of interviews in a given company, network even more. There is a marked tendency to let up and slide, thinking that since you interviewed so well, you've got the job—hands down! You might even think, "I'm in. No one else on the planet could have interviewed so well!"

This last item reminds me of a CEO client of ours, I'll call him Lee. He had very impressive academic credentials and a track record of results. I asked him one day how he was doing. Lee cheerfully informed me that he had 12 bona fide offers pending. I challenged him to continue to network. The reality is that six or more executives are competing for any one job. As such, Lee was in keen competition with 60 other equally attractive executive candidates, like himself. "Lee, there are no guarantees that you'll get *any* of these jobs! Don't let your guard down. You are setting yourself up for a huge fall psychologically and emotionally," I extolled. Lee dismissed my concerns and countered that he was much too busy managing all the last-minute issues, such as house hunting for the most attractive (albeit, pending) offers, from California to Miami. Two days later, I stopped by Lee's office. What do you think happened? That morning, five opportunities went away. Lee was shocked but was trying to rebound. Within three days, the remaining seven offers were extended too and accepted by others. Lee was devastated. After a long getaway weekend with his wife, he came back, resolved to never get caught resting on "sure things."

The moral of the story: Never assume you've got the job. Keep pushing yourself to be focused on your search efforts. Use the positive buoyancy you feel to set up additional network meetings and interviews. Keep working at your search—until you've accepted an offer and beyond. During your active campaign, work diligently to schedule three to five networking or interview meetings every week. Having many job offers will improve your confidence and enhance your candidacy to a prospective employer.

Keep interviewing until you accept a position with which you are happy. You may wish to continue to interview with companies even after you start work, if the new job is not truly what you want. If the job market is extremely tight, and likewise your finances, you may need to accept an interim position. That is, a transitional job you are planning to keep only in order to meet your financial obligations as you continue your job search. If the job is clearly transitional and not permanent, you probably do not want to be in this interim position more than 12 to 18 months. Beyond 18 months, people might accuse you of settling for something considerably less than your skills if you do not position it as a consulting assignment.

CHAPTER 17

230 TOUGH INTERVIEW QUESTIONS

Handle the Tough Questions

It is imperative that you anticipate what an employer may ask in an interview. For each interview question in this chapter, write out your responses and practice your answers out loud (sometimes known as role-playing, or reading for a part). Role-playing is one of the best ways to master a natural response to tough interview questions. You don't want to memorize your answers and sound robotic. Nor, do you want to appear too slick, either. Much of the fear of an interview comes from not being fully prepared or the fear of being rejected and being seen as less competent. To that end, I recommend that you write out a script for each of these questions and go on at least four "throwaway" interviews early in your search. "Throwaway" interviews are ones you really don't care much about. You use a throwaway to practice being more emboldened and forthright, asking really penetrating questions with little concern about wanting/needing to work there. Indeed, your goal is to master interviewing in your throwaways to the point where you are able to generate an offer. Obviously, it's best if you have some experience handling difficult questions in advance of the interview for your ideal job.

Think about the types of positions the company has to offer and review your skills, abilities, and results achieved. Then try role-playing out loud, with yourself or your spouse, partner, or a friend. Have a friend play the role of the employer, asking you questions. Legitimize your friend being relentless and curious, wanting to know more about what, why, and how you did things. Think of this process like peeling back the onion, one layer at a time. If you can confidently communicate with a friend or loved one, you will do great with a bona fide interviewer.

Many employers decide in the first few minutes whether they are interested in you or not. Remember, offers go to people who may not be technically the most qualified; offers go to people who are best at job hunting and interviewing.

Read the following questions, and *write out how you would answer them*. Consider the impact your responses might have on the interviewer. Consider how you might elaborate on them to make them better. Develop your own list of questions. Keep track of the questions asked of you in all of your actual company or role-play interviews and practice answering them.

130 Difficult Interview Questions

Personal:

1. Why don't you tell me about yourself? (Verbal Résumé: 15-second, 60-second, 3-minute sound bites)
2. How would you describe your operating style?
3. What are those traits of which you are most proud? Why and how do these manifest themselves on the job?
4. What would you like to improve about yourself? What have you done about this? "What gets in the way of you achieving what you want?"
5. Academically, how well did you do in school? What notable successes did you achieve? How much more could you have achieved? Why didn't you?
6. What have you not yet realized in your career? Impact of not achieving this? What are you committed to doing about this?
7. How did your early family life influence your career?
8. Who had the greatest influence on you that shaped who you are now? Personally? Professionally?
9. Name your top five core values. How do these values manifest themselves in your life?
10. How authentic are you? How do you define authenticity? How does your authenticity show up in the workplace?
11. How important is it that colleagues operate authentically? What are the pros and cons of operating authentically? What are the pros and cons of *not* operating authentically?
12. What gets in the way of people operating authentically? Describe a time in which you did *not* operate authentically?
13. What triggers defensiveness in you? How do you behave when you become defensive? How do you know when you've become defensive?
14. What are your professional objectives?
15. What are you doing to reach those objectives?
16. What have you failed to achieve that you highly value?
17. How do you define success? According to your definition of success, how successful are you in your career?

18. What legacy do you want to leave? How do you want your epitaph to read?
19. Do you consider yourself lucky? Why so?
20. What significant life-changing events have you had in your life, and how have they influenced you

Professional Attributes:

21. What is the span of your current responsibility?
22. What were your operating budget responsibilities?
23. How many people did you lead?
24. What are your most significant career accomplishments?
25. In your current or most recent position, what parts of your role did you like most? Like the least?
26. What frustrates you the most in your role? What have you done about it?
27. Tell me about your most notable professional *failure* and what you learned from it. How have you applied these lessons in the last 12 months, and what was the impact, intended and unintended?
28. Tell me about your most notable professional *success* and what you learned from it. How have you applied these lessons in the last 12 months, and what was the impact, intended and unintended?
29. What were the biggest decisions you have made in the last 12 months? Tell me how you went about making them and what alternatives you considered.
30. What was the most difficult ethical decision you have made? What was the outcome?
31. What was the worst decision you ever made, and what was the unintended impact on the organization?
32. What has been the major motivator in your career?
33. How would you describe your occupation?
34. What would your *bosses* say about you regarding your leadership capabilities, interpersonal style, goal-setting skills, ability to execute, and the results that were obtained? what has been your overall impact on your organization?
35. What would your *peers* say about you regarding your leadership capabilities, interpersonal style, and ability to execute plans?
36. What would your *subordinates* say about you regarding your leadership capabilities, personality style, how well you create a compelling vision, goal-setting skills, ability to execute, and the results that were obtained through them? what has been your overall impact on the organization?
37. What components of a job are most important to you?
38. Tell me about a major project or assignment for which you had responsibility. What problems did you resolve, and what were the results?

39. Describe a situation at work that required two critically important things to be done at the same time. How did you handle them, and what was the result?

40. What are some of the best ideas you ever sold to, the Board, a peer, or your manager in your organization? What was your approach, and what was the result?

41. Describe a situation in which your first attempt to sell a key idea (to a peer or supervisor) failed. How did you feel, what did you do, and what was the result?

42. How have you gotten around obstacles that prevented you from completing projects or assignments? Describe the conditions under which obstacles most often occurred for you.

43. Give me examples of different approaches you have used when persuading someone to cooperate with you.

44. When dealing with individuals or groups, how do you determine when you are pushing too hard? How does it look, and what do you do about it?

45. Describe a time in which you upgraded the talents and capabilities of your team and created a collaborative environment. What was the intended and unintended impact?

46. In your current or former job, how is performance measured, and what constitutes doing a good job? What would others say to the same question?

47. Explain the gaps of employment in your résumé.

48. I'm concerned that you've only worked for <u>only one</u> company throughout your career. I'm looking for someone who has a breadth of experiences. What is the breadth of your experience, and how can it be applied here?

49. I'm concerned that you've, worked for <u>many</u> companies throughout your career. Because you haven't been any place long enough, how do you know you've really contributed to your organizations' growth and profitability?

50. What would make up a typical day for you? How many hours in a day do you usually work? On average, how many hours do you typically work in a week?

51. Do you work harder, about the same, or less than your superiors? Peers? Subordinates?

52. Tell me about some times when you were not very pleased with your performance. How did it influence others? What did you do about it?

53. In your job at _____, what were your standards of success? What did you do to meet those standards?

54. Describe a tough negotiation that you led. What preparation did you undergo, and how did you influence the outcome?

55. Given what you know of this job, what do you consider the most important elements of success?

56. Rank your functional skills from strongest to weakest. Why this ranking? What is the unintended impact on you and the organization?

57. Tell me about some projects you generated on your own. What prompted you to begin them, and what was the result?

58. What is your long-term career strategy? Why? How will you realize this? How well on target are you at this point? How will this position contribute to your achieving this strategy?

59. How have your career moves and company changes fit into this long-term career plan?

60. Why have you chosen this particular field? What do you feel are the biggest challenges facing this field? This industry?

61. If we hired you, what are the top three goals you would like to see this department achieve?

62. If you could start your career over again, what would you do differently? What unfulfilled goals do you have, and when will you achieve them?

63. How creative are you? How do you define creativity? Give me some examples in which you were particularly creative. What was the P&L impact?

64. Describe a situation in which you demonstrated sound judgment and solid leadership skills.

65. What is the most adverse situation you have dealt with professionally? Personally? How did you deal with it? What was the result?

66. Describe the characteristics of those subordinates that did not work out, as opposed to those employees that did.

67. Explain a time in which you delayed addressing declining performance. Why the delay, and what was the impact?

68. When did you last fire someone? What were the reasons, and how did you handle it? What was the employee's response?

69. What do you see as the most difficult task in being a leader?

70. What prompted you to contemplate leaving your previous positions before? When was this? What kept you there?

71. Why haven't you found a new position before now?

72. How would others evaluate you as a candidate in this role and in this organization?

73. What would your boss, peers, subordinates, and customers say about you in reference checks? Why would that be so?

74. What would your greatest business *opponent* say about you? Why is this person an opponent?

75. What would your greatest business *proponent* say about you? Why is this person a proponent?

76. How have you helped increase sales? How have you helped increase profits?

77. In what business environments are you most experienced? Which ones do you like the best? Least?

78. What are your thoughts about relocation?
79. What is your compensation? What are its components?
80. How satisfied are you with your total compensation? Are you ahead of, equal to, or behind in your total compensation in comparison to your peers in the marketplace?
81. Under what conditions would you take less money?
82. What do you feel this position should pay? What salary do you want?
83. How do you feel about corporate politics?
84. How well do you "manage up?" Give me some examples.
85. What attributes did your last three bosses ascribe to you?
86. How much of a businessperson are you? By what definition?
87. Describe the team that reports to you. Tell me about their personalities, their background, capabilities, developmental needs, and key accomplishments.
88. If I were your boss, how would I optimally manage you?
89. How do you react to criticism on the job? What judgments do you have toward the criticism and the person sharing their observations?
90. What restrictive covenants do you have with your current or former company? (noncompete, nonsolicitation, noninterference, etc.)
91. Are you still employed? Are you on the payroll? Do you still have benefits coverage?
92. Are you in outplacement? With whom? What is the greatest learning you've had while in outplacement?
93. Regarding your current employment situation, how and when did you lose endorsement with your boss? With others?
94. What is the one major accomplishment that best defines you as a person?

Organization:

95. Tell me everything you know about our organization, our products, our customers, our competitors, and how we can be more successful.
96. How might the industry serve its customers and society better? Our company?
97. How have you kept current in your field or industry?
98. What do you see as the three most significant issues facing our industry, and notably our company, in the future? What do you recommend we do to ready ourselves for these issues?
99. Please give me your definition of the position for which you are being interviewed.
100. Would you recommend that we run our business for pure growth, sacrificing profit, or would you recommend that we run it for profitability and why?
101. Why do you want to work for us?

102. What interests you most about this position? How does this relate to your long-term career strategy?

103. Why should we hire you? What can you do for us that someone else can't do?

104. How long would it take you to make a meaningful contribution to our organization?

105. How long will you stay here in our company? What would cause you to leave our company?

106. What other positions or companies are you considering?

107. Any objections to psychological tests?

108. What questions do you have of me?

109. What aspects of your current job would you consider to be crucial to the success of the business? Why?

110. What was the least relevant job you have held? Why? How did you feel about it, and what did you learn?

111. How would you evaluate your progression up through your organization? What would you have done differently?

112. Describe how and when you get stressed. How do you display it or act it out? What do you do to eliminate the stress?

113. How long have you been looking for a position?

114. Have you ever been criticized unjustly? What were the circumstances? How did it adversely impact you? What did you do about it? What did you learn from it?

115. How have your previous jobs equipped you for greater responsibility?

116. How did you manage to get the time off for this interview? (If still employed.)

117. How will your boss react when you tell him that you have accepted another job? How will your subordinates feel?

118. When you leave your organization, what impact will this have on the projects you are working on? What is your obligation to your company? What will you do to ensure that nothing is dropped?

119. Describe a time in which you fell out of favor with an executive senior to you in your organization. Why did this occur? What did you do to lose favor? What was the impact of this loss? How successful were you at reestablishing trust?

120. Describe your interpersonal and operating style.

121. Notwithstanding that you've only recently met me, describe my interpersonal style. Carried to an extreme, what might my overplayed strengths look like, and what might be their impact?

122. What judgments do you have about people whose style and behavior is significantly different than yours?

123. Given our respective operating styles, how would you adapt your behavior to more closely align with mine?

124. Describe your leadership style.
125. What do you suspect my leadership style and traits might be?
126. What are the attributes of a good senior executive?
127. If you had to choose between hiring two good salespeople or just one salesperson that could sell the same as both of them, which would you choose?
128. Based on what you know about the industry, our company, our people, our challenges, and my operating style, what should change in the organization to optimize its capabilities?
129. How will I know if I can trust you?
130. Here's a sampling of actual questions that psychologists' have utilize. (usually followed by "hmmm," "really?" "tell me more," "and then what happened?"):
    • What was the last book you read that influenced you?
    • What newspapers do you read?
    • Describe your earliest childhood memory?
    • Who influenced you the most, and how do you manifest these influences?
    • What else should we know about you?

WORKSHEET 42

Why Are You Leaving Your Company?

To this tough question, employers are favorably impressed with a clear, concise, direct, and positive response. Do not be vague or hesitant. And, please, please, please, do not have a long preamble story. It undermines your credibility. Explain the situation in 25 words or less. If the interviewer wants more detail, he'll ask. Think through: Is your explanation reasonable and logical? Employer concerns include the following:

- Are you a job hopper?
- Were you let go for a cause?
- Will you stay long enough to contribute?
- What problem might you be running away from?
- How is your relationship with your boss and company now?
- Just how beat up are you for being terminated?
- How will hiring you help or hurt my credibility with the Board?

Sample response: 25 words or fewer

> *My company was recently acquired, and many senior executive positions were eliminated, including mine.*

The sample response above: 14 words. Simple, crisp, matter-of-fact, nonapologetic, and easy to understand.

More detail:

> *While I had the opportunity to look for another position within the company, I elected not to put my career on hold for three to five years. As such, I am looking with the full knowledge and support of my company.*

(At 41 words, not too bad a length, though not as crisp as the response with only 14 words.)

Practice your response:

WORKSHEET 43

Tell Me About Yourself

If you have not done so, prepare your various elevator speeches for this most frequently asked interview question. Refer back to your Verbal Résumé in Chapter 9, "Your Verbal Résumé—Sound Bites That Grab 'Em." Practice, practice, practice your response to this innocent, yet tough question. Surprisingly, many people stumble here. This happens because we know ourselves so well, we let our guard down and are not very concise. Refer back to your sound bites in Chapter 12, "Power Networking."

This is your chance to make a strong first impression that will greatly improve your chances for an offer. This is a very important question that deserves careful preparation. Companies are interested in your ability to present your ideas in a rational and straightforward manner. They are interested in knowing if your career has been upwardly mobile and logical. Have you progressed during each move, and how have your moves added to your career? If you have had frequent job changes, talk about the experiences in terms of your career expanding. Give evidence that you are stable, dependable, and would like to find a firm to which you can make a serious long-term commitment. Companies are also keenly interested in your interpersonal or operating style. Will you be compatible with other employees, or will you become disruptive?

Practice your Verbal Résumé:

WORKSHEET 44

What Are Your Greatest Strengths?

This is one of the top 5 most common questions asked in every interview. Virtually every interviewer wants to know how you view yourself and what you consider to be your greatest strengths. Sometimes strengths are asked as competencies, capabilities, or attributes. Since you are not really sure if the interviewer is asking about your personal strengths or technical strengths, you can presume the question to be open-ended: "I'd like to talk about both my technical strengths and my personal strengths." Proceed to your technical strengths first, then your personal strengths.

Refer back to Chapter 5, "Career Strategies and Options" to refamiliarize yourself with how you packaged your strengths and developmental needs. Why will interviewers throw these potentially unnerving questions at you in the interview? What do they really hope to gain, and what do they hope to hear you say? These "impossible questions" are usually, open-ended and designed to see how quickly and flexibly you can think on your feet. Open-ended questions provide an opportunity for you to create a context that is appropriate and that relates to the previous discussions. These kinds of questions test how concise and articulate you can be when the pressure is on.

Prepare in advance at least 7 to 10 job-related strengths. Rehearse them, and shrink them down into one or two sentences. Then support each using a good, example with a quantifiable result that you can cover in less than 30 seconds.

Sample response:

> I am a collaborative, technically competent, broadly experienced general manager with significant P&L responsibility. I have a record of attracting, developing, and retaining top talent that greatly contributes to the growth and profitability of my companies.

1.

2.

3.

4.

5.

6.

7.

8.

9.

10.

Practice Your Response:

WORKSHEET 45

What Are Your Greatest Weaknesses?

First of all, don't be intimidated by this type of question or even the trick question "What are your top five weaknesses?" The interviewer is interested in knowing that you are able to handle difficult questions and can reassure him or her that hiring you would not be a mistake. Don't be fooled into thinking that because the interviewer asked you for five weakness that you have to respond with five. Give your top one or two main overplayed strengths, and indicate that "those are the two main ones." Ironically, that trait that you deem, to be your greatest strength will always be viewed by others as your greatest liability or weakness, if you overextend it or use that strength inappropriately. Refer back to Chapter 5, "Career Strategies and Options" and insights that you previously developed.

To this question of weaknesses, the interviewer is looking for a serious and appropriate response and does not appreciate any joke about your weaknesses. Responses such as "I have no weaknesses" or "I don't golf too well" are unacceptable responses and can portray you as an individual who is inappropriate, or flippant, or that you have little insight into yourself. Remember: Tell the truth, but not the whole truth. Keep your responses nice and tight and concise. When you do, you'll be all right.

There is a formula for identifying weaknesses without damaging yourself:

- State your strength.
- State the excess of the strength.
- Tell how it shows up.
- Tell how you manage it so that it is not a significant problem.

Sample responses:

Strength: *I am driven by goals and deadlines.*

Excess: *I am aware that I can become a bit intense and push the team if we are not meeting our goals or if we are not being fiscally responsible.*

Shows up by: *When that happens I tend to work longer hours and do not relax, which sometimes shows up as my being overly focused on enhancing the organization's performance and profitability.*

Managed by: Modifying my behavior when I start to become intense. My colleagues and I hold ourselves and each other accountable, so they readily give me straight feedback. A favorite phrase that I ask myself is, "What's another perspective,? What's another way we can realize the outcome." When I utilize feedback and an objective perspective I am able to effectively avoid this intensity becoming an issue.

Practice your response:

Strength:

Excess:

Shows up by:

Managed by:

WORKSHEET 46

What Is Your Personality Style?

This question is similar to asking you about your strengths and your leadership or operating style. Employers are interested in knowing two things when they ask this question: (1) How well do you know yourself and (2) How compatible is your personality with the department's and the organization's culture. While you might be technically qualified to do the work, if you're not able to get along with your colleagues, it would be unlikely that you would be hired. Decision makers are not interested in the organizational "clutter" that always accompanies a "high maintenance" executive. Additionally, by describing your personality style, you would have an opportunity to describe your values and work ethics. Keep these general at first, and then if the interviewer is interested in specifics, be prepared to define your traits and provide examples of them.

Sample response:

In terms of my personality, I can best be described as open, straightforward, ambitious, and enthusiastic. One of my strengths is my ability to see the big picture and develop trends from many pieces of information while being able to effectively operate at a very fine level of detail. I am intellectually curious and thrive on challenges. I am result-oriented, approachable, warm, and supportive of others.

Practice your response:

WORKSHEET 47

Why Should We Hire You?

Respond as if the question was asking about your strengths, abilities, or accomplishments. Talk about things the employer probably sees as valuable, given those insights that you have already gained in the interview.

Sample response:

You should hire me because of my ability to quickly contribute to an organization's growth and profitability. The challenges and opportunities that this position represents fit nicely with my track record and my interests. The long-term plans for your organization in this function closely parallel my personal and professional growth plans. You should hire me because of my ability to secure widespread endorsement in ways that probably will enable this operation and team to be more effective.

Practice your response:

WORKSHEET 48

What Went Wrong in Your Company?
Were You Fired?

Why you are looking for employment outside your company, or your reasons for leaving are always of great concern for employers. They want to know if you are merely transferring your problems from one organization to another or to what extent you have any personality quirks or technical flaws that would get in the way of your performing effectively. While things may have gone wrong in your past (or current company), this is not a time to reveal everything. "Wrong" denotes error and, quite possibly, something bad. It is appropriate to reveal only those things that were correct and justifiable that have led to your seeking employment elsewhere. So, keep it general, and develop a story consistent with your references.

Sample response:

> *Nothing went wrong in my former organization. As I mentioned, the organization was restructuring and the streamlined operation eliminated a number of duplicated functions and positions, including mine. While I might have had the opportunity to remain with the organization in a lesser capacity, I did not want to put my career on hold for three to five years.*

Practice your response:

WORKSHEET 49

How Do You Feel About Your Company Eliminating Your Position?

Be careful not to be drawn into a discussion in which you and the interviewer criticize terminating managers and share experiences of being "zapped" and in which both of you express sympathy for each other's unfair treatment. It can be a subtle trap. Even if the interviewer is regaling you with stories of his or her own termination and how difficult it was to find meaningful employment, do not agree or say, "Yes, that's certainly the way it is for me too." Maintain a respectable distance from any discussion that sounds like dissatisfaction or anger. You may wish to consider saying something like:

Sample response:

While I am disappointed in the situation, I fully recognize the need to make that decision. If I were in the identical decision-making role, I would have certainly made the same choice. I understand that, I fully accept it, and am positive and enthusiastic about the next chapter in my career. That is why I am so pleased with the opportunity that you and I are discussing, because it certainly seems to fit those things in which I am interested.

Practice your response:

WORKSHEET 50

Why Are You Interested in Working for This Company?

This question gives you an opportunity to apply some of the information you uncovered in your research on the company prior to the interview, as well as in the actual interview. Consider relating back to your earlier responses or your values, strengths, and ideal job. Employers are interested in hearing about your desire to contribute to the company and not your desire for job stability, compensation, and benefits. In fact, issues of wages, hours, and working conditions should be the last items you talk about.

Sample response:

In researching your company and when speaking with some of your vendors and employees, I have heard only praise. Your innovative products, emerging technologies, and attention to quality are all things I believe in. When I put together the list of the top 10 companies I would like to work for, you were among the top five. In addition, I am excited about the opportunity to contribute to the company's growth and profitability.

Practice your response:

WORKSHEET 51

What Did You Like *Best* About
Your Current/Former Company?

Questions in Worksheets 51 to 54 are similar in nature. Each question requires that you answer positively and realistically, while providing the optimal amount of background information without revealing areas that might be of concern to the executive recruiter or a prospective employer.

In response to the question, "What did you like *best* about your current/former company?" Here's an opportunity to speak realistically and positively. Do not criticize your organization or find fault with it unless specifically asked to do so, and even then, be *very* cautious. Even though you may have had a bad experience with your company or with several executives in it, now is not the time to vent your frustration. The only thing that venting does for you is diminish your professionalism and usher you out the interviewer's door faster.

Be positive and realistic, keeping your responses somewhat general. If you become too specific, you run the risk of identifying dimensions the interviewer might not relate to. Be watchful of becoming flowery or overly philosophical. Present your observations with a positive, matter-of-fact tone. Otherwise, you run the risk of not being seen as credible.

Sample response:

My organization could be best described as a professionally managed organization with talented individuals in key roles. We have a good product line, are well respected in the industry and in the marketplace, and take quite a bit of pride in what we do. The organizational environment is one in which people are able to communicate openly and straightforwardly with each other. It seems as if the good of the organization takes precedent over individual needs and that we are all operating in a team basis, with no one person's interest ahead of the team's goals. If you talk to other individuals from my company, you will discover that there is a great deal of dedication and loyalty for the philosophy and mission of the company. I am only sorry that the streamlining of the organization is creating a surplus of individuals, including myself. While I am disappointed that I have to search for employment, I have been flattered and pleased with the kinds of results my job search has produced so far.

Practice your response:

WORKSHEET 52

What Did You Like *Least* About
Your Current/Former Company?

Your response should be similar to the previous question, "What did you like best about your former company?" Guard against being drawn into a more detailed discussion of what you felt was wrong with the company. Keep your responses general, upbeat, positive, *and brief*!

Sample response:

As you can tell, I am an enthusiastic supporter of my company. I don't have a whole lot to say negative about the company. The company is populated with great talent. It's got leading edge products and is a formidable competitor in an extremely tough global marketplace. It has created an environment in which people have an opportunity to grow and to learn to the best of their abilities. I guess if pressed, the thing that I would indicate is that the organization is reluctant to hire people unless the need was more than justifiable. While I do not dispute that, it meant that we worked very hard with a very lean staff.

Practice your response:

WORKSHEET 53

What Did You Like *Best* About
Your Current/Former Position?

Sample response:

I liked the challenge and that I was able to structure my job pretty much the way I wanted it, with guidance from my boss. I welcomed the challenging stretch goals, which forced me to reach deep within myself and to perform to the best of my abilities. I worked in an environment that was demanding, professional, warm, and supportive. My coworkers set high performance standards for themselves and others. We operated as a team and had the right to confront each other on poor performance if it was going to damage the organization. I like that caring, supportive, and straightforward environment in which people help each other.

Practice your response:

WORKSHEET 54

What Did You Like *Least* About Your Current/Former Position?

Again, be careful here. Ensure that your answers are positive and very supportive of your current or former boss and organization. Issues like "constant 70-hour workweeks" or "90 percent travel" are better responses than "I did not have enough to do" or "my organization was in chaos, and it drove me crazy!"

Sample response:

Well, I am pretty sold on the organization and position that I had. I do not really have much to complain about. I think the only downside about my position was that I had too much work to do. That, coupled with my tendency to be a bit of a workaholic, made for some very long hours. However, two personality traits reinforce that. One, is that I have difficulty saying no when an individual comes to me for help. Second, I know that I am experienced and have the ability to generate quite a bit of work. I know that at some point in time I will be able to get it done.

Practice your response:

WORKSHEET 55

Describe Your Current / Last Boss

Never say anything negative about a former employer. Your prospective employer will probably assume that if you like to complain now, you will assuredly continue complaining if and when you are hired. No one wants to be the next former employer who is poorly spoken of. The interviewer will be evaluating your ability to assess the "big picture," which certainly includes the dynamics of an interview. Portray your boss in a positive and realistic manner. The interviewer will appreciate your candor and insight.

Sample response:

She was very strict, which worked well in our area given the regulatory nature of our work and the time pressure to generate results. You always knew where you stood with her, as she set very high standards of performance for herself and others. I liked that. I believe people should get straight feedback on how well they are doing.

Practice your response:

WORKSHEET 56

What Significant Accomplishments Have You Achieved in Your Career?

Respond to this open-ended question by choosing two to three major accomplishments that reflect the breadth of your experiences and talent and that complement the company's needs as expressed by the interviewer. Sometimes, this type of question is asked: "What is the single most important accomplishment that you have achieved in your career to date?"

Sample response:

> *What I'd like to do is talk about my accomplishments in a broad manner and then provide specific examples that support my broad-based contributions, if that's alright. I feel that my single greatest accomplishment or skill is my ability to quickly diagnose a situation, present practical and cost-effective recommendations, and help others to implement these options. I manage things in such a way as to quickly improve productivity or set the stage for additional development or growth. Examples of this are . . .*

Practice your response: (Review and memorize the results in your résumé!)

WORKSHEET 57

Explain the Gap in Your Employment History

If you have an employment gap, explain it as briefly and convincingly as you can. Most employers understand your need to conduct a job search if your position was eliminated because of a consolidation. *Note*: If you have been unemployed for more than 12 months, it is imperative that you develop some convincing rationale beyond merely "taking some time off." Solid rationale might include consulting, conducting due diligences as part of your exploratory relationship with a private equity firm, managing your investments, assuming an interim senior executive role as part of a turnaround, and so on. Write your response to this question, and explain it to others. Have others provide feedback to you to ensure that your delivery is credible.

Sample response:

Well, there really isn't any gap. After the reorganization, I provided consulting support to several multinational companies. My role was to help them sort out the major roadblocks to their success, facilitate the development of the strategic plan, and act as internal turnaround consultant. While I have greatly enjoyed my role as consultant, I miss being inside the organization executing the strategies as part of the executive team.

Practice your response:

WORKSHEET 58

Tell Me of a Time in Which
You Were Unfairly Criticized

Careful. This question is fraught with danger if you reveal too much. However, it is also an opportunity to demonstrate how you handle yourself in difficult situations. Employers are anxious to know if you are able to learn from your mistakes or misunderstandings and to what extent you become defensive. Choose a criticism that was made that you took to heart and then appropriately modified your behavior or approach. Highlight a relevant accomplishment to show that you grew from it. If you are hurt or angry about anything in your old job or company, you will always injure yourself in interviews because this question may rekindle upset that previously happened and that may have led to your separation. Get the emotional ups and downs handled before the interview, before you permanently injure your career success.

Begin taking control of your upset by clearly recognizing what emotionally triggers you. Take ownership of your upset. You are the one, no one else, that keeps generating all that emotional energy. You have a choice to get hooked . . . or not. Other people just do what they do. You are the one who adds the emotional kicker to it. It is quite revealing to understand what you are "getting out of" your upset (such as, sympathy, attention, proving that you are right, etc.). Ask yourself, "How do I gain from these emotional outbursts? What is it costing me to hold on to my upset? How long am I willing to pay that cost?"

Sample response:

I respond favorably to constructive criticism. I know that I am able to grow from the experience if I pause and reflect on what is being said. Even if I do not feel the observations are accurate, it is up to me to clarify another person's perception of a problem, rather than disregard his or her belief or reaction. I feel that it is important to see another's point of view as being valid.

Practice your response:

WORKSHEET 59

What Salary Do You Want?

Discussions about compensation are often awkward and uncomfortable. You may even feel that you and the employer are adversaries, in that you feel you are worth more than what the company is willing to pay. While questions about salary are asked many different ways, your answers should be uniformly consistent, as outlined in the sample responses below.

If asked *early* in the interview about salary, try to defer revealing specifics until later in the interview, when you have more information (unless you are speaking with a search firm).

Sample response:

I am somewhat uncomfortable talking about money this early. I would like to defer talking about my specific compensation requirements until later in the interview, when I have a better handle on the scope of the job, and we know if we have mutual interest.

or

Thank you for asking about money requirements. It's important, and I want to discuss it, but I would like to do so in a context. As you might imagine, this is an important career step for me. I am looking for a challenging position that will allow me the opportunity to influence the strategic direction of the organization. Would it be all right if we looked into this area first a bit deeper before we get into the money? If the opportunity is right, I'm flexible on the economics.

If the person agrees to defer the discussion, immediately ask several exploratory questions about the greatest needs in the company in your area of expertise, the expectations for the job in the next year or two, and the position's most significant challenges. This gives you an opportunity to discern the needs of the company and to respond with your matching abilities.

If you cannot defer salary discussions or if asked later in the interview, see if the employer will reveal his or her intentions first.

Sample response: You ask the following.

> *You have asked about compensation; what do you have in mind?*

or, you share the following:

> *I am currently in the $250,000+ range with a management incentive, stock options, and generous benefit package. While money is important to me, it is not the only consideration. The opportunity to contribute to the growth and profitability of the firm is most important, as well as opportunities for advancement, personal satisfaction, and long-term stability. How does that fit into your expectations?*

or, you could share more detail, as in the following:

> *My total compensation is in excess of $250,000, with a base of $185,000. I am currently looking at career opportunities less than $185,000 and also situations considerably higher than that, depending on the job, company, and location. As I indicated, while money is important to me, it is not the only consideration. Minimally, I am interested in remaining whole, salary-wise, over a 6-, 12-, and 18-month period of time. What kind of income did you have in mind?*

Practice your response:

WORKSHEET 60

You Are *Under*qualified for This Position

It is not uncommon for interviewers, from search firms or prospective employers, to ask tough questions to see how smooth you handle delicate or confrontive situations. If you are told that you are "underqualified" upon revealing your compensation, it is appropriate to make several key points only *after* you get some specific feedback from the interviewer as why he or she feels this way.

Practice asking questions that counter objections in a manner that does not appear to be threatening to the interviewer or defensive on your part.

Sample response—you could ask for clarification. I recommend a simple, open-ended question as it requires the recruiter to elaborate on his or her reasoning.

Oh, why do you feel that?

Or, you could make a clarifying statement:

Thank you for being candid. Regarding compensation, I would like to make two key points. First, I recognize that I have been behind in compensation, but I have not been willing to leave my company simply for more money, even though search firms have come knocking previously. I felt that the experience that I was gaining was well worth the investment of deferred income. While money is important to me, it is not the only consideration. Second, I have always been promoted into positions of increasing responsibility and been able to successfully assume these bigger roles with little difficulty.

Practice your response:

WORKSHEET 61

You Are *Over*qualified for This Position

Being told you are overqualified poses a similar kind of challenge as being told you are underqualified. If you reveal your compensation requirements early in the interviewing process, you cannot effectively counter the charge of being overqualified because you may not have enough information about the position or the organization. If you have asked probing questions to ascertain the organization's adverse financial condition and you know how you are able to turn it around, you have what I call *leverage*. If you defer discussions about compensation until later in the interview, you will be in a much better position to talk about being *fully qualified* versus overqualified. Accordingly, you will have a much better basis to discuss your credentials meeting specific needs of the employer.

Sample response:

Really? Why do you see me as overqualified?" [Pause.— Wait for a response.] Thank you very much for acknowledging that I am well compensated and have good credentials. I am very proud of what I have been able to accomplish. My company has consistently rewarded individuals who have performed in an outstanding manner. While I am interested in remaining whole with regard to compensation, experience has shown me that it is more important to be in a position in which I am well qualified and able to significantly contribute to the P&L.

or you could say something like this:

You mentioned overqualified. I don't believe that I am overqualified. Rather, I see myself as 'fully qualified,' given that the organization needs someone of my ability and track record to contribute immediately and assume increasing responsibilities. Since you currently do not have the executive talent on board to readily achieve your business objectives and since you're willing to recognize and reward outstanding performance, I'm not worried about compensation in the long term. This is exactly the kind environment in which I thrive and would love to participate. That being said, I know that I will pay for myself many times over in the profitability enhancements and incremental revenue gains.

Practice your response:

WORKSHEET 62

What Do You Know About Our Organization?

This question is almost always asked. The more prepared you are, the more you will stand out from others applying for the same job. It's been my experience that most job seekers do not do an adequate job preparing for interviews. If you do prepare, you will really shine. Be prepared to rattle off data on sales size, number of employees, type of product lines or business groups, locations, competition, legislative trends, if any, and future company plans that you might know of.

- You should be knowledgeable about the following:

- Organization for which you are being interviewed

- Major competitors, domestically and internationally

- Emerging competitors with similar and/or advanced applications

- Private-equity firms that have been investing in this sector

- Current or emerging technologies that have leapfrogged the company for which you are interviewing

- Current or pending legislative trends that may impact the industry

Sample response:

I know that the ABC Corporation is a global, $8 billion diversified consumer products company with major brands that are recognized and respected worldwide. There are five major business sectors, employing 25,000 people. You have an enviable track record of growing your top line and margins. Your stated strategy for continued growth through acquisitions, strategic alliances, and new ventures is very exciting. It would appear that one of your challenges might be having a deep enough executive bench to keep pace with and realize ABC's long-term business goals to be the dominant player in the consumer products arena. As evidenced by your recognition in your *industry's Best Company to Work For, the company's general reputation is excellent. The product line is varied and seems to meet a growing market need. Additionally, your company is consistently developing new products and technologies. While I know some things about your company, I would certainly like to learn more about it today.*

Practice your response: (Identify important dimensions you want to explore)

WORKSHEET 63

What Questions Might You Have
About Our Organization?

Ask some questions that you already know part of the answers to, then elaborate on them. People are usually proud of their company and want to talk about it. In addition to the following, see the section, "Your Turn: Penetrating Questions *You Get to Ask*" in this chapter for an extensive list of sample questions.

Sample responses:

How did your business get started?

How have you earned your international reputation?

To what would you attribute your success?

How does business growth look for the next year or so?

What reorganization might have occurred in the last 12 months? How extensive was it, and what has been the P&L impact?

Why is this position open?

What internal candidates were considered for this role? Why are you looking outside of the company?

What has been working well in this area?

What areas need improvement?

Practice your response:

Discriminatory Questions: How to Handle Them and What to Do

Surprisingly, well-intentioned interviewers still ask questions that are blatantly discriminatory or close to being considered so. It is often less a function of outright discrimination and more an issue of an inept executive asking the questions. Nonetheless, companies who allow this practice to go unchecked not only run the risk of turning off well-qualified candidates, but they are also unwittingly vulnerable to discrimination litigation.

If you find yourself in an interview in which you feel you are being asked discriminatory questions, do not stiffen up immediately. Rather, make a mental note to verify that this is, indeed, the case. Employers are legally constrained from making employment, salary, promotion, and termination decisions based on age, race, sex, religion, national origin, or physical handicap. A question may be posed like the following: "Do you have any health problems or physical limitations that might prevent you from performing the job as described to you, including travel, if required?"

For example, you may get asked about your age, or about the age of your children, or how your spouse/partner views your working for "this" company.

You have three choices when this occurs. The first one is to close out the interview. The second is to meekly comply and give the answer. You may not wish to respond in either of these two manners. The first loses a good possible job opportunity because of a poorly prepared interviewer. The second may harm your self-esteem and reinforce negative behavior.

There is another choice. The third way is to look behind the bad question for a good question that you can answer in such a way that you respond to a genuine and legitimate concern of the interviewer. Becoming hostile or defensive in the light of an inept interviewer does not serve you in the long run.

For example, you may be asked about your age. Consider that behind that question may be a very legitimate concern about older people sometimes not being active and having stamina for long hours or tough, hands-on work.

A professional, nondefensive response to discriminatory questions, in general, is to pause briefly and then state something like the following:

> *I think I know what you are getting at. If you are concerned about my ability to be energetic and have stamina, not to worry. Given the breadth of my experience, confidence, and drive, I am generally more productive and operate more effectively than colleagues many years my junior. Does that answer your question?*

Or, if you are asked about your husband's view of working wives or some similar, obvious sexist questions, you could respond by saying something like the following:

> *My being able to keep pace with demanding roles in my past companies, which also included international travel, has never been a problem. As you can see from my record of results, I am an effective*

executive and am very committed to my career, as you probably are. You'll note that I've had three promotions since returning to the workforce and have stayed with my last firm for six years. You can count on me, if we reach a fair offer, to be very committed to XYZ Corporation. Does that answer your concern?

Or, if the interviewer should be so thick as to persist in this line of biased questioning, you can also turn the heat up a little with a slightly more assertive response, such as:

I am frankly a bit puzzled about how that information is important to my job performance. If you could ask the question another way so that it relates to the job itself, I'm sure I can give you an answer that would reflect how I can provide value to your company.

Consultative Interviewing

Turnabout Is Fair Play: The interview should not be a one-sided affair with the employer dominating the question-asking. You have to know about the job, the company, and the people in your future employment situation. It is necessary to use your judgment to determine how and when to ask questions in an interview, as well as the number of questions.

Asking open-ended, penetrating questions help you "peel back the layers" of a company and demonstrate that you're interested and capable. It will also help distinguish you from other candidates. Obviously, neither the interviewer nor you will be asking all of the tough questions posed in this chapter. If you did, it would feel like an interrogation. I recommend that you study these and select the ones with which you are most comfortable and that are most important for you in a given job situation. Additionally, you might also wish to review your "Position Selection Criteria" sheet (Worksheet 22 in Chapter 5) for some areas of high importance.

Your Turn: 80 Penetrating Questions *You* Get to Ask

Position:

1. What is the scope of the position's responsibility, authority, and accountability, and how challenging is the position?
2. What is needed and wanted in this job?
3. What has worked or not worked well in this role previously? What did the previous incumbent not do that was needed?
4. What are the major roadblocks to accomplishing these? What are the five major accelerants to success?
5. Why is this position available? How long has it been open? Can I speak with the person who had this job previously?

6. What people in the company are under consideration for this job? What are their backgrounds and track record? If I get the job, how will they feel and act?

7. What is the organization of the department? How do the roles and responsibilities relate and sync?

8. What career growth and promotional opportunities are present beyond this current position? Give me an example of when someone was successfully promoted and why?

9. What are the five most significant things that need to be accomplished by this position within the first year?

10. How are these priorities linked to the key objectives of the company as a whole?

11. Imagine looking out two years and that I am very successful. What might have I accomplished, and what would the ROI have been?

12. How visible is this role to top management and the Board? How might I interface with them?

13. How much autonomy would I have to run my area once a budget has been approved? Can you give me an example of when this was effectively demonstrated by a direct report? An example of when it was not done well?

14. How is performance measured . . . and by whom?

15. To whom does this position report? What's his or her background and management style?

16. How would employees describe the extent to which they are informed, involved, developed, and promoted?

17. How are decisions reached in the department and in the company, and to what extent will I be involved?

18. What support does this position have from other functions, and how would I negotiate for this help?

19. Would you prefer to read written reports before we'd meet, or do you prefer real-time briefings?

20. What does the CEO see as her most important roles in the organization?

21. What is it like reporting to the CEO? What are his likes/dislikes?

22. How does the CEO provide constructive criticism?

23. How does my background meet your needs? What is not present?

24. When will a decision be made on this search?

25. What is the next step?

Organization:

26. What are the company's main strategies for growth in the future, including achieving its financial objectives? Where does the company want to be in three years?

27. What are the roadblocks and accelerants to the company achieving its annual and strategic plans? How can I help?
28. How does the strategic plan get developed? Who is involved?
29. What are the corporation's primary financial objectives and performance measures? How well are these metrics understood and focused on?
30. To what extent are these objectives uniform across all product lines?
31. How are the priorities for business opportunities established? Can you cite an example of a business opportunity successfully being realized?
32. What is the company's philosophy about its obligation to its shareholders? To its employees? To its customer regarding product quality, value, price, consumer safety, and customer satisfaction?
33. What emphasis does the corporation place on short-term results, as opposed to long-term successes?
34. What are the corporation's primary sources of capital and plans for expansion?
35. What is the company's attitude toward profitability and reinvestment in equipment, facilities, and people needed to stay ahead/abreast of changing technology and competition?
36. What image does the company want the *customer* to have of this company?
37. What image does the company want the *employees* to have of this company?
38. What image does the company want the *shareholders* to have of this company?
39. Describe the corporate culture or "personality" of the company.
40. Outline the organizational structure.
41. Who are the key executives in the organization, and what are their personalities, backgrounds, abilities, accomplishments, and professional/personal goals?
42. Describe the nature of the present decision-making process and the level of risk-taking throughout the organization.
43. To what extent does the corporation encourage and reward entrepreneurial managers? Provide examples, please.
44. What emphasis has the company put on professional managers versus entrepreneurial managers? How might this look going forward? Please elaborate.
45. Describe the company's philosophy on human resources, its programs, and the manner in which these programs are being achieved.
46. What is the mind-set of the leaders regarding being results-driven and risk-oriented as it relates to business and people issues?
47. To what extent is ROI a major measurement of management performance? How well do people operationalize that focus into their everyday lives? Can you give me an example of this?
48. How much do senior leaders rely on business practices such as scorecarding benchmarking, performance metrics, total quality management, open systems organization, and participative management?

49. How effective are managers in recruiting, hiring, and retaining quality personnel?

50. How effective are your managers in identifying poor performers and coaching them to a significantly higher level of performance? What have they done? What happens if a subordinate does not perform to expectations?

51. How often are performance reviews conducted? What do you like <u>most</u> about the process? Like <u>least</u> about the process?

52. How is success defined, and how is it measured, both informally and formally, including compensation?

53. Tell me about the people who fit the best in this organization. Describe them to me and what they are noted for.

Business Prospects:

54. What is the history of the company, including present and past product lines and the markets that they serve? Cite several notable successes and notable failures.

55. What is the company's business strategy regarding growth in the current product lines as opposed to development of new product lines or acquisitions?

56. Who are the corporation's major competitors?

57. How does the corporation anticipate maintaining its current sales levels? Anticipate maintaining its profit margins?

58. How vulnerable is the company to loss of key executives or a possible takeover?

59. What is the scope of the company's domestic and international operations in terms of revenues and employees? Total numbers and percentages?

60. What are the company's 1-year and 5-year sales objectives?

61. How much does management support/emphasize investing in the development of target business areas and in the divestiture of marginal products or business groups? Provide some examples. What is the intended and unintended P&L impact?

62. In what stages are products on the "growth curve?"

Strategic and Operating Plans:

63. Describe the nature of the planning process. How are decisions concerning the budgeting process made?

64. Identify the key corporate participants in the annual/strategic planning process?

65. What operating guidelines are used to monitor the planning process, the resources required, talent gaps, and the results?

66. What is the system of accountability to ensure the attainment of the operating and strategic plans?

67. How often and in what form does the company report its results internally to employees? What, if any, organizational surveys are conducted results?
68. How are results acknowledged and rewarded to the executive team and staff?
69. What are the repercussions of having a significant variance to the operating plan?
70. What is the company's typical response when a business unit manager does not make plan? How does this response contribute to or inhibit the attainment of the business plan in the future?

Dealing with Company Ownership Issues and Founders:

71. Of what aspects of your business and its people are you most proud?
72. What kind of legacy do you want to leave?
73. What are your aspirations for the company during the next five years? Ten years?
74. How confidential are the particulars of the company, such as sales size, number of employees, locations, specific names of key accounts, etc.?
75. Who is the person you rely on the most in the company? What role is this, and why do you rely so much on him or her?
76. How involved are your heirs in the business? What roles do they occupy?
77. How ready are your heirs to assume greater P&L responsibility? What else needs to occur to enhance their leadership capabilities and seasoning?
78. Who is on your Board, and what role does it play in your business?
79. What was the greatest calculated risk you took in growing the business, and what were the results?
80. What are the greatest challenges that your business will face in the next 5 to 10 years?

Interview Critique—Fine-Tuning Your Success

Your ability to learn from your interviews will be greatly enhanced if you critically evaluate each interviewer's needs, the company's demands, and how you can contribute in the role.

I recommend that after interviewing in an organization you complete the "Interview Critique Sheet." Before another interview, your review of these sheets will reinforce those things that went well and raise your awareness (and resolve) to eliminate your stumbling in the next interview.

If you keep these critiques current and diligently review them, you will find that you are able to master interviewing in a way you never thought possible. Your responses will be tighter, your answers more crisp, and your confidence raised. You'll also experience that your credibility is greatly enhanced and your enthusiasm highly contagious.

WORKSHEET 64

Interview Critique Sheet

Following each interview, complete these three questions. Use the information below when you write your thank-you letters and prepare for your next interview. Fill out this information immediately—before driving off. *Do not* wait until the next day to complete this, as your memory will grow stale on you.

1. What is one significant thing, said by each person you met, which could be a "hook" that you can refer to in a follow-up letter?

Name   Statement/Need

2. What are the most significant needs in the company (identified by each person you interviewed) that your skills match?

Name   Statement/Need

3. What should be mentioned in any follow-up letters that might improve your candidacy? This might include things to reinforce something about you or cover something that was omitted. Note: Always express your continued interest.

Name   Statement/Need

CHAPTER 18

DIGGING DEEPER— COMPETENCY-BASED INTERVIEWING

"What are you going to do for me?"

—All CEOs

What Is It?

Competency-based interviewing, also referred to as behavioral-based interviewing, is a selection system that focuses on job-related experiences, behaviors, knowledge, skills, and abilities. While this type of interviewing has been around for decades, it is formally coming back into greater use, notwithstanding few interviewers are truly skilled in this approach.

The premise of competency-based interviewing is this:

Your past behavior and performance is a predictor of your future behavior and performance.

The competencies relevant for you are those personal characteristics associated with the organization's culture and the traits that superior performers have demonstrated behaviorally. These competencies are unique to the job and company because they are culture- and values-driven.

While each organization has its own competencies by which it evaluates candidates for hire (and for compensation and promotional considerations), the process is often highly informal with little regard to structure. In fact, you'd be surprised by how few companies actually have *any* kind of integrated interviewing strategy or objective approach.

 Mastering competency-based interviewing will give you a leg up on your competition for the perfect job. If you do, I can guarantee that you will have superior interviewing skills to 90+ percent of your interviewers.

Admittedly, every organization will have its own core competencies that influence its personality and corporate culture and how people behave. However, the following is a list of the 10 essential executive competencies. These competencies are universally applicable to the vast majority of organizations, whether large or small, for-profit or non-profit, service or manufacturing, or publicly traded or privately held. Later in the chapter, in the "Executive Competencies and Targeted Behavioral Questions" section, we will work with each of these in greater detail.

10 Essential Executive Competencies

- Authenticity
- Self-management
- Intellectual agility
- Organizational awareness
- Interpersonal skills
- Communication skills
- Building effective teams
- Command skills
- Customer focus
- Integrity

Behaviorally, What Skills Do Employers Zero in On?

Employers zero in on functional skills, adaptive skills, and command skills:

1. *Functional skills.* These include the knowledge and skills that you have exhibited throughout your career and enabled you to achieve the role you have. *Functional knowledge* encompasses areas of responsibility, like manufacturing, distribution, marketing, and human resources, to name a few. *Functional skills* include "softer" issues, such as organizing, managing, developing, communicating, and so on.
2. *Adaptive skills.* These skills enable you to consciously make adaptive shifts in how you think, feel, and behave to accomplish a given task. Examples of this might be your interpersonal flexibility, your coping mechanisms, your positive expectancy, your biases and perspectives, and your personal drive, to name a few.
3. *Command skills.* These leadership skills include creating a compelling vision, managerial courage, drive for results, biases for action, timely decision making, and presentation skills.

What Types of Interviewing Questions Are There?

Hypothetical Questions

These questions place you in a hypothetical situation and test your intellectual ability to demonstrate your wisdom, judgment, experience, and interpersonal agility. The questions test your memory or commonsense skills more than in evaluating how you actually performed. For example: *If you had to develop a successor, what major traits and skills would you emphasize?* Or, *What competencies do successful leaders have?*

Leading Questions

Questions that telegraph what the interviewer is seeking are considered biased, as they "lead" the job candidate to the answer. For example: *You don't mind reporting to a younger boss, do you?* Or, *Don't you think that people at all levels should be allowed to work from home?*

Behavioral Questions

These types of questions ask you to provide examples of behavior from your past that demonstrate the kind of person you are and how closely aligned to the position's and company's competencies you are.

Most behavioral questions are "open-ended" and often begin with *Tell me, Who, What, Where, When, How*, and *Why*. As open-ended questions solicit an "essay" response, they are usually preferred. Nonetheless, there are times when "close-ended" questions are used to confirm specific information (You have your PhD, correct?). Of all the open-ended questions, *Why* and *What* probe the best beneath the surface as to your motivation for something. (*Why* did you get your PhD? *What* prompted you to write your dissertation on migrating executives?) A good example of *Tell me* questions are "Tell me something that you accomplished in the last three years of which you are particularly proud. Conversely, tell me something that you did in the last three years that did not work out so well."

Preparing for the Competency-Based Interview

The following are some tips for handling this type of interview.

- Perform your due diligence on the company.
- Evaluate the position specification.
- Match the position's competency with your results.
- Anticipate, prepare, and practice, practice, practice.

Let's look at each of these in turn.

Perform Your Due Diligence

Collect data. If you know the name of the organization, the role, and the individual to whom the position reports, research the organization, its competitors, and anything else that might seem to be relevant as it relates to its positive or adverse impact on the company.

- For public companies: study the annual report, 10K, proxy, and quarterly reports. If you are going in for an interview at the company, ask the hiring manager to send you some information beyond what you already have. Ask for product brochures, copies of several current and back employee newsletters, history of the company, and the like. If you are seeing the search firm, this information should be supplied by the executive recruiter, though not always.
- For private companies, request any information that is available, and check the company's Web site. If you deem it to be important, then you may wish to pay for a D&B (Dun & Bradstreet) report. Note: Not all the data that is in a D&B report is accurate, as many owners of private companies do not disclose confidential information.
- Investigate the interview schedule: How long, by whom, in what order? You may wish to give some thought to being the last interviewee (usually preferred). If you are the first person interviewed, you may educate the interviewer to ask increasingly better questions as the interviewing schedule progresses. All things being equal, you have a better chance of differentiating yourself from others if you have the opportunity to interview last.
- Evaluate online research capabilities: Start with *Hoover's* (www.hoovers.com), *The Wall Street Journal* (www.wsj.com), and recent magazine articles for personal background information on key executives in the organization that interviews you.
- Network: Contact people who might be able to speak knowledgeably about the company's culture, executive personalities, marketplace image and reputation, competitive advantages, major customers, and its history.

Evaluate the Position Specification

- Examine carefully any statements in the Personal Characteristics section regarding values, principles, beliefs, philosophy, behavior, and style. Based on discussions with the recruiter (or others), determine which of the personal characteristics are most important.
- Determine (or hypothesize) if specific competency statements were created because of the successes or failure of the previous incumbent.

- *Do not* just skim and say, "That's me!" Drill down and ask yourself to write out demonstrable proof and specifics, as if you were the recruiter.

Match the Position's Competency with Your Results

- Identify those characteristics that are most like you, and provide examples of when you performed or contributed to the P&L while displaying these competencies.
- The Career Summary statements on your résumé are typically statements of professional experiences, achievements, scope of influence, and the mosaic of your values. While they do not mention specific results, the statements point to behavior that is reflective of your competencies.
- The accomplishments on your résumé are expressions of actions and results. Statements of the "situation" or context are typically inferred or are embedded in your résumé accomplishments.
- Your first task is to add the situation or context of the accomplishment.
- Your second task is to weave in the competencies of the job spec into the story of your work history and accomplishments.

Anticipate, Prepare, and Practice, Practice, Practice

Since competency/behavioral-based interviewing is more deliberate and structured, so must you be. If you merely show up, thinking that your charisma, intellect, or enviable academic pedigree will land you the job, you will be disappointed and sadly mistaken.

By definition, competency-based interviewing is more challenging. While you might have great relationship skills, you have to prove that your personality, values, experiences, and results closely fit the organizational demands. All the more reason for you to *anticipate* competency and behavioral questions, *prepare* (as in write out) numerous S.A.R. (Situation, Action, Result) statements that closely align with the position specifications, and *practice, practice, practice* your responses so your delivery is smooth and you are confident and emboldened.

Peek Behind the Curtain

I'm giving you a peek behind the curtain so you can minimize the probability of being rattled in an interview that has a different set of rules. The four primary steps in the competency/behavioral interview are as follows:

1. Introduction
   - Begin mutual introduction.
   - Develop rapport.

- Set clear expectations as to how the interview will be conducted, the roles, and the scope of questioning.
- Outline the interview format and time frame.

2. Background review
   - Verify candidate's credentials: work history, education, and contact data.
   - Determine the fit of qualifications.
   - Ask why he/she is interested in being employed by the company.

3. Targeted interview questions
   - Interviewers will normally only ask one to two questions per competency, unless you are not clear or concise enough.
   - Interviewers do not tell you what competency they are asking about.
   - Interviewers rate your level of competency based on your responses. The three evaluative levels are Not Qualified, Entry-Level Experience Demonstrated, and Experienced-Level Demonstrated.

4. Summary/close. The interviewer—
   - Clarifies next steps. (The candidate moves to second interview or washes out).
   - Answer questions from the candidate.
   - Completes the rating and evaluation of candidates.

From the Employer's Perspective

Competency/behavioral interviews are significantly different from traditional interviews. In *traditional interviews*, the interviewer and the interviewee are on more or less equal footing. There is the normal ongoing give-and-take in a lively interview where both parties are asking questions and responding to them. Additionally, the interview process may be somewhat informal and unstructured.

Competency/behavioral interviews are different in that the interviewer is the only one asking the questions. The interviewer asks penetrating questions to elicit behavioral responses that indicate the level of demonstrated experience and skills. Also, the interview follows a fairly formal structure and process. Typically, if the organization will be employing the competency/behavioral interview approach they will inform you ahead of time. Specifically, you will be informed of the structured nature of the interview, including that this meeting will be interviewer-led with very little opportunity for the candidate to ask questions in the first interview.

As promised, let's drill down into each of the 10 essential executive competencies. We are going to take a look at a typical format that an employer might utilize when assessing executive candidates, utilizing a competency/ behavioral interview approach.

Executive Competencies and Targeted Behavioral Questions

Competency 1: Authenticity

Targeted Interview Questions:

- Describe a situation in which you candidly spoke the truth when others were holding back. What was the impact of that?
- Tell me of a time in which you were open and transparent when it was uncomfortable and you were at risk.
- Describe a time in which you were willing to admit that you were wrong. How were you wrong and what was the result of your acknowledgment?

Competency 2: Self-Management

Targeted Interview Questions:

- Describe a time when you did not insist on a direct report completing a project the way that you would have done it. What was the lesson for you, and what was the project's outcome?
- Tell me when you had to generate you own motivation to finish a challenging task, even though you were given little direction or were working alone. What were the circumstances, and how did you motivate yourself?
- When did you disagree with your boss's position on something important? What strategy did you employ to convince him of the merits of your thinking? What was the impact?

Competency 3: Intellectual Agility

Targeted Interview Questions:

- Describe a time in which you saw a solution to a perplexing problem that no one else did. What did you do, and what was your thought process that enabled you to have a broader perspective?
- When did you overcome an obstacle in an innovative manner? What was your strategy, what was innovative about it, and how did you get others to accept your suggestions?
- How have you helped others to expand their perspectives and see deeper nuances?

Competency 4: Organizational Awareness

Targeted Interview Questions:

- Tell me about a time when you had significant obstacles to overcome at the Board, staff, and organizational levels. Be specific about the process you used and the result.

- Describe how you keep informed of your organization's shifting climate, and what you do about it.
- What is the personality of your organization, and how does that personality impact how you lead and how decisions are made?

Competency 5: Interpersonal Skills

Targeted Questions

- Tell me about a time when you were able to adapt to a person from a background or culture different than your own. Why was it important to do so? What steps did you take to make this relationship work? What was the result?
- What has been your most positive interaction with a customer? What has made the relationship so great? How was the relationship established, and how do you maintain it?
- We all have difficult relationships. Tell me about a challenging situation where you had a difficult boss. What was your approach to "winning him or her over," and what was the result?

Competency 6: Communication Skills

Targeted Questions

- Give an example of a time you had to influence someone's view on a subject whose view was opposite of yours. What was your approach? How successful where you in changing his or her view?
- Let's talk about a time in which you had to provide a clear explanation of a difficult subject to someone with limited knowledge. What was the situation? How did you handle this? What was the result?
- Describe a situation with a lot was at stake where you were able to overcome a significant difference of opinion with a customer. How did you work through the situation with whom a lot was at stake?

Competency 7: Building Effective Teams

Targeted Questions

- Explain a situation where you contributed to a team's ability to reach a decision or goal. What steps did you take to convince others to understand your views or ideas? What were the results?
- Tell me about a time when you led a group with members with different interests, backgrounds, and perspectives. What differences in the group did you notice?

What part did you play in ensuring these differences did not get in the way of the group's objective?
- Describe a time you had to work closely to achieve a goal with people with whom you had little in common. What was the situation, and what did you do to ensure success? What was the result?

Competency 8: Command Skills

Targeted Questions

- Tell me about two of your current business objectives, and what you are doing to meet them.
- What have you done to turn a major project or the business around? How did you overcome resistance to your strategy, and what was the impact?
- Describe a time when you faced incredible odds but prevailed. Why was it so difficult, and what did you do to overcome this resistance?

Competency 9: Customer Focus

Targeted Questions

- Tell me about two ways you are currently working to better serve your customers. How have these efforts been successful?
- Share with me a time when it was important to get along with someone under difficult circumstances. What were the major issues, and how did you address them?
- Discuss the most difficult customer issue you have had. How did you address it, and what was the end result?

Competency 10: Integrity

Targeted Questions

- Tell me about a time when you made a decision that was unpopular with others. What was the situation, what did you decide, and what was the reaction? How were you able to resolve your differences? What would you do differently if you had to do it over again? Why?
- Describe a time when you were asked to do something you knew was wrong. What did you do? What was the result?
- Sometimes it seems processes get in the way of getting the work done. Describe a time when you questioned the value or usefulness of how something was done. What alternative methods did you offer? What was the outcome of your efforts?

S.A.R. It to Me! Answering Competency-Based Questions

Only a S.A.R. response is effective.

Situation.   Give an example of a situation in which you were directly involved.
Action.   Tell what action you and your team took.
Results.   Identify the soft and hard results and its impact on the organization.

I recommend that you use the three-minute rule. If you *practice* keeping your responses to three minutes or less, you won't be accused of talking *ad nauseum*. Your goal is to balance reporting the facts in a punchy manner while telling a story that weaves and leverages your behavior that matches the organization's competencies.

Example: Linking Competency to CIO's Résumé

- *Executive competencies:* Command Skills, Customer Focus
- *Résumé statement:* "Generated $80 million in incremental sales from the launch of the e-commerce site in its first year."

Table 18-1   Example of CIO's S.A.R.

Situation	The organization wanted to conduct business through an e-commerce portal. The market through online purchases was estimated to exceed $500 million annually. The company was headquartered in Amsterdam, with major divisions located in 20 countries. This was a major challenge since there was some resistance to this new approach.
Action	I assembled a top-notch, global, cross-functional team. I created a compelling vision for e-commerce and challenged people to exceed the company's expectations. I got alignment and commitment from the group. We collaborated and agreed on a three-phase approach—from communication to rollout—and developed a schedule and milestones for each phase. I met with the team weekly and the stakeholders monthly to report progress and get feedback.
Results	We launched the e-commerce site under budget and ahead of schedule, and we generated $80 million in incremental sales in the Web site's first year.

Example: Linking Competency to CFO's Résumé

- *Executive competencies:* Intellectual Agility, Building Teams
- *Résumé statement:* "Saved $25 million annually through effective lease negotiations for national retail store rollout."

Table 18-2   Example of CFO's S.A.R.

Situation	The corporation's strategic plan called for an aggressive campaign to go nationwide with retail stores for our active outdoor apparel business.
Action	I led a cross-functional team that set negotiating strategy, leasing cost parameters, and deadlines required to achieve the national rollout on time. I also served as chief negotiator.
Results	Leases were negotiated ahead of schedule at 20 percent below targeted rate on average and for a longer term, which was a major action in stores, achieving profitability six months in advance of plan. Eliminated $25 million annual rent exposure.

Your Turn—Creating Your S.A.R.s

Turn to your résumé, and flesh out all the accomplishment bullet points for at least the last five years. You may certainly go back further than that if previous S.A.R.s demonstrate a broader competency base. While there only three blank S.A.R. charts that follow, you may use the format from the downloadable exercises on RL's Web site. Good luck and happy S.A.R.-ing!

WORKSHEET 65

Your S.A.R.

Instructions: Refer back to the 10 common executive competencies highlighted earlier in this chapter. For each S.A.R. statement that you want to create, identify one to three competencies, and tie these competencies back to one specific results statement in your resume. Use short, crisp, punchy language as your identify the **situation,** the **action** that you took, and the quantitative or qualitative **results** you achieved.

Executive competencies: _____

_____

_____

Résumé statement: _____

_____

_____

Situation
Action
Results

WORKSHEET 66

Behavioral-Based Interview Questions

Instructions: To sharpen your interviewing skills, answer the following competency-based questions. Keep in mind that you will be requested to describe situations followed by a series of questions that probe deeper into what happened, your learning, the action that you took, and the results.

Give me a specific example of a time when your boss criticized your work in front of others. How did you respond? How has that event shaped the way you communicate with your boss? (Interpersonal skills competency)

Tell me about a time when your work or an idea of yours was unfairly criticized in a larger meeting. How did you respond? How has that event shaped the way you communicate with that person? (Authenticity competency)

Give me a specific example of a time when you sold a key customer on a leading-edge idea or concept. How did you do it?   What was the result? (Customer focur competency)

Describe the system you use for keeping track of multiple projects. How do you track your progress so that you can meet deadlines? How do you stay focused? (Command skills competency)

Describe a specific problem you solved for your employer. How did you approach the problem? What role did others play? What was the outcome? (Intellectual agility competency)

Describe a time when you got coworkers who disliked each other to work together. How did you accomplish this? What was the outcome? (Interpersonal skills competency)

Tell me about your most notable failure. What things did you fail to do? What were the repercussions? What did you learn? (Self-management competency)

Describe a time when you put your needs aside to help an employee understand a task. How did you assist him or her? What was the most effective way this person learned? What was the result? (Building effective teams competency)

Describe a politically charged mess that you were thrown into the middle of and you failed. What was at stake? What did you do? How did you fail? What didn't you do? What could you have done differently? Where did you hold back? What was the outcome? (Organizational awareness and integrity competencies)

Tell me about a time when you blurted something you regretted. What did you actually say? What were you trying to say? What was the impact? What is your learning about what unconscious belief you were holding onto that led to your blurting what you did? (Communication skills competency)

Give me two examples of when you showed great leadership. Why did you chose these examples? How do you define great? What did you do that was great? If I talked to your boss, what would he or she say was great? What was the P&L impact? What were the "soft" results? What made these "soft" results great? (Command skills competency)

How Does the Process Work from an Employer's Perspective?

The following table outlines the steps of the interview process from the employer's perspective.

Table 18-3   Steps in Competency-Based Interview Process

Step One	The hiring manager and HR identify specific competencies for the job and are incorporated in the job specification. Interviewers are selected.
Step Two	Interviewers asks job candidate open-ended questions about best/worst work experiences in the last three years. Prompts are used to capture behavioral terms as well as expressions of thoughts and feelings.
Step Three	Candidate's statements are transcribed, analyzed for relevant behaviors, and evaluated for quality and intensity. Typically, each interviewer numerically rates the candidate.
Step Four	Resultant competencies are compared to the job spec and recommendations are prepared: "Good fit" or "Bad chemistry." Ratings are compared from all the company's interviewers, and a final decision "Hire" or "Not Hire" or "Hold" is made.

Readiness Is Essential

Do Your Research

"Know thyself . . . and thy competencies." The text and worksheets in this book will help immeasurably in getting you grounded in who you are and polishing your skills and accomplishments.

You will absolutely want to know what this role encompasses and what competencies it (and you) will be measured against. If the company representative or the executive recruiter does not have a prepared set of competencies, take brief notes that capture the competencies "headings." Most recruiters have a position specification from which you'll be able to guesstimate the relevant competencies.

Get Prepared

The reality is that you need more preparation and practice for competency-behavioral interviewing than a traditional approach.

Regardless of whether you know the company and exact role for which you are being considered, when it's your turn to ask questions it is recommended you do two things in the context of the top 10 Executive Competencies.

First, identify your major competencies and calibrate them against the top 10 Executive Competencies. For each of your major competencies, develop stories/vignettes from your experiences that crisply and powerfully illustrate a number of S.A.R.s *and* competencies. Do not forget: You should be able to deliver each vignette in three minutes or less. If you get caught up trying to impress the interviewer with 25,000 well-chosen words, you've lost.

Second, develop your own list of questions that correspond to the executive competencies so that you interview the organization and boss, similarly using the behavioral interviewing format.

Listen for Opportunities to Leverage

If you listen deeply to the messages and the meanings of the interviewer's words, you will get most, if not all, of what you need to successfully communicate your competencies and capabilities. When your competencies and behaviors are presented naturally and fluidly in the conversation, you will have impressed the interviewer with your genuineness, but you also created great leverage for your candidacy. If you are well prepared and rehearsed, you will be able to focus intensely on the interviewer, versus being distracted composing your responses when he or she takes a breath.

Partner Up and Get Straight Feedback

The only way any of us will advance in our learning or skills is by getting straight, honest feedback that is focused on helping us improve. Practice with a confident and authentic partner. If possible, have your partner videotape your delivery and provide unvarnished feedback aimed at improving your skills. Legitimize your partner giving you straight feedback, and commit to not becoming defensive or feeling disappointed when you didn't produce the result you wanted—at that time.

Remember: Defensiveness is always rooted in feelings of shame, humiliation, and of "losing face." My suggestions:

- Lighten up; take what you *do* seriously, not yourself.
- View such feedback as a gift to master your interviewing skills.
- Shift your focus to what you will gain from this experience.
- Thank your partner for being willing to risk telling you the truth.

Summary

Now is the time to roll up your sleeves and invest in yourself. Networking is the key to getting your foot in the door. Interviewing is what gets you behind the desk in the corner office. While I realize mastering the techniques in Chapters 16 through 18 can be daunting, it is essential for your job search. Take a few questions a day; sit down and begin. Answer the first question right now.

STEP 6
MANAGING THE CAMPAIGN

CHAPTER 19

MANAGE YOUR CAMPAIGN— SUSTAIN THE MOMENTUM

Successful Career Search Formula

The quote below from Robert Browning describes how I feel about a successful career search campaign. A successful campaign will stretch you. And you will grow considerably, personally and professionally, in the process.

 "Ah, but a man's reach should exceed his grasp, or what's a heaven for?"
—Robert Browning

With that in mind, there is a formula to a successful career search.

- If you make 20 really solid networking calls a day, you'll probably reach five people and generate at least three networking meetings. The rest will be voice mails that you will need to follow up on.
- Making 100 networking calls a week will yield 15 or more commitments for personal meetings, spanning 30 days. Accordingly, 75-plus voice messages are in your networking pipeline to be followed up on over the next few weeks.
- Given this ongoing level of activity of being able to get at least three networking visits for every 20 calls, you should be able to *generate at least five meetings a week* without any trouble, if you sustain your efforts.
- Experience has shown us that for every 10 networking meetings, one of these can be considered a bona fide interview versus merely networking.
- Determine your daily/weekly networking goal, factor in some slippage, plot the timetable, commit yourself to the task at hand, and never, never give up.

Manage Your Search . . . Versus Having It Manage You

It's not uncommon for you to feel a bit overwhelmed by all that you have to do to get that ideal job. Any task with multiple elements might seem overwhelming at first, until you organize your activities into smaller pieces with definitive outcomes and timetables. Yes, I admit that there are many nuances involved to getting the right job.

Be committed to your success. Don't let anything distract you from your goal. These tips, tools, and techniques are all successful and proven with executives like you. How well they work for you depends on how diligently you work at mastering them.

Why Establish Career Search Goals?

As the Cheshire Cat said to Alice when she was lost, "If you don't know where you are going, then any road will take you there."

 Your job hunting will probably take three times as long as you would like and will require 10 times the patience you thought you had.

Rather than have you wander aimlessly like the characters in Lewis Carroll's *Alice in Wonderland*, I want to help you develop a strategy to get what you want. To achieve your career search goals, you obviously need to know the following:

- Where you are headed
- How to get there
- A timetable for accomplishment
- Contingency plans for problems
- A method to measure when you're successful and when you're not

Plan of Action

How well you achieve your search goals will depend on how deeply committed you happen to be and how well you develop a detailed plan of action. A contractor would not think of building a house without detailed blueprints and material specifications, regardless of how experienced he might be. Yet it is ironic that people, perhaps even yourself, launch a career search without hardly any advance planning. If you identify your desired outcomes, become committed to your successfully reaching these goals no matter what, and diligently work your plan, you greatly increase your chances of success.

"I don't care how long you worked or how hard you worked. The only thing that matters is results. Ultimately, you are paid for results!"
—Anonymous

Record Keeping

Maintaining accurate, up-to-date records will greatly aid you in keeping organized and increasing your search momentum. Nothing is more embarrassing than receiving a phone call from a prospective employer and not being able to link up the name of the caller with an organization. However, if you establish a simple, easy-to-use system early on, you will not be in the position of having to create one once you actively begin networking and interviewing.

After Mailing to Search Firms and Target Organizations—Nine Ways to Create Momentum

1. Each evening, identify the 10 most appropriate search firms and interesting target organizations you want to contact. Write them down and gather contact data, including why you might be a good fit. Also, select 10 new personal contacts to call.
2. Research the search firms and target organizations (using networking, the Internet, directories, phone calls to the firm's receptionist, etc.). Develop a file of reprints on your core target companies, the competition, and the industry. When you network into your target organizations, utilize this information in your conversations with them.

    Identify the key contacts in your target search firms and organizations and possible areas of interest or concern to these companies. These would be the people you would most likely be closely interacting with if hired.
3. Call several of your network contacts and ask them if they know anyone in your newly identified target organizations. (This includes anyone they know that may know someone in these organizations.)

    While you are talking with your networking contacts, you'll also want to get names of additional search firm partners and additional leads. Remember, follow up on the leads your contacts give you immediately, and get back to your contacts to keep them posted on your success with their contacts. They will appreciate it.

4. Don't cut into prime networking hours (from 7a.m. to 9 p.m.) by compiling your notes and getting focused. I recommend that you conduct your research and get organized the night before. That way, you can begin calling these key search firm and organizational contacts right away before an assistant is present to be a gatekeeper. Briefly leverage your personal contacts, introduce yourself, your capabilities and interest in meeting for purposes of PAIR (Personal Advice, Information, and Referrals).

5. When you contact your target companies, seek to set up an interview with each key contact, again for purposes of introduction. Failing that, secure a commitment to a follow-up phone call sometime in the near future, even if it is to periodically inform them of your status. Before ending this conversation, add value about your credentials/capabilities.

   Note: Everyone's time is precious. Don't be discouraged if you get rebuffed as you seek meetings. Even if you have a fantastic referral from an accomplished senior executive, you still may not be able to get any face-to-face time with a senior recruiter.

6. Develop a personalized thank-you letter for each telephone interchange you have. If you spent time on the telephone with one of your key people a thank-you note is appropriate. Keep in mind, only a fraction of job seekers write thank-you letters. Become the tough competitor to beat by doing something that distinguishes you from others. Again, you may use e-mail or a hand-written note card as your means of transmitting your thanks.

7. Go on "interviews". An introductory meeting is counted as an "interview" even if there is no immediate, visible opening. After each interview, write a thank-you letter individualized for each person you saw.

8. Set up a follow-up plan including next-step strategies and specific dates on which you will telephone, write, or visit. Mark the dates on your calendar or in your PDA. Commit to executing your plan and following through on these follow-up dates.

9. Select 10 more firms and 10 more contacts. Start the process again. If you didn't make your goal, don't be discouraged. Just keep focused and committed to moving forward each day.

Job Hunting Success Strategies

In order to conduct an active search, one which yields results, I recommend you create a significant amount of focused activity around your search. The following Success Strategies address each of the four main career search avenues by your probability of success.

Personal Contact Networking

Up to 80 percent of executive positions are filled through networking, in some form or fashion. When you network effectively you are able to identify opportunities in both the "hidden marketplace" and the "open marketplace." Networking can be an exhilarating experience with strangers graciously extending themselves on your behalf. Networking can also be frustrating, as some people may not support you as much as you would like because you caught them by surprise. You may have presumed you had a better relationship than you do or you might have mangled your request for help, including not helping them help you. They may have honestly thought they didn't have any appropriate contacts or leads to pass on. Or, even though they may genuinely want to help, they get busy and do not follow through with information promised to you.

Remedy:

- Maintain 100 percent accountability for the effectiveness of your networking and search success. Keep the perspective, "If it is to be, it's up to me!" If your networking is not yielding the results you desire, evaluate what thoughts, feelings, and behavior you must change for you to be successful.
- Before calling, know your agenda and the goal of your call. Always be sure you know precisely what you want from your personal contacts **before** you approach them.
- Give your contacts a typed list of your top 10 to 30 target search firms and/or organizations. Ask whether they know any senior executive employed there or if they know of someone *else* who would know an executive employed there.
- Prepare and practice your responses to some basic questions to demonstrate that you are composed and confident. Even with business acquaintances be prepared to answer such things as, Why are you leaving? What are you looking for, role wise? What are your short-/long-range objectives? What are three of the most significant things you have accomplished in your career?"
- Refresh your memory by turning to Chapter 12, "Power Networking—Unlocking the Secrets to Career Success." Remember to do the following with your contacts:
  1. Inform people of your status.
  2. Ask for help and information concerning:
     - Executive search firm contacts
     - Target organizations
     - Personal leads
     - Opportunities
  3. Legitimize sending your résumé, *and* following up periodically to see if your contact has any additional leads or information for you.
     - Never e-mail when you can call.
     - Never have a detailed phone conversation when you can meet someone.

○ Personal communication is the best way to network.
○ Make a complete list of everyone that you know—50 to 2,000 people. Prioritize these people in A, B, C categories. Work the list of your "A" priorities above all other search avenues. If you recall, I mentioned that 80 percent of all executive jobs come through networking. Look up names of people you know from where you work, go to school, exercise, worship, as well as relatives, neighbors, vendors, consultants, and salespeople whom you know.
○ Initiate a minimum of 20 calls per day. Your goal is to speak with at least 10 people daily.

My commitment is _____ conversations per day.

Retained Executive Search Firms

Executives connect through a direct recruiter contact in approximately 15 percent of the time. Accordingly, if you were to network into a search firm, your probability of success would be higher. Retained executive search recruiters are in the people business. Like so many of us, they have multiple roles. They sell their services to client firms, they search for talent, and they sell the concept of a career change to qualified executives. The dilemma. Recruiters like to meet people, *and* they are invariably overwhelmed with requests from executive job-seekers wanting to meet. The challenge for you, then, is how to most appropriately network in without being seen as a burdensome obligation or chore. This push-pull is one of the main reasons why it can be pretty tough to get a call back from a recruiter.

Remedy:

• Ask your personal contacts for the names of search firm executives they respect and would recommend. Have your contact call on your behalf or, minimally, use your contact's name to obtain a personal discussion. As search firm executives are inundated with candidates seeking a personal audience, you will need to persevere and be patient to get through.
• Maintain or update your file on "open positions" in which search firms have used you as a network resource. You are simply calling back for a return favor.
• Call the search firm partner back once or twice to let the recruiter know that you are really interested, but then back off unless you have time to burn and you really want to talk. Recognize, though, if the recruiter does *not* return your calls that the chances are slim there is anything very interesting there. You might also wish to zero in on those firms that you know specialize in your field.
• Watch advertisements in professional trade journals from search firms who place repetitive ads for jobs within your discipline. Even if the particular ad does not

exactly fit your experience, they might have something else they are not advertising.

Again, never agree to pay anyone a fee for finding you a job. Standard industry practice relies on the company to pay the fee and all reasonable expenses.

- National search: Network with 50+ search firms. Mail to 300+ firms.
- Local search: Network into 25+ search firms. Mail to 100+ firms.
- Continue to expand your list of those you inform of your candidacy. Use your personal contacts to network into the practice partner in charge of your specialty or industry after a few weeks to ensure that they filed your credentials under your area of expertise. Your goal may be to leverage an interview.
- Use your network contacts to open the door into three to four search firms per day, connecting with key account executives.

My commitment is _____ connections with search firms per week.

Target Organizations

Only three percent of executive roles are filled by "cold calling/writing" directly to companies. On that basis alone, you should not spend a lot of time pursuing this low-yield search venue. Well-known companies receive a tremendous number of employment inquiries. It is not uncommon for a high-visibility organization to receive thousands of letters each week. Because of the time and expense involved in responding to each letter that comes in, you may not receive a personalized return letter or call if you were networking. Be mindful of your probable emotional response when you get a postcard acknowledgment of your résumé: "If this is how they treat people, I do not want to work there." Ironically, *that* company may be the best place in which to work, given its reputation. After all, look at how many people wish to connect with them.

Remedy:

- If your reject letter was personally written by the decision maker you wanted to reach, you may wish to write a follow-up letter. For a good example of an effective letter, turn to Chapter 8, "Create Powerful Marketing Letters That Evoke Action!" By doing so, you will definitely be in the minority of candidates responding a second time.
- Follow up on your letter with a call approximately a week later to attempt to establish a relationship and solicit leads. In effect, you turn the prospective employer who "rejected" you into a personal contact. Will you get rejected often? Absolutely, in the vast majority of time. But when you strike a lead, it's great!

- Acknowledge to the employer that while the company might not have any current openings, you would like very much to be considered when something develops.
- Network into your target organizations if you want to be noticed. I used to think that it was productive to mail your résumé, with a cover letter, to hundreds of target organizations. Not anymore. As I previously mentioned, less than 3 percent of direct mail contact (e-mail/snail mail) leads to offers. If you have organizations in mind, why not network into them and increase the probability from less than 3 percent to 80 percent?
- By making follow-up calls to the specific individuals identified at each target organization, you will be able to considerably expand your networking base. Have a goal to never hang up without at least one lead, though don't be overly adamant, lest you lose.
- There is good news–bad news concerning mailings to target organizations. The *good news* is that you might feel that you are actively engaged in your campaign. You've done exhaustive research on the Internet, you have invested money in databases, and you've identified your prime target companies. You have produced a solid, clear accomplishment: sending out lots of résumés, albeit unsolicited.

  The *bad news* is that mailing to hundreds or thousands of target organizations is a "C" priority. Such a mailing lulls most job searchers into sitting back and thinking that the calls and offers will come pouring in. There is a direct correlation to the size of the mailings with the reluctance to network. The greater the trepidation, the greater the tendency to retreat into passive (e.g., nonproductive) search activity. While I acknowledge that mailings to organizations does work, I liken it to the adage, "Even a blind squirrel stumbles across an acorn occasionally." Mailing directly to someone you do not know does generate interviews, though very rarely. Your best bet, by far, continues to be networking into your target organizations. That's your "A" priority search strategy.

My commitment is to network into___ organizations weekly.

Advertisements—Internet and Classifieds

Along with target organization mailings, ads generally represent the lowest yield for job candidates—less than 2 percent. Since executive clients at all levels have successfully connected by responding to ads—"open and blind"—we recommend that you continue to respond to them. However, do not spend hours scouring the Internet or classified advertisements. Don't get sucked into seeking your job through ads, thinking that, at least, there are bona fide job openings on the Internet or in the papers.

Remedy:

- Commit to spending no more than 30 minutes a day exploring open positions on the Web. There will not be a huge number of executive jobs listed there, anyway.
- Master the use of search agents on the major search engines. To effectively explore this venue, while expending less than 2 percent of your effort, I recommend that you revisit Chapter 15, "Into the Vortex—Internet Career Searching—(Plus Traditional Classified Advertisements)."
- In the case of positions listed in the classifieds, if you have not heard back from the prospective employer within 20 days, respond again with your résumé. Your original correspondence and résumé may have been misplaced. To renew interest, refer to Chapter 8, "Create Powerful Marketing Letters That Evoke Action!"
- If the ad identifies the company, call the company and ask to speak to the head of the department. Explain your situation and express continued interest. Go for it! You have nothing to lose and everything to gain! Correspondingly, when you craft your letter to this decision-maker, you'll be able to personalize the letter.
- Like direct mailing to target organizations, ad responses only lead to a job offer in 2 percent or so of the cases. Nonetheless, when you see an advertisement that resonates with you, respond. Respond to a minimum of six ads per week via the Internet or in the classified section of your local or target city newspapers.
- Look for and respond to ads that fit your objective. "Blind ads in the newspaper" are OK. Respond to those that fit, highlighting in the insert sections of your cover letter the things that the ad specifies. Write out your response immediately so they don't pile up! *Date your cover letters three days after the ads appear*, then mail your letters at that time. Why wait? More than 70 percent of all ad responses come in within the first week of the ad's appearance. You want your résumé to appear in the trickle, not the flood of résumés.

My commitment is to respond to____ ads per week.

20 Tips to Empower Your Campaign and Keep It on Track

1. Be open to the possibility of successfully getting connected utilizing any one of the job search avenues, not just the way you connected the last time when you looked for a job.
2. Take complete responsibility for follow-up to your contacts or companies. Don't accept "Don't call us, we'll call you" as valid.

3. Spend 80 percent of your time on those activities which generate 80 percent of the action. That's networking, in case you've had a lapse.

4. Do not give up on one (or more) of your prime target organizations after they tell you, "Sorry, we do not have any openings." More than 50 percent of our clients create their own jobs in organizations in which there was no bona fide opening previously.

5. Use the positive feelings that you have after a super networking call or interview to aggressively pursue additional opportunities because you want multiple offers from which to choose.

6. Contact your networking contacts more than once. Contact your search firm recruiters more than once. Contact your target organizations more than once.

7. Write timely thank-you letters that provide value and make the reader think about what you have said and the position you espoused.

8. Create an "article file" of relevant and timeless articles of interest. Few people send articles of value to key interviewers or network contacts after a conversation. If you do so, you will be seen as unique and distinctive. My article file is pretty eclectic and covers the gamut: leadership, creativity and innovation, change management, change agents, teaming, creating synergies, organizational alignment, etc.

9. Do not become cocky in the second and third interview, thinking "the job is mine." If you do, you'll invariably ratchet back your drive, energy, and efforts to continue to network and secure additional interviews.

10. Always remember that you are up against very stiff competition, so you need to look for ways to create additional positive exposure for yourself.

11. Always evaluate the impact your behavior and words have while networking and in interviews so you are constantly assessing your "story" against how it might sound to others.

12. Remember: Executive search firms work for the employer; they don't work for you.

13. Become known in companies and to others as a talented person *before* you come out of your organization (next time) and *before* there are openings.

14. Write individualized thank-you letters to multiple interviewers in the same company.

15. Develop a "consultant's perspective" while interviewing, which will enable you to legitimately probe, observe, and challenge the interviewers. Additionally, become skilled in writing "mini–proposals," thereby creating a significant distinction between you and your competition.

16. Do not identify salary data in a letter in response to an ad because it stated, "Only résumés with salary history and requirements will be considered." If your background is interesting and fits, you will get called.

17. Do not believe that blind ads necessarily mean actual jobs—they may be placed by search firms wanting to "round out" their files or by companies seeing who is in the market.
18. Respond to newspaper advertisements a second time within 20 days if you have not heard back from them the first time. It is recommended that you respond within hours of ads posted on the Internet, given the level of competition.
19. Use the bad experience from one interview to reaffirm your commitment to always be prepared. See this experience as a valuable learning opportunity—not defeat.
20. Do not project your fears into situations that don't call for them. For instance, when you do not get a timely call back, resist the temptation to rationalize ("I wouldn't want to work for such a rude company!") or beat yourself up unnecessarily ("I'm not seen as a player; that's why I'm not getting any calls back.").

Handle Rejection with Wisdom and Grace

No one likes to be rejected. While rejection for a job is more of a business decision, it stills feels personal. Here you are, exposing yourself, being vulnerable, and you get rebuffed. It may hurt or it may not. You *will* get rejected for a lot of reasons—some valid, some not. The challenge is to sort out the valid rejects from the invalid ones and turn them into your advantage. To a good salesperson, a "no" is almost the same as a "yes"; it just requires a different strategy to win. In this process of job changing, you may get stuck. You may feel as if you are off track or are not moving forward like you should. Don't worry; this is a normal part of the campaign. All is not lost. There are remedies to handle rejection and to get going again. Consider these ideas contained herein as part of your turnaround strategies. Don't beat yourself up or blame others. When you feel victimized by rejection you are powerless to change the situation.

By assuming complete accountability for creating the rejection, and the feelings you attach to it, you have the power to change the circumstances. You are the only person that is able to get your head, your heart, and your gut back into the game. Play ball!

Consulting or "Trial Employment"

There are a number of innovative ways to get hired in companies. This section outlines one possibility. As part of your search strategy, you may wish to consider consulting or "trial employment" with a company that might be reluctant to commit to full-time employment, for whatever reason. Trial employment is utilized when you or the company is not yet 100 percent committed to a permanent, full-time employment relationship. Trial employment usually looks like project-based consulting and has a given time limit. For you, trial employment is a great hands-on way to demonstrate your capabilities. For the company, trial employment is a golden opportunity for you to accomplish something significant and begin to identify with the company culture, its people, and its challenges. Organizations are becoming increasingly, receptive to trial employment as part of a short-term consulting engagement or as an easy way to move from "temp to perm" employment. This is also an excellent method of evaluating the suitability of a candidate, and it represents a tremendous opportunity for you to scrutinize the company as well.

Caution: Do not undertake a consulting assignment or temporary employment if it will not lead anywhere. Your career search momentum may be severely damaged if you consult for a company on an extended basis if it does not further your career goals. However, if you are running low on funds or you have been unemployed for an extended period of time, let's say more than 12 months, having a consulting engagement or two helps explain your extended search. Plus, having a successful consulting engagement is a great way to become reenergized, confident, and grounded again in you capabilities and talents.

The Challenge of an Elongated Search

Many very talented executives have elongated search campaigns. Some are unwilling to relocate. Some individuals are committed to breaking out of their industry niche where they have spent 25 years, and it's difficult to convince recruiters and employers that their leadership skills are readily transferable. Other executives are seeking higher level positions or different roles. This often occurs when a SVP seeks to become a COO or CEO. Or, a CFO in a large privately held company is seeking to become the CFO of a public company. Likewise the senior staff attorney vying for a GC role faces the same challenges. Given the pressure to perform and execute flawlessly, employers and Boards of Directors are reluctant to risk hiring someone who is not currently a "sitting" CEO, COO, CFO, or GC. That's the reality that you face if you are dramatically changing your focus including, moving up, or shifting functions.

Still others have elongated campaigns because of some personal attribute, for example, if the person is painfully shy and has a difficult time projecting boldness, confidence, or enthusiasm. Or, there might be some job-hunting deficiency, such as the lack of networking ability. I have discovered that the lack of success in career changing is more attitudinal than it is a permanent, unchangeable flaw.

If your search is elongated or in danger of becoming so, there are some definitive actions you can take, albeit they might be somewhat uncomfortable. The challenge and opportunity is to objectively examine what is working well and what is not working well. While you might not wish to gain straight feedback from others, as they might tell you to begin doing the very thing you fear the most—like networking—it is important to do so. It's been my experience that whenever I feel uncomfortable about proceeding down a path I know to be correct, I'm invariably holding onto a disempowering belief that erodes my confidence, positive action, and forward momentum.

If you have an elongated search, I invite you to examine your disempowering beliefs. Try a different tact. Experiment with thinking, feeling, and behaving differently, and see if that might produce a better result. Recommit to mastering those career search elements that you resist the most. You know which they are. You are worth the effort. Quit contributing to your greatest roadblocks.

Shhh, I've Retired—Don't Tell Anyone

When talented executives have a protracted search campaign, I always look for extenuating circumstances. I always look for and ask, "What's going on here that is getting in the way of successfully finding that perfect job?"

I had a candid, straightforward conversation with one of our clients who had unknowingly retired. The only problem was that he hadn't yet admitted it to himself. Protests to the contrary, he had withdrawn from the race. It was quite obvious to me that this very talented, yet frustrated, executive-entrepreneur was filled with excuses and complaints. Bottom line: He feared rejection. He thought networking was beneath him. Equally revealing was the fact that this highly resourceful client employed few, if any, of the strategies we jointly created on how to overcome his disempowering beliefs and behavior. All these things, coupled with his extended trips, led me to hypothesize that he had, indeed, retired. In fact, he sheepishly admitted that he had needed the nudge from us to legitimize it with his wife.

Another case in point: Early one afternoon I spent two hours with one of our clients who was rounding the curve on being out of the job market for two years. I had called him three months ago to set up this meeting. However, when I called, he informed me that the very next day he and his wife were off on a 45-day junket to Asia, followed by several weeklong golfing trips around the United States and Ireland. So, today was the first available time he had for a discussion that he said he desperately wanted. His bottom line: Since selling his business for $33 million two years ago, he retired without declaring so. He was the envy of his golfing buddies, traveling worldwide and very successfully managing his investments. A large part of my meeting was focused on helping this executive feel okay, whether he was retired or not. For example, he now had the money and time to take the trips he never took before, given the press of his business. He spent a lot more time with the inner-city youth support organization as a board member. He also treated his wife to her dream—a series of gourmet cooking classes in Provence, France.

The point is this: It's okay to retire if you have the means. While you've earned the right to retire, my only caveat is retire for the right reasons. Run happily *toward* a more enriched lifestyle; don't run *away* from your discomfort of networking, for example. If you decide to retire, honor the contributions you've made over the years and the legacy you've left. Rejoice in your ability to move into a new phase of your career and life.

 Remember the adage: "Plan your work and work your plan."

CHAPTER 20

REVITALIZE YOUR CAMPAIGN— WHAT TO DO WHEN YOUR CAMPAIGN IS STALLED, STUCK, OR DERAILING

On Your Roller Coaster—Hang On!

Managing a highly intense job search can be very heady; much like riding a world-class roller coaster. There are some exhilarating ups and some heart-stopping plummets. Plummets occur when the number of interview trips declines suddenly, when the phone goes silent, or when you are repeatedly the runner-up for the ideal job.

The point is, even if your campaign rides like a roller coaster, hang on! One never gets off a roller coaster when it is still moving. Do not operate every day as if it were a life and death matter. You have the tools to do the job. Remember, you have been successful before . . . you will be successful again.

Patience, Patience, Patience

Ironically, now is the best of times and the worst of times. This is a time when you may feel both exuberant and depressed. There is a psychological high after having "launched" into the marketplace. You wait expectantly for the harvest of positive phone calls and letters. They may come sparingly. You know that patience is required, yet you wish your situation would be different, that you would get 12 calls the next day.

Experience has shown that these calls do come, but at a much slower pace than is comfortable. Regardless of this advance warning, you will probably experience feelings of being let down, abandoned, even betrayed. After all, you did your part; you sent out your résumés and so on.

On the other hand, if your situation is such that three days after you broadcast your job search you get flooded with calls, great! You are in the minority, and we applaud the success of your well-cultivated network, your market approach, good fortune, and great timing. But even with a highly successful campaign, you need to be aware of the normal emotional swings from highs to lows.

This part of the campaign requires you to balance your expectations with plenty of patience. Remember, thousands of people like you have been there—thousands of times before. Patience! Have confidence—the process will work for you if you work at mastering it.

Stress and Its Impact

Stress in a search campaign is inevitable. No matter how enthusiastic and optimistic you might be, stress comes to all. If you tend to be a "half-empty-glass person," you will probably be more pessimistic and stressed. Unless you manage your stress, it's likely that you will be consumed by it. Correspondingly, you'll have some rough times. How does stress reveal itself?

WORKSHEET 67

Common Physical Stress Sensations

CIRCLE all those physical traits that you are experiencing. These sensations might be symptomatic to acute stress. Consult your physician if you are experiencing these physical sensations on a prolonged basis.

Drained	Insomnia
Lifeless	Fatigued
Empty	Cold extremities (hands, feet, nose)
Out-of-body	Shaken
Drifting	Tunnel vision
Falling	Jittery/fidgeting
Tight	Clammy skin
Muscles clenched	Slurred/interrupted speech
Teeth/jaw ache	Inappropriate behavior
Headache	Low tolerance for noise/light
Joints/muscles ache	Reddened complexion
Diminished	Pale complexion
Uneasy	Tight clothing
Nauseated	Suffocating
Weak	Frequent need to urinate
Listless	Spastic colon
Roaring in head	Dilated pupils
Slow motion	Tingling scalp and skin
Fast motion	Light headed
Clumsy	Difficulty swallowing
Under/over eating	Lump in throat
Oversmoking	Overdrinking
Hyperventilating	Over medication
Biting nails	Overly loud talking
Spots in vision	Overly soft talking
Not hearing words said	Feeling crowded

WORKSHEET 68

Common Emotions When Under Stress

CIRCLE all those emotions or thoughts that you are experiencing. These sensations might be symptomatic to acute stress. Consult your physician if you are experiencing these emotions and thoughts on a prolonged basis.

Unloved	Apathetic
Discarded	Used
Worthless	Unappreciated
Unclean	Loss of sexual appetite
Impotent	Lost
Emotionless	Scolded
Alone	Forgetful
Disjointed	Sudden attack of doubt
Giddy	Depressed
Hair-trigger temper	Attacking others
Indecisive	Need to be neat
Blaming others	Afraid to trust
Ignoring differences	Attached/threatened
Denying being terminated	Low self-respect
"Replaying" events	Low self-worth
Name calling	Sadness
Powerless, incapable	Unable to dissociate from former employer

Common Thoughts When Under Stress

I'm not as good as I thought.

It's not my fault!

I need to defend my position.

Effective people do not get stressed!

I am not stressed!

Others are biased and prejudiced; not me!

Broken promises are the rule of the day.

There is only one way to learn—the hard way!

I will now manipulate others for my gain; that's the way.

Oh, no, not another problem! I can't cope!

If I ignore this problem, it will go away.

I have been taking on problems that are not mine.

I can't seem to say no.

Most situations are impossible!

Can't anyone do anything right anymore?

It is not fair! How come? Why me?

Take Accountability . . . and Shed Your Stress!

When you are stuck in your stressed state, you'll experience discord in many parts of your life. When you are deeply stuck, do not expect to be fully aware of it. Your body and unconscious mind know it first, though, and stress may quickly build.

You may divert your responsibility from how your career and life looks by blaming others or by making excuses for everything that has happened to you such as: It was not your fault that the first e-mailing blast did not hit the way you thought. It was not your fault that the interview did not produce an offer. And it certainly wasn't your fault that the Internet ad for the perfectly matched job you answered did not yield a reply.

At the same time, you may experience yourself finding fault with everything that others are doing (or not doing) on your behalf. Your friend was supposed to get back to you with the key name from a major target company, and she has not. The executive recruiter has not called back yet, even though you were told you are the lead candidate. Things do not seem to be working. How might you get back on track? Take accountability! Don't blame your lack of success on anything or anyone. I recommend that you:

1. Do not blame yourself; rather, acknowledge that the ownership for your success or lack of it is solely your responsibility.
2. Diagnose what could be done differently to realize a better result. This means assessing the gap between what was really done and what could have been done.
3. Evaluate your commitment to mastering this career search process and your performance herein. (A lack of search success is more about an undisclosed need or disempowering beliefs and less about lack of skills, drive, and commitment.)

4. Determine what you truly want to do, in specific terms, not generalities. Capture it in writing, and identify what resources and help you'll need to achieve your goal.

5. Identify your roadblocks to success. These roadblocks unconsciously get in the way of your realizing your potential. They are your disempowering old habits, sabotaging behavior, or blame-oriented tapes that you play in your mind to avoid addressing the tough issues about yourself, including achieving career success.

6. Identify your accelerants to success. These accelerants are your empowering beliefs, attitudes, and behavior that propel you to greatness. I am a firm believer that when you are in your empowered state, you have the ability to realize optimal performance. With this mind-set, you naturally focus on possibilities, options, and abundance. Not blame. Not roadblocks. When you are operating in such an empowered (mental and emotional) state, roadblocks become mere logistical issues to overcome; not impossibilities.

Stress Comes from Change and Irrational Beliefs

Stress comes from the somewhat idealistic view that life should be the way we want it to be. However, we also know that "wishing makes it so" only exists in the world of Disney.

While your eyes may be the window to your soul, your language is reflective of how you think, feel, believe, and behave. Upset will emerge when you find yourself living in the context of your expectations versus reality, the way life really is. Even the trials and tribulations of everyday life can set us reeling and cause upset.

See if you use any of the words under the Expectations column in Figure 20-1. You might wish to circle those words and add any other words that you use.

> The greater the difference between our expectations of how life should look and how it really is, the greater the potential for stress.

Exercise: Immediate Stress Relief

Before you can revitalize your stuck or stalled campaign, you need to reduce, then manage your stress. First of all, realize that while this might be one of the most taxing experiences of your life, you are by no means the first to go through it. It is actually quite common. Then realize that since you cannot live your life today

Figure 20-1   Your Expectation—Source of Potential Upset

Expectations of Life . . .

Must be	Should be
Ought to be	Needs to be
Has to be	Want it to be
Wish it were	Could be
Got to be	Will be

The greater the difference between your expectations and life's reality, the greater the potential for . . .

1. Anxiety
2. Frustration
3. Disappointment
4. Anger
5. Sadness
6. Fear

Life's Reality . . .

The way it really is . . . here and now

Note: Carried to an extreme, the end result is *failure*. Reality has failed to live up to your expectation of it. The only thing constant about life is change. If you find yourself frustrated or upset, the reason is probably because something has occurred differently than you imagined.

Remedy

Lighten up and examine both how realistic your expectations are and how you might effectively close the gap between where you are now and where you want to be.

completely free of stress or distress, it is important to develop effective ways for dealing with that stress.

1. **Temporary Fight or Flight**
   - Take a break; put the search aside for a while, and get out of your house. Take a long walk or run; exercise your muscles as much as you can.
   - Breathe slowly and deeply from the abdomen, concentrating on blowing out slowly and evenly.
   - Ask a friend to listen while you blow off steam in private. Saying whatever you want will relieve your tension. It does not have to be true or highly responsible. The object is to feel relief from the stress.
   - If you have been drinking a lot of coffee, reduce your intake of caffeine for a while.
   - Mentally take a step back, take a good look at your total job search project, and recommit yourself to the task.
2. **Imaginary Flight**
   Physical—Isometric Tension and Release:
   - Quietly tense and relax your toes, legs, abdominals, spine, back, neck, then facial muscles, all the while exhaling deeply as you relax. Repeat this motion

five times, slowly allowing the tension, stress, and strain to drain out of your body and head. Nobody has to know what you are doing. It can even be done in a meeting without attracting attention.
- Grip your chair tightly, and sway back and forth on your tiptoes.
- Take more deep breaths.

Nonphysical—Humor:
- Look for the humor in the situation—what is ridiculous about it. You never decided to have this happen. "How did a nice person like me get into this? I never deliberately set out to have a bad day, did I?" Look at the situation as if it were right out of the Sunday comics.
- Attach new meaning to your most tense situation to shift your focus into perspective and to lower the intensity of your emotions. Instead of being outraged at being terminated, mildly view it as a "slight bother." Rather than being devastated at not getting the job offer that you wanted, view it as something "not meant to be. I'm glad I didn't talk my way into that company if they weren't excited about me."
- Imagine yourself somewhere else—in a place where you would really love to be, a place where you always feel peaceful and relaxed.

3. Direct Honesty
- Take responsibility for your search. "Own" your career *and* your life. You are the source of the problems, as well as the solutions. *Recontextualize* the problem by shifting your perspective as to how you view a problem and are entangled by it.
- Admit your feelings and take responsibility for them, without blaming or accusing yourself or another.
- Admit your stress and your need to do something immediately to relieve it . . . and then go and do it.
- If you have made a mistake, admit it and move to correct it.

4. Plan Your Work and Work Your Plan
- Recognize that just as inaction is at the source of your upset or emotional distress, *so is action the best source of pushing past your feelings that hold you captive.*
- Plan a series of five or six action steps you can actually execute within the next six to eight hours. Ask yourself, "What are all the things I can do right now?" Then do them! It works. Success breeds success.

5. Lighten Up!
- The time when you need to secure a job most is the time when you will least likely get it . . . because you're probably uptight and projecting a sense of desperation.
- Soooo—relax. Lighten up. You've found this job, you'll find another one.

The Reality of Rejection

The Cold Reality

- You *will* be rejected. A search, like any marketing campaign, is not 100 percent successful even though you might like it to be different. When you are unable to secure an interview or you are turned down for a job you really wanted, it very much feels like rejection.
- You can be hurt deeper than you thought possible and are willing to admit.
- Highly competent and perfectly rational people will turn a deaf ear to you, even after previously indicating that they would support you.
- Executive assistants will thwart your well-rehearsed attempts to get past them to their bosses.
- People will not return your phone calls, especially executive search recruiters.
- Your search will take *3 times longer* and will be *10 times tougher* than you imagined.
- Your mailbox contains only bills and reject letters.

The Warmer Reality

- People *do* care about what happens to you—even strangers.
- Help will come from many unexpected sources.
- There will always be opportunities out there for those who believe in themselves; so keep on working the process.
- If you are committed to your success, so will others be.
- Success may come from a phone call "out of the blue."
- You *have* accomplished a great deal. As soon as these accomplishments are matched to a need, you *will* be called.

Commitment—The True Difference

Individuals involved in the search process come in all different sizes and shapes, temperaments, and makeup. Why is it that some career searchers are really on fire for themselves and others seem to be limp?

The difference is commitment. *Committed people cannot be stopped.* Committed people exhibit a special kind of motivation that keeps them moving unerringly toward their goal, regardless of obstacles or issues of personal convenience. Certainly, your personality will play an important part in the level of outward display of enthusiasm. However, it will not necessarily determine your commitment to your success, *per se*.

The military has a simple phrase to express commitment to a task at hand which I would like you to make operational in your life:

Hunker down and move forward.

Are You Really Committed to Your Success?

Do you … ?

1. Create challenging personal career goals and develop realistic and viable action plans to obtain them?
2. Keep in balance the things you would *like to do* against the things you *have to do*?
3. Maintain positive expectancy about your life and search efforts? Do you have the feeling you cannot fail? Do you create the same level of enthusiasm in others?
4. Distinguish between being patient and being stuck?
5. Take responsibility for those things you have control over and not feel guilty about life's circumstances over which you have little or no control?
6. Continue to work when it is easier to quit? Is your operating philosophy, "It's OK to be down; just never give up?"
7. Critically assess the status of your campaign and have the discipline to put it back on track?
8. Commit to being the best you can be?

If you answered "Yes" to seven or more of the questions above, congratulations on being "on fire," deeply confident, and positively expectant! If you answered "Yes" to five then you have a positive frame of mind, overall. If you answered "Yes" to less than three questions, then you most likely run the risk of being knocked down fairly often by life's circumstances, feeling powerless. My recommendation is that you should reread this chapter and also Chapter 19, "Manage Your Campaign—Sustain the Momentum."

Success Can Be Stressful

You may feel that once you have an offer or two, your worries are over. Not necessarily. Be advised that you may be both excited and troubled by the prospect of successfully ending your campaign. In fact, you may be more anxious and troubled with two or three offers than when you first were separated.

Why is that? The consequences of your career move are far more significant and *lasting* than the time frame in which you conduct a career search. The time involved in a

Figure 20-2   Success Can be Stressful

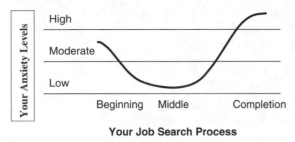

search is measured in months, but the time spent in the right (or wrong) career move is measured by years! Figure 20-2 illustrates how your anxiety level may be heightened at the conclusion of your search.

15 Things You Can Do to Be Unstoppable

1. Observe and then verbalize where you are on your emotional roller coaster of mad, sad, shame, fear, and glad (Figure 1-1). Be honest with yourself; this is for your benefit—no one else's. Make a copy of the emotional rollercoaster, post it in a highly visible spot, and refer to it often.

2. Give yourself permission to be angry or depressed and still have the capability to conduct an aggressive campaign. In other words, it is okay to be in whatever emotional state you find yourself. Having emotions and getting stuck is a normal part of life. However, permit yourself to be in this emotional state only for a limited period of time—say, three minutes. If you are mad, rage with all of your intensity for three minutes; no more. Take a deep breath, then move on to something productive, feeling cleansed and refreshed. (If you're like me, you won't be able to sustain your high-octane kicking and screaming, cathartic rage for more than about 90 seconds.)

3. Focus your attention on the emotional state that you are in, and determine what the real reason is, no kidding, that is making you angry or depressed. Develop and then employ those strategies that will get you out of your diminished emotional state and into a powerful, confident state.

4. Make the distinction between yourself and your behavior. While you certainly are responsible for your behavior, you yourself are not your behavior.

Just Because . . .	**Does Not Mean That . . .**
Your campaign fails . . .	You are a failure
Your campaign succeeds . . .	You are a success

Ask yourself:

- Where am I stuck?
- How do I know when I am stuck?
- When do I get most stuck?
- What do I gain/lose when I am stuck?
- What do I gain/lose when I am unstuck?

If you draw a blank, ask yourself:

- What is it that I am afraid to admit . . . the one thing I will never reveal?

5. Recognize that you gain tremendous personal power when you control your circumstances rather than allowing your circumstances to control you. When you assume responsibility for your life, you generally will experience a sense of freedom—freedom to be yourself.

6. Master your time. Establish your daily priorities the night before by identifying your next day's objectives and the corresponding "To Do's." Identify your prime (optimal) working hours, and schedule your most important or difficult tasks then. Establish specific "business hours" for yourself when you are at work and times when you let your voice mail take over. Being disciplined and having a routine is critical for your success. The added benefit is that the people that live with you will appreciate knowing your schedule and what your "business hours" are.

7. Identify your top five time wasters. Observe what triggers these time wasters. Might it be your fear around making a tough networking call, the prep time needed to get ready for an important interview, or the dread of exercising? Change only comes after you are aware of what is driving you/stopping you. As you note your tendency to get off track by certain things, commit to learning techniques that eliminate or minimize them. Some common ones include telephone interruptions, visitors, home projects, socializing, the siren song of the golf course, lack of clear personal goals, general procrastination, poor scheduling, lack of self-discipline, and a thousand other ways in which we avoid doing what we know we have to do.

8. Concentrate on the successes you have had. While it is far easier to zero in on failures, continue to focus on your campaign *successes* and *progress*. This continued push will encourage additional successes.

9. Focus on target areas (personal contacts, for example). Identify goals that are measurable and represent a challenge. Initiate 20 calls per day.

10. Commit yourself to the task whatever that might be. If you become overwhelmed by the enormity of a seemingly impossible challenge, break major points into bite-sized activities that could move the larger task forward, while continually having the end goal in mind.

11. If you become stuck, identify and explore multiple perspectives and options. Ask yourself, "What are five possible solutions to the problem?"

12. Connect with others. Do not drift into being a hermit. Even though it is easier to operate independently, it's not healthy or productive. Recall me saying that 80 percent of the executive jobs are consummated through networking? A large part of networking success comes from face-to-face discussions, not merely telephone connections. So, stay in contact with people. Being with others can be invigorating; it can boost your morale, spark new ideas, and affirm you personally if you feel isolated. Maintaining your social, business, and professional contacts is a must.

13. Ask for support from others in being successful in your career search. The support could range from asking someone to be a willing listener during tough times to critically evaluating a business strategy you have developed.

   Caution: Most people do not know how to ask for nor receive honest feedback from others. Generally, we see it as too embarrassing, too brutally honest, or as an imposition on the person's time. If you are fortunate enough to receive honest data upon asking for it, graciously profit from it.

   A great way to boost your own morale and energy is to give back to someone else who might need a helping hand. It is impossible to generously give back to someone or something, without feeling buoyed in return. Try it—you'll like it.

14. Exercise at least three times a week. Build a fitness program into your day. Most people report that exercise improves their creativity and energy levels. Physical activity increases oxygen flow to the brain and improves your thought processes. Looking good and feeling good are essential to your mental and emotional well-being.

15. Hang on and keep doing what you know is right and needs to be done—even when it is uncomfortable, not showing immediate returns, or easier to quit. *Anything worth doing requires effort.*

 Success comes before work *only* in the dictionary!

STEP 7
NEGOTIATIONS

CHAPTER 21

NEGOTIATIONS—GAIN LEVERAGE AND GET THE COMPENSATION YOU DESERVE

Be Realistic in Your Salary Demands

Reaching the end of a job interview, the human resources person asked a young engineer fresh out of MIT, "And what starting salary were you considering?"

The 21-year-old engineer enthusiastically replied, "In the neighborhood of $200,000 a year and an attractive housing allowance, plus a comprehensive benefits package."

The interviewer said, "Well, in addition to those requests, what would you say to a 5-week vacation, 14 paid holidays, full medical and dental, company matching retirement fund to 50 percent of your salary, and a company car leased every two years, say, a 5-series BMW?"

The young engineer sat up straight and said, "Wow! Are you kidding?"

The HR interviewer countered, "Yes, but you started it."

 You only get paid what you negotiate.

Truer words have never been spoken. You don't get paid based on an organization's need, your education, your experience, your capabilities, your charm or charisma—you get paid what you negotiate. *That's unfair*, you cry. So what if you deem it to be unfair. Tiger Woods does not have one of the most lucrative endorsement contracts in sports because he is nicer than other golfers. He is paid this king's ransom because he (and his agent) negotiated it. You may feel that your MBA from an Ivy League university entitles you to a sweeter deal. However, you need to powerfully demonstrate how you're worth more and effectively negotiate for it. And, like our young friend fresh out of MIT, you also need to be realistic in your salary demands.

Long gone are the days in which you could merely show up with your credentials and track record of accomplishments in hand and get the big bucks. The competition is tough, and the line is long of equally qualified executives vying for the same job you are. So, you have to sell yourself and negotiate to secure a favorable employment package.

Simply put: If you don't sell yourself, why would anyone else?

Myths and Realities of Negotiation

Myth 1:   *Companies won't pay you what you're worth.*
Reality: Companies will pay whatever it takes to get the person they are convinced can help them achieve their goals. The salary structure is considered an interesting guideline, but nothing rigid for the right person.

Myth 2:   *If you've been terminated or currently unemployed, you don't have much leverage to negotiate.*
Reality: In fact, you have as much leverage as you are willing to believe in and seize. If you behave confidently and during the process previously indicated that you are exploring other options, your leverage will be greater. Even if you are desperate for the job, don't let the prospective employer or recruiter see you sweat. Be enthusiastic without being manic. Be calm, cool, and collected without appearing disengaged, or uninterested. Keep in mind, you are talented, and you will significantly contribute to the organization far greater than your compensation. So, hiring you is a "no-brainer." Plus, the reality is that if you are unemployed, being unencumbered by a full-time job enables you to pursue a number of opportunities, potentially leveraging multiple offers against one another.

Myth 3:   *Companies always negotiate.*
Reality: Well, you'd think so, particularly if you are the ideal candidate the company needs and wants. However, there are exceptions, and we have seen clients blow up offers if they haven't done a masterful job building solid relationships and gaining widespread endorsement for their candidacy. I look at negotiations like a dance; there's always a give and take—a time to be assertive and a time to yield. Minimally, you don't want to be seen as inflexible and difficult to deal with; that's what gets offers pulled.

In my experience, an attempt at negotiating a better package can result in one of three responses. The first response might be "Yes." If so, great! The second the response might be, "No, there is no additional room in the package. We've gone as far as we can go." In that case, you need to decide if want the job, if the discussion is completely dead, or if you can finesse to have the discussion again at some other time. Which leads us to the third response. This response sounds and feels like, "Not now, perhaps later we can revisit elements of your package." Even if your prospective boss does not say those exact words, you want to do so, if nothing more than to save face and have the discussion of a "catch-up" strategy. (We'll talk about the nuances of a "catch-up" strategy later in this chapter).

Myth 4:   *If you ask for severance pay, including outplacement costs, you cast yourself in a poor light.*

Reality: Most companies acknowledge that employment uncertainty is a way of life, especially for senior executives. Having a comprehensive separation agreement is a cost of doing business competitively at the executive level.

Myth 5:   *You should never take a lesser job or lessor compensation package.*

Reality: There might be any number of reasons why you should consider accepting one or both of these options. You might very well step back if you are switching industries or if you are being groomed to be the CEO who will retire in 18 months. You take a lateral move to learn a new venue or function, and so on. The real question is, "How does this help me/hurt me in my long-term career strategy?" If it helps, take the lesser role or package. If it hurts you, you might reconsider taking the job.

Get Grounded. Be Positive

Contrary to what you might think, compelling negotiations do not begin in this negotiations chapter. Rather, it occurs much, much earlier. Your persuasiveness in your negotiations begins way before you get the offer or even before you develop your résumé or conduct your first interview. Having a positive and confident mind set is directly related to your knowing and believing that you are talented and can significantly contribute to an organization's growth and profitability. Much like a black belt in aikido grounds himself in his stance for optimal stability, so likewise, you get to ground yourself in your beliefs about yourself as you reflect on your capabilities and visualize success. When I think of the term *grounded*, I think of words, such as rooted, stable, unflappable, majestic, enduring, unhurried, persistent, above the fray, magnanimous, smooth, calm, and regal. Wouldn't you love to be calm, magnanimous, and regal in your offer negotiations?

As a way to gain leverage in the offer negotiations I recommend that you incorporate the following Keys to Success into your daily routine. As you consistently apply these keys, you will have significantly enhanced your confidence and your chances of bettering your package.

1. Know your outcome.

What is it that you really want to achieve? Do you want a new job? That is easy—there are plenty of minimum-wage positions available, and you could probably could get one tomorrow. You want to make sure it's the right job. If you want to make a meaningful career move, then invest the time and energy in this activity, not unlike the time you invested in getting your education or completing a major project.

2. Master thy self.

I can predict with a high degree of certainty which executives are going to be successful in their career search and, most notably, in their negotiations. Simply stated: the more confident and interpersonally agile you are, the greater the probability of success and greater compensation.

3. Be committed to achieving your career/life goals.

Determine your life's priorities, and make your campaign a top priority. What would your campaign look like if its priority was the same as, let's say, breathing? Would that change how you approach learning the nuances of this search process, especially networking? If you were deeply committed to your success, what could you accomplish?

4. Evaluate everything in your life against your goals.

Ask yourself the question "What is the best use of my time, energy, and talent *right now*?" If, in your opinion, you deem a given activity to be a high priority and it supports you in pursuit of your outcome, then keep on doing it. If you suspect it is not an "A" priority, critically assess it and then reprioritize it.

5. Develop personal intensity and a high sense of urgency.

People who achieve significant results universally have a high degree of intensity about their beliefs and possess a high degree of urgency. This burning desire to accomplish your outcome will help create the momentum you need to push beyond those times when it is inconvenient or uncomfortable to continue working. Plus, employers know that everything of significance was achieved only after someone was highly focused and driven to succeed.

6. Work your plan, and eliminate what is not working or adding value.

Once you have established your plan and are satisfied with its soundness, work the plan. If you find that during the course of your plan's execution you need to modify some things, then do so. When you drive your car, you are constantly fine-tuning the controls in your car to produce a desired outcome, including stopping when needed or successfully navigating a curve. The same fine-tuning and attention to detail is required for your campaign strategy to be successful.

7. Make a decision, manage the decision, and enjoy the outcome.

After you have an offer (or offers), you will be evaluating it against your Position Selection Criteria for the ideal job. If you recall, this template encompasses position responsibilities (short term and long term), challenges, compensation, personal chemistry between you and others, and other dimensions important to you. Determine if the opportunity is right. If it is, accept the offer and don't second-guess yourself. You made a perfect decision because you made it based on all the available information you were consciously and unconsciously aware of. To that end, it was perfect; nothing else needed to be added or subtracted.

8. Keep discovering.

After you have been employed for a while, if you are not completely satisfied, you will have new data by which to evaluate your decision. At that point you might conclude that you might have made an employment mistake. Rather than jump ship immediately, first take stock of your situation. Look beyond your own expectations, and identify ways to contribute to others in your new organization. Discover what others want and need in this new relationship. Continually look for ways to add value to another person, the team, and the company. Once you add value and as your relationships begin to flourish, your employment satisfaction will invariably increase.

Receive and Analyze Offers

While the employment process and job offers are clearly business transactions, it will feel as if you are entering into a personal relationship. Intuitively, you understand that personal chemistry between you and others in the company makes all the difference in the world. You might be offered the best job in the world, but if the people relationships do not feel right going in, the situation may not work.

Receiving an Offer

- Be enthusiastic. Sound pleased. Express your interest in working with your new boss and for the new organization.
- Take notes on the starting salary, reporting relationships, title, start date, and other benefits. Feed back your understanding.
- If the offer is low, react positively to the possibility of contributing to the organization, and observe that the offer is not yet fully competitive. You might wish to introduce the concept of a catch-up strategy here if the reaction is

somewhat shocked to your push-back. Or, you could wait until you get the offer in writing to introduce the catch-up strategy. (This strategy enables you to create a compensation package that guarantees to pay you increasing amounts of monies over a 6-, 12-, 18-month period of time to remain economically whole over time.)

- Ask when the company needs your decision. Or, after you have received the offer, you might tell your prospective boss (after you indicated how pleased you are) that you are "committed to several, already arranged interview trips. Further, you intend to make a decision by "X" date; would that be OK with them?

- Ask that the offer details be sent to you in writing. Until the offer is in writing, consider it "smoke," which could evaporate at any time. The verbal employment agreement that you have so carefully cultivated with your potential boss is in jeopardy if he or she is transferred or leaves the company. To that end, it is clearly better to have the hiring specifics in writing. If it is not company policy to confirm offers in writing, then you send a confirming letter or e-mail to your new boss with these particulars.

- If on the phone, sign off warmly, thanking him once again for the opportunity.

Analyzing an Offer

- Refer to your notes on the following worksheets:
  Worksheets 17 to 21, "Liked Best/Liked Least"
  Worksheet 22, "Position Selection Criteria"
  Worksheet 23, "My Ideal Job"

  Examine the relevancy of those factors compared to your offer(s). Make any necessary modifications to that list based on how you have grown and what you have learned during your search.

- Ask yourself, "Does this offer(s) and the opportunity meet both my short- and long-term needs?" If so, how? If not, why not?

WORKSHEET 69

Analyzing an Offer

PART I: Revisiting What You Know to Be True

1. What does the ideal job look like for me? In terms of:
   - Duties/projects/responsibilities/challenges
   - Work team/leader relationships
2. What elements of the ideal job are present/missing in this position?
   - Present
   - Missing
3. What do I like/dislike about the position?
   - Like
   - Dislike
4. What reasons do I have to accept/decline this job?
   - Reasons to accept
   - Reasons to decline

PART II: Finessing the Tactics

5. What might prevent me from accepting this position? Evaluate:
   - What other offers have been made? How do they compare?
   - What specific action can I take to generate additional offers?
   - Without damaging the relationship with my prospective employer, what action might I take (or request be taken) that could effectively delay my acceptance/rejection decision?
   - How long can I realistically delay accepting the offer before I turn off my potential employer; or worse, before the offer is withdrawn?
   - How is my financial situation? Do I need to accept this offer to "keep bread on the table"?
   - Should I take this job now and continue to search?
   - How is my fear of changing jobs and being zapped again getting in my way of accepting this offer?

PART III: Employment Offer Checklist

We have always believed that clients begin to negotiate conditions of their new employment offer from the moment they start their transition. The negotiation commences with the assessment, résumé, and credentials preparation and is inherent in each and every step of the career search process. As your campaign progresses, the checklist below is intended as a guide for your consideration as potential offers are being discussed and drafted. *Note*: Do not expect to secure every single item mentioned.

General

___ Job title
___ Reporting relationship
___ Principal accountability/scope of responsibility/job description
___ Start date
___ Offer subject to satisfactory: Drug test/reference check/background credit check/physical exam
___ Offer response date

Restrictive Employment Agreement(s)/Covenants and Duration

___ Confidentiality/nondisclosure (confidential and proprietary information)
___ Nonsolicitation (focused on employees)
___ Noninterruption (focused on business and customers)
___ Noncompete (focused on direct competitors)
___ Nondispragement (focused on not blaming either party)

Compensation

___ Sign-on bonus; when paid
___ Bonus repayment stipulation if you leave the company
___ Base monthly/annual pay
___ Next scheduled salary review date; "catch-up" strategy
___ Annual bonus: target percentage; payout features; first-year guarantee; prorated for current year
___ Long-term incentive compensation plan: eligibility, plan design, and payout features
___ Other special incentive plan participation: eligibility, plan design, and payout features

Equity Building Opportunity

___ Profit sharing
___ Retirement plan: defined benefit or defined contribution
___ Supplemental retirement plan
___ 401(k) plan: matching features, etc.
___ Deferred compensation plans
___ Stock option plans: Estimated annual amount, plus plan features
___ Stock grants
___ Employee stock purchase plan: discount features, etc.
___ S.A.R.s, phantom stock, etc.
___ Other

Insurance and Benefits

___ Vacation: at appropriate level for position
___ Medical: Any preexisting conditions
___ Dental
___ Prescription drug/vision
___ Disability income (short-term and long-term)
___ Life: Your plan/spouse-partner/family member
___ Accidental death and dismemberment
___ Business travel insurance

Perks

___ Leased auto/auto allowance (operating costs included)
___ Preferred parking
___ Business travel: first class/business class
___ Country club (family members included)
___ Health and fitness club (family members included)
___ Spouse career transition assistance
___ Dues paid, expense reimbursement for attendance at professional/trade association meetings
___ Executive physical exam
___ Spouse physical exam
___ Executive coaching
___ Home office: high-speed Internet hookup, other home office equipment purchase or lease
___ Tax preparation assistance/estate planning
___ Laptop, Blackberry, other technology tools or services

Relocation Assistance

___ Repayment stipulation if leave the company

___ House-hunting trip(s) to new location: Number of trips family members included

___ Movement of household goods/furnishings, including temporary storage (Ideal: no monetary cap)

___ Temporary quarters expense reimbursement: How long? Caps on amount?

___ Lease cancellation penalty reimbursement, if renting

___ Purchase of existing home

___ Marketing assistance, existing home

___ Carrying costs of existing home: P&I, insurance, taxes, maintenance

___ Closing costs, existing home

___ Closing costs, new home: new home mortgage points, etc.

___ Mortgage rate differential/location cost differential payment (if new location higher cost)

___ Bridge loan or mortgage arrangement assistance (equity advance)

___ Gross up of taxable relocation expense reimbursement

___ Discretionary relocation expense allowance (one month's salary, specified amount, etc.)

___ Commuting expense reimbursement: While in temporary quarters or if family delays relocating.

Termination or Separation Clause

___ Involuntary or voluntary termination severance plan:
for "good reason" or for reasons other than "cause," (i.e., severance package is triggered because of change of control/ownership/leadership/ title role/responsibilities; business dissolution; adverse impact of change in conditions of employment, such as geographic location, title, reporting relationship, or perceived status; etc.)

___ Number of months of base pay and current year prorated bonus to be paid

___ Lump sum or paid at regular pay periods

___ Benefits continuation, COBRA, etc.

___ Executive outplacement support: Employee choice of firm? Amount or limits on cost commensurate with role.

___ Relocation expense reimbursement for return to city of origin (if desired)

Note: The inclusion or absence of any of these employment offer components reflects the organization's culture and philosophy. Generally, an overly conservative compensation package and a rigid approach to negotiations *might* indicate that the organization is cautious and conservative. Be wary of the common tendency to judge the company or the hiring manager as unsophisticated, myopic, inflexible or that they undervalue talent. We have had clients project these negative labels onto the company without beginning to even negotiate an offer package. Unfortunately, such negative thinking undermines your relationship with your prospective company.

Housing Cost Differential

If relocation is a possibility or necessity, the cost of housing may play a significant role in your employment decision making. While you may have received an attractive offer, it may not be fully competitive if you lose ground financially because of higher housing costs in the new location. To that end, you may wish to ask for some form of housing differential, increased base salary or additional stock options, for example. There are a number of Web sites that will help you determine the relative cost of living differentials (and salary comparisons) in different cities to aid you in your salary negotiations.

Leverage Offers Against Each Other

Having been made an offer, it is not uncommon for you to become quite anxious. For many, it's the best of times and the worst of times.

It is a time to do some serious evaluation of those career/life plans you have developed earlier. If the offer presented to you is truly a once-in-a-lifetime opportunity, your choice is clear. But ironically, the offer for your "perfect job" might still be eluding you or it hasn't yet materialized, though you feel it definitely is in the queue. Murphy's Law rules again!

- Objectively evaluate your employment options, the number of offers (actual or pending), how well you "fit," your sense of the company's desire for you, etc.
- Determine the longest acceptable delay, and secure the OK from the company offering you a job offer. You could say:

  I am very excited about coming to work here. However, I would like to follow through on my commitments to finalize discussions with several other companies.

- Recontact organizations that had previously shown interest. For example:

  I am in the midst of receiving some fine offers and would like very much to include your organization in my decision making. Where do you stand on making a decision?

Companies drag their feet on extending offers for a wide variety of reasons: there are other business priorities, you might not be the strongest fit, the plans have changed and the position is not going to be filled, or perhaps there is a pending acquisition that may materially affect hiring decisions.

Rather than remain uninformed, contact the hiring authority and request feedback on your candidacy and the company's timetable.

What to Do When the Offer Is Low

Bummer. A less-than-fantastic offer can be a downer. Because salary offers feel so personal and they seem to be closely tied with feelings of self-worth, you run the risk of not responding as positively as you should. Worse, you might even "blow up" an opportunity if the offer is significantly less than expected. Receiving a lower-than-anticipated compensation package often feels like rejection. You may be hurt, embarrassed, confused, and perhaps even angry. If you're like most people, you may not handle this as confidently and powerfully as you did the interview. Even though the salary or title may not be what you want, it is vitally important not to show your disappointment. Don't lose your cool. Rather, begin to negotiate!

Manage the Paradox

That's what I recommend you do when you receive a disappointing offer. By the way, you might think the offer is all about money; in fact, compensation is but a piece of the offer.

Managing the paradox is distinguishing between two diametrically opposed points of view; like, feeling sad and glad simultaneously. It is common to have a "collapsed distinction" when you are disappointed or feeling a bit humiliated by a low offer.

On the one hand, you have an offer from an organization that you are excited about (positive distinction). On the other hand, the offer is much less than you wanted, and you are feeling weird about it (negative distinction). A collapsed distinction refers to the comingling of these two emotions and distinctions. In other words, the distinctions (both positive and negative) are collapsed into one another. The ability to separate these two diametrically opposed emotions is a powerful lever in your negotiations.

If the offer is low, first express your enthusiasm for the opportunity to partner with your prospective boss and to contribute to the company's growth and profitability (positive distinction). Second, briefly indicate your disappointment in the job offer, which is the conflicting position (or negative distinction). To that end, you might say something like the following:

> *Thank you for the offer. The opportunities at XYZ sound terrific and I am looking forward to contributing to the team. However, I am disappointed in the overall compensation package, and would like to explore how we can reach a mutually agreeable arrangement.*

Once you have briefly stated your position, be quiet and let the prospective employer respond. Too much talking on your part here may be interpreted as nervousness, not confidence. Set your keen problem-solving abilities aside for a moment, and let the employer respond.

The next section, Catch-Up Strategy, illustrates how you can incorporate the tactics from this section with specific recommendations to create a competitive offer, albeit over 12 months. Just because the offer is low initially does not mean you cannot successfully negotiate a great package.

Catch-Up Strategy—Negotiate When the Heat Is On

When the offer is unacceptable as is, indicate your desired compensation package, and ask if some form of satisfactory accommodation can be worked out for both of you. For instance,

> *Thank you for the offer. The opportunities at XYZ sound terrific, and I am looking forward to contributing to the team. However, I am disappointed in the overall compensation package and would like to explore how we can reach a mutually agreeable arrangement. While money is important, it is not the only career consideration, as we both acknowledged. My interest is to remain whole, salary-wise, over a 12-month period of time. I would like you to consider some options that might include a hiring or sign-up bonus and/or guaranteed 6-month and 12-month salary increases. I understand that career moves like this are a "leap of faith" for both of us. I am willing to sacrifice some money up front because I am confident that through my contributions, any deferred dollars will be made up over time.*

Improve Offers by Focusing on Organizational Needs, Not Money

If the employer is reluctant to move on your compensation package, you may want to influence the decision maker by respectfully highlighting what the company will likely get (talent-wise) for the money being offered.

Help the recruiter or decision maker examine the organizational needs and challenges *first*, then zero in on the credentials required to do the job and the compensation—in that order. Remember, if the offer is significantly less than you think you deserve, and if the company is truly unwilling to go higher, you may be overqualified, given their commitment. The company may clearly *need* a person with your talents but may *not want* to pay the price. Your challenge, then, is to get the employer to know the extra value that you can bring.

Figure 21-1 is a model that you may find helpful as you attempt to educate, then shift the employer to a more generous (and appropriate!) salary offer. While we recognize that your compensation levels and background will be different than the following example, let us use this person's compensation as an example. You will have an opportunity to complete your own worksheet if you find yourself in this situation. But first, let's dissect the model.

A. *Salary offer.* The base salary of $175,000 and a performance bonus plan targeted at 15 percent does not reflect the immediate and desperate need that this company has to accelerate its sales, provide leadership to the dysfunctional sales organization, and balance the product mix.

Figure 21-1

A. Salary Offer	B. Company Wants/Needs/Requires
• VP—Global Sales • $175,000 salary • $25,000 relocation benefits maximum • Medical benefits—complete • 401(k) plan: 25% matching • $300 per month car allowance • Target performance bonus of 15%	• Senior Vice President–Sales and Marketing • 15–20 years sales/marketing mgmt experience • Experienced executive with record of results building and leading highly motivated sales and marketing teams that penetrate accounts, increase sales and profits, and turn around companies • Ability to build sales from $200 to $800 million • Succeed retiring EVP/COO in two years
C. Company Likely to Get	**D. Optimal Offer**
• Territory management experience • 8–10 years selling experience • Limited managerial experience • Medium-sized company background	• $265,000 base salary • Bonus: 40%; options; long-term incentives • Car allowance: $800 per month + operating costs • Complete relocation benefits, plus gross up

It is appropriate to fully identify what is included in the salary offer, including often overlooked details such as deferred tax/compensation plans like 401(k) plans and comprehensive medical and life insurance plans. As this job requires relocation, the $25,000 cap is much too conservative, given the senior executive they need to hire. A more realistic relocation benefit is one with no limit on the costs associated with real estate commissions, transportation, and "points" on both ends with about 90 days temporary living allowance. Also, given the required senior sales management role, a car allowance and incentive bonus are normal and customary.

B. *Company wants and needs.* Through in-depth interview discussions and probing questions, it was obvious that this company was in deep trouble and the other senior executives were counting on this executive to lead them out of difficulty. The sales organization was in disarray: salespeople sold more lower profit margin products because it was easier, order entry was in shambles, wrong products were shipped, filled orders were often not what the customers wanted, dealers were unsatisfied and not performing, and the sales force turnover eroded the customers' confidence and the company's effectiveness. Plus, on the marketing front, this was a company in search of a vision and focus.

Clearly, the troubled company needed and wanted a seasoned sales expert and leader who could turn it around and position it for further growth. However, given its cash flow dilemma, it did not feel it could afford to pay the executive's salary demands.

C. *Company likely to get.* While $175,000 is a fine offer for individuals growing into a territory manager's position or currently handling approximately $50 million in sales, given national salary range norms, it was too light for a troubled $200 million company (desiring to be $800 million) with eroding profits and market share. In the executive's favor, he knew the company could not financially afford to have the person in this role make a mistake or learn on the job. A person was required to hit the ground running, adding value immediately. The company desperately needed a seasoned leader. The challenge for this executive (and you when/if you face this situation) is to respectfully and in a nonthreatening way, point out the reality of quadrant C. The person most likely attracted to the compensation structure in quadrant A would most likely not be strong enough for the company's needs, although he or she may fit the "compensation profile." If you are in this discussion, while you admittedly run the risk of portraying yourself as overqualified, you can significantly minimize this impression by doing your research on the company and by asking penetrating questions throughout the interview that support the need for a person like you versus one who may accept a much lesser salary.

D. *Optimal offer.* The "optimal offer" represents that total compensation package you feel is appropriate for the company's opportunity and challenges, your credentials, and what other companies would be willing to pay. Your goal is to move the company from being out of sync with what they want, need, or require and the salary offer. You are trying to move them out of operating quadrants A and B into B and D, which properly aligns the job's demands with its compensation.

WORKSHEET 70

Profile Your Job Offer

Complete each quadrant fully with your intent to develop counterarguments that justify a higher compensation package.

A. Salary Offer	B. Company Wants/Needs/Requires
C. Company Likely to Get	D. Optimal Offer

17 Tips to Improve Your Offers

To help the decision makers or the recruiter safely explore this disparity and to make the shift, it is recommended that you do the following:

1. Thank them for the offer. Be enthusiastic.
2. Ask them how they determined the compensation package. Express appreciation for the process and the "rightness" of the research.
3. Acknowledge that you feel the offer is not yet fully competitive, given what the company needs, wants, and requires.
4. Legitimize the offer. Acknowledge that the offer is valid given their cash flow dilemma and where they are with the talent that they have currently.
5. Gain leverage by highlighting both what the company needs (to be turned around), wants (strong commitment to hire the right person), and requires (seasoned sales and marketing leader with a 15- to 20-year record of turnarounds and accelerated revenue and profit growth).
6. Briefly summarize your skills, abilities, accomplishments, capabilities, and fit for this job now and in the future.
7. Ask for feedback: "Given my record of accomplishments, what kind of results do you think I could achieve?" Pause and let them respond. Ask: "What concerns might you have about my ability to improve top line revenues, far in excess of my compensation?"
8. Thank them for acknowledging that you could do the job well and you are an ideal fit for their short-term and long-range plans, including being a viable successor to the EVP/COO.
9. Share with them the compensation elements and salary you are discussing with other prospective employers that coincide with the "ideal offer."
10. Again, ask for feedback: "How does this sound?" Pause. Wait for a response. Now, if the decision maker starts to grab his chest and gasp for air, you probably telegraphed a salary a bit too high.

    Short of having to administer CPR, you should smile and acknowledge that you, too, recognize a discrepancy between the company's offer and what you are finding in other companies as an optimal offer for an individual with your skills and needs of the company.
11. Help the decision maker focus on the salient points of the situation by crisply summarizing the main issues, which hopefully prompt him or her to say "yes!" Let's see how you might cut through all the rhetoric with this target firm."

Your Response	**Company's Response**
Clearly you need a person to help the company turn around, right?	*Right!*
You indicated that for every month in which the wrong person is in the job it is costing the company millions, right?	*Right!*
Based on what you and your team shared with me, I am stronger than the current national accounts manager?	*Right!*
So, if I was in place doing what needed to be done one month sooner (versus hunting for the person to fit the job at $175,000), I would more than offset the difference in your original offer and the sales I would generate, right?	*(Hopefully they would say) Right!*

12. Reiterate that

I do not see myself as overqualified, rather fully qualified for this position. While money is important to me, being in a challenging role is most important. As I may have indicated previously, I am willing to work with you on how we might structure a total compensation plan, not just salary. I would be willing to discuss a "catch-up" strategy. This might include a significant number of options that are currently worth only pennies on the dollar, a percentage of the money saved or new sales generated, a hiring or sign-up bonus—whatever you feel is appropriate to keep your cash flow healthy.

13. Express appreciation for the company's willingness to openly discuss the opportunities and challenges and the means to accomplish that through being flexible and responsive. ("Being flexible and responsive" is the subliminal message that they will, indeed, be open to increasing the compensation package in a timely manner.)

14. Ask, "What is the next step?"
    - "Is there anyone else who needs to be involved in the discussion at this time?"
    - "Would you like me to summarize our discussion and outline in an e-mail what I feel is a more competitive package?"

15. Prepare a summary of your discussion, possibly utilizing the worksheet format as the basis for your write-up. Before you share your worksheet or summary with your prospective employer or recruiter, you may wish to have someone whose judgment you trust preview the material. You certainly want to guard against language that makes it seem you are *demanding versus discussing*. Your best intentions mean nothing if your prospective employer feels you are overly demanding and disrespectful. Your proposal should be intriguing and compelling to the ultimate decision-maker, the CEO.

Ideally, meet in person to go over these items point by point. The least preferred next step is to simply e-mail it. If you do, you will not be able to observe the employer's reaction, a valuable source of data during delicate discussions.

16. If you must mail or e-mail the letter, do so, though a word of caution: Before mailing or e-mailing the letter to the employer, call ahead and emphasize that the items outlined are discussion points based on your previous meetings and should not be considered as mandates or absolutes. This letter in intended to be a basis of further dialogue. Please note: If you have any concerns about being misunderstood, do not mail/e-mail your summary. It is far too easy for employers to agree to be open-minded about salary discussions before they read your observations. Handle this communication piece with great care, as it is very easy for the employer to reach the conclusion that you are too expensive. To emphasize that point: unless properly introduced, this letter could be a "deal-breaker."

17. Follow up very soon after the time when the employer should have received the letter; again, face-to-face meetings are preferred. Ask for feedback. Listen carefully and respond respectfully. This is a time to be very supportive of the prospective employer or recruiter.

Employment Agreements/Contracts

Surprisingly, many employers are nervous about the language of "contracts," yet they will willingly enter into an "employment agreement." If an offer letter has signatures on it (yours and/or a company representative's), it is a contract. As such, a contract is a legal document. So, take care and know to what you are committing.

Employment contracts are formal legal agreements between an organization and a new employee that identify the terms and conditions of employment and the compensation and benefit package. Typically, employment contracts are reserved for senior executives or persons undertaking unusual, high-risk, or foreign assignments or are engaged in consulting for a definite period of time.

Letters of Agreement

If the organization does not provide an employment contract or confirming letter to you, you may wish to write a detailed "letter of agreement" that outlines your understanding and acceptance of the offer. At the very least, you will be able to spell out the specifics of the offer in detail, including title, reporting relationships, and total compensation provisions (including options or any special compensation "catch-up" steps). Say,

Thank you for the offer and agreeing to these points. Before I make my final decision, I would like to see the offer in writing. Is that possible? When do you think you will be getting that out to me?

Caution: Do not use the letter of agreement to gain things that you have not previously secured. Items still under negotiation can be mentioned in your letter but need to clearly be identified as still under consideration and in a preliminary stage.

Guidelines for Accepting an Offer

At this stage of your campaign, you have:

- Been extended an attractive offer (at least one), and perhaps effectively negotiated for more responsibility or more money
- Expressed enthusiasm for the opportunity to be of mutual benefit and to contribute to the company's growth
- Received a confirming letter outlining offer details
- Evaluated this offer in light of other opportunities and your targeted career plans
- Made the decision to accept the employment offer

Because employment relationships are so personal, it is advisable to personally contact your potential manager, the HR head, or the search firm partner, whomever is most appropriate to call first. I recommend that:

- Call your new manager first, accept the offer, and settle any last-minute details. If you feel comfortable doing so, send a confirming letter outlining the major elements of the offer.
- If your new organization asks you to sign and return the offer letter sent to you, do not balk. However, read the offer letter carefully, as returning it signed constitutes a contract binding on both parties.
- When in doubt, or if the stakes are particularly high, have an employment attorney review the letter for any issue that may be a problem if you and the company elect to part, hopefully not soon.

Guidelines for Rejecting an Offer

Most people would love to be in the position of having more than one offer to choose from. It is a heady experience. It's also described as scary, confusing, exhilarating, and "the best of all possibilities."

On the other hand, you may have the dilemma of only having one offer at a given moment, and it is for a well-paying position that you really do not want. Or, you need to go back to work so you are contemplating taking an unsatisfactory job for any number of emotional, psychological, or financial reasons. What to do?

First, critically evaluate the offer in light of your short-term and long-term career interests, needs, and promotional opportunities, as previously developed. Second, determine what condition your finances are in. Do you need to accept this position to keep yourself financially together? As distasteful as it might seem, you may need to accept an offer knowing that it may only be on a temporary basis.

If the employment opportunity is not acceptable and your finances are OK, it may be appropriate to decline the offer. It is recommended that you communicate your decision on the phone (or in person), indicating your specific reasons. Do not reject a company's offer hoping that you can negotiate a better deal. If you want the job, say so and negotiate. Only reject an offer if you are fully prepared to walk away from the opportunity with no strings attached. While you are reflecting on this decision, I recommend that you recontact any other employers or search firms with viable openings to communicate that you have a pending offer. While it is a stretch, ask them if something else could quickly materialize.

Before rejecting an offer, you may wish to talk it over with someone you respect, then decide. Talk it over with your family members or close friends. Let them be a sounding board during this time. Also, sleep on the decision to decline the offer for 24 hours.

Over the years we have had a number of executives who were excited about opportunities at first blush. We evaluated these offers against the research they had done: corporate cultures, the succession plans, the personality fit between them and others, the total compensation package, and the opportunities to really contribute and drive the corporate strategies. When all was said and done, many an opportunity did not stand up to the scrutiny in the clear light of day. To say no to an offer in hand is tough. After you reject a bona fide offer, be alert to a possible onslaught of conflicting physical sensations, feelings, and emotions. People who have rejected opportunities that were not right for them expressed that they reexperienced the emotional ups and downs of their job loss. While this experience was difficult, they also knew it was the correct course of action to take.

The Offer

1. How to evaluate an offer:
   - Compare your current income and your value in the marketplace.
   - Compare companies.
   - Compare total compensation.
   - Use your Position Selection Criteria as a guide.
2. How to keep your options open:
   - Buy some time with each offer.
   - Allow time to compare offers.
   - Request more time if you are anticipating another job offer.

- Ask to see additional facilities or key people in the company (possibly even board members or outside investors) so as to slow down the hiring process, enabling you to speed up other opportunities.
3. How to evaluate multiple offers:
   - Compare base salary and bonus (short- and long-term incentives).
   - Compare benefits.
   - Compare options and stock grants.
   - Measure against your career goals and objectives.
   - Use the "Position Selection Criteria" worksheet.
   - Examine what your head, your heart, and your gut say.

To tap into a client's gut feel about an offer, I sometimes tell her that the offer will be withdrawn in three seconds, at which point she needs to make a decision: 1, 2, 3! Decide. Once she has decided, we'll dissect her reasoning, and note the distinctions between her "head" and "gut" data. Invariably, clients make the right choice.

The Counteroffer—If You Are Still Employed

If you are still employed, extracting yourself from your company may not be simple or easy. Increasingly companies are making counteroffers. The dollar cost of sweetening your compensation pales in comparison to the expense of possible search fees, relocation, stock/option buyouts, learning ramp-up, turnover of key subordinates, and so on. We estimate that the cost of replacing an exiting executive can top 10 times base pay. So, the least expensive decision the Board can make is a counteroffer.

Most executives are not prepared for the counteroffer. It can be disorienting and flattering for the resigning executive to suddenly be courted by the company that only recently could not or would not meet his promotional or compensation objectives. Ironically, the executive that announced his exit is now given a raise, promotion, or some other promises to stay.

However attractive, there are some issues to consider. How has the counteroffer addressed those factors that led to the executive being enticed away? If compensation is the only factor embodied in the counteroffer, the executive will likely become dissatisfied again and leave at a later date.

Once an executive expresses a desire to leave the company, top management is uncertain as the person's loyalty going forward. Often bosses feel that they have been blackmailed into a counteroffer. Senior executives may reason that if this person can be "disloyal" now, he will be disloyal again. Indeed, there's a high probability that the organization will launch a discreet search to replace the "dissident" employee. If you suspect that your organization might operate like this, you should ask yourself, "What are my long-term career advancement prospects and opportunities?"

When in doubt about your short-term/long-term advancement potential, have a candid discussion with your boss. Ask what areas you need to shore up, and inquire as to how you are viewed inside the organization. Such a discussion may provide some clues about whether you should begin a discreet search or whether your future is bright in your current organization.

Responding to Michele Cannon's Employment Agreement

Michele, I've had a chance to review your offer. First of all, congratulations! It is a fine offer. My two cents follow:

Section 1: Term of Employment :   Ideally, I'd prefer a two-year *evergreen* contract, as it never expires. It just keeps rolling along with the same provisions as this limited two-year agreement. Executives, like yourself, start to get antsy to either renew the contract or start actively looking for a job if the finite employment agreement is not renewed at about the six- to nine-month mark before the expiration of the agreement. From your perspective, you wisely need to hedge your bets, as the company has not declared its ongoing commitment to you through a contract extension.

Section 3 (b) Bonus: I'd prefer a *guaranteed* bonus of something like $150,000. Calculation was based on five months multiplied by your 50 percent target bonus. Guarantees are simple, and everyone knows what the dollar amount means. No disputes around failed memories.

Section 4 (b) Auto Allowance: What if you like your current car, and you do not want to buy or lease? The benefit language here is too restrictive. Simpler approach is for your company to provide you $15,000 for annual auto expenses—Period. You should not have to prove/provide receipts; the $15,000 is part of your W-2 regardless of how it is spent or utilized. If your car is 100 percent paid for, great! Then all you are incurring is operating costs and maybe putting a little in your pocket. Consider that amount extra base compensation.

Section 4 (c) Life Insurance: Do you have the option to buy more at low rates? Might be a good investment . . .

Section 4 (e) Relocation Allowance: I prefer no cap on expenses, including complete tax gross-up. Have you gotten estimates on moving? With real estate fees, temporary living, and so on, it might be in excess of $130,000 if house purchase or extended house rental is included while your house is being built (if that is the direction you might go). There is no advantage to you to capping this fee. Speaking of house purchase by your employer, you might wish to see if you can get that provision in the contract if you do not sell your house within six months. Happens all the time, though not as frequently as it once did.

Section 6 (b) 2nd Paragraph Disability or Death: Recommend that you insert the concept/language that encompasses your estate *or heirs for the duration of the severance period*. Also, you might wish to evaluate the policy manual regarding vesting of options upon death or disability to make doubly sure that your estate or heirs have the ability to exercise your options when it is most advantageous taxwise.

Section 6 (c) (i) Termination without Cause: A severance of 12 months compensation (base and bonus) is good—18 months is better, especially at your level. In my opinion, requiring a dollar-for-dollar offset for any amount earned while on separation pay (even as a director) is pretty petty. These types of restrictions are clearly reflective of the culture and the slightly punitive mind-set of the CEO or Board. My advice: Be mindful of this undercurrent, and be watchful of this CEO/Board being punitive in the early stages to "whip you into shape to show you who's boss."

Executive Outplacement: You definitely want to include this in any separation provisions. You want the freedom to make the final decision which firm to use. Don't worry, outplacement is a normal for benefit senior executives and considered merely the cost of doing business.

Regarding Benefits during Severance: Find out what you can still do. Can you still contribute to 401(k) (probably not), receive/buy options, and so on?

Triggering Events: This section is totally missing. I've attached an offer checklist for your review. These triggering events acknowledge the reality of executive turnover. Witness changes at your old company. We can talk more about this, but let me highlight some of these events that trigger the severance benefits:

- *Change of control*. When 50-plus percent of ownership changes hands, as defined by SEC.
- *Change of leadership*. When less than 50 percent of ownership changes hands and if/when a new leader (by whatever title) takes over. Most people think that change of control covers it all, but this loophole is sometimes used by acquiring firms that decide to employ this tactic on unsuspecting company officers who lose out when their big change of control packages don't apply.
- *Change of title, role, responsibilities, reporting relationship, or compensation*. If there is a clear and documentable diminishment of any of these terms, you have the option to take advantage of your severance benefits (usually within six months of the event, but it should be spelled out).
- *Change of geography*. A required move of more than 50 miles constitutes a triggering event.

Section 7 (b) (i) Noncompete: If possible, have the organization identify a limited number of direct competitors. Likewise, you want a limited number of products and services deemed to be in any restrictive covenant. Also, the noncompete time frame needs to be in relative balance with the severance. For instance, a noncompete period of 2.5 years may be too skewed in favor of the company, especially if they only offer you 12 months of pay. Are all these services currently being extended? I may be all wet; however, it appears that some of them may be wish lists (like consulting). You do not wish to be constrained from becoming a consultant because the company is contemplating it at some time in the future, perhaps, if luck prevails.

Michele, it's a fine offer; one of which you can be rightfully proud. I look forward to hearing more about the next step.

Best regards,

Clyde

 "Success is getting what you want. Happiness is wanting what you get."

—Dale Carnegie

STEP 8
THE NEXT STEP

CHAPTER 22

EXECUTIVE ONBOARDING— ENSURE SUCCESS IN YOUR NEW JOB

Reality Check—Make Sure That Love Is *Not* Blind

Before you throw your objectivity to the wind, this is a time for a sober, reality check.

Three years or less, then you're out and casting about in the marketplace again. Whoa! If you are like most people, you think that's outrageous! Yet that's what the average career life expectancy is for executives now. Times have certainly changed. In our parents' generation it was common to retire from a single employer. Early in my career, if a person changed jobs more than four times, the person was considered a job hopper, disloyal, and opportunistic.

The reality of a global economy, something we've been acknowledging for more than 25 years, has contributed to massive downsizings. Global outsourcing, short-term Wall Street mentality, employment-at-will legislation, ballooning personal debt, and lack of wrongful discharge litigation have all contributed to high levels of employment uncertainty. This uncertainty is both good news and bad news.

The bad news is that valued contributors are often too easily discarded without much angst or commitment to enable the executive to be successful. It was, and largely still is, a time of sink or swim for new employees. The good news is the loud and clear message that all employees from the CEO on down must take complete responsibility for his or her career success. You are totally accountable for your success in your roles. If you have an entitlement mentality that deludes you to think that you are guaranteed an easy career without your having to work at it, you'll be sadly mistaken. What *are* you doing to achieve leadership mastery? How *are* you differentiating yourself and being indispensable? What is your *brand*? Your technical expertise is not enough. Generating results is not enough. They are important, and they need to be balanced with interpersonal and leadership mastery. You need to take charge of your career by being 100 percent accountable for its outcome!

Ten years ago, articles lamenting the malaise of quick career moves and capricious terminations were headlined with—"Employer and Employee Loyalty Is Dead." It's even truer today. We recently conducted a survey of 1,900 executives and executive search firms. The survey revealed that 80 percent of all employed executives were either actively or discreetly looking for work or receptive to exploring an attractive opportunity, if called. That's a huge percentage of executives opting to bail out of their organizations if the right opportunity materialized.

I know that I am biased toward people taking complete responsibility for the quality of their business (and personal) relationships. If you do not have the widespread organizational advocacy and endorsement that you'd like, then figure out how you are going to achieve it—that is, if you want to have some longevity in your career. Now, while I am clearly biased toward not making excuses if your relationships blow up, I am not naïve. I know that there are many situations that are incredibly unfair. I know that you might be in a situation in which you never had a chance to win. You might have been at odds with your boss or the Board because of diametrically opposed values. You might be a victim of your boss's hidden agenda (she wants to bring her own staff onboard from her previous company).

I've personally been in some situations that I thought were stacked against my success. Nonetheless, when I strip aside all my "hot" emotions (mad, sad, shame, and fear), I am still responsible for the quality of my relationship with my boss. So what if I think he's not as supportive toward me? The questions I pose to myself are, "What am I doing that is creating this negative response from my boss? What does my boss *need* and *want* from me, and how am I, no kidding, delivering against these needs? What attitude do I have toward my boss, and how is my attitude affecting my behavior toward him? If I were my boss, what would I think of my attitude and behavior? If I don't trust or respect my boss, what attitude and behavior must I change to create the desired level of trust and respect?"

I acknowledge that I've derailed some circumstances because of my own insecurity, fear, and small-mindedness. Correspondingly, there have been times that I've been taken advantage of by others because of a lack of integrity that was rooted in their deep-seated fears.

And when it was all said and done, I was *still* responsible for the quality of the relationship. My responsibility was twofold. First, I had to determine what I could do to solidly build rapport. Many times, that meant viewing the person as if I *did* respect him. I viewed him with different eyes. Second, I behaved toward my nemesis as if I was truly his friend. That meant lightening up, stopping being nervous or hesitant, and eliminating any emotional "hair triggers." I have to confess. Being calm, cool, and collected with one obnoxious colleague, in particular, was a Herculean effort, but I did it. Surprisingly, this person subsequently apologized for his hostile attitude toward me.

My firm's approach to relationship building is holistic. It is a process that is designed to empower clients to be more aware and confident in their ability to contribute and

EXECUTIVE ONBOARDING—ENSURE SUCCESS IN YOUR NEW JOB   *431*

successfully weave through their company's organizational minefields. If you read the Preface, you know that I did not do a very good job of building my relationship with my boss years ago.

I started Robertson Lowstuter on the core belief that while everyone intends to do well, there is often a disconnect between what we intend and how we behave. In fact, I hold myself out as the poster boy for this disconnect when I got zapped years ago.

 Success is a conscious act. Taking charge of your career is a radical act.

What Is Executive Onboarding?

Executive onboarding is a formal, planned strategy to align your and the organization's values, needs, and goals. A well-executed onboarding strategy will enable you to gain widespread support and endorsement from others and contribute in an accelerated manner. The bottom line is your successful integration into the organization. See Figure 22-1. This strategy is coupled with deliberate and conscious action on your part, involving others.

While all of us have the capacity to operate effectively in new roles or in new organizations, having a deliberate strategy significantly enhances the probability of your success.

What Onboarding Is *Not*

Executive Onboarding is not just having a luncheon with your new staff, although that's nice. It's not just having a beer after work with several of your peers. It's not just keeping

Figure 22-1   Pillars of Onboarding Success

Onboarding Success for Authentic Leaders

Alignment | Endorsement | Contribution | Integration

your antenna attuned to the buzz in the lunchroom. And, it's a lot more than getting an orientation of the office layout from your assistant.

Common Career Derailers

There are myriad reasons why careers derail, regardless of whether it results in an exit. I'm sure that some of the derailers cited below are common to you, and no doubt you have experienced a number of others that are unique to you.

As mentioned, my major career derailer was that I had an entitlement mentality that led me not to build strong enough endorsement with my direct manager. If you have ever had bumps in your career, you might have experienced a derailer. I invite you to identify your career derailers.

WORKSHEET 71

Career Derailers

To raise your awareness of something that might unintentionally undermine your effectiveness, CIRCLE the career derailers that apply to you and your situation.

There is a lack of …

Authenticity, encompassing openness, and genuineness in your organization's culture

Fit, personal chemistry, or endorsement with your boss or the board

Straightforwardness in behavior and communication

Clarity of role or performance expectations

Compelling vision

Leadership effectiveness and sound decision making

Willingness to be influenced or receive feedback (you or others)

Aligned values: authenticity, openness, straightforwardness

Interpersonal agility and flexibility

Life/work balance

Awareness of unintended impact

Strategic view or plan

Sense of urgency and ability to execute

Support from direct reports, peers, or top management

Respect for your role, authority, decisions, and knowledge

Understanding of the nuances of the job

Adapting quickly enough to your organization's unique culture

Being a part of the internal network and informal communication channels

Confidence and boldness in creating your vision and rallying others around it

Creating momentum in establishing a high-performance team

Being able to maneuver through the "wake" of the history that surrounds your role and position

Learning and mastering new skill sets that are needed and wanted in your new role

An environment that is nonpolitical

Collaboration, interdependence, and commitment of people serving the greater organizational good

What We've Learned About Going In/Coming Out

Your employment status and future promotions will basically rest with your performance reputation established within your first 30 days on the job. Obviously, your goal is to achieve the reputation of a technically competent and authentic leader who effectively builds widespread organizational endorsement while adding value. One way to do this is to repeatedly ask yourself "What's *needed* and *wanted* on the job, in the company, and in my relationships?"

A well-accepted Japanese business axiom is the paradoxical "Slow down, so as to speed up." Since I am a visual and physical person, it always helps me to explain this concept when I stretch out my arms, shoulder height, to my side and hold my palms facing up. In my right palm is the reality of needing to slow down and meet people to build alliances and endorsement while assessing the need and asking for feedback as to what can/should be improved. In my left palm is the challenge to balance the need of speeding up my contribution and making a difference. There is always huge pressure to jump in and begin to act immediately. Over the years I have coached hundreds of well-intended executives whose careers have blown up because they sped off in the wrong direction trying to contribute and in the process alienated top management and gained little endorsement. To be successful, slow down . . . and speed up.

Figure 22-2 illustrates that while technical knowledge and task skills are important (indeed, they are essential to doing the work), the real driver to success is interpersonal and leadership skill mastery. It's probably no surprise that when we are in school, the emphasis is on technical knowledge. Early in our career we are called upon to apply what we learned. The circle of task skills recognizes the value of integrating education with practical hands-on application, leading to results. Interestingly, as we advance in our careers, our technical knowledge and task skills, while still important, are significantly overshadowed by the need to have interpersonal/leadership competency.

Figure 22-2 Leadership Balance

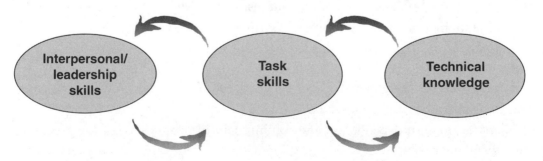

Truly successful executives have mastered their ability to manage themselves, to quickly read others, and to effectively lead. Without having solid interpersonal or leadership skills, an executive's talent will be suboptimized. When I look at this model, with its three circles, I think of an 18-wheeler, tractor-trailer rig (see Figure 22-3). The Interpersonal/leadership circle is the engine, the tractor, if you will, pulling a trailer that is composed of the remaining two circles. A fully loaded trailer without a tractor is a storage shed, at best. But when all three spheres are fully integrated, significant results are routinely realized.

Figure 22-3

As I mentioned earlier, executives are hired into organizations because of *fit, personal chemistry, and endorsement*—technical capacity notwithstanding. Executives exit their organizations not because of a lack of talent or technical competency, but rather because of a lack of fit, personal chemistry, and endorsement. If you can't get along with others and be interpersonally agile, it doesn't matter how bright or talented you are, you will not realize your potential.

Why Is It Important to Create an Onboarding Strategy?

- You want to be successful.
- You don't want to get caught unaware.
- You want to beat the three-year odds for career longevity, if it's appropriate.

I often ask executives:

- How many of you deliberately planned your careers—every step?
- How many of you have ever consciously planned your own exit?

Simply put, you don't want to get caught unaware. Less than 5 percent of our executive clients indicated that they deliberately planned their career steps, especially the abrupt, involuntary ones. These executives revealed that their career paths evolved more or less by accident. Some observed that they were in right place at the right time and they were willing to take a risk on a move. Most executives, however, acknowledged that their career progression seemed to have a life of its own.

Despite the due diligence and preparation before entering a new role, many clients feel that they initially are in over their heads as they enter a new position. Indeed, you may have also felt the same way. The challenges are immense in that you are expected to be able to embrace the complexities of the new organization, learn and understand the business challenges, manage new boss relationships, and get to know how other people with whom you interact within the organization think and act. Coupled with the speed at which business must be conducted, even the best of players are up against the edge of their comfort zones. All the more reason during this time of vulnerability to have a plan of attack on how you will get up to speed quickly, build widespread endorsement, and achieve the results you want.

The 4-Score of Effective Onboarding

You might ask yourself, "So, how do I close the gap between what I intend and how I behave/perform?" Seek to apply the 4-score of effective onboarding:

1. *Awareness.* Be cognizant of those personal inhibitors or career derailers and drivers to your success.
2. *Alignment.* Develop congruency of your talents, innate strengths, and passions.
3. *Accountability.* Takes complete responsibility for the outcome and being accountable for the impact of your behavior—intended and unintended.
4. *Authenticity.* The core of effective onboarding. You need to be grounded in your genuine, natural self to be optimally successful.

All four of these elements, as shown in Figure 22-4, need to be present in the development of your strategic onboarding action plan, which we will work in the next few pages.

Figure 22-4   Score of Effective Onboarding

Growth Questions Designed to Unlock Answers

We do not easily change our behavior, and our history does tend to repeat itself. Before starting your new job, I encourage you to pause and reflect on your learning from your organizational transition or your previous job prior to your promotion. If you are interested in discovering how you could have achieved more at your previous employer, what you could have done differently, and perhaps why you didn't, great! No time like the present to "peel back the layers."

I recommend that you answer the following worksheet questions candidly and completely.

WORKSHEET 72

Growth Questions

What was the reason for your leaving? What would others say was the reason for your leaving?

What could you have done differently to have been more successful? Why didn't you?

In the past 12 months, how differently have you been operating from your normal style?

What signs were there that you and your boss were drifting apart?

What did you do to protect yourself inside the organization *and* hedge your bets outside in the marketplace?

If you did not do anything "protective," what did you gain by *not* taking protective measures? What did you lose?

If you could have been more proactive in your discreet job search, why were you not? What barriers were present that prevented you from acting?

If you were a victim of politics, what can you do to manage them next time?

What experiences, on and off the new job, will be instrumental in achieving your goals?

What specific action will ready you to achieve your 5- and 10-year goals?

How do you plan to keep your network alive and healthy and yourself appropriately active and visible in the marketplace?

What are the top five responsibilities in your new job?

What are the top five challenges or demands in your new job?

Who might be the greatest proponents, supporters, or advocates for you in this new position? What has created this being the case?

Who might be the greatest opponents, the people who will resist or challenge you the most? What has created this being the case?

What functions do you know least well? Who is in charge, and when will you learn more about each one?

If you did not receive the kind of position that you wanted on this move, what experiences are you missing? How will you gain that experience?

What is *needed* and *wanted* by the Board of Directors, your boss, your boss's peers, your peers, your subordinate team, and other parts of the organization?

The Tool Kit—Strategic Onboarding Action Plan Worksheet

Refer to www.RobertsonLowstuter.com to access the worksheet entitled, Onboarding Tool Kit for you to create your own onboarding action plan. The Tool Kit will help you get focused on the highest priority onboarding activities. Complete the worksheet to the best of your ability. When finished I also recommend that you share your insights with a person who knows you well, as well as your new boss to calibrate your plan and to legitimize this endeavor. The eight columns in this worksheet are:

Column 1: **Outcomes.** Identify your top five onboarding outcomes.

Column 2: **Action.** Identify the action you will take to achieve these outcomes.

Column 3: **Roadblocks.** Identify the most likely self-limiting and disempowering roadblocks.

Column 4: **Accelerants.** Identify the key accelerants or drivers to successful onboarding.

Column 5: **Impact.** Identify the estimated P&L impact.

Column 6: **Timing.** Identify when you will successfully achieve this result.

Column 7: **Accountability.** Identify how you will hold yourself accountable.

Column 8: **Status**. Use a red light, green light, or yellow light to indicate progress at a glance. As currently configured, there is enough room to make cryptic comments.

Accountability Partners

Find someone who will help you be successful in your onboarding efforts. Enlist this person as your accountability partner. Having an accountability partner is analogous to having an advisor who has a strong interest in your success.

By the way, it is best if you and your partner establish some ground rules as to the role you want the other person to play. How much honest, straightforward feedback are you willing to accept? Where, how often, and how long will you meet? It's better to meet more frequently for shorter periods than to wear out your welcome after the first meeting or call.

Your accountability partner's role is to support you in your successful transition. The role might include career coach, sounding board, provide objective perspective, keep you focused, and help you understand organizational/interpersonal dynamics, and measure your contributions in quantifiable metrics. Your accountability partner's role is *not* to rescue you or make you dependent on him or her. Nor is it to merely tell you what you might wish to hear.

Your Psychological Contract

Intellectually, you might nod your head and agree that you are committed to creating your onboarding strategy. However, declaring your commitment out loud to other people significantly helps to cement in your commitment. Given the average job life expectancy of three years or less, having a dynamic onboarding strategy that you update on an ongoing basis might be the difference between moving on and staying to contribute.

Here's one easy way to begin to craft your formal action plan. On an index card, write down what will you say "Yes to" and "No to" in your onboarding transition and integration. Share your insights and your Yes to/No to with someone whom you trust. Lastly, keep your Tool Kit and your index card handy so you might refer to these from time to time.

Additional Tips—Your First Few Months

- Become a "consultant" in your new role, creatively problem-solving and resolving conflicts or confusion.
- Learn how to contribute value to everyone with whom you come in contact. If you don't feel you are adding value, then do some research, and figure out how you can help. Do not talk much (if at all) about how things were done at your

former employer, and do not be too quick to volunteer solutions which, at first glance, look just like something you encountered previously. If you don't stop and ask questions, you run the risk of being embarrassed by your incomplete analysis and premature recommendation.

- Identify those individuals whom your function impacts and meet them. Get to know their needs, interests, and motivations. Learn about their roles and responsibilities. It is critical to your own success that you know what seems to work with your new colleagues.
- If you are replacing a person, you may wish to ask the following questions to key people:
  ○ How did you view the other person?
  ○ What was done well?
  ○ What could have been improved?
  ○ If you could have anything you want from this position, going forward, what would it be?
- Learn to gain support and endorsement of others (superiors, peers, and subordinates) by informing and involving them in your thoughts, feelings, ideas, and intentions.
- Do not confuse your using people as sounding boards with the need to gain approval or consensus decision–making. Rather, strive to balance your need for information gathering with your colleagues' need for a given outcome. Rarely will they expect more than that, and if you ask for their input, most people are pleased to provide it. As you know from personal experience, involvement fosters commitment.

12 Onboarding Strategies

1. *Leverage your strengths* in your new role and relationships.
2. *Assess the needs of the organization* as a whole and those of your internal/external customers. Be responsive to areas in which you could assist others.
3. *Gain feedback* to be aware of and calibrate what is working well/not working well. Continually solicit information from your associates as to what can be improved and assist them in being successful.
4. *Identify proponents/opponents*, but be careful not to align too quickly. Turn opponents into your greatest advocates by addressing their needs and by adding significant value.
5. *Contribute quickly* by judiciously responding to immediate needs, not by being overly cautious or deliberate. Jump in the deep end right away with your eyes wide open, ensuring that you are doing the right things for the right reasons.

6. ***Communicate up*** to your immediate managers and those above to solicit their input and advice on major projects and their views regarding their needs. Clarify expectations and metrics, being 100 percent accountable for your relationships.

7. ***Support across*** to your peers, championing their sound ideas, initiatives, and projects. Operate as a partner looking for opportunities to affirm and support your colleagues while speaking your mind.

8. ***Develop down*** to your direct team, enabling them to feel more empowered, bold, and confident. And, of course, provide them with constructive, authentic feedback.

9. ***Gain alignment*** from others for your compelling vision by involving them and building a synergistic alliance.

10. ***Network internally/externally*** for the purposes of expanding your knowledge base of experts, ideas, and different perspectives.

11. ***Maintain your personal/work life balance*** by adopting the operating philosophy, "Work hard and play hard." Doing so will enable you to keep your sanity and perspective.

12. ***Continue to invest in yourself and your career*** by creating opportunities to speak and contribute your time, money, and energy to causes you support. Seek out professional and personal growth workshops or forums that enable you to stay sharp, innovative, and current.

To help you gain insight as to your natural onboarding style and the vulnerabilities you might have, please complete the following Worksheets 73 and 74.

WORKSHEET 73

Onboarding Strategies

Step 1: Most Comfortable

Reread the 12 Onboarding Strategies in this chapter. Select the single strategy that you are <u>most comfortable with</u> and relate to most directly.

What is it about this strategy that you identify with most readily?

What values are embedded in this strategy, and why do you relate to them so closely?

When you are busy executing this strategy, what might you be avoiding and why?

Step 2: Least Comfortable

Of the 12 Onboarding Strategies, select the single strategy that you are <u>least comfortable with</u>.

What about this strategy makes you uncomfortable?

What do you think and feel, and how do you behave, when you engage in this strategy?

Regardless of how you feel about your least comfortable strategy, how might you recontextualize it and be comfortable and successful?

Step 3: Committed to Working On

After reviewing again the list of the 12 Onboarding Strategies, identify the one strategy that you will commit to mastering.

What is it about this onboarding strategy that appeals to you?

What will you do differently going forward?

What will be the outcome, and how will you know you've been successful?

WORKSHEET 74

Integrating into the New Job— What Has Worked for You?

What strengths have made you successful in your career so far?

What additional skills and abilities will be needed in your new role? How will you gain these skills?

Briefly describe what you did previously that led to your most successful integration into a new role and organization.

What top three personal strengths did you utilize in this successful integration? (Examples: ability to develop rapport, desire to add value and serve the greater organizational good, ability to focus, drive for results).

What did you learn from exiting your previous organization(s) that you will apply in transitioning into your new company?

Strategic Survival Plan in Your New Position

- Learn from your notable successes and notable failures. I'm sure you have grown more from your mistakes, because you've probably reflected on them, ascertaining what could have been improved or avoided. Don't merely breathe a big sigh of relief without educating yourself and assuming accountability for any blow-ups.
- Maintain some healthy emotional distance between yourself and the company. Remain objective and professional in your approach to your job. Create a balance between your business life and your personal life.
- Don't be political. This can be permanently damaging. Therefore, refuse to discuss personalities, and do not take sides. Don't make excuses or blame others if you get burned at some point in the new job. If your relationships are not as strong or as effective as you'd like, confront the issue, and modify how you behave to ensure the result you want.
- Always gauge shifting winds. Watch for changes. Be alert to new directions or trends or people in power. Become more known and visible when this happens.
- Know more about your business and company than you need to know. This requires an inquisitiveness that won't quit. Read the company's annual report, the operating plan, and employee communication vehicles. If you need help deciphering the financials, ask someone you know and trust in finance. Ask about new products or new projects or programs in other departments. Learn how the company operates, and become known to as many people as you can.
- Always have a business/operational plan to help you measure performance. If your goals are not being met or have little chance of being met, increase your pressure to succeed.
- Review monthly what you have done. Measure your own performance against your own goals. Set next month's accomplishment goals. Give yourself a quarterly performance review. Be tough on yourself. Expect results, not perfection.
- Status quo is death. Successful organizations expect action . . . all the time. Keep things moving. Make things happen. Do not sit on yesterday's successes.
- No business will ever replace good gut instincts, personal courage, and a high sense of urgency. Be demanding, firm, fair, and above all, be genuine with others.
- Everything you do will have a direct positive or negative impact on the bottom line. Prudence dictates performance—better performance.
- Lastly, have fun!

Post-Search Strategy

One of the insights you might have gained during your search was the importance of networking with search firms, target companies, and personal/professional acquaintances.

1. Commit to taking a contact (search firm account executive, or professional colleague, or friend) to lunch, at least once a month. This will help you promote yourself in a nonthreatening manner, and you will maintain your visibility appropriately.

2. Continue to be a networking source to others in need. Do you remember how gratifying it was to receive support from others when you were casting about for leads or even a friendly voice on the other end of the phone? Now it's your turn. Add value to other job seekers when they call—more than merely providing names. Inquire about the status of their search, and don't be afraid to ask penetrating questions. Be a friend to a stranger. Provide straight feedback.

   Make some time available for people who are trying to network with you. However, guard against overextending yourself by providing too much support, as you don't want to create the impression that you're carrying on your campaign.

   Caution: Do not "bowl people over" with your keen careering insights, no matter how correct they may be. Earn the right to volunteer information by asking what role the caller wants you to play. Then provide your observations, and recommended action steps which have worked for you.

3. Approximately 30 days after you accept the new position, send a mailing to 50 to 100 contacts, including companies, search firms, and personal contacts indicating your changed status. For a correspondence sample, please refer to the "New Position Accepted" letter at the end of Chapter 8, "Create Compelling Marketing Letters That Evoke Action."

Commencement—A New Beginning

Excited, stressed, tired, restless, elated, deflated, energized, anticlimactic, relieved—these are common emotions at the conclusion of a well-run search. Now that the dust has somewhat settled on your search campaign and before you leap into your new career, it is advantageous for you to develop the onboarding strategies vital for your success.

 What do you want your life and career to look like? What do you need to do to realize these goals? Now, go out and *achieve it.*

Best wishes for your continued career success, and may you always . . .

"Create Uncommon Results!"®

Clyde C. Lowstuter

RESOURCES

The following resources are intended to broaden your perspective and help you master the nuances of the career transition process.

Careering:

Dikel-Riley, Margaret, and Frances E. Roehm. *Guide to Internet Job Searching*. New York: McGraw-Hill, 2006.

Kroeger, Otto, with Janet M. Thusesen. *Type Talk at Work: How the 16 Personality Types Determine Your Success on the Job*. New York: Dell Publishing, 2002.

Lencioni, Patrick. *Silos, Politics, and Turf Wars*. San Francisco: Jossey-Bass, 2006.

Lowstuter, Clyde C., and David P. Robertson. *Network Your Way to Your Next Job Fast*. New York: McGraw-Hill, 1995.

Lubit, Roy H. *Coping with Toxic Managers, Subordinates ... And Other Difficult People: Using Emotional Intelligence to Survive and Prosper*. Upper Saddle River, NJ: Financial Times Prentice Hall, 2004.

MacKenzie, Alec. *The Time Trap*. New York: AMACOM, 1990.

Neff, Thomas J., and James M. Citrin. *You're In Charge Now What?* New York: Crown Business, 2005.

Smart, Bradford D. *Topgrading: How Leading Companies Win by Hiring, Coaching, and Keeping the Best People, Revised and Updated Edition*, New York: The Penguin Group, 2005.

Wackerle, Frederick. *The Right CEO: Straight Talk About Making Tough CEO Selection Decisions*. San Francisco: Jossey-Bass, 2001.

Watkins, Michael. *The First 90 Days*. Boston: Harvard Business School Press, 2003.

Zander, Rosamund Stone, and Benjamin Zander. *The Art of Possibility: Transforming Professional and Personal Life*. Boston: Harvard Business School Press, 2000.

Entrepreneuring:

Block, Peter. *Flawless Consulting: A Guide to Getting Your Expertise Used.* San Francisco: Jossey-Bass/Pfeiffer, 2000.

Harper, Stephen C. *The McGraw-Hill Guide to Starting Your Own Business: A Step-By-Step Blueprint for the First-Time Entrepreneur.* New York: McGraw-Hill, 2003.

Lesonsky, Rieva, and the staff of Entrepreneur Magazine. *Start Your Own Business.* 3rd ed. Irvine, CA: Entrepreneur Press, 2004.

Lowstuter, Clyde C. *Entrepreneurial Characteristic Profile.* Bannockburn, IL: RL Communications, Inc., 2007 (Access at www.robertsonlowstuter.com).

McConnell, Ben, and Jackie Huba. *Creating Customer Evangelists.* Chicago: Dearborn Trade Publishing, 2003.

Palo Alto Business Pro Plan Premier 2007. Palo Alto, CA: Palo Alto Software, 2007.

Parks, Steve. *How to Fund Your Business: The Essential Guide to Raising Finance to Start and Grow Your Business.* Upper Saddle River, NJ: Prentice Hall, 2006.

Poynter, Dan. *The Self-Publishing Manual: How to Write, Print, and Sell Your Own Book.* 15th ed. Santa Barbara, CA: Para Publishing, 2006.

Root, Hal, and Steve Koenig. *The Small Business Start-Up Guide.* Naperville, IL: Sourcebooks, Inc., 2006.

Shenson, Howard L. *How to Develop and Promote Successful Seminars and Workshops: The Definitive Guide to Creating and Marketing Seminars, Workshops, Classes and Conferences.* New York: John Wiley & Sons, 1990.

Mergers & Acquisitions, Private Equity and Venture Capital Arenas:

Frankel, Michael E.S. *Mergers and Acquisitions Basics: The Key Steps to Acquisitions, Divestitures, and Investments.* Hoboken, NJ: John Wiley & Sons, 2005.

Harding, David, and Sam Rovitt. *Mastering the Merger: Four Critical Decisions that Make or Break the Deal.* Boston: Harvard Business School Publishing, 2004.

Levin, Jack S., Martin D. Ginsburg, and Donald E. Rocap. *Structuring Venture Capital, Private Equity and Entrepreneurial Transactions.* Fredrick, MN: Aspen Publishers, 2006.

Leadership:

The Arbinger Institute. *Leadership and Self-Deception*. San Francisco: Berrett-Koehler Publishers, Inc., 2002.

Bennis, Warren. *On Becoming a Leader: The Leadership Classic Updated and Expanded*. Reading, MA: Addison-Wesley, 2003.

Blanchard, Kenneth, William Oncken, Jr., and Hal Burrows. *The One Minute Manager Meets the Monkey*. New York: William Morrow, 1989.

Bossidy, Larry, and Ram Charan. *Confronting Reality*. New York: Crown Business, 2004.

———— *Execution: The Discipline of Getting Things Done*. New York: Crown Business, 2002.

Cashman, Kevin. *Leadership from the Inside Out*. Minneapolis, MN: TCLG, 1999.

Collins, Jim. *Good to Great: Why Some Companies Make the Leap and Others Don't*. New York: Harper Collins, 2001.

Drucker, Peter F. *The Effective Executive: The Definitive Guide to Getting the Right Things Done*. New York: Harper Business Essentials, 2006.

Gardner, Howard. *Changing Minds*. Boston: Harvard Business School Press, 2004.

George, Bill. *Authentic Leadership*. San Francisco: Jossey-Bass, 2003.

Gladwell, Malcolm. *Blink*. New York: Little Brown and Company, 2005.

Kanter, Rosabeth. *Confidence*. New York: Crown Business, 2004.

Kotter, John P. *Leading Change*. Boston: Harvard Business School Press, 1996.

Lencioni, Patrick. *The Five Dysfunctions of a Team*. San Francisco: Jossey-Bass, 2002.

Lennick, Doug, and Fred Kiel, Ph.D. *Moral Intelligence*. Upper Saddle River, NJ: Wharton School Publishing, 2005.

Lowstuter, Clyde. "Change Agents: Be Accountable!" Bannockburn, IL: RL Communications, Inc., 2003 (available at www.robertsonlowstuter.com).

Morris, Besty. "The New Rules." *Fortune Magazine*: July 2006, pp. 70-87.

Redmond, Andrea, and Charles A. Tribbett, III, with Bruce Kasanoff. *Business Evolves, Leadership Endures: Leadership Traits that Stand the Test of Time*. Westport, CT: Easton Studio Press, 2004.

Ruiz-Miguel, Don, and Janet Mills. *The Four Agreements Companion Book*. San Rafael, CA: Amber-Allen Publishing, 2000.

Ryan, Kathleen, and Daniel K. Ostreich. *Driving Fear out of the Workplace*. 2nd ed. San Francisco: Jossey-Bass, 1998.

Sirkin, Harold L., Perry Keenan, and Alan Jackson. "The Hard Side of Change Management," Harvard Business Review, October 2005.

Welch, Jack, and Suzy. *Winning*. New York: Harper Collins Publishers, Inc., 2005.

Whitworth, Laura, Karen Kimsey-House, Henry Kimsey-House, and Phil Sandahl. *Co-Active Coaching*. Mountain View, CA: Davies-Black Publishing, 2007.

INDEX

ABOUT THE AUTHORS & FIRM

CLYDE C. LOWSTUTER, MCC
President & CEO   Robertson Lowstuter, Inc.

Clyde Lowstuter is a seasoned peak performance executive coach. He has been awarded the MCC, Master Certified Coach, from the International Coach Federation, awarded to less than 1 percent of coaches worldwide. Robertson Lowstuter, his executive development firm, has coached thousands of executives in career transition to optimize their unique leadership capabilities and to take charge of their careers connecting into meaningful traditional and innovative roles. He is particularly skilled in reawakening creativity, aliveness, and authenticity in his clients while enhancing their effectiveness and profitability.

Clyde is a prolific writer and sought-after speaker as the author of McGraw-Hill books. *In Search of the Perfect Job* and *Network Your Way to Your Next Job ... Fast!* He has written, narrated, and produced leading-edge audio programs: *Six Figure Networking*, *Power Interviewing*, and *Empower Your Career and Your Life*. He regularly creates and presents the *Executive Forum*, a highly interactive leadership experience. Clyde lives in the Chicago area.

CAMMEN B. LOWSTUTER

Cammen Lowstuter is the collaborator of this book. She is an accomplished staff writer and workshop co-developer for Robertson Lowstuter. Cammen also works in marketing and public relations at Colorado Free University. Cammen lives and works in Denver.

About Robertson Lowstuter

Robertson Lowstuter is an executive development consulting and coaching firm. Since 1981, RL has partnered with executives, teams, and organizations to enhance the authenticity, contributions, and impact of their leaders through Executive Coaching, High Performance Team Building, Career Coaching, and Change Leadership. Visit us at www. robertsonlowstuter.com.